Nassau County

From Rural Hinterland to Suburban Metropolis

Edited by

Joann P. Krieg and Natalie A. Naylor

A Long Island Studies Institute Publication
from
HOFSTRA UNIVERSITY

Empire State Books
Interlaken, New York
2000

HOFSTRA UNIVERSITY
Hempstead, New York 11549
Library of Congress Catalog Number: 99–69565
ISBN: 1–55787–155–8 (cloth)
ISBN: 1–55787–156–6 (paper)
Manufactured in the United States of America

Papers presented at Centennial Conference
"Nassau County:
From Rural Hinterland to Suburban Metropolis"
March 18-20, 1999

Sponsored by
The Hofstra Cultural Center,
The Long Island Studies Institute, and
The Nassau County Centennial Committee
Hofstra University, Hempstead, Long Island, New York 11549

Cover and dust jacket photographs: Samuel Velsor farm, c. 1910
and Hofstra University, 1989 (see p. 166).

A *quality* publication by
Heart of the Lakes Publishing
Interlaken, New York 14847

Contents

The Nineteenth Century and Earlier

Changes and Transformations

Health Care

Aerospace Heritage

People and Places

Illustrations, Maps, and Tables

Photographs from the Nassau county Museum Collection in the Long Island Studies Institute at Hofstra University are abbreviated in the credits throughout as *NCM Collection, LISI at Hofstra.*

Foreword

James M. Shuart

We have so much to celebrate in Nassau County's centennial—a hundred years of a community which has grown and prospered since its break with Queens County. I must admit, however, that I was born and grew up on the other side of the county line, in College Point.*

My family had come in the mid-nineteenth century, when College Point was still quite rural. For them, College Point was home. All of the older people viewed the community as a small town in its own right. Most of them didn't want to be annexed by Flushing, let alone New York City.

My mother told me that the old timers, mainly German and Irish immigrants, opposed annexation by New York City and voted "no" to defeat the move. Educating the multilingual voter was not very well done in those days, and, after the vote, there were many of those old Germans and Irishmen who were very upset that a vote against annexation should have been "yes." They felt cheated that they had been swept into New York City in an ambiguous vote, and they carried their resentment to their graves. Nevertheless, Queens did become one of the "outer boroughs" of Greater New York and Nassau became a county in its own right.

I came out here at age seventeen to go to college, and I found a home here at Hofstra. Nassau County gave to me what my parents and relatives had had earlier in College Point. We have a very rich history, something that we should work very hard to preserve and to pass on to succeeding generations. That doesn't happen all by itself. It takes people like you and me to pass it on, to make sure that it's accurate, and to make sure that the information is accessible.

Finally, it is important to promote the enterprise, even though as scholars we prefer to believe that the search for knowledge should be its own reward. It is tempting to take a scholarly stance against publicity and self-promotion and say, "Well, we don't do that." But there are no accidents in life, and the preservation of our history, like truth and justice, doesn't just happen. It has to be promoted and supported.

That's why universities came into existence. Ever since the first one in Bologna, universities have kept that lamp of learning alive. We, with our

*The president of Hofstra University, James M. Shuart, welcomed those attending the conference at the evening dinner. His remarks (which were transcribed and edited), constitute a fitting foreword to this conference volume.

computers, are allied with our colleagues from the Middle Ages who kept knowledge alive with their scribes. That is still our mission; it isn't finished. We have wonderful libraries and technology to serve our purpose, but it takes human beings who believe in it to make it happen.

Cynics would say that winners re-write history and I am sorry to say that this has happened in too many instances. That's why professional historians must stay with it and work so hard to keep the record straight. The preservation of our heritage doesn't just happen. Whether you look back to Dutch roots or English roots, both of which we have here in Hempstead, what you see is that Long Island brought together two old world civilizations and from there we built our own through all of the phases of American history.

It can be a lot of fun going back through the history of Nassau County and Long Island to revisit the Duke's Laws, the Revolutionary War, the Civil War, or the early 1900s when our good friend Teddy Roosevelt was president. Long Island played a very prominent role in all of that. But history doesn't stop there.

In this century, Long Island has the distinction of leading the way. After World War II, it housed the returning veterans and built the very best educational institutions, from pre-kindergarten right through colleges and universities. But none of that just happened. There were many, many people who were so dedicated to their communities and gave of themselves all along the way. They've done a wonderful job. Hofstra University is extremely proud to have the opportunity to join with you in saluting the men and women who have worked so hard to make Nassau County what it is, and even more, to create its potential for the future. The challenges of yesterday may be under control—or at least, we are working on them. There will be more challenges in the future. We can be very confident that the men and women of Long Island who have taken care of business in the past will continue to do so very well into the future.

I've been in higher education for most of my adult life. I started as an administrator in 1959, and I'm still here, even after twenty-three years as president. But for five years in the early 1970s, I had a wonderful opportunity to join Nassau County's government and to work with wonderful people like Joe Driscoll and John Kiernan, people who have added so much to this conference. And I had the privilege of a first-hand exposure to and experience in this thing called local government—working with the people who carry on the official business of our community.

I'm a born New Yorker and I have all the cynicism that all New Yorkers have. I've read them all, *New York Times,* the *Daily News,* the *New York Post,* and I was as cynical as the rest toward local government when County Executive Ralph Caso invited me to join Nassau County's government. He said to me, "You're a social scientist over at Hofstra University, why don't you join me as the Commissioner of Social Services?" I wrestled with that and then I said, "Why not, I'm going to do it!" That decision opened up an adventure for me. I met people from every walk of life who came together in county government.

Down in Washington they think county government is child's play. And up in Albany they also look down at local government as not the real thing. But it is at the local level that things really happen. That fact came through in the conference's panel on local government with John Kiernan, Joe Driscoll, and Farrell Jones. Local government is where people deal with their very everyday existence. This is their community, and they control their destiny on a day-to-day basis. And from that position they mediate with these other areas of government.

Here in Nassau we're very lucky that we've had sensitive men and women who have been at the leading edge of society in meeting both opportunities, and problems as they arise. While I was in county government, I made some discoveries that I would like to share with you. Whether it was Ralph Caso, his administration and people, or the previous administration, Gene Nickerson, and others, the people were very helpful to each other in getting the job done. They were people of quality, people who were totally committed to serving the needs of the folks here at home.

Joseph Jaspin who was the County Attorney at the time said something to me that really impressed me. He said, "If you were to take any municipal government, any local government, and look at its departments and their dates of establishment, you would see a history of crisis and crisis resolution. So of course you begin with the police, then health, and then public works, and others in the order of their establishment, and in a very real way, you'll have a history of that community."

To interpret the history of Nassau County, whether under Gene Nickerson, Ralph Caso, Fran Purcell, or today's Tom Gulotta, you have to think about it in Joe Jaspin's terms. In Nassau County, in addition to those initial bedrock departments, we went on to be pioneers in mental health—one of the first counties in the state to do so. People in Albany didn't get it. They thought, "Why are the people in Nassau County pushing us on this new mental health stuff?" We were at the leading edge and continue to be there.

Then, not too long ago, when I was in county government, things like learning disabilities came to the fore along with concepts of early childhood intervention. Perhaps it was difficult for the taxpayers to shoulder those new developments, but this community had recognized the needs and organized to meet them.

It was the same with drug and alcohol abuse. Ralph Caso was the first county executive in the state of New York, probably in the whole country, to recognize the severity of that problem. I don't know whether Ralph will ever get credit for that, but I'd like to make my bid to recognize his contribution. He had the foresight and creativity to see that problem for what it was and still is, and he had the courage to do something about it. We were pioneers also in women's services, services to the aged, and more recently, when I was a member of the commission in revising the Nassau County charter, in creating a new office for minority affairs.

Joe Jaspin, what an intelligent guy you were! You clearly saw that Nassau County rose to every one of these challenges before any mandates were put forth by the state or federal government. Sometimes, we were on the battle lines with the state people and with the federal people, and we were considered "pains in the neck" at the time. But we were, and I hope we will continue to be, ahead of them.

As an unabashed booster, let me point out that the population of Nassau County is larger than twenty-two states in the Union. If we were a city, we'd be the sixth largest city in the United States of America, right behind Cincinnati. Working in government, you became aware of that, and of the fact that a community of this size has a great deal to offer.

Nassau County has had its bashers and we've had people who say, "Long Island is so bad that we're gonna move out of here, high taxes, etc., etc. . . ." An objective view of the situation, though, shows that it's one of the greatest places that one could ever hope to live. Our services are superb, and although we'll argue about the cost, and we'll argue about the specific kinds of things that we want in our everyday life, we are served very well by the people who are elected—from whatever party—in the villages, the towns, and the counties. And, I must also add that our representatives to the state and to the nation are tops.

Nassau County is one of the finest municipalities, communities, locations—however you want to define it—in the entire country. Here on Long Island, we have perhaps one of the finest array of colleges and universities in the nation. We're the envy of the rest of the nation.

Our history at Hofstra parallels that of the county. We have an institution which, not too long ago, only sixty-some-odd years ago, was nothing. We started in 1935 as Nassau College-Hofstra Memorial, a branch of New York University, and in 1938 initiated the move to become a separate institution. Those were also the years in which Nassau County adopted and implemented its new charter. Since then, the development of Hofstra clearly parallels that of Nassau. Even when Hofstra was in financial trouble twenty-three years ago, we were still better than 95 percent of the colleges in the nation and we are much stronger than that now. Today, Hofstra is a vital part of Nassau County's educational and cultural resources. In a short period of time we've come into our own; we're not a back-water institution in any way. We are standing tall, a beacon for students from the rest of the country and around the world. You always hear about Boston as *the* place for higher education, but when you walk the campus here you hear quite a few Boston accents. They're even coming down from Boston to go to Hofstra. We are doing very well.

Some years ago I listened to people who always talked about how good it was in other places, but then I learned first hand, working in government, here at Hofstra over the years, and with the various commissions that I've had the opportunity to work with, that we are not behind on anything. We are leaders.

In a historical conference like this we are obviously going to look at the warts of our community and things that have gone wrong. But we should also look at the strengths of this great community as our people reacted to their problems. We've handled every major disaster, whether wars, airplane crashes, or community upsets, very, very well.

That does not rule out problems in the future, but if there are people in this country who want to create a new community, I suggest they look at the history of Nassau County and adopt the outlook and the values of the people who live here. Regardless of group differences, however they are defined, there's a mutual respect in Nassau County that's hard to find anywhere else in this nation. The record will show that we take care of our own. We work hard at it and we have a great history. Even better than that, through the study of history, we can recognize the potential for the future and plan for it. In other words, the best is yet to come.

Hofstra began its classes in 1935 in this house built for Kate and William Hofstra in 1904. They called it the Netherlands; today it is Hofstra Hall. Photograph courtesy of the Hofstra University Office of Public Relations.

Nassau County Courthouse, c. 1910. The courthouse was the first building erected by the new county in 1900 and has been a symbol of county government ever since. *NCM Collection, LISI at Hofstra.*

Introduction

Natalie A. Naylor

Anniversaries provide appropriate occasions to reflect upon the past. Nassau County was formed on January 1, 1899, by the three eastern towns of Queens County (Hempstead, North Hempstead, and Oyster Bay), after the western towns had become part of greater New York City in 1898. Hofstra University commemorated the centennial of Nassau County by holding a conference on March 18-20, 1999, under the auspices of the Hofstra Cultural Center, the Long Island Studies Institute, and the Nassau County Centennial Committee. The conference featured forty-five speakers discussing various aspects of the history of Nassau County. The range of topics was broad and extended back to the nineteenth century, but a conference (and this ensuing conference volume) inevitably is not a comprehensive treatment. However, important aspects were included, and this book is a significant contribution to the history of Nassau County.

Hofstra University President James M. Shuart spoke at the conference dinner. His perspective was unique since he had had experience serving in county government before becoming Hofstra's president in 1976. His welcome reflected his pride in Nassau County and Hofstra University and his genuine appreciation of history. Dr. Shuart's transcribed and edited comments constitute the Foreword to this conference volume. His personal knowledge of the oral tradition in College Point, Queens, about the vote on the consolidation of New York City, is an interesting footnote to that event which spurred the formation of Nassau County. Hofstra University's significant development in the last quarter of the twentieth century is a credit to Dr. Shuart's leadership. The creation of the Long Island Studies Institute in 1985 is one aspect of the legacy of his administration. The Institute itself is a cooperative endeavor between Hofstra University and Nassau County. This Nassau Centennial Conference in 1999 was the twenty-second conference sponsored by the Institute, and this is its twenty-seventh publication.

National Perspectives

Jon C. Teaford, Professor of History at Purdue University in Indiana, was the keynote speaker at the conference. In "Nassau County: A Pioneer of the Crabgrass Frontier," he discusses Nassau County's history in the broader national perspective of the development of America's urban and suburban metropolitan areas. Nassau was "born in the age of urban imperialism," Dr. Teaford observes, but "it owes its very existence to a desire to remain apart."

Its villages incorporated to protect their suburban residential lifestyle and accepted fragmented rule with special districts. Efforts to centralize and unify government were resisted for decades until Republican leader J. Russel Sprague crafted a compromise charter which centralized some functions and provided for an elected county executive—the first in the country. The post-World War II years brought not only population growth, but also business and industry, shopping centers and industrial parks. More recently, Nassau has become a mature suburb and, as Professor Teaford states, "pioneered an alternative future."

"Myths and Realities of Suburban Politics" is a revision of Marjorie Freeman Harrison's comments at a panel discussion on "Nassau, The Quintessential Suburb." She maintains that suburbia "is a topic worthy of study in its own right" and not only as "an adjunct of the neighboring big city." Harrison challenges stereotypes of suburbia as "innately conservative" and "uniformly white and middle class." Examining broader national trends in politics, she argues that Nassau County Republican leaders played an important role in national GOP politics as architects of centrist "Modern Republicanism."

The Creation of Nassau County

"The Formation of Nassau County" was the topic of a panel discussion at the conference with Nassau County Historian Edward J. Smits; Jeffrey A. Kroessler, an historian who has written extensively on Queens County history; and George Lankevich, Professor Emeritus of History, CUNY, and author of books on New York City history. Since they had previously published their research, their discussion is not included in this volume.[1]

When the cornerstone of the 1900 county courthouse was opened at a centennial event in July 1999, a contemporary account, "The Erection of the County of Nassau," was discovered. This documents the role of United States Senator Thomas C. ("Boss") Platt in securing the successful passage of the bill creating Nassau County through the New York State legislature. This important document, with its accompanying supporting letters, is included in this volume, with an introduction by County Historian Edward J. Smits, under the title "'Boss' Platt's Role in Creating Nassau County."

When greater New York City was created it included Long Island City, the Towns of Newtown, Jamaica, and Flushing (the three western towns of Queens), and portions of the Town of Hempstead. Geographer Patricia T. Caro carefully analyzes "The Location of the Queens-Nassau Border" by tracing the boundary between Jamaica and Hempstead from colonial times and indicating the significance of the Welles Line, first drawn in 1684. With consolidation in 1898, New York City wanted Jamaica Bay, and the Rockaway Peninsula was a key segment. Hempstead did not protest the loss of this territory in 1898, but after the creation of Nassau County, a strip on its western border, including the areas of Inwood, Lawrence, and Elmont, was returned under the Doughty Bill.

The location of the courthouse was a persistent issue for Queens County in the nineteenth century. The courthouse was the center of county government and one of the first concerns of the new county. The Nassau Board of Supervisors scheduled the dedication and laying of the cornerstone for Nassau County's courthouse when its most famous citizen could attend. At the ceremonies, Governor Theodore Roosevelt of Oyster Bay spoke of the responsibility of public officials and the civic duties of citizens. James W. Foote incorporated Roosevelt's speech in his first-person presentation at the conference dinner, and TR's speech is included in this volume.

Goverance and Political Leadership

Local historians have given little attention to the impoverished residents of their area, although provision for the poor has been a responsibility of local government from the early colonial period. Ruth Shackelford examines "Institutional Poor Relief in Nassau County, 1899-1999," focusing her attention on the towns' almshouses and the county children's home in the early decades of the county. State regulations and inspections led to a Temporary Home for Children and to new buildings with improved conditions for the almshouses. The emergence of specialized institutions, widows' pensions, and a shift from institutional care to foster homes for children led to the closing of the county children's home in 1919, and to the almshouses serving primarily the aged and infirm. After briefly summarizing changes in recent decades, Professor Shackelford concludes, "Nassau County stands as a model for its dedication to its more unfortunate citizens."

"Political Leadership" was the topic of a conference session and three articles in this volume. Marjorie Freeman Harrison, in "Italian-American Inwood and the Making of the Modern Nassau Republican Party," examines how Inwood, one of the Five Towns in southwestern Nassau County, "served as a crucial proving ground" for the Republican Party's political strategy of community organizing. She analyzes how Peter DeSibio built a "potent political operation" through Italian-American networks in Inwood. He was an effective fundraiser for the Republicans, delivering votes, and dispensing patronage jobs. G. Wilbur Doughty and J. Russel Sprague used these same techniques in building the county Republican Party, and in the process brought ethnic communities and newcomers into political participation.

In "Executive Power: A Comparison of Styles," James Shelland compares the executive styles of Nassau County's first four county executives: J. Russel Sprague (served 1938-1953), A. Holly Patterson (1953-1961), Eugene H. Nickerson (1962-1970), and Ralph G. Caso (1971-1978). In the late 1960s and 1970s, Shelland interviewed three of these county executives, many of their assistants, and others involved in county government. Acknowledging the variety of factors affecting their different approaches, he characterizes Sprague and Patterson as having a business and conservative approach to county government. Although Nickerson was a Democrat and Caso a Republican, they shared a commitment to expanding government to provide services.

Herbert D. Rosenbaum, Professor Emeritus of Political Science at Hofstra University, has long been interested in local politics and government. He moderated two sessions at the conference and this volume includes his "Reflections on Nassau County's Suburban Politics." The suburbs are now a significant force in federal and state politics. Dr. Rosenbaum discusses individuals such as Leonard Hall, Peter DeSibio, J. Russel Sprague, Eugene Nickerson, and Joseph Margiotta, and he places the Nassau County situation in the larger context of state and national politics.

"Preserving Nassau County's Heritage in Museums and Parks," by Mildred Murphy DeRiggi, describes the development and growth of the county's extensive park, preserve, and museum system. Beginning with the acquisition of Salisbury (now Eisenhower) Park in 1944, the county has established an impressive number of parks and an unparalleled museum system. Parks and preserves range from the large Eisenhower Park with its three golf courses to waterfront parks on the north and south shores, and more than a dozen others with swimming pools, ice skating, and other recreational facilities. The museums include natural history (Tackapausha), archaeology and Native Americans (Garvies Point), a nineteenth-century restoration village (Old Bethpage), Gold Coast mansions (Falaise and Hempstead House), and a Cradle of Aviation Museum.

John B. Kiernan chaired the Charter Revision Commission in 1993-1994. As he points out in "The Creation of the Nassau County Legislature," this was "the most dramatic change in the way Nassau County has been governed since the county charter/county executive form of government was adopted in the 1930s." Mandated by a federal court decision to change to a more representative system, the Commission recommended a nineteen-member legislature. This was approved by the Board of Supervisors and the voters in a referendum in 1994. The legislature has been in operation only a few years, but has already brought about changes in county governance, as Kiernan notes.

The Nineteenth Century and Earlier

Nassau County's centennial was being commemorated, but a few of the articles deal primarily with earlier aspects of its history, when Nassau was part of Queens County. James M. McKenna, in "The Hempstead Plains: A

Capital Field for Military Exercises, 1700-1898," traces the use of the Plains from colonial times, focusing on military encampments during the Civil and Spanish-American Wars. Though overshadowed by the aviation fields in the twentieth century, the training camps at Camp Black and Camp Scott, which McKenna describes, are an important part of Nassau County's heritage.

Most motorists driving on Sunrise Highway probably don't realize that they are traveling on a road built over pipelines for Brooklyn's water supply. As Brooklyn's population grew in the nineteenth century, it needed more water than its wells could supply, and it looked westward to Queens County. In "When Nassau Supplied Brooklyn's Water," Richard A. Winsche explains how Brooklyn purchased land south of Hempstead for a reservoir, and other parcels of land for its water supply, despite protests from Queens County. Soon after Brooklyn became part of New York City in 1898, its water came from the Catskills, and Brooklyn's more than two thousand acres of watershed lands in Nassau County eventually became the backbone for the system of state parks and parkways which Robert Moses constructed, beginning in the 1920s.

The designation "Nassau" for the new county did not originate in 1899, but has a much longer history which Dorothy Horton McGee traces in "The Naming of Nassau County." The Nassau family dates to the eleventh century in Germany, and the House of Orange-Nassau to the sixteenth century in the Netherlands and to William III, Prince of Orange, who ruled England with his wife Mary from 1689-1702. Unsuccessful efforts to divide Queens County in 1869 and 1876 had included proposals of the name Nassau for the new county and, although Matinecock, Norfolk, and Bryant were also proposed as names in 1898, the name Nassau was adopted.

Changes and Transformations

In "An Ecodeterminist View of Nassau's Growth," Edward J. Smits analyzes how the "natural environment and ecology have influenced its development pattern from the time of colonial settlement." The Hempstead Plains became a center for horseracing beginning in the colonial period; in the twentieth century, it was the cradle of aviation and spurred the aviation industry. Long Island Sound and the ocean attracted wealthy New Yorkers who built country homes and estates on the Island, and hotels and boarding houses brought those of more modest means. Recreational opportunities abounded and golf, yachting, polo, fishing, and duck hunting flourished. The Long Island Rail Road facilitated suburban growth in the 1920s. Levitt and other developers spurred growth in the post-World War II years, facilitated by parks and parkways and the abundance of recreational opportunities which continue to influence the development of Nassau County.

Kenneth M. Foreman details the growth of "Public Education in the Bellmores, 1850-1950." The Bellmore districts are typical of many Long Island school districts which had one- and two-room country schools offering an elementary education (through grade eight) during much of the nineteenth century when attendance was not compulsory. As population, enrollments, and state funding increased, more teachers were hired, graded elementary schools evolved, and the teachers received better training. The struggle for secondary education in the early years of the twentieth century began with Bellmore parents seeking reimbursement for tuition in neighboring high schools. When Baldwin High School no longer had room for the 125 Bellmore students, in 1934 the Bellmores took advantage of a state law which encouraged districts to join in forming a Central High School District, and opened Mepham High School, named for the superintendent who had proposed the idea.

In "From Orchard Street to Sunrise Highway: The Establishment of Jewish Communities in Nassau County, 1897-1999," Martha Kreisel traces developments from early peddlers in the mid-nineteenth century to the formation of the first synagogue in Glen Cove in 1897. The Hempstead Hebrew Congregation, the Farmingdale Hebrew Association, and synagogues in Lawrence soon followed. Anti-Semitism from the Ku Klux Klan in Nassau County in the 1920s and financial problems in the 1930s presented difficulties to Jews and their congregations on Long Island. In the post-World War II years, the Jewish population boomed, and new synagogues were built. Although the total Jewish population in Nassau has declined in recent decades, Iranian and Iraqi Jews have moved to Great Neck and Orthodox families from New York City to the Five Towns.

Hugh A. Wilson examines Nassau County as a case study in "The American Welfare State and the Growth of Suburbia." New Deal banking and mortgage policies underlay the post-World War II housing boom which was spurred by the GI Bill, federal housing legislation, and deduction of mortgage interest. Thus, the federal government subsidized Levittown and other suburban developments. The GI Bill also financed higher education for veterans, and federal programs provided funding for college dormitories. Enrollments at Adelphi, Hofstra, and C. W. Post Colleges expanded. Nassau County benefited greatly from federal expenditures for the defense industry, since Grumman, Republic, Sperry, Fairchild, and other aviation companies employed thousands of Long Islanders. The postwar American welfare state thus aided and abetted the growth of suburbia in general and Nassau County in particular.

Health Care

The several essays in this section constitute the beginnings of an exploration of a hitherto largely unexplored aspect of Nassau County's history. We are grateful to Thomas Joseph Palmieri who organized this session for the conference, and the physicians who participated. Dr. Palmieri examines "The History of Hospitals in Nassau County," beginning with Nassau Hospital, a medical dispensary in West Hempstead in 1896 (now Winthrop-University Hospital in Mineola), to the recent mergers and affiliations of hospitals in the county.

Some of the other articles in this section also include information on the history of hospitals in the county. Doctors L. D. George Angus and Dina Fahmy trace "Trauma Care in Nassau County," from Long Island Rail Road accidents, flu and polio epidemics, and frostbite from blizzards in the early decades of the county to the development of trauma centers, burn centers, and Emergency Medical Systems in recent decades. Trauma care has become a specialty, and the effectiveness of Nassau's trauma centers was demonstrated in the Avianca crash in Cove Neck in 1990.

In "A History of Heart Surgery on Long Island," Dr. B. George Wisoff discusses cardiac surgery programs which began in the 1950s at various hospitals in Nassau County. Long Island Jewish Hospital has a residency teaching program for heart surgery. Basic research is conducted in the hospital laboratories and at the Cold Spring Harbor Laboratory. We can be proud that Long Island hospitals rank high in coronary bypass surgery.

Dr. Adrian R. Coren dates the beginning of "The History of Orthopedics in Nassau County" to the arrival of the first orthopedic specialist at Nassau Hospital in 1929. The first formally trained, full-time orthopedist in Nassau County was Ortho Hudson who opened an office in Hempstead in 1930. Dr. Hudson traveled to many Long Island hospitals and trained other orthopedists. Dr. Coren mentions many doctors who pioneered various orthopedic procedures at local hospitals.

Dr. Jack David Gorvoy in "Pediatric Care in Nassau County" focuses on developments since 1930. Earlier, most babies were born at home, and few doctors in Nassau specialized in pediatrics. When Meadowbrook Hospital opened in 1935, it had a pediatrics unit, nursery, and a contagious disease unit which cared for victims of the polio epidemic that year. Well baby clinics began in Nassau County in 1938.

"Surgery in Nassau County in the Twentieth Century" is addressed by Dr. Stanley D. Berliner. He contrasts the situation of persons with a hernia or breast cancer in 1900 and the medical treatment available today for these "two most common surgical procedures." The progress in these fields has been enormous, and it is a tribute to our local hospitals and to surgeons as well as to the general advances in medicine over the years.

Aerospace Heritage

Nassau County has a rich aerospace heritage, which is the topic of two papers in this volume; earlier Institute publications also addressed this important topic.[2] Roy Douglas traces "The Origins of Airplane Manufacturing in Farmingdale, New York: 1917-1928." This village was one of the "cradles" of aviation manufacturing. In 1918, Sydney Breese built Penguins—ground trainers, not designed to fly. Before his untimely death in 1923, Lawrence Sperry built unique amphibian triplanes, the single-engine Messengers, and the record-setting R-3 racer in his Farmingdale factory. Sherman Fairchild began making planes designed for aerial photography in what had been Sperry's plant and expanded in 1928 to a larger factory and airfield in East Farmingdale, east of the county line. In later years, Liberty, Republic, and other companies in Farmingdale would continue the tradition of airplane manufacturing.

Thomas J. Kelly, Father of the Lunar Module, gave a slide presentation at the conference, "From Long Island to the Moon: The Project Apollo Lunar Module," explaining Grumman's role in the Apollo moon landing in 1969. In 1961, in the midst of Cold War competition with the Soviet Union, President John F. Kennedy committed America to landing a man on the Moon within the decade. Grumman proposed a Lunar Orbit Rendezvous for the Apollo mission and became the prime contractor for the Lunar Module, which landed on the Moon. Six of the Lunar Modules manufactured and assembled at Grumman's plant in Bethpage remain on the Moon. Kelly concludes his article by briefly summarizing the legacy of the Apollo Program.

The conference featured a session with several films on Nassau's aviation heritage. *Daredevils and Dreamers,* a 1998 documentary, includes vintage footage from the Golden Age of aviation in the 1920s and 1930s, focusing on Roosevelt and Curtiss Fields. *Grumman at War: The Hellcat* profiles Grumman's most famous World War II fighter. *The Cradle of Aviation Museum* describes plans for the extensive new museum Nassau County is creating, which will highlight aircraft flown or manufactured on Long Island.[3]

People and Places

Theodore Roosevelt was Nassau County's most famous citizen, and has received much attention from historians over the years. In 1990, Hofstra University had a three-day conference, "Theodore Roosevelt and the Birth of Modern America," and the conference volume, *Theodore Roosevelt: Many-Sided American,* dealt with many aspects of his multifaceted life and career.[4] In "Theodore Roosevelt in the Local Arena," Natalie A. Naylor focuses on his local public activities, which have received little attention.

Oyster Bay greeted its adopted son with impressive receptions when he returned home from the Spanish-American War in 1898, from Africa in 1910, and from Brazil in 1914, as well as after his political campaigns. Roosevelt held receptions for his friends and neighbors at Sagamore Hill, spoke at local celebrations, laid cornerstones, and dedicated monuments. As Professor Naylor concludes, Roosevelt was "active in a wide range of civic activities—an exemplary first citizen in the local arena."

The conference included a session, "Spotlight on Communities." Every community is in some respects unique, but many share certain similarities, though the specific timing and individuals involved, of course, vary. Long Beach is one of the unique communities. It was the vision of one man and is one of only two cities in Nassau County. In "Sandbar to City: William H. Reynolds and the Planned Community of Long Beach, 1906-1922," Roberta Fiore and Elizabeth Coffin Allerhand explain how Senator Reynolds developed the barrier island. Reynolds dredged the channel, imposed a rectilinear grid, built a concrete boardwalk, provided water and sewage systems, put telephone and electricity lines underground, erected a town hall, hotel, and golf course, and imposed restrictive covenants to ensure a unified appearance. The original homes were large and very expensive; later he built and marketed more modest "Reynolds homes" and prefabricated bungalows. Despite the bankruptcy of his development company in 1921, Reynolds continued his control and, following the incorporation of Long Beach as a city in 1922, William H. Reynolds was elected its first mayor.

William J. Johnston, in "Farmingdale's History: A Reflection of Nassau County's First Century," traces the early development of Farmingdale and focuses on its history in the twentieth century, noting parallels throughout to Nassau County's history. The village was incorporated in 1904 and grew steadily, but slowly, until the post-World War II years. That growth is reflected in the increase from one school to nine schools in a decade stretching between the 1950s and 1960s, and in greater ethnic and religious diversity. Farmingdale's business district on Main Street thrived, but the opening of shopping centers in Hicksville and Massapequa, and discount stores on Route 110, have brought changes. Many of the traditional stores were replaced with restaurants and more service-oriented businesses. Farmingdale is a microcosm not only of the history of Nassau County, but also its history is fairly typical of many other communities in the county as well.

A number of contemporary comedians grew up in Nassau County, including Lenny Bruce, Eddie Murphy, Billy Crystal, and Jerry Seinfeld. Joseph Dorinson examines two comedians associated with Nassau County in "From Soup to Nuts: Laughter in the Suburbs—Alan King and Billy Crystal." King was raised in Brooklyn, but has lived in Nassau County for most of his career. Billy Crystal grew up in Long Beach where he began his career, but moved to the west coast for a career in film. Dorinson dubs King, the urban expatriot, "America's foremost suburban comic."

In "Women in the Clergy in Nassau County: Breaking Through the Stained Glass Ceiling," Linda F. Burghardt profiles four contemporary clergywomen, detailing the personal journey each took toward her religious vocations and examining the cultural and religious climate in which women clergy perform thier leadership roles today. While Nassau County is more receptive to women in the clergy than many other areas of the country, and great strides have been made to allow them a full voice in religious leadership, there are still major gains to be made in the area of pay equity, equal job opportunities, and congregational acceptance. The Institute's conference volume, *Long Island Women: Activists and Innovators,* touched on some of the work of women in Catholic religious orders.[5]

Janet Wagner, in her article, "A Century of Authors and Literature," chronicles the more than three dozen twentieth-century writers who have roots or resided in Nassau County. Some, such as Frances Hodgson Burnett, Sinclair Lewis, and F. Scott Fitzgerald, resided here only briefly, but did some of their important work here. Others, such as Christopher Morley, lived in Nassau County for most of their career. Morley's writing studio, The Knothole, is preserved in the county park in North Hills which now bears his name.[6]

Other Conference Features

County Executive Thomas Gulotta delivered greetings from the county at the opening of the conference. "Governing the County" and "Nassau: The Quintessential Suburb" were topics for panel discussions as well as the previously mentioned session on "The Formation of Nassau County."[7] There were other conference speakers whose presentations are not included in this conference volume, but virtually all the sessions were audiotaped and are available in the conference files at the Long Island Studies Institute.[8]

A few of the sessions featured films and videos. "Levitt's Town" was one chapter in Allen Oren's *Long Island, Our Story,* produced for Cablevision News 12 in 1998. *Building the American Dream: Levittown, NY* was produced by Stewart Bird and Cablevision in 1994. Other videos focused on Robert Moses: *The World That Moses Built,* from the PBS *American Experience* series (1990), and "A Man Called Moses," a segment from Oren's *Long Island, Our Story.*[9] A computer slide program by Edward Magnani on the "Nassau County Centennial, 1899-1999" was shown in the Rochelle and Irwin A. Lowenfeld Conference and Exhibition Hall in the Joan and Donald E. Axinn Library.[10]

Guest curator Linda B. Martin prepared the conference exhibition, *Nassau County at 100: The Past and Present in Photographs,* by selecting twenty-five archival photographs from the turn of the century and photographing contemporary views of the same sites. The exhibition was in the Lowenfeld Exhibition Hall in the Axinn Library from January 25 to March 23, 1999. The exhibition catalog, published by the Hofstra Museum and the Long Island Studies Institute, provides a permanent record of the exhibition; the publication includes all the photographs (with the contemporary color works reproduced in black and white) and twenty additional historic photographs.[11]

A staged reading of a 1934 play by Christopher Morley, *Soft Shoulders: The Commuters' Comedy,* was presented by the Hofstra Cultural Center and Hofstra USA Productions in the Student Center Theater, under the direction of Bob Spiotto. The satire on the lives on Long Island commuters was last produced in 1940 at the Millpond Playhouse in Roslyn.[12]

Acknowledgments

I am grateful to Hofstra University for its continued support of the Long Island Studies Institute which makes our publications and conferences possible. Joann P. Krieg's editorial pen has improved the readability of this book. I selected most of the illustrations in this book which are from the Collection of the Nassau County Division of Museum Services in the Long Island Studies Institute at Hofstra University. Mildred Murphy DeRiggi of the Nassau County Museum System has been gracious in securing copies of photographs. The credit line throughout has been abbreviated as *NCM Collection, LISI at Hofstra.* Barbara M. Kelly was co-director of the Nassau County conference and assisted with this conference volume.[13]

Many of the contributors assisted the publication by providing their articles on computer disk. The Institute secretary, Victoria R. Aspinwall, continues to be an invaluable editorial assistant, proofreading and providing editing suggestions, as well as entering manuscripts and corrections on the computer. Dorothy B. Ruettgers has been my grammatical consultant. Walter Steesy of Heart of the Lakes Publishing has been patient with my fine tuning page proofs. My thanks and appreciation to all who have assisted publication of this book.

Notes

1. See Edward J. Smits, "Creating a New County: Nassau," *Long Island Historical Journal* 11 (Spring 1999): 129-44; Jeffrey A. Kroessler, "The Greater City and Queens County," *Long Island Historical Journal* 11 (Fall 1999): 1-14; and George J. Lankevich, *American Metropolis: A History of the New York City* (New York: New York University, 1998). A reprint of "The Formation of Nassau County," by Natalie A. Naylor, from the *Nassau County Historical Society Journal* 53 (1998): 8-10, was distributed at the conference. On New York City consolidation, see also David C. Hammack, *Power and*

Society: Greater New York at the Turn of the Century (New York: Russell Sage Foundation, 1982); "Imperial City," in *Gotham: A History of New York City to 1898,* by Edwin G. Burrows and Mike Wallace (New York: Oxford University Press, 1999), 1,219-36; and *The Encyclopedia of New York City,* edited by Kenneth T. Jackson (New Haven: Yale University Press, 1995).

2. See two books by Joshua Stoff, Curator of the Cradle of Aviation Museum: *The Aerospace Heritage of Long Island* (Interlaken, NY: Heart of the Lakes Publishing 1989) and (for younger readers), *From Airship to Spaceship: Long Island in Aviation and Spaceflight* (Interlaken, NY: Empire State Books, 1991); and articles in Institute conference volumes: Joann Lynn, "Woman's Cradle of Aviation: Curtiss Field, Valley Stream," in *Evoking a Sense of Place,* edited by Joann P. Krieg (Interlaken, NY: Heart of the Lakes Publishing, 1988), 85-95; Joann Lynn Harvey, "First Women in Aviation," in *Long Island Women: Activists and Innovators,* edited by Natalie A. Naylor and Maureen O. Murphy (Interlaken, NY: Empire State Books, 1998), 43-56; and Henry M. Holden, "The Life and Times of Harriet Quimby," in *Long Island Women,* edited by Naylor and Murphy, 57-64.

3. The films *Grumman at War: The Hellcat* and *The Cradle of Aviation Museum* are in the collection of the Cradle of Aviation Museum at Mitchel Field, Garden City. *Daredevils and Dreamers* is in Hofstra University's Collection at the Long Island Studies Institute, which also has in its collection some earlier films on the Cradle of Aviation including vintage footage of pioneering flights.

4. *Theodore Roosevelt: Many-Sided American,* edited by Natalie A. Naylor, Douglas Brinkley, and John Allen Gable (Interlaken, NY: Heart of the Lakes Publishing, 1992).

5. See Sister Edna McKeever, "Mother de Chantal Keating, CSJ: A 'Notable, Noble American,'" in *Long Island Women: Activists and Innovators,* edited by Naylor and Murphy, 126-32; and Sister Lois Van Delft, "Women of Faith: The Spiritual Legacy of the Founders of St. Francis Hospital," in *Long Island Women,* edited by Naylor and Murphy, 146-53.

6. Cedarmere in Roslyn Harbor, the country home of William Cullen Bryant, a nineteenth-century poet, is also part of the Nassau County Division of Museum Services. Cedarmere and the Knothole are open seasonally (for information, call 516-571-8130 or 572-0257).

7. "Governing the County," moderated by Edward J. Smits, featured John B. Kiernan and two former Deputy County Executives, Farrell T. Jones and Joseph H. Driscoll, Jr. Kiernan's comments on the Charter Revision Commission are included in this volume, (137-42); an audiotape and transcript of the session, including questions and answers, are in the conference files in the Long Island Studies Institute at Hofstra University's West Campus. Barbara M. Kelly, curator of the Long Island Studies Institute and co-director of the conference, spoke at the panel discussion on "Nassau: The Quintessential Suburb."

8. Papers presented at the conference, but not included in this volume, are: "Leonard Hall: A Country Politician," by Owen Smith, Professor at C. W. Post Campus of Long Island University (some of his points are summarized in Herbert Rosenbaum's article in this volume, "Reflections on Nassau County's Suburban Politics," 118-25); "Set in Nassau County: Image and Identity in Cinema" (movies filmed in Nassau County), by Monica Taller Albala of the Nassau County Division of Museum Services;

"Long Island in Air and Space: Past and Future," by Tom Gwynne, Senior Operations Planner for the Cradle of Aviation Museum at Mitchel Field; "75 Years of the Nassau County Police Department," by George Maher, Nassau County Police Department Historian; "The Mineola Fair: Mirror of a County's Growth," by Gary Hammond, historian with the Nassau County Division of Museum Services (published in the *Nassau County Historical Society Journal* 54 [1999]: 23-30); "Living on the Bay: A Study of Long Island's Traditional Waterfront Architecture," by Nancy Solomon, a folklorist and Director of Long Island Traditions; "Old Time Base Ball on Long Island," by Ken Balcom and Gary Monti, the Supervisor and Volunteer Coordinator of the Old Time Base Ball program at Old Bethpage Village Restoration; "Cold Spring Harbor Laboratory Research in the Twentieth Century," by Bruce Stillman, Director of the Cold Spring Harbor Laboratory; "Mineola—County Hub, Seat of Independence," by Cecilia Bergstein; and "Change of Venue: Nassau County and Malbone Street Tragedy" (a 1918 accident in Brooklyn), by Anthony C. LaVecchia and Jon Sterngass. Audiotapes of these presentations are in the Long Island Studies Institute conference files at Hofstra University, West Campus, 619 Fulton Avenue, Hempstead, NY 11549; 516-463-6411.

9. The *Long Island, Our Story* videos and *Building the American Dream* are in Hofstra University's Collection at the Long Island Studies Institute, which also has considerable footage from the Long Island State Park Commission on building parks and parkways in the New York metropolitan area (nine videos, six hours; some unnarrated raw footage). The Institute also has another video showing the building of Jones Beach and the 1939 World's Fair, a 1962 CBS documentary, *The Man Who Built New York,* and WNET's *Conversation with Robert Moses* (1977).

The Long Island Studies Institute sponsored conferences: "Suburbia Re-examined" in 1987, and "Robert Moses" in 1988. Those interested in more on these topics should consult the conference volumes: *Suburbia Re-examined,* edited by Barbara M. Kelly (New York: Greenwood Press, 1989); *Long Island: The Suburban Experience,* edited by Barbara M. Kelly (Interlaken, NY: Heart of the Lakes Publishing, 1990); and *Robert Moses: Single-Minded Genius,* edited by Joann P. Krieg (Interlaken, NY: Heart of the Lakes Publishing, 1989).

Several films on Nassau politics and government were shown at the conference and are mentioned in notes 2-4 in Herbert Rosenbaum's essay, "Reflections on Nassau County's Suburban Politics," p. 125. The aviation films were mentioned earlier in this Introduction; see also note 3 above.

10. This is accessible on the web: www.co.nassau.ny.us.

11. Linda B. Martin, *Nassau County at 100: The Past and Present in Photographs* (Hempstead: Hofstra University, 1999), is available from the Long Island Studies Institute.

12. A videotape of the *Soft Shoulders* production is in the conference files at the Long Island Studies Institute.

13. Although conference credits appeared in the conference program, I would also note here the valuable assistance of the Hofstra Cultural Center and, in particular, the efficent work of Athelene A. Collins-Prince, Assistant Director of the the Cultural Center and Conference Coordinator. Edward J. Smits, Chairperson of the Nassau County Centennial Committee, assisted in organizing the conference. A number of Hofstra faculty served as moderators of sessions. The Friends for Long Island's Heritage provided financial support for the conference.

This cartoon, entitled "The Dream of the Tiger," appeared in the *Hempstead Record* (October 1957), published by the Town of Hempstead Republican Committee. It vividly expressed the desire to remain apart from New York City. "We do not want to become 'The Borough of Nassau,' the tail of the Tammany Tiger or any part of it," J. Russel Sprague proclaimed in the accompanying editorial which urged a "No" vote on holding a state Constitutional Convention in 1959. *NCM Collection, LISI at Hofstra.*

Nassau County: A Pioneer of the Crabgrass Frontier

Jon C. Teaford

Nassau County's history, viewed in the broader context of metropolitan development in America, has a significance that raises its centennial observance to a higher level of importance. Nassau County has been a pioneer along what has been called "the Crabgrass Frontier."[1] It was one of the first areas to attract a large suburban population, having accommodated thousands of commuters to New York City as early as the 1920s and 1930s. It was also one of the first areas to develop scores of independent political entities, towns, cities, and villages, housing families whose breadwinner commuted each day to the central city for work. Yet Nassau was also one of the first areas to become what has been called post-suburban, that is, an area once suburban that has developed characteristics more commonly associated with a major central city. In the decades following World War II Nassau County became increasingly a center of retailing, manufacturing, and office employment, not just a collection of bedroom communities. It could boast a major daily newspaper, which today has the sixth largest daily circulation in the United States. And Long Island is home to a major-league hockey team, which, by choosing the name "Islanders," clearly identified itself as a team primarily representing Nassau and Suffolk counties. But Nassau was not only a pioneer in suburban and post-suburban development, it also was one of the first suburban regions to reach maturity. By the 1960s it had reached its full population growth, and since that time it has pioneered a new stage of metropolitan development, that of mature post-suburbia. Nassau has been, then, in many ways, in the forefront of metropolitan trends that have transformed America as a whole.

This centennial is of even further significance because it marks not only one hundred years of Nassau history but also the close of the twentieth century. And it is especially appropriate that the centennial and the end of the century coincide, for in retrospect it is apparent that the twentieth century has been the century of suburbia. Whereas the previous century witnessed the phenomenal rise of large American cities, the twentieth century has been characterized by the dispersion of population among outlying towns and villages and the ascendancy of a new way of life. The nineteenth century was the century of New York City, the urban giant which grew from a mere 61,000 people in 1800 to a gargantuan 3.4 million in 1900, but the twentieth century has been Nassau's century. Nassau is a prime example of the prevailing tendencies of twentieth-century American development.

From its beginning, Nassau was a political unit dedicated to reversing the trend toward big city expansion so characteristic of the nineteenth century. The late 1800s and first decades of the twentieth century formed the great era of urban imperialism in the United States. From 1850 to 1920 the largest American cities absorbed extensive tracts of land, annexing unincorporated territory and consolidating with existing smaller municipalities. In 1854 the city of Philadelphia absorbed twenty-eight other local governments and extended its boundaries to include the entire 129 square miles in Philadelphia County. During the 1880s, Chicago engaged in an aggressive annexation campaign that expanded its area fivefold. And between 1900 and 1920 Los Angeles acquired most of its present territory, annexing its port at San Pedro and the vast San Fernando Valley, absorbing new territory larger in size than all of Nassau County.[2]

But, of course, the greatest example of this urban imperialism was the creation of Greater New York in the 1890s. As a result of the consolidation of 1898, New York City's area increased more than sixfold from 44 to 299 square miles. Moreover, some of the same factors inspired this consolidation scheme as did other annexation campaigns elsewhere in the nation.[3] Every city wanted to improve its rank among the hierarchy of metropolises in the nation, and annexation was necessary to improve one's rank, or in the case of New York City, to maintain first place among America's cities. Chicago's rapid growth and its land grab of the 1880s startled some New York boosters who recognized that the western upstart might some day surpass a New York City confined to Manhattan Island and the southern part of the Bronx. In 1894, the *New York Times* claimed it was "a foregone conclusion" that unless the city "extends her borders at once, she will be outstripped by Chicago."[4] The *Times* estimated that if New York City retained its existing boundaries, Chicago would surpass it in population in 1902 and become the nation's greatest municipality. According to the *New York Times* and other such boosters, the "real" New York included the then independent municipalities on western Long Island, and the census figures should reflect this.

Moreover, many of the outlying areas favored annexation because of the improved public services and government that the central city could provide. The superiority of central city services was evident in urban areas throughout the nation, and the New York City area was no exception. This was especially evident in Queens County's largest municipality, Long Island City, whose local government had such an odious reputation that the voters supported consolidation with New York City by a margin of better than four to one. In the age of urban imperialism during the late nineteenth and early twentieth centuries, annexation to the big city was generally popular both in the city itself and in the areas to be annexed. The city would gain in stature and population; the annexed areas would receive the superior services that the large municipality could provide. Consequently, big city expansion was both popular and prevalent in the 1890s.

Nassau County, of course, represented an early exception to this prevailing trend. It owes its very existence to a desire to remain apart, to *not* become a district within the big city. In the 1890s one proponent of withdrawal from Queens County summed up the Nassau attitude, one which has largely prevailed throughout the county's history. He warned: "It is probable that there will be extra trouble when the outskirts of greater New York are in our midst. Provision against impending danger is wisdom."[5] The big city was, in the minds of Nassau's founders, an impending danger and the creation of Nassau was a provision against this danger. Thus Nassau County's founders were pioneers of a separatist trend that would become more prevalent in American metropolitan areas after 1920 and would influence suburban development throughout the remainder of the century. From its very beginning Nassau was defined as that part of Queens which was not urban and not eager to become so. It was that part of Queens outside of New York City, and that continuing sense of being outside the city and offering a better alternative to the city has defined much of Nassau's history. This same sense of being gratefully beyond the city has also defined the suburban mentality throughout the United States in the twentieth century. From its earliest beginnings, then, Nassau offered a foretaste of the suburban era of the future. Though born in the age of urban imperialism, it was an exception to the rule during that era.

In the decades following its creation Nassau would provide a low-density alternative to life in New York City, as suburban developments attracted thousands of new residents. From 1900 to 1920 the population more than doubled from 55,000 to 126,000, as it already experienced an influx of new residents during the county's first decades. During the 1920s, Nassau witnessed an even greater wave of suburbanization as its population more than doubled in a single decade. By 1930 more than 300,000 people lived in the county, and the population density figure was about 1,100 people per square mile (see Table). With such density, the county could hardly claim to be rural any longer, though numerous expanses of countryside survived. It was clearly one of the nation's premiere suburban areas. Moreover, real estate agents and subdivision developers of the 1920s lavishly extolled the virtues of this prime example of suburbia. It was a haven of clean air, open spaces, and socially desirable neighbors, yet within only forty minutes of Manhattan's Pennsylvania Station. For example, in 1928 a promoter of a subdivision in Great Neck advertised homes for "people of refinement who recognize the opportunity of settling in an exclusive community" and who could enjoy "the wholesomeness of life in the suburbs." A developer of Sands Point promoted

Population and Density of Population, Nassau and Suffolk Counties, 1890-1990

	Population		Population Density Per Square Mile	
	Nassau	Suffolk	Nassau	Suffolk
1890	45,760	62,491	167	68
1900	55,448	77,582	202	84
1910	83,930	96,138	306	104
1920	126,120	110,246	460	120
1930	303,053	161,055	1,106	175
1940	406,748	197,355	1,356	214
1950	672,765	276,129	2,243	299
1960	1,300,171	666,784	4,334	723
1970	1,428,838	1,127,030	4,942	1,211
1980	1,321,582	1,284,231	4,609	1,409
1990	1,287,348	1,321,864	4,489	1,451

Source: U. S. Census data from 1930-1990, Jon C. Teaford, *Post-Suburbia,* 12, 47, 95, 163; 1890-1920, *Historical Population of Long Island Communities 1790-1980* (Hauppauge: Long Island Regional Planning Board, 1982), 15-16 (density calculated using land area in 1930 *Census of Population*).

properties that were "near enough to New York for convenience" but which were "quiet and comfortable at all seasons of the year" and adjoined "the extensive holdings of well known and cultured people." Moreover, an East Williston developer told prospective buyers: "Being in Nassau County the home owner has the advantage of progressive local government without the delays, annoyances and taxes of the big city."[6] As these advertisements presented it, Nassau was quiet, wholesome, refined, exclusive, and beyond the control of crude, cigar-chomping Tammany politicians. Nassau was eminently accessible to the big city, but it was not part of that city. By living in Nassau, one could partake of Manhattan but one could also escape it. Nassau was the suburban dream, supposedly embodying the best of both city and country. This was the ideal of the suburban haven which was winning adherents throughout the nation. And during the 1920s Nassau developed as the preeminent example of this ideal.

While the suburban lifestyle was flourishing in Nassau, a suburban form of government was also developing. Whereas the big city was governed by one large government centered in a downtown city hall, the characteristic suburban government was a small municipality which provided government for a fragment of suburbia that was tailored to the special needs and interests of that fragment. In Nassau and other emerging suburban areas, residents thus rejected not only the big city way of life but also the big city way of government. This fondness for village government was evident in the soaring number of municipalities within Nassau's boundaries. In 1920 there were only twenty village or city governments in Nassau, but by 1930 this figure had more than doubled to forty-seven, and by the mid-1930s it was up to sixty-five. Moreover, despite a recommendation by the New York State Conference of Mayors that the village form of government was inappropriate for communities of 7,500 or more, most Nassau villages, no matter what their populations, resisted city status. Of the sixty-five municipalities, sixty-three were villages and only two, Long Beach and Glen Cove, were cities. Many of the villages had a larger population than the cities.[7]

Many of these entities were created to protect a desired way of life, a goal typical of suburbia. For example, many of the new municipalities in the northern half of the county were estate communities which incorporated in order that the local gentry would have the legal authority to exclude unwanted development and maintain a low-density estate lifestyle. Saddle Rock, Centre Island, Old Brookville, and Old Westbury were all estate communities, with municipal governments dedicated to preserving the status quo of their aristocratic residents. Incorporation in Nassau, and later in suburban areas across the nation, was often a protective device, a means by which to build a wall around a fragment of suburbia.

As such the suburban municipality deviated sharply from the big city which boasted of its size and was eager to attract as many new residents as possible. In the nineteenth century communities incorporated to become cities; in the twentieth century suburban villages incorporated in order to not become cities. In the big cities which developed in the nineteenth century, municipal government existed to nurture growth and provide the services necessary for the city to expand and prosper. In Nassau the role of the municipalities that incorporated in the 1920s was quite different. It often was to preserve a lifestyle, to preserve the status quo rather than to create a dense urban environment. Nassau was pioneering a new conception of municipal rule.

These new governments were also developing practices and procedures that differed markedly from those of the big cities. Though a Republican party organization dominated county and town politics in Nassau, at the village level traditional partisanship was not so appreciated. In suburban villages the leaders were not supposed to be politicians but instead civic-minded volunteers who contributed their time and talents to the community's government just as they did to the Kiwanis or Rotary. Moreover, in sharp contrast to the nation's democratic ideals, in some suburbs the idea of the contested election was abhorrent. In 1946 the village report of Garden City boasted that in twenty-seven years of municipal existence "at no time ha[d] there ever been more than one ticket placed in nomination for the offices of mayor and trustee." Consequently, "partisanship and disunity ha[d] been avoided," and candidates had been "selected on their merits without political pressure."[8] This rejection of the democratic ideal of competitive elections was not evident in every suburban community; many villages experienced sharp factional conflicts. But Garden City residents and like-minded citizens believed that partisan competition between Republican and Democratic slates with its overtones of conflict and division seemed inappropriate for suburban havens. The big city was an arena of clashing forces and harsh competition, but the suburban village was expected to be a refuge from such crass conflict, even though it often was not. In Nassau and elsewhere, as suburbia developed, a new ideal of civic-minded government, with neither Republican nor Democratic slates, emerged as most suitable for the scores of freshly minted villages. It was appropriate that the basic constitution of Garden City government fashioned in 1919 was known as the Gentlemen's Agreement, for village government was expected to be a gentlemanly affair in distinct contrast to the disturbing rough-and-tumble politics of the big city.

By 1930 Nassau had pioneered a suburban pattern of life and government that was to become characteristic of other suburban areas throughout the nation. In Nassau, as elsewhere, suburbia was to be a residential haven accessible to the big city but offering a lifestyle which the city could not match. Moreover, fragmented municipal rule by scores of village governments was the prevalent suburban pattern as opposed to the big city pattern of control from a distant city hall and administration by a gargantuan bureaucracy. By 1930 the suburban alternative was firmly planted in Nassau County, and this alternative was to be replicated in metropolitan areas across the nation.

Suburbia, however, bred certain problems as well as solutions. And these problems were going to force some compromises with the ideal of the suburban haven. Nassau and other areas had to deviate from the ideal because that ideal was either too impractical or too costly. And again Nassau was a pioneer, an innovator of pragmatic compromises that would ensure surburbia's survival.

This pattern of compromise was evident in the development of Nassau's county government. By the 1930s Nassau not only comprised sixty-five villages and cities but 173 special district governments. There were fifty-three lighting districts, fifty-two fire districts, and thirty-eight water districts. A survey of Nassau County's government reported: "There are so many local jurisdictions that it was not possible to prepare a map of the county or even of one town showing local unit boundaries." According to this investigation, there were within a single tract of 120 acres, twenty-four governmental units exercising authority, "or one for every five acres of ground."[9] In the minds of most public administration experts such extraordinary fragmentation of government was inefficient and resulted in costly, irresponsible government. Residents had a difficult time fathoming who was in charge, and excessive duplication of effort supposedly increased costs and hampered coordination necessary for improved service.

As early as 1914 a good-government group called the Nassau County Association was lobbying to correct some of the problems in the pattern of local rule. This group won state legislative authorization for the creation of a commission to propose reforms in Nassau's framework of government. The commission's report issued in 1918 asserted that change was necessary and noted a demand "in particular for a greater centralization and responsibility of authority."[10] Thus it called for a transfer of authority to an overarching county government which supposedly would overcome the inefficiencies resulting from the division of responsibility among excessively small governmental units. In reporting on the commission's findings, the *New York Times* announced that the reformed framework would govern Nassau "like a big city."[11] This was a red flag for many of Nassau's residents who sought to avoid such big city government at all costs.

During the following two decades, however, Nassau residents disagreed over attempts to correct the existing governmental fragmentation and create a more centralized and unified system of rule. In 1921, New York voters approved a state constitutional amendment that permitted both Nassau and Westchester counties to adopt new forms of government. In both 1925 and 1935 Nassau citizens rejected by large majorities proposed county charters that would have centralized authority in the hands of the county government and abridged some of the traditional prerogatives of the cities, towns, and villages. A key factor in their defeat was the opposition of the county's powerful Republican organization. In 1925 one spokesperson for the Republican organization made a characteristic argument when he contended that "the charter would mean the surrender by the Towns, villages and cities of their inalienable right to local government."[12] Such exaggerated claims swayed the voters, but the statements of Governor Al Smith did not help the cause of reform. In 1928 he told the New York City Bar Association that "within the next five years Nassau will have to be a city." A Nassau County real estate developer offered a more realistic assessment when he remarked: "The people of Nassau County want decentralization rather than the opposite. The fact that Nassau County is composed of a number of individual villages governed by the residents themselves is one of its strongest selling points."[13]

Recognizing the merits of reform arguments but at the same time alert to the separatist feelings of local residents, the Republican organization headed

This cartoon, "Let's Consolidate Everything, It's Easier to Grab That Way," appeared in the *Hempstead Record* (October 1955), published by the Town of Hempstead Republican Committee. It was in response to a Democratic election campaign charge that "new residents weren't attracted to Nassau," because it was a "jurisdictional jungle." *NCM Collection, LISI at Hofstra.*

by J. Russel Sprague agreed on a compromise solution in 1936. The organization backed a charter proposal which created a county executive with a qualified veto over the actions of the county board of supervisors. The new charter centralized authority over welfare, health, and tax assessment in the county, and authorized a county planning commission to adopt a master plan to guide the county's development. In November 1936 Nassau voters approved the charter which preserved the small-scale village governments but made some concessions to those who believed that centralization of authority was necessary.

By adopting the charter Nassau again established itself as a pioneer along the crabgrass frontier, for it became the first county in the United States to create an elected executive office, an innovation that would spread across the nation during the following six decades. By1987 at least 391 counties in thirty-one states had elected chief executives comparable to that in Nassau County.[14] Moreover, the elected executive has been a feature of government in many of the largest suburban counties. Both Westchester and Suffolk counties followed Nassau's example as did Oakland County, Michigan, and St. Louis County, Missouri, two of the nation's most populous suburban counties. The Nassau model was a cross between the traditional board-governed structure of county government and the mayor-council government of the big city. As such it was well suited to suburban counties which felt compelled to retain the fragmentation of authority dear to the hearts of suburbanites, but at the same time impose the coordination inherent in a single elected executive. Thus Nassau and the other counties that followed its example had a county executive comparable to a big city mayor but they did not embrace the unitary, centralized rule characteristic of the largest central cities. The Nassau model of government was a pragmatic compromise which preserved the suburban ideal of small-scale rule while overcoming some of the shortcomings inherent in the fragmentation of authority.

By the 1940s and 1950s Nassau was not only compromising with regard to its structure of government, it was accepting certain necessary changes in suburban lifestyle. The traditional ideal of the bedroom community had certain definite drawbacks. Bedroom communities lacked the retailing and job opportunities available in the big city, necessitating long and irksome commutes for both shoppers and workers. Moreover, bedroom communities were most often woefully lacking a lucrative tax base, a factor of increasing significance after World War II as Nassau's homes became crowded with school-age children who required more teachers, more school buildings, and consequently more tax dollars for education. In the face of these realities, the ideal of the suburban haven yielded, and the years following World War II witnessed a marked change in Nassau. Between 1947 and 1963 the number of persons employed in manufacturing in the county almost quadrupled, and the advent of the industrial park marked a new era of detente between suburban manufacturing and residential development. In 1957 a Nassau County publication observed that "the industrial park . . . promises to be a vital contributor in terms of greater employment opportunities and a more equitable sharing of local taxes." This publication further noted of the industrial park: "One of its chief attractions is that it need not clash aesthetically or otherwise with the existing suburban nature of Long Island's two Eastern Counties."[15] Clean industry on landscaped sites could thus yield needed jobs and tax revenues without too seriously disturbing the prevailing suburban environment.

An expansion in retailing was likewise changing the face of Nassau. The giant Roosevelt Field shopping center opened in 1956 with a branch of Macy's, scores of other stores, and 11,000 parking spaces.[16] A far cry from the quaint village shopping districts of the pre-World War II period, Roosevelt Field marked a new era in Long Island retailing. Gradually, Nassau would declare its retailing independence from Manhattan.

By the 1960s Nassau was deviating from the suburban ideal of an earlier era. It had accepted some degree of county government coordination superimposed on the multitude of towns, cities, villages, and special districts. Nassau residents had embraced an elected county executive who more closely resembled a big city mayor than a traditional county official. The bedroom community was meanwhile giving way to a more balanced economic pattern with large scale retailing and thousands of manufacturing jobs. While maintaining a form of government, a physical environment, and a lifestyle which contrasted sharply to that of New York City or other large central cities, Nassau was becoming more urban and less traditionally suburban.

By the 1960s Nassau was also entering a new phase of its development and once again it would prove a suburban pioneer. For Nassau was one of the first suburban areas to reach maturity, in other words, achieve full population. Nassau's population increased slowly during the 1960s, peaked in 1970, then slowly declined and has remained relatively stable in the 1990s (see Table p. 30). In any case, by the 1960s and 1970s Nassau was no longer an area where potato fields were being transformed into vast housing developments. That era of suburbanization was over. Instead, Nassau was pioneering a new stage in metropolitan development. Within the following two decades an increasing number of areas throughout the nation would enter this new era of maturity.

Maturity did not necessarily mean economic decline in these mature suburban areas. Many communities experienced soaring real estate values, and in the 1970s and 1980s commercial development continued. So neither Nassau nor other mature suburban regions were necessarily "over the hill." But they were not experiencing rapid population growth as they had in earlier years.

From 1899 to 1999, Nassau has been in the forefront of suburban and post-suburban development. It has pioneered stages of development that would become characteristic of metropolitan areas throughout the nation. In the early twentieth century it spawned commuter suburbs that opted for independent municipal existence in a pattern replicated from New Jersey to California. By the 1930s it was fashioning new institutions of government suited to the prevailing ideals and practical demands of suburbia. Under the Nassau model, localities would retain their autonomy whereas the county would provide some overarching coordination. This was a scheme repeated in heavily populated suburban counties elsewhere. In the second half of the twentieth century Nassau pioneered a new age of suburban commercial development typified by the shopping mall and industrial park. Finally, it was in the forefront of suburban maturity, having achieved its full population by 1970. The year 1999 marks the centennial of Nassau County and one hundred years of development in an area which from its very birth was dedicated to not being part of a city, to not being one more conquered territory of central city imperialists. This is the centennial of a world apart, a world that rejected the urban past and over a period of ten decades has pioneered an alternative future.

Notes

1. The allusion is to Kenneth T. Jackson, *Crabgrass Frontier: The Suburbanization of the United States* (New York: Oxford University Press, 1985).

2. See Jon C. Teaford, *City and Suburb: The Political Fragmentation of Metropolitan America, 1850-1970* (Baltimore: The Johns Hopkins University Press, 1979), 33, 36, 43-46, 61.

3. Teaford, *City and Suburb,* 57-58, 76.

4. *New York Times,* October 30, 1894, 5.

5. P. Halstead Scudder, quoted in Geoffrey Mohan, "Nassau's Difficult Birth," in *Long Island: Our Story,* by Newsday (Melville, NY: Newsday, 1998), 234.

6. *New York Times,* July 11, 1926, sec. 10, p. 5; July 15, 1928, sec. 11 and 12, p. 4.

7. In 1930, the population of Glen Cove was 11,430 and Long Beach, 5,817. The incorporated villages with larger population than the two cities in 1930 included: Floral Park, 10,016; Freeport, 15,467; Garden City, 7,180; Hempstead, 12,650; Lynbrook, 11,993; Mineola, 8,155; Rockville Centre, 13,718; and Valley Stream, 11,790. The number of villages and unincorporated communities with larger population than the cities is even greater in the 1990s. The city of Glen Cove's population was estimated to be 24,546 in 1998 and Long Beach, 35,030, whereas the village of Hempstead's was 47,250 and Levittown, an unincorporated area, 52,601. See *Historical Population of Long Island Communities 1790-1980: Decennial Census Data* (Hauppauge: Long Island Regional Planning Board, 1982), 20-36; and Long Island Power Authority (LIPA), *Population Survey* (Uniondale: LIPA, 1998), 7-12. The number of municipalities in Nassau in 1999 is sixty-six. In Suffolk County, for comparison, there are no cities; the number of municipalities increased from twelve in 1920 to twenty-six in 1930; there are thirty in 1999. The Village of Hempstead began to take steps in late 1999 to incorporate as a city in order to secure a share of the county sales tax revenues. (Editor's note.)

8. *Annual Report of the Incorporated Village of Garden City, New York, 1946* (Garden City, NY: Village of Garden City, 1946), 11-12.

9. Thomas H. Reed, *The Government of Nassau County* (Mineola: Nassau County, 1934), 4, 58.

10. Jon C. Teaford, *Post-Suburbia: Government and Politics in the Edge Cities* (Baltimore: Johns Hopkins University Press, 1997), 33. In addition to Nassau and Suffolk Counties, the other "edge city" counties examined in this book are: Oakland, Michigan, north of Detroit; DuPage, Illinois, west of Chicago; St. Louis County, Missouri, west of the city of St. Louis; and Orange County, California, south of Los Angeles.

11. *New York Times,* March 17, 1918, sec. 3, p. 11.

12. *Hempstead Sentinel,* October 29, 1925, 1.

13. *New York Times,* March 4, 1928, 1; December 28, 1930, sec. 11 and 12, p. 3.

14. Jon C. Teaford, "Local Legislative Institutions," in *Encyclopedia of the American Legislative System,* edited by Joel H. Silbey, 3 vols. (New York: Charles Scribner's Sons, 1994), 1: 245.

15. Edgar Gray and William N. Leonard, "Park That Industry," *Long Island Business,* October 4, 1957, 4.

16. Teaford, *Post-Suburbia,* 55.

Myths and Realities of Suburban Politics

Marjorie Freeman Harrison

The celebration of Nassau's centennial comes at a time when scholarship is starting to catch up with the fact that, by population distribution at least, the United States may be characterized as a suburban nation. The academic literature on suburbia, an increasingly sophisticated body of work which constitutes a growing sub-speciality of urban studies, is nevertheless marred by oversimplifications and an elitist strain common to much writing about the American working class, middle-class life, and "middle brow" culture.

Suburban voters comprise the largest single block of voters in presidential elections. In 1960, the suburbs accounted for a third of the national vote; by 1988, that proportion had increased to 48 percent (Schneider 1992, 35). The reapportionment of Congress following the 1990 census resulted in 170 congressional districts that are primarily suburban, 98 primarily urban, and 88 primarily rural (Schneider 1992, 37). In the presidential elections of 1992 and 1996, the suburban electorate was perceived as a key swing vote; Bill Clinton's ability to win over suburban voters, especially those who might otherwise cast Republican ballots, greatly contributed to his victories. However, the history and dynamics of suburban politics has not been studied in the kind of detailed way needed to forecast how the suburban dimension will shape the future of American politics.

A series of notions pervading much writing and thinking about suburbia obscures rather than illuminates the dynamics of suburban public life. What follows aims to contribute to the process of defining and clarifying analytical frameworks that are useful in studying suburbia. It is hoped that these will help guide researchers to those questions and perspectives that have a good chance of yielding depictions of suburban history and contemporary life that are accurate and reflect the diversity and dignity of suburban residents and their communities.

First, research about Nassau and other suburban areas promises to be more productive if undertaken from the point of view of suburban development as a topic worthy of study in its own right, not only in comparison to or as an adjunct of the neighboring big city. Obviously, the politics of urban-suburban metropolitan areas operate in a myriad of interdependent ways, but as suburban areas have grown in population to rival their city centers, they have developed their own economic infrastructures and substantial job markets, and, as their governmental systems have matured, spheres of suburban public life have taken on more autonomous dynamics influenced, but not necessarily dominated, by the city.

Second, expressed either implicitly or explicitly too often in academic work and journalistic commentary on suburban politics, are notions which assert that suburbia is innately conservative. These assumptions posit characterizations that need to be teased out and examined. For example, it is argued that the people who chose to move to the suburbs left cities for racially-motivated reasons; they did not want to live in multiethnic, multiracial areas. Corollary to this is the assertion that homeownership exerts a conservative undertow on suburbanites' political consciousness. A related problem that has become less widespread as scholars such as Barbara Kelly provide more accurate frameworks for studying suburbia, is the tendency to portray suburban areas as predominantly upper class and affluent, portrayals predicated on misunderstandings of the economics of homeownership. Despite the spate of work done on Levittown, renowned precisely because its relatively small houses were affordable for working-class families, the fallacy remains that to get a mortgage, a family must be middle class.

The challenge for contemporary analysts of suburbia is to draw on the work of those scholars and journalists whose publications have contributed to the development of cohesive and historically accurate depictions, and to effectively rebut those misconceptions which inhibit clear-eyed understanding of suburban politics and its relationship to the larger national picture. Kenneth T. Jackson's *Crabgrass Frontier* offers an excellent starting point, precisely because it looks at the specific housing policies that shaped people's choices in the postwar period. In the context of an acute housing shortage following World War II, federal mortgage policy made it cheaper for whites to purchase a suburban home than to renovate a residential building in an urban neighborhood. Jackson demonstrates, based on his examination of Home Owners Loan Corporation (HOLC) maps, that this federal agency engaged in redlining, thereby reducing the flow of mortgage dollars into urban neighborhoods with minority residents. Jackson is wise in not making the mistake of conflating racially-based governmental policy with the motivations of thousands who took advantage of favorable mortgage opportunities. It is unclear that racial biases were a more powerful "push" out of the city than the "pull" of the "more for your money," subsidized, and economically attractive option of suburban homeownership.

On this point, the work of historian Andrew Wiese on black suburbanization provides crucial insights, for he documents the consistent efforts of African Americans, throughout the twentieth century, to create suburban communities. Wiese reasons that with suburbs now the place where most Americans live, "[a]rguably, to be suburban is to be American" (Wiese 1993, 31). Examining three black suburban communities around Cleveland,

Detroit, and Cincinnati, Wiese found that suburban "black pioneers explicitly desired many of the same things as their white counterparts." Their "vision included a good job, such as only the city could provide, but it also contained such nonurban things as open space, a private home designed to their own specifications, a plot of land that they owned, a garden and small livestock, and the sense of a community that they could control" (Wiese 1993, 31, 32, 51).

Wiese contributes powerfully to the clarification of the class characterization of suburbia by showing that even though the residents of the black hamlets he studied were poor, and their neighborhoods did not enjoy the same amenities as found in many middle-class, white suburbs, these black communities on the peripheries of cities were indeed suburban. He contests Kenneth Jackson's definition of American suburbia as "affluent and middle-class" (Wiese 1993, 33; Jackson 1985, 6). While "postwar American suburbanization may be characterized by the dominance of white middle-class suburbs, this is by no means exhaustive of the suburban experience in the twentieth century. Suburbanization must be understood not just as middle-class sprawl but as the whole expansion of American cities beyond their bounds—economically, politically, and socially" (Wiese 1993, 33).

Moreover, by implication, Wiese makes it clear that the growth of suburbs like Nassau was not simply a matter of white flight. While black and white suburban aspirants faced different barriers, what was shared was summed up by a black resident of a Cleveland suburb: "Everybody . . . wanted a little place of their own." For black homeowners, it was not their residential preferences that separated them from other suburbanites, but rather "race and class that distinguished these individuals from millions of white 'Levittowners' or affluent 'country club' suburbanites" (Wiese 1993, 42, 51).

That the desire for suburban homeownership cut across racial and class boundaries confounded 1950s critics of trends in American culture and working-class politics. Evaluations of the labor movement paralleled, in many ways, criticism of suburbia. In numerous analyses of the postwar union movement, journalists and academic commentators, such as William H. Whyte, traced the apparent decline of 1930s labor militancy to the suburbanization of industrial workers who now showed "scant enthusiasm" for strikes for fear of falling behind in their installment payments on home appliances (Lester 1958, 44). The ascribed preoccupation of workers with raising their standard-of-living, aided and abetted by homeownership and mortgage payments, is contrasted with the militancy workers showed during the industrial union battles of the Great Depression era. It became a truism that blue-collar workers were in desperate pursuit of a middle-class lifestyle and middle-class status (Marchand 1982, 164-69).

What this analysis failed to take into account were the actual economic conditions working families faced, postwar inflation and housing shortages key among them. Nor does this view pay adequate attention to pent-up desires for a more comfortable, stable life that were seared into people's consciousness by the deprivations and insecurities of the Depression and World War II decades. These deep-seated motivations found an outlet in the idea of suburbia, but the dynamics creating these popular needs were not caused by the development of suburbia.

Union leaders faced "bottom up" pressure from rank-and-file members who want to share, with their families, the benefits of the American postwar economic boom. Given urban housing shortages and federal mortgage policies which favored suburban homeownership, it is not at all clear what housing options blue-collar families, on a large scale, could realistically have availed themselves of, other than suburbia, during this period.

The critique of working people's desire for "more," a criticism often aimed generically at the "suburban lifestyle," tends to confuse consumption with consumerism, and to conflate all suburban neighborhoods with those most affluent ones where ostentatious conspicuous consumption may be on display. (It is interesting to note in passing that often those who make the consumerist critique of working-class patterns fail to extend their disapproval of materialism to those who show "good taste" and have the resources to engage in patterns of spending that include expensive city apartments and the accoutrements of high culture.) In the postwar period, moving into a suburban home and attaining the "essential luxuries" of middle-class life, to use Daniel Bell's apt phrase, can be seen as a matter-of-fact choice among the relatively limited options available to people with moderate incomes who needed to live where the jobs were.

The impact of homeownership on suburbanites' ideological orientations is difficult to measure. The fact that many suburbs that were Republican before their growth booms remained Republican does not in and of itself explain as much as it might seem to on first blush. It is a commonplace of party life that newcomers will tend to register with the majority party, but it is not at all clear what that registration affiliation tells us about voters' thinking, ideology, actual opinions of the parties, and election-day choices.

The evidence from Nassau's history shows that while the Republican Party has maintained the dominance it has enjoyed since the early days of Nassau's century, the party has seen a steady erosion of its overall registration and electoral advantage, a secular trend throughout the state, as an increasing number of voters register as independents and as voters in general continue to show a considerable proclivity toward "ticket splitting." Political observers note that in some cases it is the third party vote—Conservative or Right-to-Life—that puts the Republican candidates over the top, with the straight Democratic-Republican vote being very close. The returns, in selected races, for Democrats such as Senator Daniel Patrick Moynihan, Governor Mario Cuomo, presidential nominee Bill Clinton, congressional candidate Carolyn McCarthy, and 1993 Nassau County Executive contender Ben Zwirn, to name a few, show that the Nassau electorate displays independence, pays attention to national issues, and votes Democratic not infrequently, giving Democrats far more votes than would be predicted by party registration numbers.

There is another level of analysis, beyond electoral outcomes, which offers deeper insights into the nature of suburban political ideology, and the corollary assumption that suburban Republicanism signifies suburban conservatism. My studies of the evolution of the Nassau Republican Party during the five postwar decades have persuaded me that to really understand what a party or a party vote actually signifies, it is crucial to understand what the *content* of that vote or that affiliation is for people in Nassau who cast the ballots.

The question becomes: What can we learn from the way the Nassau Republican Party projected its image, its identity, its ideology through campaigns, candidates, policies in government, and public-issue pronouncements? What is clear from a study of party materials, newspaper reports, and oral history interviews is that during the postwar period, the party hewed to the center of the political spectrum precisely because it perceived that that was where the voters were. Large numbers of Democrats moved into the county after World War II, and even if many changed their party affiliations to Republican (because, they were told, that was the way to get a pothole fixed or a job), the party was sophisticated in its grasp of the public's adherence to certain basic political precepts, shaped by the New Deal period, about the role of government.

In general, the advocacy of right-wing issues was not the party's practice. Key GOP and governmental leaders such as mid-century Nassau County Party Chairman and County Executive J. Russel Sprague, and one of his successors in the 1960s, New York State Assembly Speaker Joseph Carlino, explicitly eschewed issues that might alienate voters in the middle, that is, Democrats and independents. It is not surprising that the Conservative Party of New York State, in its early days during the 1960s, directed particularly harsh criticism at the moderate Nassau GOP.

Certainly there were clear differences between the Nassau Democrats and Republicans on issues such as school busing, public housing, Vietnam protests, abortion, and the feminist movement. These placed the Republicans clearly on the right side of the political spectrum and caused Democrats and others to see the GOP as a conservative-leaning party.

The parties took different positions on racial issues that were close to home, such as busing to achieve racial balance in public schools. The degree to which Republicans made a generalized racial appeal to the white electorate resists simple measurement. Partisans of Republican campaign practice argue that GOP references to "public housing," or to its intention to protect Nassau's quality of life against incursions from "high rises like in the city," were non-racial reassurances to suburbanites who disdained the crowding and noise of the city. Democrats and their allies reject this rationale, stating that the GOP's supposedly anti-urban postures were, in the context of New York City's very visible neighborhood racial transitions, barely veiled signals to white voters that the Republicans would block integration in Nassau, while Democrats, if elected to local posts, would allow racial change to take place, in keeping with the racially-liberal platform of the national Democratic party.

What needs to be determined is to what extent voters perceived these "wedge" issues to be particularly relevant to their choices for local, town, and county posts. While activists deeply engaged in matters related to the county's administration of such programs as social welfare or health care argued to the contrary, for the most part, issues of municipal governance were presented as non-ideological. The Republicans benefited from this perception and their dogged self-promotion as the guardians of a comfortable, suburban way of life, marred though it was by the endemic racism of American society.

The key point here in terms of generic representations of the "suburban vote" is to cull out from the study of Nassau, an important postwar-growth county, what can be learned about the character of its voters. Historical analysis of what people thought they were voting for when they voted Republican on the local level does not support the contention that, in general, racial issues aside, a GOP vote was an ideologically conservative vote. For some voters of definite right-wing leanings, a Republican vote presumably was a conservative vote, as it was in the minds of those who were left-of-center.

This perspective about the particular content of voting Republican in a specific locality links into another contention that identifies suburbanization as a causal factor in the country's national political move toward the right in the 1950s. This tautology fails to factor in the rightward drift in politics that was evident during the late 1930s and 1940s. A prime example of this shift was seen among a group of key New Deal intellectuals, in and around President Franklin Roosevelt's administration, who gravitated toward the center. As Alan Brinkley shows in *The End of Reform,* key Democratic policymakers migrated toward a "vital center" that relied less on direct government intervention and activism, substituting policy prescriptions which endorsed a greater role for the "private sector" in federal economic policy. This ideological and programmatic repositioning within the New Deal leadership reflected generic trends in national politics, and there is little in the historical record to suggest that these changes were tied to anything specifically suburban.

Similarly, the cultural and political shifts of the Cold War era derived not so much from specific demographic American developments as they did from the longstanding American practice of anti-communism and the particular needs of politicians and ideological leaders within the context of postwar international dynamics. Anti-communism and the "McCarthyism" that exemplified the Cold War domestic epidemic went beyond the career of any one politician, but a study of the career of Senator Joseph McCarthy shows that the Wisconsin Senator made his dramatic turn toward hard-hitting anti-communism after being a relatively moderate Senate Republican, because his lackluster record as a Senator elicited only lukewarm support from his state's conservative newspapers. He needed an issue to jump-start his re-election efforts. Causal links with suburbanization do not emerge here as central to the driving narrative of right-wing postwar politics.

On this cluster of issues concerning the evolution of the postwar national political landscape, initial research into Nassau's history points to conclusions that run directly counter to hypotheses that link suburbia to the nation's postwar rightward political trajectory. In fact, what emerges from a study of the role of key Republican Nassau-based politicians in the 1950s is the story of a group of leaders, who on the local, state, and national levels, exerted considerable influence aimed at steering the GOP toward the political center and away from historic and contemporary pulls toward the right.

There is an episode in presidential politics that serves as a microcosm of the dynamics of Nassau's moderate suburban Republicanism, played out on the national political stage. The victory of Dwight D. Eisenhower at the 1952 Republican nominating convention was a defining moment in the evolution of the GOP and of postwar politics; it also exemplified a number of factors relevant to an analysis of the place of suburban politics within the larger universe of American mid-century public life.

To a significant degree, Eisenhower's success was due to the organizing skill of New York Governor Thomas E. Dewey and his key political lieutenants, chief among them Nassau's J. Russel Sprague. The campaign waged by Dewey, Sprague, and other moderate Republicans on behalf of Eisenhower, who had also been wooed by Democrats who wished him to be their party's nominee, represented one effort amid decades of work driven by Republican centrism. Dewey, as governor and GOP presidential candidate in 1944 and 1948, and Sprague, as a key leader in state politics and as a member of the Republican National Committee, often engaged in sharply partisan campaigns against the Roosevelt administration and its supporters. However, they were also determined to prevent the triumph of that wing of their party, represented at the 1952 convention by presidential hopeful Ohio Senator Robert A. Taft, which they viewed as too stridently in opposition to New Deal-era programs embraced by the majority of the electorate.

In the daily, blow-by-blow reportage on the convention in major newspapers, Sprague emerged as the hero of the day, the master tactician in a contest in which the two contenders, Eisenhower and Taft, ran neck and neck. The conservative image of suburban politics is belied by the role of Sprague and others, such as Leonard Hall, chairman of the Republican National Committee and congressman from Nassau's Oyster Bay Township, who were the architects of Eisenhower's moderate, centrist "Modern Republicanism." That these individuals remain relatively obscure in American party histories, far more so than if they had been mayors of cities comparable in size to Nassau, constitutes one measure of how much needs to be done to fully integrate understanding of suburban politics into the national political narrative.

Sprague's and Hall's involvement presaged later conflicts in which Nassau GOP leaders fought rightward movement of their party nationally. During the 1960s, Nassau County GOP Chairman and Speaker of the New York State Assembly, Joseph A. Carlino, a backer of New York's moderate Republican Governor, Nelson A. Rockefeller, refused to support the party's 1964 presidential nominee, Barry Goldwater, arguing that the candidate's extremely conservative positions would alienate the suburban elec-

Leonard Hall holding a bust of Theodore Roosevelt in 1958 during the TR centennial. Hall's father was Roosevelt's coachman. *NCM Collection, LISI at Hofstra.*

torate. He was proven correct and was himself swept out of his Assembly post and later his party position due to the landslide vote for Democratic President Lyndon B. Johnson, whose coattails were particularly long, even in Republican Nassau.

Interviews conducted by the author with Carlino and others reveal that during the postwar decades, suburban voters, their expectations of government shaped by the Depression and the New Deal, were keen to ensure that basic entitlements were protected and local services provided. They would not brook rhetoric suggesting or policies aimed at significant roll-backs of key programs. Thus the local GOP had to bend to accommodate itself to ex-urbanites, to voters who personally enjoyed benefits from federal programs, to people who might have family traditions of Democratic affiliation but who might consider voting Republican on the local level if the party seemed to be managing local affairs and providing services competently, while presenting a relatively tolerant social persona. This tradition of rhetorical moderation continued through the presidential campaigns of 1992 and 1996, when Nassau GOP leaders were quoted, repeatedly, warning their national leaders and candidates to stay away from divisive right-wing policies and rhetoric.

How the long-dominant party will adjust its approach in the wake of startling Democratic victories in the 1999 elections for County Legislature and Town offices, particularly three victories for Hempstead Town Board on which no Democrats had served since 1907, remains an open question as the country's second century unfolds.

References

Brinkley, Alan. 1995. *The End of Reform: New Deal Liberalism in Recession and War.* New York: Alfred A. Knopf.

Jackson, Kenneth T. 1985. *Crabgrass Frontier: The Suburbanization of the United States.* New York: Oxford University Press.

Kelly, Barbara M. 1993. *Expanding the American Dream: Building and Rebuilding Levittown.* Albany: State University of New York Press.

Lester, Richard A. 1958. *As Unions Mature: An Analysis of the Evolution of American Unionism.* Princeton: Princeton University Press.

Marchand, Roland. 1982. "Visions of Classlessness, Quests for Dominion: American Popular Culture, 1945-1960." In *Reshaping America: Society and Institutions, 1945-1960,* edited by Robert H. Bremner and Gary W. Reichard, 163-90. Columbus: Ohio State University Press.

Schneider, William. 1992. "The Suburban Century Begins." *Atlantic Monthly* 270: 33-44.

Wiese, Andrew. 1993. "Places of Our Own: Suburban Black Towns Before 1960." *Journal of Urban History* 19: 30-54.

"Boss" Platt's Role in Creating Nassau County

Edward J. Smits

Historical celebrations, such as Nassau County's observation of its Centennial commemorating its creation, on January 1, 1899, as an independent county separated from Queens County, are good opportunities to revive interest and acquaint local citizens with their heritage. Nassau's 1999 celebration had this objective, but also had the surprise result of solving one of the most significant historical questions concerning its origin.

As part of Nassau's Centennial, a ceremony was held on July 11, 1999, to commemorate the laying of the original cornerstone of the Old Courthouse held on the site on July 13, 1900. It was decided to open the original cornerstone and remove the contents of its metal box. The contents had been recorded in newspapers of the day, but there was anticipation that perhaps some additional unknown historic items may have been included. None were, but what was listed as a short history of the county was, in actuality, a typed manuscript entitled, "A Short History of the Political Methods Employed by the Writer in Securing the Erection of the County of Nassau, the 61st County of the State."

The general outline of the political and civic efforts to establish a new county on Long Island are well known and documented in my essay "The Creation of Nassau County," which has been published in various formats since 1960.[1] From 1869, residents of Queens County's eastern towns of Hempstead, North Hempstead, and Oyster Bay led several attempts to separate their towns and some adjacent Suffolk towns to create a new county. They were unsuccessful until 1898 when Greater New York City was created and the three towns were left in limbo outside the city line but still within Queens County. A citizen committee met in January, and a committee chaired by lawyer Halstead Scudder from the Town of Oyster Bay soon began efforts to secure a new county.

Although the author of the cornerstone historical document indicates his intent "to conceal his identity," it is most likely that Halstead Scudder is the writer. Not only was he central to the activities delineated, but the attached letters backing up his account would have been available only to him or a close associate. His account finally lays to rest the historical enigma of the final legislative approval of Nassau's creation. Although newspaper accounts of 1898 trace the difficulties and political debate over the desirability of creating the county, they were silent on how it was eventually approved in the state legislature despite opponents in both Republican and Democratic camps. It seemed certain that state Republican boss Thomas Platt, who was responsible for expediting the creation of Greater New York City, must have been involved in Nassau's attempt, but there was no written evidence. This manuscript history and copies of correspondence prove Platt's detailed and direct efforts to secure the legislation creating Nassau.

Scudder obtained a letter of introduction to Platt from B. F. Tracy, one of Platt's closest associates, who was President of the Commission that drafted the New York City Charter. Subsequently, Platt then requested D. P. Witter, who led the city charter reform in the Assembly and controlled government legislation, to advance the county bill. When it stalled in the Senate, he wrote the Republican Senate leaders Timothy E. Ellsworth and Clarence B. Lexow to support and move the measure on March 26.

In a final step, Platt indicated to Scudder that he had sent a telegram to Governor Frank S. Black, who approved the legislation despite a delegation of Queens leaders urging his opposition in a meeting on April 26.

This set of documents now provides a fascinating and significant record of the previously hidden details of political activities vital to secure the creation of Nassau County. Ironically, it would never have been revealed without an innocuous special event celebrating Nassau County's Centennial. The documents preserved within the cornerstone time capsule certainly are, as Scudder envisioned, of great interest to the generation one hundred years later.

A Short History of the Political Methods Employed by the Writer in Securing the Erection of the County of Nassau, the 61st County of the State, dated July 13th, 1900

Mineola, Nassau County, N.Y.
13th day of July, 1900.

It has occurred to me, an individual who had every opportunity to observe and to know the inner workings of the political machines of both the democratic and republican parties, and the conditions which prompted certain prominent men in the State of New York to favor the erection of this, the 61st county of the State, that perhaps to generations who are to come, and whose political methods may have, and I trust, will have, very materially changed from those in vogue to-day, it may be of interest to learn what were the methods employed by the men who in the face of the fiercest opposition on the part of the so called practical politicians of both parties succeeded in erecting this county.

It is the present intent of the author of this message to posterity to conceal his identity so far as the signing of this short history of the erection [?] of the county goes.

Around about 1870-75 a number of gentlemen prominent in political and financial circles in both Queens and Suffolk Counties, conceived the idea that a county erected out of the eastern portion of Queens and the western part of Suffolk would be an improvement over the then existing conditions, eliminating from the municipality of Queens that portion of the county more cosmopolitan than rural and joining with the rural end of Queens that part of Suffolk which was not so far removed from the City of New York as to be entirely separated from the influences which tend toward the development of a semi-rural, semi-suburban population. The scheme prospered to the extent of receiving the approval of the lower house of the Legislature of the State of New York, but died in the Senate, owing to political jealousies.

All question of the division of the three historic counties of the Island died out until, upon the consolidation of the various municipalities now forming the City of Greater New York, there developed a condition which seemed to those who had at heart the best interests of the towns situated in the eastern end of Queens so onerous as to preclude any development along the lines formerly followed by those communities and to inspire great anxiety among the more conservative residents of these towns. By the operations of the Charter the County Board of Supervisors of the County of Queens was made a body composed of eight members, five of whom, hailing from that portion of the county within the Greater New York limits, had absolute power to make any expenditure and to impose any tax which they saw fit, up to the constitutional limit, upon the eastern portion of the County of Queens, in defiance of the protests of the three members from the eastern towns of the County, and that without placing any burden whatever upon the constituents of the five supervisors so doing, the Greater City charter having taken from the Board of Supervisors of the entire county any power to levy taxes or incur expenses for that portion of the County within the Greater City. Such a condition, of course, could not continue, and, without going into tiresome details as to why, suffice it to say that the cleanest solution of the problem that confronted the people of eastern Queens was to secure a separation from that part of the County embraced within the Greater City limits.

A mass meeting of the citizens of the three eastern towns was called by Halstead Scudder, a man who had attained some little prominence in the independent politics of the day. In response, there assembled, on the 24th day of January, 1898, some six hundred and odd of the conservative thinking people. The meeting was called to order by the Hon. Benjamin D. Hicks, and after considerable discussion, a committee composed of William G. Miller and Lott Vandewater, of the Town of Hempstead; Joseph H. Bogert and

Wilbur R. Lewis, of the Town of North Hempstead, and Gen. James B. Pearsall and James H. Ludlam, of the Town of Oyster Bay, with Halstead Scudder as Chairman, was chosen by those assembled, who, together with the Supervisors of the respective towns, namely, George W. Smith, of Hempstead; Augustus Denton, of North Hempstead; and Samuel J. Underhill, of Oyster Bay, were charged with the duty of preparing a bill to erect a new county out of the three eastern towns of the County of Queens, and to provide for a new and separate municipal body.

The committee selected John B. C. Tappan of Glen Cove, and Wilmot T. Cox, of Mill Neck, as legal advisers. The latter two, in collaboration with Halstead Scudder, prepared a bill, which on submission to the committee was finally adopted and forwarded to the Assemblyman, the Hon. George Wallace, representing the three eastern towns of Queens. Mr. Wallace introduced the bill in the Assembly, where it was referred to the Committee on Internal Affairs. The politicians of both the democratic and republican parties held aloof from all connection with the meeting at Mineola, and not until the bill as prepared by the counsel for the committee had been printed and published in the local papers did they awaken to a realization of the fact that an effort was being quietly made to do away with many of the abuses which had grown up under the regime of the men who had fattened in the old County of Queens.

The governmental scheme proposed by the committee had as its essential feature the abolition of all fees in the county offices and the substituting therefor of fixed salaries for county officials, and the turning into the County Treasury of such fees as had formerly been the perquisites of the officials. It can well be understood that such a radical departure from the methods pursued for generations would incite the utmost degree of opposition on the part of those who saw their privileges so in danger of curtailment.

That local faction of the republican party which at the time was out of power aided the committee, and as a result, when Mr. Wallace reported to the committee that he was unable to secure any advancement of the bill from its resting place in the pigeon-holes of the Committee of Internal Affairs of the Legislature, the committee [was?] enabled, by means of a letter, hereto annexed, from Gen. Benjamin F. Tracy, Ex-Judge of the Court of Appeals of the State of New York, to the Hon. Thomas C. Platt, to obtain a very patient hearing, and finally to obtain from Senator Platt, who then, and at this time absolutely dominates the republican party, what amounted to a command to the Hon. D. P. Witter, to at once advance the bill and report the same out of Committee to the Assembly. Upon the delivery of Senator Platt's order to Mr. Witter, which is hereto annexed, the bill was immediately advanced to a third reading, and at a later day passed the Assembly and in the usual course went over to the Senate. The faction of the republican party in Queens

County, led by the Hon. William J. Youngs, and representing the office holders rather than the tax-payers, despairing of defeating the bill in the Assembly, in view of the support given it by Senator Platt, directed every effort towards its defeat in the Senate, and had succeeded in making arrangements whereby the bill was to be buried in the Internal Affairs Committee in the Senate until such time as to preclude its passage owing to the adjournment *sine die* [indefinite] of the Senate. The committee having the bill in charge, learning of this condition of affairs, again appealed to Senator Platt, and he, realizing the advantage to be obtained by him in playing off one faction of the republican party against the other, issued orders in the form of letters, hereto annexed, to Senator Timothy E. Ellsworth and Senator Clarence E. Lexow, directing them in general terms to see that the bill was carried through the Senate. When reported from the Assembly to the Senate, in deference to Senator Platt's direct mandate the bill was referred by Lieutenant Governor Timothy L. Woodruff to the Committee on Judiciary of the Senate, and by that committee reported out the next day, and then and there passed by a unanimous vote of the senate, the democrats conceding that there was nothing in the nature of the bill to warrant any opposition to it.

The fight against the enactment into law of the Nassau County Act on the part of the disgruntled local democratic and republican politicians did not cease with its passage through the Legislature, but was continued before Governor Black, and every effort made to get him to withhold his signature. Gen. Tracy, Senator Lexow, Lieutenant-Governor Woodruff and Senator Platt were again appealed to by the committee, and they uniting in a request, which on the part of Senator Platt was equivalent to a demand, that the signature of the Executive be affixed, the bill became a law.

Such, in a few words, is the present condition of legislation in this State. It is impossible to procure the enactment into law of any measure, however meritorious, unless it has first been vised by the man dominating at the time the party in the State.

This act erecting the County of Nassau contained no jobs, created no places, and afforded no opening wherein it could be successfully assailed from the standpoint of good government and the protection of the best interests of the people at large. On the contrary, it inaugurated a new era in the development of municipal government in this State, yet, despite the fact that it was only assailed by those whose personal perquisites and pickings were cut off by its operations, yet until the dictum went forth from the one man, namely, Senator Thomas C. Platt, who controlled the workings of the republican party in this State, it was impossible to secure its enactment into law.

That when read, it may be one hundred, it may be two hundred years hence, this short history of the political situation now existing as regards legislation for purely unselfish ends may prove of interest to the descendants of those who have gone before is the earnest and sincere hope of the author.

Attached Letters

New York, March 4th, 1898.

Hon. Thomas C. Platt
Senate Chamber, Washington, D. C.
My dear Senator;

This will introduce to you my friend, Mr. Halstead Scudder, of Queens County, who, in common with all that part of Queens County not included in the City of New York by the new charter, is earnestly urging the creation of a new county. The proposed county will be Republican, Judge Wallace having carried it I am informed by about one thousand. Unless there is some reason not apparent to me against it, I think good politics requires the creation of this county, thus permanently separating that part of Queens County which is included in the Greater New York from that part which is not. Mr. George Wallace, the present member of the Assembly from the district which will constitute the new county, if created, is earnestly in favor of the bill.

You will find Mr. Scudder to be a gentleman, a man of intelligence and of high character, and you can assume that he believes everything he says on the subject of this county. I hope you will hear him fully.

Very truly yours,
(SGD) B. F. Tracy

Hon. T. C. Platt,
Senate Chamber, Washington, D. C.

New York, March 12th, 1898.
49 Broadway.

Hon. D. P. Witter,
Assembly Chamber,
Albany, N. Y.
My Dear Witter: -

My attention has been brought to the extraordinary conditions now existing in Queens County, owing to the operation of the Charter of New York City. The people of Eastern Queens are seeking relief from the burdens imposed upon them through the operations of the Charter, and have, so I am informed, had prepared a bill erecting a new county out of the three eastern towns of Queens not included within the Greater City. I understand that the bill to effect the County of Nassau is unassailable from the standpoint of good government and constitutionality. I am particularly desirous of aiding in the relief of these people, and shall esteem it a favor if you will kindly use your influence in advancing the bill at as early a date as possible.

Yours very truly,
(Signed) T. C. Platt.

COPY

New York, Mar. 26, 1898.

Hon. Timothy E. Ellsworth,
Senate Chamber,
Albany, N. Y.
Dear Sir: -

This will introduce to you Mr. Halstead Scudder of Queens, Chairman of the Committee of Citizens who have had prepared the Nassau County bill to erect the County of Nassau out of that part of Queens County not included in New York City.

I have been over this matter very carefully. One of its strongest features is that it cures evils existing in eastern Queens without amending the Greater New York Charter.

I have every assurance that the bill is unassailable from any standpoint. The Senator from the Queens District, Mr. Koehler, is a Democrat and, of course, cannot be expected to push the measure.

I trust therefore that you will extend to Mr. Scudder in view of the early adjournment every assistance in your power to assure the passage of this bill.

Very truly,
(Signed) T. C. Platt.

COPY

New York, Mar. 26, 1898.

Hon. Clarence E. Lexow
Senate Chamber
Albany, N. Y.
Dear Sir: -

This will introduce to you Mr. Halstead Scudder of Queens, Chairman of the Committee of Citizens who have had prepared the Nassau County bill to erect the County of Nassau out of that part of Queens County not included in New York City.

I have been over this matter very carefully. One of its strongest features is that it cures evils existing in eastern Queens without amending the Greater New York Charter.

I have every assurance that the bill is unassailable from any standpoint. The Senator from the Queens District, Mr. Koehler, is a Democrat and, of course, cannot be expected to push the measure.

I trust therefore that you will extend to Mr. Scudder in view of the early adjournment every assistance in your power to assure the passage of this bill.

Very truly,
T. C. Platt.

COPY

UNITED STATES SENATE,
Washington, D. C., April 5th, 1898.

Mr. Halstead Scudder
16 Exchange Place, New York
My dear Sir:

I have your letter of yesterday regarding the Nassau County bill and have this morning telegraphed the Governor expressing the opinion that the bill was a meritorious measure and urging his approval of the same. I trust that he may see fit to give the bill his official sanction.

Yours very truly,
T. C. Platt

Note

1. See *The Creation of Nassau County* 1960 (Reprint; Syosset: Friends of the Nassau County Museum, 1979); "The Creation of Nassau County," *Long Island Historical Journal* 1 (Spring 1989): 172-76; and "Creating a New County: Nassau," *Long Island Historical Journal* 11 (Spring 1999): 129-44.

Halstead Scudder (1861-1909). Scudder convened the January 1898 organizational meeting and enlisted Boss Platt's aid to secure passage of the bill creating Nassau County in 1898. He deserves recognition as "The father of Nassau County." *NCM, LISI at Hofstra.*

The Location of the Queens-Nassau Border

Patricia T. Caro

One hundred years ago a boundary line was drawn that shaped Long Island's dual nature throughout the twentieth century. The Nassau-Queens border, set in 1899, now separates suburbia from city. In the minds of many, it defines "The Island" to the east from "The City" to the west. Today, everyone in the area knows that taxes, schools, municipal services, and ethnicity change at the border. However, when the line was set it cut through a largely homogeneous rural area, and almost no one foresaw how meaningful the placement of that boundary would become. The location of that boundary line, and the factors that influenced it, are the focus of this paper.

The border exists because Queens County was split on January 1, 1898 so that its western third could be annexed to the new expansive municipality known as Greater New York. One part of Queens County thus became a constituent part of New York City, while the eastern two-thirds remained independent of it. This anomalous arrangement lasted only a year, however, as the portion of Queens County not consolidated into Greater New York broke away to form the County of Nassau on January 1, 1899.

At first, the western border of the new county lay somewhat east of its present location. That boundary resulted from the language of the bill creating Greater New York that was enacted by the State Legislature in February 1894.[1] It designated the portion of Queens County to be included within Greater New York as areas to the west of the eastern boundary of the Town of Flushing, and west of a straight line drawn from the southeastern corner of the Town of Flushing to the middle of the inlet between Rockaway Beach and Shelter Island at the Atlantic Ocean. Thus, in the north it corresponded to a pre-existing boundary line (the border between the Town of Flushing and the Town of North Hempstead), but in the south it broke new ground since it only approximated the boundary line between the Town of Jamaica and the Town of Hempstead. The boundary sliced a significant wedge of land from the westernmost part of the Town of Hempstead for inclusion within Greater New York. Part of that wedge was returned to Hempstead in April 1899 when some of the original town line was restored, and so defined the western boundary of Nassau County that, with only very small changes, still exists today (Fig. 1).[2]

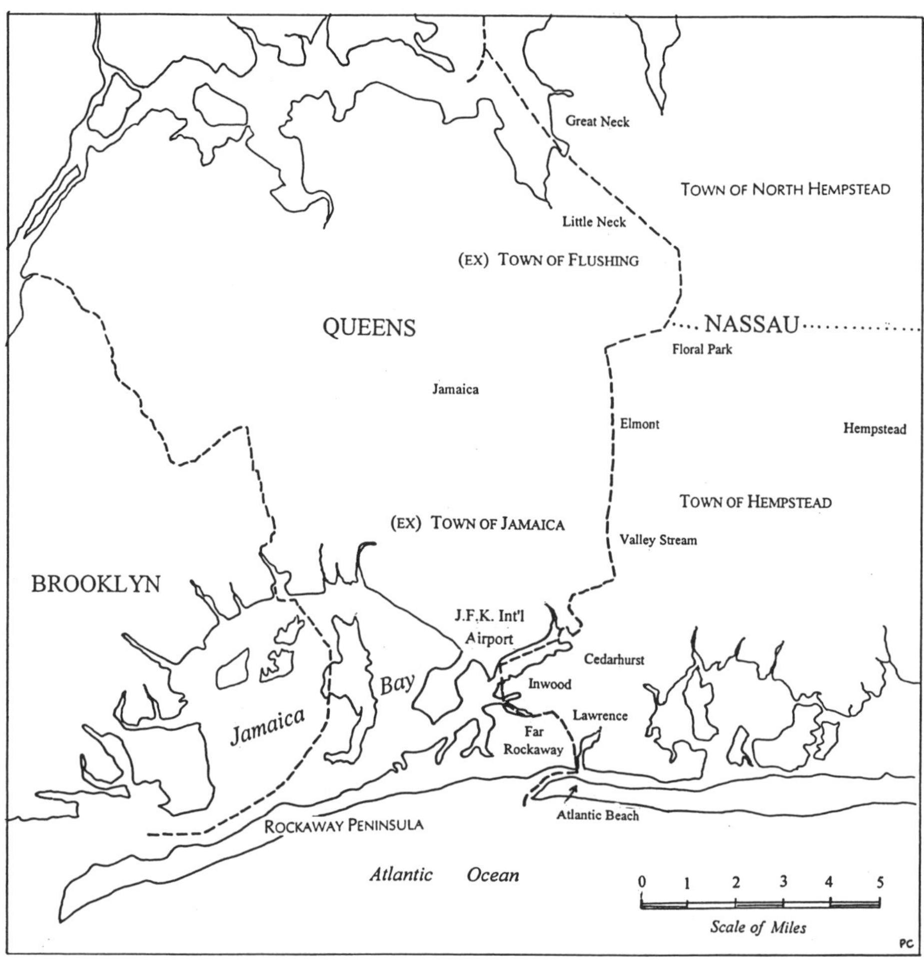

Fig. 1. The Queens-Nassau Border Area, 1999

Early Town Boundaries

Most of the Queens-Nassau border of today corresponds to the boundaries separating the towns of Flushing from North Hempstead, and Jamaica from Hempstead as they existed in 1897. Although three of the towns were founded in the seventeenth century and North Hempstead was a late eighteenth century spin-off from the Town of Hempstead, their boundaries emerged slowly. At first they were more like frontier zones than fixed lines, and served mainly to separate minuscule numbers of Europeans into administrative units whose main function was that of granting land ownership to their inhabitants. Early town records occasionally cite the need for boundary clarification, but usually there is no mention of the actual changes made.[3] Manuscript and published maps drew the boundary lines imprecisely and often in contradiction to one another.

Attention to town boundaries increased as the population and responsibilities of the towns grew. By the nineteenth century, the functions of the towns included the creation and maintenance of highways, jails, and poorhouses; the demarcation of election districts; and, of course, the allocation of resources and property, both on dry land and undersea. The cost of highway construction in particular prompted each individual town to stake out its jurisdiction with precision.

The boundaries separating towns were well established by the late 1800s, when the idea of consolidating territory to form a Greater New York began to be seriously considered. By the time of consolidation, Flushing shared about six and a half miles of border with North Hempstead and one and a quarter miles with Hempstead, while Jamaica shared twenty-two and a half miles with Hempstead, of which nearly sixteen miles were along the Rockaway Peninsula.[4]

The Northern Portion of the Boundary Zone

Borders in the Flushing section have changed very little since 1788, shortly after North Hempstead seceded from Hempstead and its boundaries were recorded in the *Laws of New York.* [5] Only very minor shifts occurred during the nineteenth century, and none in response to impending Consolidation. However, it took almost a century after North Hempstead's founding before most maps depicted the legal boundary of 1788 consistently and accurately. Before 1886, most maps show the Flushing-North Hempstead boundary as composed of just two straight lines, one running southeast from Little Neck Bay and another almost due south to Jericho Turnpike. They ignore the third line, a diagonal beginning about half a mile north of Jericho Turnpike, which today runs from the intersection of Langdale Street and Hillside Avenue southwestward to Jericho Turnpike just east of Tulip Avenue. Most nineteenth-century maps also misrepresent a small section of Flushing's border with Hempstead by including within Flushing a small triangular wedge south of Jericho Turnpike.[6]

In all likelihood, these cartographic errors resulted from sloppy map rendering of a small area crowded with roads, railroads, and boundaries of minor civil divisions. However, their persistence on reputable maps until 1886 gives the false impression that Flushing's southeast border was jockeyed in the 1880s perhaps as a reaction to the early talk about Consolidation. In fact, the proposed Greater New York boundary of 1894 was applied without dispute to the "shrunken" Flushing whose eastern and southern limits had been generously enlarged by a century of cartographers. Curiously, the cartographic errors of the nineteenth century occur in a section of the Queens-Nassau border area that many people still find surprisingly homogeneous, a zone where place names (Bellerose, Floral Park), street patterns, and architectural features are remarkably similar on both sides.

The Southern Portion of the Boundary Zone

The Jamaica-Hempstead stretch of the Queens-Nassau boundary has a longer and more significant history of change. From colonial times, persistent attempts to adjust the territorial extent of their jurisdictions have preoccupied the towns of Hempstead and Jamaica, and later Hempstead and Greater New York. Two changes were major. In 1898 the Rockaway Peninsula was permanently given to Greater New York by the Town of Hempstead. At the same time, a narrow north-south strip from Elmont to Lawrence, later known as the Doughty Strip, was also ceded to Greater New York. It, however, was returned to the Town of Hempstead sixteen months later.

Surprisingly, the Rockaway Peninsula was relinquished by the Town of Hempstead with barely a whimper, while the Elmont-Lawrence strip was the subject of considerable debate from the start. In all likelihood, tacit or covert political deals made at the turn of the century shaped these transactions, thus diminishing the chances for a full explanation of how the Queens-Nassau border came to be precisely where it is. But earlier published evidence sheds some light on why the southern portion of the boundary zone, the western border of the Town of Hempstead, became a territorial accordion at the time of Consolidation.

The Early Boundary Between Hempstead and Jamaica Town

The Kieft Patent of 1644, a document that granted English settlers town rights and title to lands in the eastern portion of the Dutch-held territory on Long Island, is the accepted legal base of the Town of Hempstead. Its western boundary, described as a straight line running from Matthew Garritson's Bay to the South Sea (that is, from Little Neck Bay to the Atlantic Ocean), left much room for interpretation. Fifty years after the issuance of the patent, the Welles (sometimes spelled Wels or Whels) Line made its first appearance on maps, a distinct north-south line in about 73° 44' 47" West longitude, running northward from the Atlantic Ocean through Rockaway Neck (at about B 9th Street in Far Rockaway today; see Fig. 4).

Like the Mason-Dixon Line, the Welles Line came to represent more than was originally intended. Named for the surveyor Philip Welles, it began in 1684 as a property line of the Cornell family. For most of the next century, however, it was viewed as the effective western limit of the Town of Hempstead on the Rockaway Peninsula. Until about 1800 it corresponded to the edge of European settlement, as the sandy dunes west of the Welles Line were shunned by settlers. As a result, the bulk of the Rockaway Peninsula escaped administrative attention until late, and in the meantime, the Welles Line became the area's principal legal landmark.

Confusion about the status of the Welles Line must have developed in the eighteenth century. As if to clarify the matter, two maps from 1791 have clear hand-written notations on the Rockaway Peninsula, just west of the Welles Line, that this land "is not included in the Patent of Jamaica"[7] or that "this neck lies within the jurisdiction of the Town of Hempstead."[8] It is clear that virtually all of the peninsula lay west of even the most generous interpretation of the Kieft Patent, yet neither Jamaica nor any of the towns in what is now Brooklyn laid claim to it. It appears that the Town of Hempstead merely assumed jurisdiction over it as European settlement spilled west of the Welles Line from the original core of Far Rockaway settlement. By 1809, deeds to land in what is now Arverne and Rockaway Park state unequivocally that they lie in the Town of Hempstead, County of Queens.[9]

Thereafter, until 1898, maps show the entire peninsula as Hempstead land, with the Jamaica-Hempstead town boundary running through Jamaica Bay, Head of Bay, and Hook Creek. A remnant of the Welles Line persisted north of Hook Creek, where the boundary between the towns continued as a straight line running nearly north-south.

Thus, by the early nineteenth century, the Welles Line on the Rockaway Peninsula had lost its designated meaning as a settlement border and its implied meaning as an administrative one. Yet it lingered as part of the vernacular geography of the area, a well-known reference line cited in publications and drawn on maps throughout the nineteenth century. As drawn on these maps, the Welles Line represents the initial appearance of a fixed straight line running north-south through the eastern edge of the Rockaway Peninsula.[10] It is interesting for two reasons. At the time it was first drawn it represented the southwesternmost reaches of the Town of Hempstead's territorial concerns. Two centuries later, it closely matched the southern portion of the Greater New York line.

The Rockaway Peninsula Within the Town of Hempstead

For the people living on the Rockaway Peninsula, being part of the Town of Hempstead rather than the Town of Jamaica made sense. Until the twentieth century, it was far easier to travel from Rockaway to the village of Hempstead than to the village of Jamaica or to other points in western Queens. Even in colonial times, Rockaway people traveled to Hempstead for essential supplies and for church-going; Hempstead was reached by a regular stagecoach run along dependable roads approximating today's Broadway in Lawrence and Peninsula Boulevard. By contrast, the path from Far Rockaway to Jamaica, which skirted Jamaica Bay to the east, was marshy and unreliable; the route became practical only after the completion of Rockaway Turnpike in 1916.

The railroad era also enhanced the links to nearby places in the Town of Hempstead, at least initially. In 1869, the South Side Railroad built a line from Valley Stream to Far Rockaway, with stops at Cedar Grove (Hewlett), Woodsburgh (Woodmere), Ocean Point (Cedarhurst), and Lawrence. Its opening prompted wealthy real estate developers to build housing and recreational facilities for the upper classes at these locales.[11] For the next fifty years, this string of communities, as well as East Rockaway, Arverne, and Rockaway Beach, were collectively known as "the Rockaways," and were perceived by the general public as a playground of the rich.

The Rockaway Peninsula was physically linked to land in the Town of Jamaica only after 1880, when the Long Island Rail Road constructed a trestle across the waters and marshes of Jamaica Bay. That link, whose purpose was to provide service to Brooklyn, prompted almost no contact between communities on the peninsula and those to the north in the Town of Jamaica. Seven years later, the "Air Line" was connected to the Long Island Rail Road's Far Rockaway branch, thus making a loop around Jamaica Bay, by way of Lawrence and Valley Stream. The connection promoted the arrival of summertime pleasure seekers from Manhattan, but it did not lead to much contact between Rockaway and other areas in Queens.

In sum, the Rockaway Peninsula was barely integrated into lands to the north or west, even by the time of Consolidation. Although just beyond the Welles Line and only gradually administered by the Town of Hempstead, its European settlers developed early and persistent contacts with the people of that town. In the nineteenth century, the town's role in the development of Rockaway was also paramount. Gas lighting was installed, roads were macadamized, and revenues were collected from taxes and shellfish harvesting licenses. Far Rockaway grew; by 1888, it had more than 3,000 people and housed the only bank within the Town of Hempstead *not* located in Hempstead Village.[12]

One wonders why, in 1898, the Town of Hempstead so readily gave it up.

Rockaway Must Go

The visionaries of Consolidation into a Greater New York saw the Rockaway Peninsula as an important component of their plan. When first proposed in 1894, the bill creating Greater New York intended to annex, among other areas, a significant portion of Long Island: Brooklyn, Long Island City, the towns of Newtown, Flushing, and Jamaica; and that portion of the Town of Hempstead lying west of a straight line drawn from the southeast corner of the Town of Flushing to the middle of the inlet from the

Atlantic Ocean between Rockaway Beach and Shelter Island. The Rockaway Peninsula, of course, lay to the west of that inlet.

Like the Bronx and Staten Island, Long Island's contribution to Greater New York included a great deal of coastline, an important consideration for the expanded city.[13] The idea of Consolidation came at the pinnacle of the maritime era and western Queens, like all of the areas to be annexed, had notable embayments that might help Greater New York achieve maritime prominence.

Jamaica Bay, in particular, held great promise in the eyes of Andrew Haswell Green, the early and powerful proponent of Greater New York.[14] It was huge, accessible to the Atlantic Ocean, and largely sheltered from its tides and storms. Its shallow water and marshes might be ameliorated by constant dredging. Its northern shore might warrant major port facilities if the narrow Rockaway sandspit continued to serve as a buffer between bay and open sea. The main entrance into the harbor would be at Rockaway Inlet, sandwiched between the western tip of the Rockaway Peninsula and eastern tip of what is now Sheepshead Bay in Brooklyn. If such were the case, the Rockaway Peninsula would be critical to Jamaica Bay harbor for two reasons: its western end would define the eastern edge of the entrance to the harbor, and its six miles of length would protect the bay and its port facilities from direct exposure to oceanic storms.

Thus the role of the Rockaway Peninsula in Jamaica Bay's maritime potential probably sealed its fate for inclusion within Greater New York. How much of the peninsula, how much beyond the shores of Jamaica Bay was needed? The southeast point selected in the Greater New York proposal—the middle of the inlet between Rockaway Beach and Shelter Island—determined that all of the peninsula would become part of Greater New York. This included the wider northeast section that merges with the mainland. Thus the Village of Far Rockaway, Inwood, and part of Lawrence would be included, for, in 1894, the inlet lay more than a mile east of the easternmost edge of Jamaica Bay.

Why did the Greater New York proposal specify a point so far east? The Rockaway Beach-Shelter Island Inlet was not so valuable in itself, but it was a visible physical feature, the first inlet from the Atlantic Ocean east of the Head of Jamaica Bay. Its possession would ensure that Greater New York received all of Jamaica Bay with plenty of room for shoreline development. If nothing else, it seemed a convenient divide.

Coveting that inlet, called Plum Gut at the time, introduced complicated boundary issues and pitted three powerful parties against one another. Plum Gut was a narrow, shallow, migratory body of water created in 1870 when a storm broke through the long sandspit that lay about 1,000 feet from Far Rockaway and Lawrence. Like other small inlets that penetrate the barrier islands formed by sandspits along Long Island's south shore, Plum Gut had been shifting westward with the set of the longshore currents.[15] Disputes over ownership sometimes resulted as the spits changed their shape and location.[16] Such was the case with Shelter Island, the spit east of Plum Gut and just offshore from a portion of the mainland property of the wealthy real-estate developer Newbold T. Lawrence.

In 1894, Plum Gut lay about 100 feet west of Bannister Creek, a stream whose course had changed very little over time and thus served as a relatively reliable landmark. To the west of Bannister Creek lay the agglomerated settlement of Far Rockaway, bounded on the north by some of the land of Newbold T. Lawrence. To the immediate east of Bannister Creek lay the residences of Newbold T. Lawrence and of other important, long established families such as the Doughtys and the Spragues. More land of Newbold T. Lawrence lay further east, partly undeveloped because of its marshy character. As it turned out, the Greater New York line ran through Lawrence's property, leaving most of his drier land to the west of the line and his marshier land to the east.

Instituting the New Boundary

Consolidating the desired land into a Greater New York had to await several formal processes: (1) passage of a bill by the State Legislature, (2) approval of the bill in a referendum to be held in the areas affected, and (3) signing of the bill by the Governor.

The idea for an expanded city had been bandied about since the 1870s, but public knowledge of it came late and piecemeal. In early 1894, newspapers began to mention a bill in the State Legislature that would allow a referendum to be held on the subject of the creation of a Greater New York. On February 9, 1894, the *Long Island Farmer* (the Jamaica-based forerunner of the *Long Island Press*) reported that "the bill does not compel consolidation."[17] A few days later, the same paper reported that "the Greater New York Bill has been amended in the Senate. All the [Queens] county towns are excluded from it and it provides for the annexation of Brooklyn and Long Island City only. It will pass in this shape or not at all."[18] The bill passed the State Legislature in February 1894, but newspapers continued to print only scanty and often inaccurate reports on its meaning. Given the paltry, often erroneous reporting, it is not surprising that the upcoming referendum generated little excitement within Queens County. The Town of Hempstead was forced to take notice, however, as it was obliged to provide special ballots on the issue of consolidation for those voters living within the affected areas.

Only a third of the eligible voters in Queens voted in the referendum, which was held during the general election of November 6, 1894. The vote, in toto, was in favor. But the Town of Flushing and Election District 19 in the Town of Hempstead (Inwood) overwhelmingly opposed it. The votes for all voting units in Queens are shown in the table below.

Referendum Vote in Greater New York Question, 1894

Locality	Vote For	Vote Against	Percent For
In western Queens			
Long Island City	3,529	792	81.6
Newtown	1,267	956	57.2
Flushing	1,144	1,407	44.8
Jamaica	1,381	1,263	51.8
Subtotal	7,321	4,408	62.4
Within the Town of Hempstead			
ED #16 - Valley Stream	8	8	50.0
ED #17- Garden City	4	6	40.0
ED #18 - Cedarhurst	87	79	52.4
ED #19 - Inwood	68	196	38.9
ED #20 - Far Rockaway	167	121	57.9
ED #21 - Oceanus	144	81	61.3
Subtotal	478	412	53.7
Grand Total	7,799	4,820	51.8

ED refers to Election District.
Source: Hempstead Inquirer, November 9, 1894.

Clearly the voters of central and eastern Queens County had muted enthusiasm, at best, for consolidation into Greater New York. But it did not matter, for the referendum was not binding on individual election districts or towns. Only the overall vote counted and that vote allowed the State Legislature to give the proponents of Greater New York the green light for their plan.

Smith's 1894 Map of Election Districts

While their votes ultimately would not count for much, voters living in all of the affected areas had to be given the right to participate in the referendum. In preparation, the Town of Hempstead hired Thomas V. Smith to prepare a map showing both the proposed Greater New York boundary as well as the Town of Hempstead election districts involved (Fig. 2).[19] As a civil engineer, Smith was entrusted to determine the precise location of the middle of the inlet between Rockaway Beach and Shelter Island, and thus

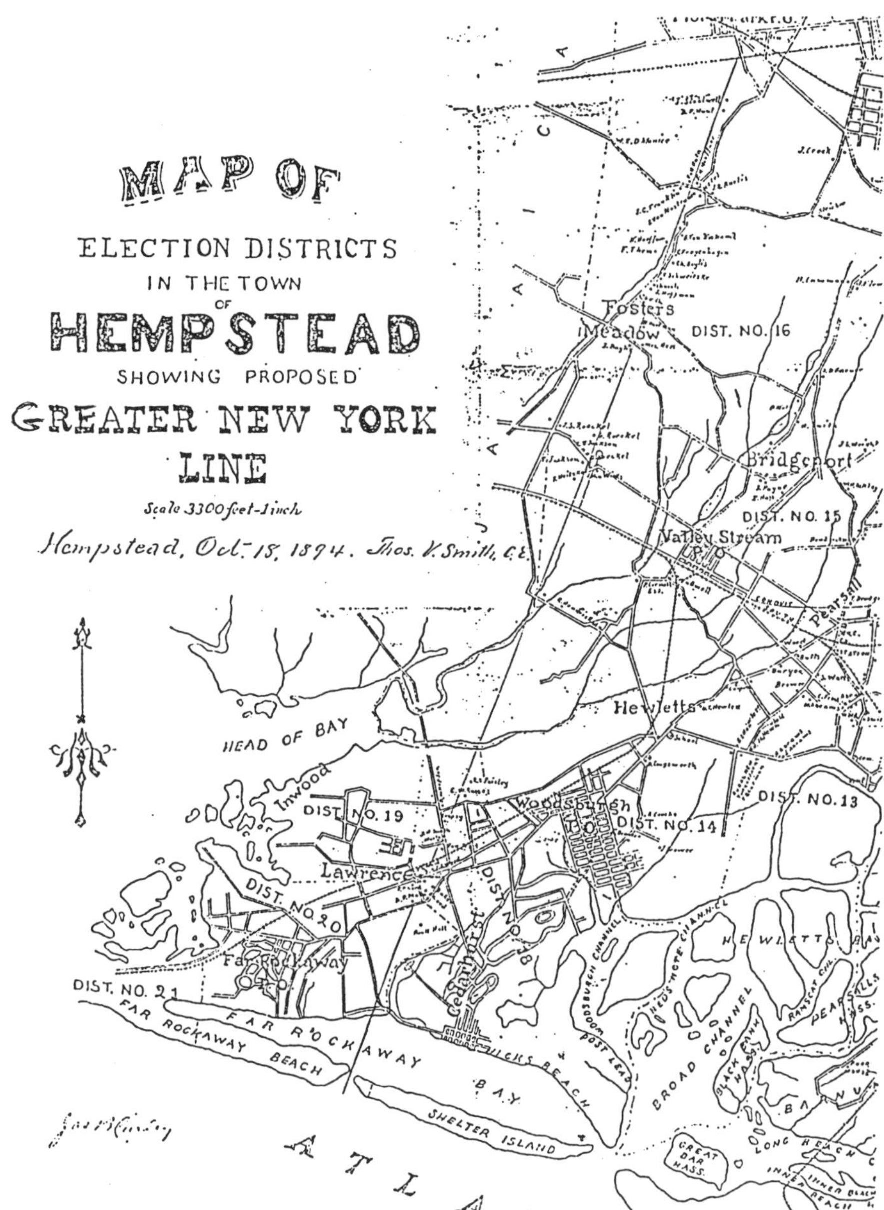

Fig. 2. Thomas V. Smith's Map of Election Districts and the Greater New York Line, 1894. Map courtesy of the Town of Hempstead Archives.

the southern point of the Greater New York boundary from which the line to the southeastern corner of the Town of Flushing was to be drawn. Although this map of October 1894 became the basis of heated controversy three years later, it was readily accepted as accurate at the time of its production.

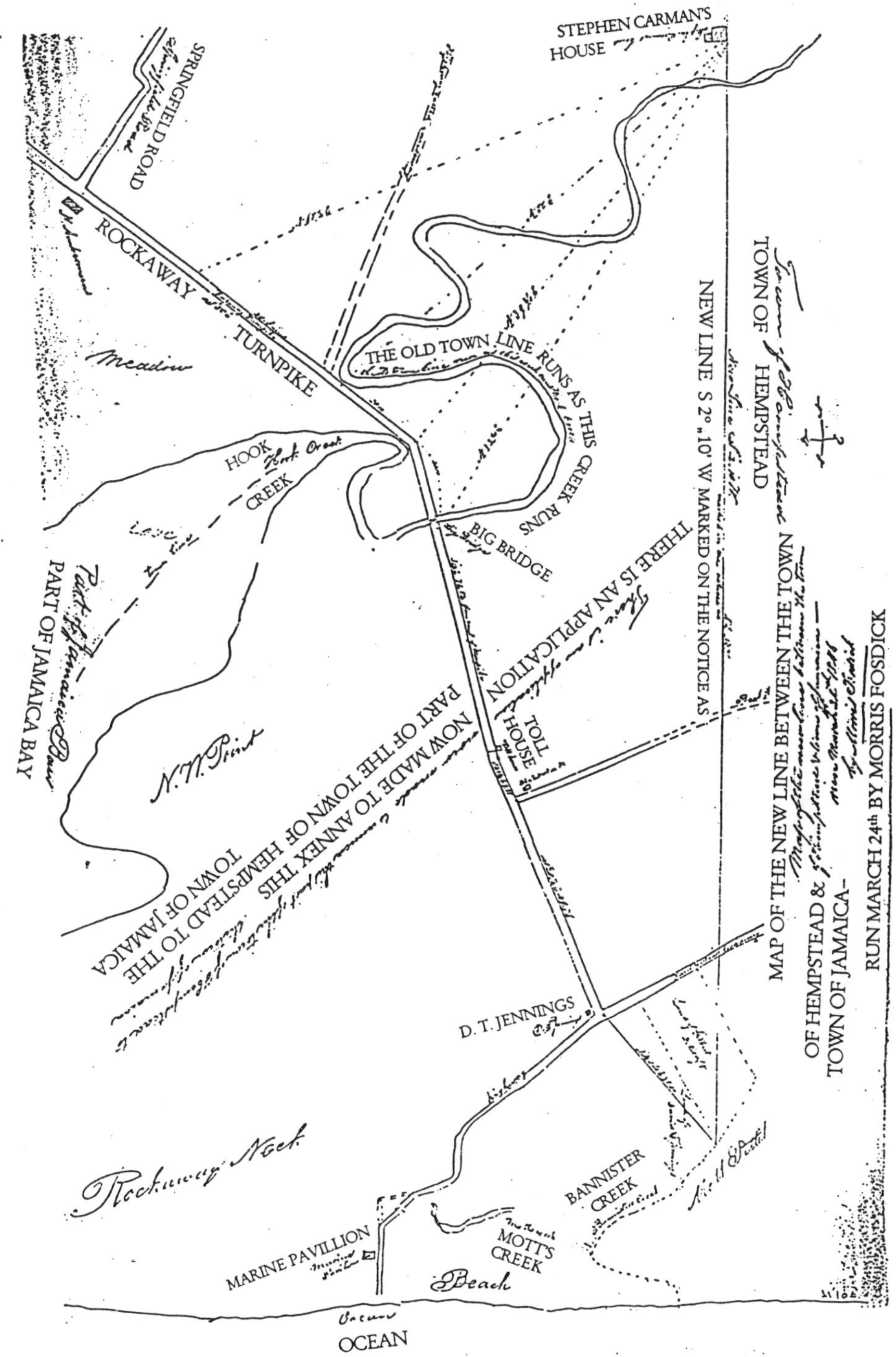

Fig. 3. Map of Proposed New Town Line Between Jamaica and Hempstead, 1846. Printed lettering has been added to enhance the legibility of the original hand-labelled map (see Appendex, 75). Map courtesy of the *NCM Collection, LISI at Hofstra.*

On Smith's map of 1894 the eastern boundary of Greater New York shows up as a straight line heading north-northeastward from the middle of Plum Gut, passing just west of Bannister Creek, continuing through a point at a conspicuous fork in Hook Creek, and stopping at the northern border of the Town of Hempstead where it meets the southeastern corner of the Town of Flushing,

Thus the southeastern boundary of Greater New York was a straight line that closely paralleled the Welles Line, or at least its seventeenth century cartographic expression. For a straight line imposed as a boundary on an already settled area, it was a relatively good line, as it bisected mostly rural land of the Town of Hempstead. But some of that rural land was in the hands of powerful and wealthy individuals who, as it turned out, were opposed to having their land within the City of New York. It also cut the Village of Far Rockaway, which over time had expanded west of the Welles Line, out of the Town of Hempstead.

The Rejected Boundary Shift of 1846

The Greater New York proposal was not the first re-appearance of the Welles Line as the intended western border of the Town of Hempstead. In April 1846, the Town Board of the Town of Jamaica rejected an application to annex certain lands of the Town of Hempstead by a vote of 4 to 1. Town records declare, "we believe that the annexation of a part of the Town of Hempstead, as proposed in the said notice and petition will materially operate to the disadvantage of many of the inhabitants of the Town of Jamaica. Resolved, that the freeholders and inhabitants of the Town of Jamaica are opposed to the annexation of any part of the Town of Hempstead to this town."[20]

The Jamaica Town records state neither the location of the property to be annexed nor the origination of the application, but the location, at least, reveals itself on a hand-drawn map made by the reputable surveyor and politician Morris Fosdick (Fig. 3).[21] Entitled "New Boundary Between the Town of Hempstead and the Town of Jamaica" and dated March 24, 1846, the map indicates a new line heading north-northeastward from Bannister Creek to the house of Stephen Carman at the fork in Hook Creek, where it joins the original boundary. Its resemblance to the southern half of the proposed Greater New York line is uncanny; although Plum Gut does not yet exist, the proposed new town line begins less than 100 feet from the location of the inlet in 1894, thus making its course to Hook Creek virtually identical to that of the Greater New York line.[22] (See Fig. 4.)

While Fosdick's boundary line ends up at a slightly different point on Jericho Turnpike, the proposed annexations of 1846 and 1894 both strive for similar results: to separate the Town of Jamaica (or, later, Greater New York)

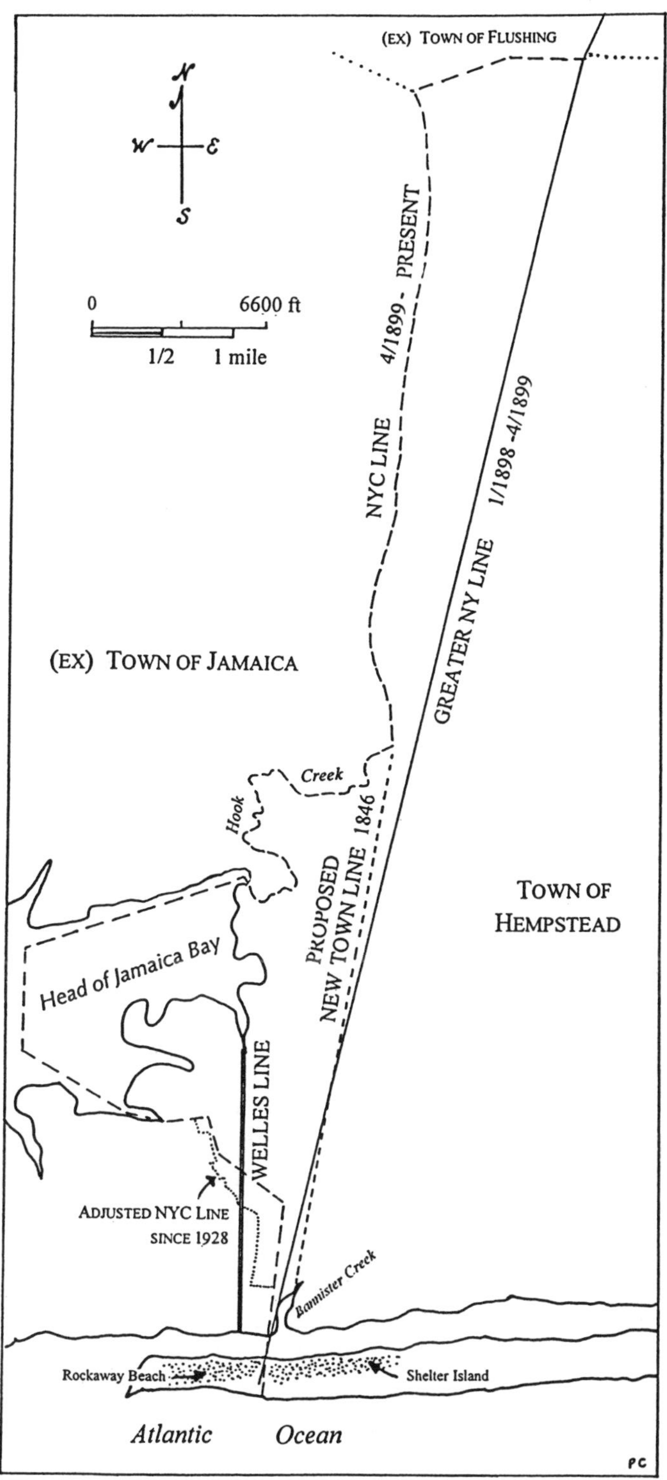

Fig. 4. Various Boundary Lines in the Western Edge of the Town of Hempstead.

from the Town of Hempstead by means of a series of straight line boundaries trending north-northwest from the spot where Plum Gut lay in 1894, and in so doing, transferring all of the Rockaway Peninsula, Inwood, and parts of Lawrence, Cedarhurst, and south Valley Stream from the Town of Hempstead to the Town of Jamaica (or, later, to Greater New York).

It is, of course, curious that the Town of Jamaica adamantly rejected the annexation of the Town of Hempstead land, and it is unfortunate that the records give no details of the discussion. Ostensibly, the supervisors claimed to want no additional burdens, since the primary objective was to serve the people within the existing town boundaries. But the Hempstead lands to be annexed, with the exception of the settlement at Far Rockaway, were occupied mostly by self-sufficient farmers, not very different from most of the inhabitants of the Town of Jamaica at the time. The farmers of western Hempstead were, of course, quite isolated from the village of Jamaica, but not much less than they had been in 1894 when Greater New York was eager to incorporate them. Thus one wonders whether the attempts to annex the same land in 1846 and again fifty years later might not stem from a nagging influence of the relic Welles Line.

Reaction to Consolidation

Three years after the Greater New York bill was passed by the State Legislature and the voters had given their approval in the referendum, the governor finally signed the bill into law on May 6, 1897; the newly expanded city would exist as of January 1, 1898. Queens began making preparations. Of all the minor civil divisions affected, the Town of Hempstead had the most complicated adjustments to make, as the Greater New York boundary ran through its land. The Town Board met immediately to deal with this problem.

In June 1897, the Town Board of the Town of Hempstead voted 3-2 to accept the Greater New York line as shown on Thomas V. Smith's map (Fig. 2, 64). This showed the boundary as described in the Greater New York Bill when it was passed by the State Legislature in 1894. But at the Board meeting of July 12, 1897, several speakers raised objections.[23] Fred Ingraham, a lawyer, pointed out that the newly accepted boundary bisected several election districts and left their voters disenfranchised.

A more fundamental objection was raised by the influential judge A. N. Weller. He claimed that the Board had not guarded the interest of the Town in voting away to Greater New York a large and valuable piece of land (much of what is now Cedarhurst and Lawrence). He argued that Newbold T. Lawrence, who owned much of the valuable land in question and whose case against the Town of Hempstead was pending in the state courts, was correct in challenging the right of the Town Board to give his land up to Greater

New York.[24] Weller's passionate discourse is the single statement of opinion on either side of the issue that appears in the Town of Hempstead records or minutes.

Judge Weller proceeded to outline a means of retaining at least some of the valuable Town land. He called in Thomas V. Smith, who testified as a civil engineer, that as of May 6, 1897, the channel between Rockaway Beach and Shelter Island had moved 3,500 feet *west* of where it had been in 1894. Weller then argued that as the channel had shifted westward from the time the Greater New York bill was passed by the Legislature to the time it was signed by the Governor, so too should its boundary line. Thus, continued Weller, the boundary line should be redrawn, beginning its straight line course to the southeastern corner of the Town of Flushing from the middle of the *new* location of the channel. Smith then presented a new map of the Town of Hempstead election districts, redrawn so that each lay entirely within or entirely outside of the repositioned boundary line. This strategy accomplished two goals: it left no citizen in an election district straddling the Greater New York boundary line, and it placed most of Newbold T. Lawrence's land safely to the east of the line. The Town Board immediately reconsidered its earlier decision, and voted to adopt the new election districts as based on the westward shift of the boundary channel by two thirds of a mile.

The right of the Town Board to change the boundary was questioned at once.[25] Queens County Clerk Sutphin applied to the Queens County Board of Supervisors to have the boundary line settled by judicial determination. In September the case was heard in Supreme Court by Justice William D. Dickey (*Gleason v Town of Hempstead*). Dickey concluded that the lawmakers meant the boundary to be where the channel was when the act was passed in 1894 in accordance with the first map drawn by Thomas V. Smith. Interestingly, the judge commented that it would have been much better to have a more stable boundary in the Charter of the City of New York. He then handed down a decision granting an alternative writ of mandamus, so that questions of fact raised at the hearing might be submitted to a jury.[26]

The issue never made it to any court. On January 1, 1898, Greater New York became a reality and it included all the lands west of the boundary line described in the Act of 1894. The Town of Hempstead instantly lost a little more than 7 percent of its land to Greater New York, and was reduced to eighteen election districts.

For exactly one year, beginning January 1898, the Greater New York boundary split Queens County into two parts: its western third, comprising five wards, lay within the City of New York, while its eastern two-thirds, comprising the Towns of Oyster Bay, North Hempstead, and the shrunken Hempstead, lay entirely outside the City.

Within the eastern towns of Queens County, political energy turned toward the creation of a new county. For decades, the eastern towns had vied with the western towns of Queens over issues such as the location of the courthouse and other county facilities. When the Greater New York proposal appeared in early 1894, the eastern towns did not resist being excluded. For the most part, they welcomed the opportunity to reorganize their political and administrative functions, tasks which had grown increasingly difficult in the latter half of the nineteenth century as western Queens became more urban and Democratic while eastern Queens had remained largely rural and Republican.

Thus, the announcement in February 1898 of the intent to create a new county called Nassau was generally greeted with enthusiasm in the three eastern towns of Queens. Perhaps making preparations for that welcomed development diverted public attention from the loss of the Town of Hempstead's westernmost lands. One year to the day after Greater New York took control of the land and people within its domain, Nassau County came into existence.

The Doughty Bill

Within a month of the creation of the new county, Assemblyman Wilbur Doughty introduced a bill in the State Legislature that would return some of the land lost by the Town of Hempstead to Greater New York. It called for the return of the area of Inwood, parts of Lawrence, and that sliver north of Inwood that encompasses the westernmost parts of what is presently Valley Stream, Elmont, and southwestern Floral Park. By April 1899, it became law and restored Hook Creek as part of the boundary (from the head of Jamaica Bay to Stephen Carman's house at the fork in Hook Creek, as well as the north-south line running from Carman's house to the southeastern corner of the Town of Flushing).[27] Further south, Doughty's bill named the northern and eastern limits of the ex-village of Far Rockaway as the southwestern limits of the Town of Hempstead. (See Fig. 4.) In so doing, it confirmed the earlier relinquishment of the Rockaway Peninsula, including the entire village of Far Rockaway, by the Town of Hempstead.

There are three interesting aspects of the Doughty Bill related to the Rockaway Peninsula. First, the northern boundary of Far Rockaway was unprecedented as a border of the Town of Hempstead, but the eastern one approximated both the Welles Line and the new town line of 1846, which was rejected by the Town of Jamaica. Secondly, the Republican Ward Committee of Rockaway Beach passed a resolution in early February 1898 requesting that Assemblyman Doughty amend the bill to include the villages of Rockaway Beach, Arverne, and Far Rockaway, all on the Rockaway Peninsula.[28] Doughty did not do so. Thirdly, the Doughty Bill was vetoed by Mayor Van Wyck of New York City after its passage in both houses of the State Legislature, but it nevertheless became law and the designated land was returned to the Town of Hempstead.[29] Later, however, mayoral vetoes effectively killed two powerful drives by Far Rockaway to secede from New York City: in 1915 and again in 1917, bills to create an independent Far Rockaway City were approved overwhelmingly by both houses of the State Legislature, but were vetoed by John Purroy Mitchel, Mayor of New York City.

Conclusion

Today's Queens-Nassau border derives from the splitting of Queens County a century ago when the Greater New York Bill defined the areas to be included in the enlarged city and led to the reorganization of the remainder of Queens County as Nassau County one year later. The rationale for including parts of the Town of Hempstead within Greater New York was not publicly stated but it appears that the inclusion of the "Doughty Strip" was an inadvertent acquisition lying west of the straight line (from Flushing's southeast corner to Plum Gut) that ensured Greater New York's deliberate and full control over the Rockaway Peninsula and all the other shores of Jamaica Bay. The Town of Hempstead's official reaction to its potential territorial loss is prophetic, for Town records outline a bold, albeit last-minute, attempt to salvage the "high and dry" areas of Lawrence and Cedarhurst, while omitting any mention of the Rockaway Peninsula.

The root of this disinterest in the Rockaway Peninsula is unclear. Perhaps Town of Hempstead officials felt that it was too critical a part of Greater New York's *raison d'être* to contest. Yet most of the Village of Far Rockaway lay beyond the shores of Jamaica Bay and its population had a long history of interaction solely with other places within the Town of Hempstead. Trying to retain it would have been just as logical as trying to retain Lawrence, Cedarhurst, and other places eventually returned as the "Doughty Strip."[30]

It is possible that the Town of Hempstead was willing to part with the Rockaway Peninsula beginning at the eastern limit of Far Rockaway Village because it never had clear title to it. It lay beyond Hempstead's land as defined in the Kieft Patent, and it lay just beyond the line widely acknowledged as the Welles Line. And as late as mid-nineteenth century, after Hempstead had assumed de facto jurisdiction over the Rockaway Peninsula, the application to annex to the Town of Jamaica the Hempstead land lying west of what amounted to the Welles Line strongly suggests that the Welles Line remained a meaningful divide in the minds of at least some people.[31]

It is, of course, highly probable that the Town of Hempstead was willing to part with Far Rockaway (and the rest of the Rockaway Peninsula) as part of a deal that would return areas considered more valuable. Certainly the

Doughty Bill returned to the Town of Hempstead areas of solid Republican leaning while clearly rejecting the re-attachment of the more Democratic Rockaways.[32] Political or other tacit dealings notwithstanding,[33] the boundary seems to recall the preceding two centuries during which a ghostly line haunted map makers and evoked the crossing of an important boundary zone.

Notes

Individuals representing several institutions graciously assisted me in locating old maps, newspapers, and other documents: Myrna Sloam of the Bryant Public Library in Roslyn, Rhoda Becker of the Town of North Hempstead, Jim Driscoll of the Queens Historical Society, John Hyslop of the Long Island Division of the Queens Borough Library, Clyde Patton of Hunter College, and the entire staff of the Long Island Studies Institute at Hofstra University, and Karen Roselli and Thomas Saltzman of the Town of Hempstead were especially generous in providing patient assistance and thoughtful insight. To them all, and to Nassau Community College for supporting my research, I extend heartfelt gratitude.

1. The original bill defining the boundaries of New York City was, in fact, called "An Act providing for the submission of the question of consolidation of the City of New York with certain territory under a single administration to a vote of the people" (1894 *New York Laws,* Chapter 64). It was subsequently amended in 1899 (see note 27 below).

2. Most of the boundary changes in the twentieth century have been minor, usually adjustments involving a home or business that straddled the border. One substantial change occurred in 1928, when the border in the Far Rockaway-Lawrence area was shifted 100 to 400 feet westward for a north-south distance of about a mile (1928 *New York Laws,* Chapter 802). The change was prompted by the opening of the Atlantic Beach Bridge, which connects the Nassau County communities of Atlantic Beach and Lawrence. After Nassau County officials claimed that bridge traffic would be slowed by having to navigate the streets of Far Rockaway, the State Legislature granted the land to Lawrence so that a new approach to the bridge, Doughty Boulevard, could be built in Nassau to replace the old McNeil Avenue in Far Rockaway. Today, Route 878 has replaced Doughty Boulevard.

3. Benjamin D. Hicks, ed., *Records of the Towns of North and South Hempstead, Long Island, N. Y.,* 8 vols. (Jamaica: Long Island Farmer Print, 1896-1904), May 20, 1751 and April 6, 1824, 4: 86, and 4: 87 (cited hereafter as *Hempstead Town Records*).

4. Once they became part of Greater New York, the towns and their political functions were dissolved. Jamaica and Flushing became "wards," their prior significance giving way to differences in zip code and unofficial distinctions of postal address. But east of the Greater New York boundary, the towns retained their identity and viability. Indeed, Hempstead and North Hempstead are two of the most populous, wealthy, and powerful towns in the country.

5. In 1788 *New York Laws,* Chapter 64. This and other laws cited are discussed in John C. Thomson, *The Greater New York Charter of 1901* (New York: Lawyers Co-operative Publishing, 1901), 23.

6. A map commissioned by the Surveyor General of New York does not show the boundaries as specified in the 1788 laws nor does the 1873 *Atlas of Long Island, New York* (New York: J. B. Beers, 1873). The first correct cartographic rendering of the changes appears on the *New Map of Kings and Queens Counties* (New York: J. B. Beers, 1886). After the publication of this large-scale map, other reputable works, such as the *Atlas of Queens County* (New York: Chester Wolverton, 1891), and various Belcher-Hyde local atlases of 1896 (Brooklyn: Hyde & Co.), followed suit.

7. Map by William Stewart, dated October 9, 1791, in the Town of Hempstead Archives, Hempstead, NY.

8. Map by William Stewart, dated 1791, in the Town of Hempstead Archives.

9. Alfred Bellot, *History of the Rockaways from the year 1685 to 1917* (Far Rockaway, NY: Bellot's Histories, Inc., 1918), 20.

10. In fact, the Welles Line *may* have been a futile, if official, attempt to clarify the border between the Town of Hempstead and the Town of Jamaica. It appears that Welles, several of whose surveys are mentioned in the Hempstead Town Records of August 24 and August 27, 1685 *(Hempstead Town Records,* 1: 490-92), was summoned by town officials after they had called a meeting to give "oure deputys ffull power . . . [in] ending ye diference Consarning the bounds beetweene oure Naybouring Towne Jamaco and us" *(Hempstead Town Records,* 1: 487). Bellot, in his *History of the Rockaways,* 17-18, quotes a description of a Welles survey which he claims is the basis of the Welles Line. The survey cited by Bellot is one of the metes and bounds defining a particular piece of property, a complicated series of landmarks, distances, and angles that bear no relationship to a straight line. Since the Welles Line that shows up on maps for the next two hundred years is notably straight, one wonders if the survey quoted really was the original survey of the Welles Line, or perhaps if town officials actually preferred a cartographic simplification of the numerous and possibly vanishing Welles markers.

11. *Village of Lawrence, N. Y.: A Brief History of a Long Island Community* (Village of Lawrence, 1977), 12-13.

12. An address delivered by Valentine W. Smith at the noonday meeting of the Exchange Club, November 13, 1934 (ms. in the Far Rockaway file, Long Island Division of the Queens Central Library). (On the history of Rockaway, see also Vincent F. Seyfried, *Old Rockaway, New York in Early Photographs* [Mineola: Dover, 2000]. Editor's note.)

13. David C. Hammack, *Power and Society: Greater New York at the Turn of the Century* (New York: Russell Sage Foundation, 1982), 196, 356-57. Hammack suggests quite plausibly that the broad territorial limits of the Greater New York proposal reflect the powerful influence of the Chamber of Commerce in assuring the city's pre-eminence as a world port.

14. Jeffrey A. Kroessler, "Jamaica Bay, The Greatest Port That Never Was," *Seaport,* Fall 1994, 22-27. Within a few years of Consolidation, plans were drawn to develop Jamaica Bay into a world-class harbor with three major shipping lines and extensive docking facilities on the north shore of the Bay. For two decades, the plan stagnated because of paltry railroad access to the intended docks. It was finally abandoned once Robert Moses proposed it as a recreational area.

15. Both Rockaway Beach and Shelter Island are gone, as is the little inlet that briefly lay between them. Much of the old Rockaway Beach, a spit of land lying south of present-day Far Rockaway, was washed away during a storm in 1903. Soon after,

real estate developers deliberately had the inlet filled in and the sandspit of Shelter Island raised and stabilized, and, by using material dredged from the bottom of Rockaway Bay, connected Shelter Island to the western end of Long Beach Island. The landfill added to Shelter Island allowed the creation of Atlantic Beach, while the dredging itself produced a new navigable waterway, north of Atlantic Beach, called East Rockaway Inlet or Reynolds Channel. The creation of Atlantic Beach and the filling in of the old inlet closed off Hicks Beach in Lawrence, the site of Newbold Lawrence's Isle of Wight development, from direct access to the Atlantic Ocean.

16. For a detailed discussion of the shifting sands of the spits and an interesting and concise summary of the laws concerning changes in property lines brought about by coastal geomorphologic processes, see the informative unpublished ms. by Edward Bentley, *The Isle of Wight,* in the Peninsula Public Library in Lawrence. *Newbold T. Lawrence* v *the Town of Hempstead* 155 NY 297 (1898) involved the legal interpretation of changing property ownership resulting from the inevitable erosion of the eastern end and deposition to the western end of these barrier islands. The decision as to who lost and who gained ownership hinged on whether the changing location of inlet and spit were erosional or avulsive.

17. *Long Island Farmer,* February 9, 1894, 5.

18. *Long Island Farmer,* February 16, 1894, 1.

19. The original map is in the Town of Hempstead Archives.

20. Records of the Town of Jamaica, 5 bound vols. (typescript in the Long Island Collection, Queens Borough Library, Jamaica), 4: 303, minutes of the meeting of April 10, 1846.

21. Fosdick was well known and respected in Queens County in the nineteenth century. He learned surveying from his father, a professional surveyor, and went on to hold several important county offices, including Commissioner of Deeds in 1838 and County Judge and Surrogate from 1849 to 1866. His signature on the map lends the application great credibility.

22. The original map is in the Nassau County Museum Collection of the Long Island Studies Institute at Hofstra University (Map M106). (See Fig. 5, p. 75.)

23. Minutes of the Town Board Meeting, Town of Hempstead Records, ms. vol. 12: 41-42. Located in Town of Hempstead Archives.

24. The case was ultimately won by the Town of Hempstead (*Town of Hempstead* v *N. T. Lawrence,* 147 AD 624 [1911]).

25. Minutes of the Town Board Meeting, Town of Hempstead Records, Meeting of August 17, 1897, ms. vol. 12: 69-70.

26. *Hempstead Inquirer*, September 3, 1897, Town of Hempstead Records, ms. 12: 111; Meeting of October 7, 1897.

27. In 1899 *New York Laws,* Chapter 379, An Act to Amend the Greater New York Charter by excluding certain territory therefrom, and annexing it to the Town of Hempstead, in the County of Nassau.

28. *Hempstead Inquirer,* February 3, 1899.

29. *Hempstead Inquirer*, April 28, 1899.

30. In fact, the Rockaway Peninsula effectively became an exclave of Queens County once the Doughty Strip was returned to the Town of Hempstead. Rockaway people can drive to other parts of Queens only by crossing a toll bridge over Jamaica Bay unless they go northeast through the communities of Inwood and Lawrence.

31. The Welles Line, that is, B 9th Street, remains as a curious relict boundary. The sliver of Far Rockaway to its east is visually and ethnically similar to Lawrence, and marked by large single-family houses. Immediately to the west begins the more urbanized portion of Far Rockaway, with high-rise apartments and a commercial core.

32. The Doughty Bill returned to the Town of Hempstead not only the residential properties in Lawrence belonging to Newbold T. Lawrence and J. Russel Sprague, but also the shore of Jamaica Bay in Inwood where G. Wilbur Doughty, Sprague's uncle, docked his boat.

33. On the role of Doughty and Sprague as leaders of the Nassau Republican Party, see Marjorie Freeman Harrison's article, "Italian-American Inwood and the Making of the Modern Nassau Republican Party," in this volume (95-108); and Michael Dorman, "A Legacy of Kings," in *Long Island: Our Story*, by Newsday (Melville: Newsday, 1998), 331, 333. (Editor's note.)

Appendix

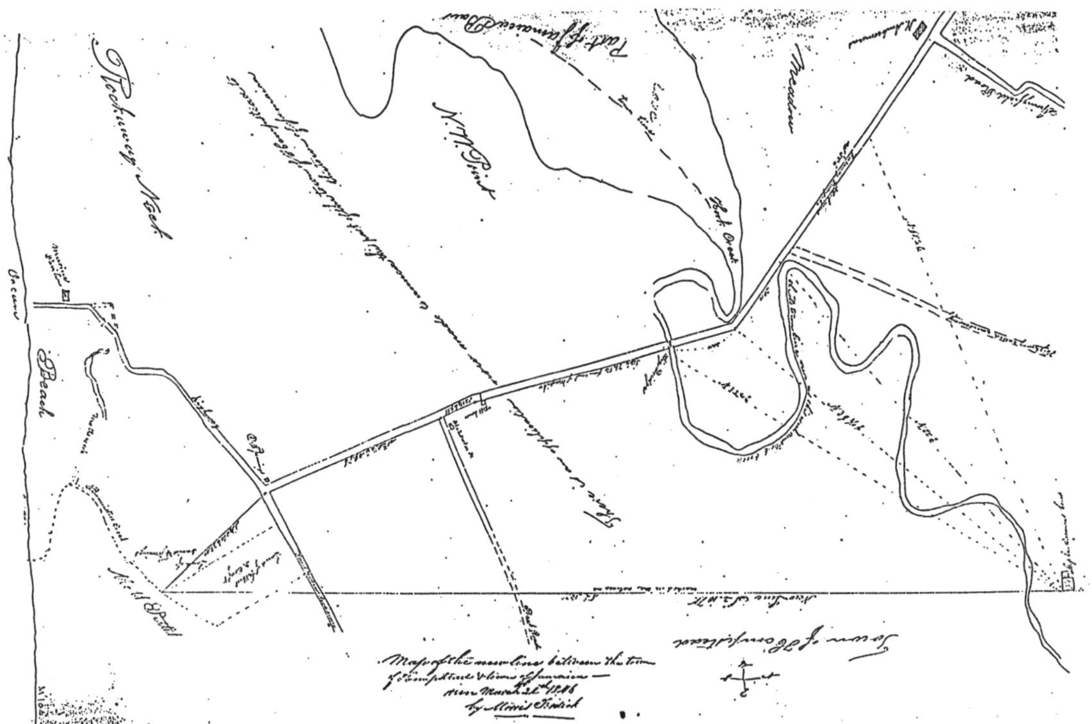

Fig. 5. Facsimile of Morris Fosdick's 1846 map of proposed new town line between Jamaica and Hempstead (also see Fig. 3, p. 65 above). *NCM Collection, LISI at Hofstra.*

Speech at the Laying of the Courthouse Cornerstone

Theodore Roosevelt

Fellow citizens, ladies and gentlemen,*

I am delighted to have the chance to be present and take part in the laying of the cornerstone of this building today, because of what is meant to the county by the erection of the building and because of what is meant to all of us as citizens by the manner and kind of work that is to be done in the building after it is erected.

There are certain deep questions affecting our civic duty which go far beyond any party opinions so long as we insist that our representatives of whatever faith possess the elementary moralities and decencies. We can't afford as citizens ever to permit our representatives, least of all those of our own party, whatever that may be, to forget there are certain characteristics we put above theories, that it is our right and duty to insist that every public servant shall show the same qualities of honesty and uprightness as in private and business relations.

We cannot afford for one moment to permit the preaching of doctrines which are good enough when preached but which are not practiced. We can't permit the kind of morality which finds promises made on one day of the week and not performed on the other six. No amount of ability will take the place of the work-a-day humdrum virtues, from the highest public official to the lowest, from all who take their way to and from the courthouse. He must know his duty and then do it. We can't accept any ability that is a substitute for honesty, which is what we want from any public servant. He must recognise the moral law by his deeds. He must have more than liberal loyalty, he must practice it.

Now for the public. Remember that the public servant will do what the public requires him to do, or, if the public is indifferent, what the public elected him to do. But you can't stop him if he goes wrong. If you permit sharp practice it will be your own fault if it is exercised at your expense. The

---

*James W. Foote, the conference dinner speaker, included in his first person presentation of Theodore Roosevelt the speech which Governor Roosevelt gave at the laying of the cornerstone of the new county's courthouse on July 13, 1900. This version is from Jesse Merritt's article, "Laying of the Cornerstone of the Old County Courthouse," *Nassau County Historical Society Journal* 17 (Summer 1956): 16-17, which was reprinted by the Nassau County Bar Association for the July 11, 1999 opening of the cornerstone. (Editor's note.)

Governor Theodore Roosevelt at the Cornerstone Laying Ceremonies for the Nassau County Courthouse, July 13, 1900. The *Proceedings of the Board of Supervisors, 1900* reported that Roosevelt "delivered a very interesting address, after which he laid the cornerstone in a very substantial way" (65). *NCM Collection, LISI at Hofstra.*

people rule and as they are or are not determined to have decency in public life, they will see to it.

Free government is not a gift that can be handed out by the celestial powers, but only by hard work under self-government and we must preserve it. Fundamentally, the average man must do his part in the work of self-government and make his representatives feel the results he wishes on the plane on which it must be and can be kept. And ultimately it is almost of greater importance that the men who do the work should be in touch with us and should respond to what is highest and best in our desires. The old lesson to remember is that the Decalogue and Golden Rule are particularly in place in public life. The public servant must be decent, upright and honest. All free men are alike in privileges, his duties and responsibilities. The average citizen must be a good husband and father, but he must also observe honesty and decency and honor in public life.

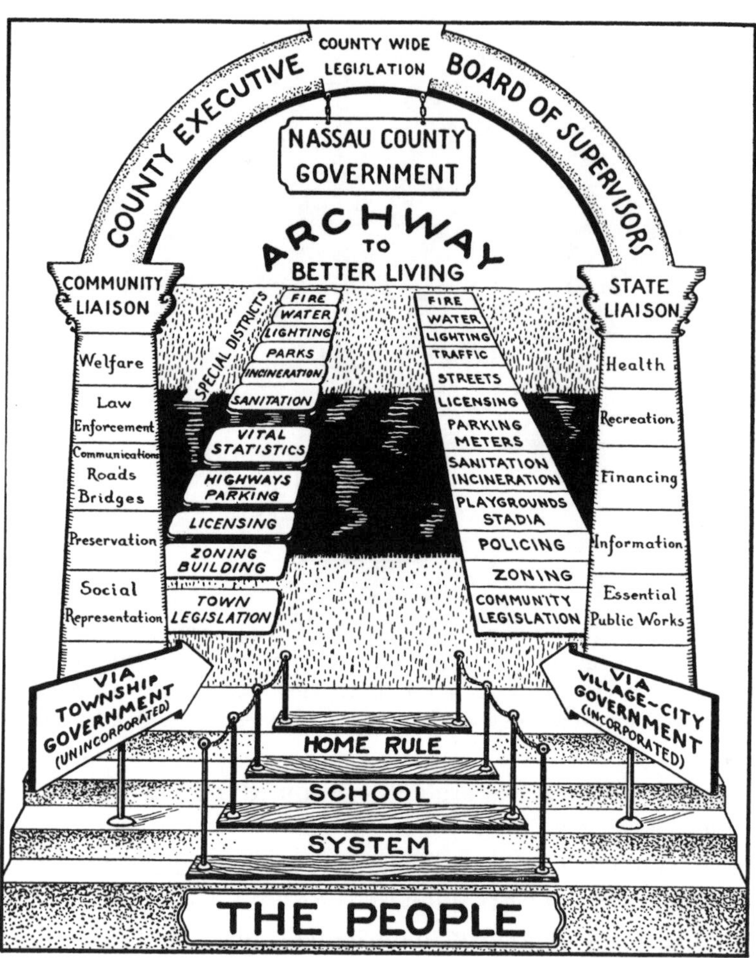

A depiction of Nassau County government under the County Executive-Board of Supervisors system which governed the county for more than half a century (1938-1996). This illustration accompanied an article, "'Nassau'—That Means 'Home Rule,'" which explained how the four divisions of local government (county, town, city or village, and school districts) work together for "the most representative government." From *The Nassau Record* published by the Nassau County Republican Committee, October 1952. *NCM Collection, LISI at Hofstra.*

Institutional Poor Relief in Nassau County, 1899–1999

Ruth Shackelford

When Nassau County came into existence on January 1, 1899, it already had in place a well-established system of public relief for its needy citizens. There was a county almshouse, two town almshouses, and a children's home. These institutions, combined with a program of outdoor relief administered on both town and county levels, provided the county's first safety net for its most fragile citizens—elderly men and women, young, unmarried mothers with nowhere to go, and children who had lost their parents or whose parents could no longer support them.[1] Over the next hundred years, Nassau County's poor relief system evolved, generally in line with changes that were taking place in social welfare throughout the United States. While these changes led to the closing of the county almshouse and the children's home, the two town almshouses proved to be remarkably resilient. Both remain in existence today, in somewhat different form—as homes for the elderly—and are still providing critically needed care for some of the county's neediest residents.

The Nassau County Almshouse had the shortest history of any of the county's public poor relief institutions. Originally established by Queens County in 1874, this institution was a "poor farm," an almshouse that provided care for the county's poor, but also was a working farm. Residents were expected to earn their keep by working on the farm, and the farm itself reduced operating costs by providing a large part of the institution's food. Because of its location, on Barnum's Island (called Hog Island prior to 1874) in southern Nassau County, the almshouse was inherited by Nassau County when the two counties were split apart in January 1899.[2] At that time, the County Almshouse consisted of ten buildings located on 450 acres of land and could provide care for more than four hundred persons. While an institution of this size may have been appropriate for the much more populous Queens County, it was more than the smaller, more rural Nassau County needed. With only twenty-seven residents in 1899, the County Almshouse was underutilized and much too expensive to maintain. For the next two years, county officials tried to cover costs and reduce expenses by selling off much of the almshouse's equipment and stock, by cutting off electricity to the island and using oil lamps instead, and by discharging all staff except for the keeper and matron. Finally, in May 1901, the almshouse was sold and the profits used to help construct the new Nassau County government

Hempstead Town Almshouse built in 1875. Postcard c. 1905, *NCM Collection, LISI at Hofstra.*

buildings at Mineola. From this point on, the county used the two town almshouses for institutional care.[3]

The Hempstead Town Almshouse was originally founded in 1773. The town purchased a seventy-acre farm on Jerusalem Avenue, east of the village of Hempstead in what is now the community of Uniondale. Initially the farmhouse on the property was used to house the county's needy residents; then, in 1875, a new building was constructed on the property. Town officials had chosen the farm site deliberately; like the county almshouse, the new Hempstead Town Almshouse was to be a working farm. All residents who were physically able to do so worked on the farm, which produced most of the vegetables, meat, grain, and dairy products consumed by the almshouse residents.[4]

Soon after Nassau County came into existence, a representative of the New York State Board of Charities, the organization responsible for visiting, inspecting, and supervising charitable institutions in the state, described the Hempstead Town Almshouse as an "attractive," "colonial style farm house" that looked "like an old-fashioned mansion" rather than an almshouse. The interior of the building, however, was less charming. While all of the rooms were clean and neat, the building was beginning to show its age. Floors and stairs were worn, laundry and bathing facilities were inadequate, and much of the building was in need of repair. The following year some improvements were made—a modern, for the time, plumbing system was installed, which pumped water from a newly-dug well into a thousand-gallon tank in the building's attic, and two new bathrooms were added, one for each sex, with flush toilets, shower baths, and sinks—but the building itself still needed "considerable repairing."[5]

In 1899, the Hempstead Town Almshouse was caring for twenty-five men and eight women, fifteen of whom were over the age of seventy. Most of the residents lived in the main building under the kindly care of a husband and wife team who acted as keeper and matron. A few residents, however, were housed in the old almshouse building, known as the "Annex," which had been left standing when the new building was constructed in 1875. The Annex appealed to the more "feeble" men who were not yet bedridden, because their rooms were on the ground floor and they could have their meals served to them there, rather than having to negotiate two flights of stairs in the new building to get from the residents' rooms on the second floor to the dining room in the basement. While the two almshouse buildings may have been somewhat shabby, visitors regularly reported that the institution was neat, clean, and orderly, that the residents were satisfied with the care they received, and that the residents were served food that was both "abundant and of good quality."[6]

The Hempstead Town Almshouse was supported by town funds. The other town almshouse, the Jones Institute, had a more unusual form of support. When Samuel Jones died in 1836, he provided in his will that the sum of $30,000 be set aside as an endowment to provide for the care of the poor of the Towns of North Hempstead and Oyster Bay. In 1840, the newly-formed Jones Fund for the Support of the Poor purchased sixty-three acres of farmland on which the first Jones Institute building was constructed. In 1878, another small parcel was added, increasing the property to sixty-five acres, and a series of bequests by other generous citizens increased the Fund's endowment to $48,000 shortly after the turn of the twentieth century. The Jones Fund was administered by a popularly-elected Board of Trustees made up of three residents of Oyster Bay and two residents of North Hempstead. In addition, the Towns of North Hempstead and Oyster Bay contributed to the support of the Jones Institute by paying half of the combined salaries of the Institute's keeper and matron, and each town also paid a small sum to the Trustees elected from their towns for each meeting of the Jones Fund they attended.[7]

The first building of the Jones Institute was located in Brookville, about four miles from Oyster Bay. Similar to the Hempstead Town Almshouse in many ways, it was an ordinary two-story wooden building surrounded by a working farm that produced much of the grain, vegetables, and meat consumed by the residents. In 1899, the Jones Institute housed twenty men and six women, half of whom were over seventy years of age. There were also a few "colored" residents, who were housed and fed separately from the white residents, a practice that was reported to be "peculiar" to this institution.

Visitors found the almshouse clean and orderly and the residents "contented," but, like the Hempstead Town Almshouse, the building was showing signs of age and wear. The barns and outbuildings were delapidated, the floors and stairs were worn, and the walls were cracked.[8]

Prior to 1884, almshouses provided the only public institutional care for needy children in what was then Queens County.[9] Following an investigation into the care of children in almshouses conducted by the New York State Board of Charities, the New York State legislature passed a law, in 1875, that required the removal of all "healthy and intelligent" children over the age of two from almshouses in the state and prohibited any further commitments of these children to almshouses. By the end of the year, most of the county and city almshouses had complied with the new law; Queens County was not among them. Lacking any acceptable local institutions to which these children could be sent, poor relief officials simply procrastinated and left the children where they were. In 1878, another law was passed requiring the removal of *all* children over the age of two from almshouses in the state, regardless of their mental and physical condition. The New York State Board of Charities strongly recommended that, whenever possible, needy children be placed in "good family homes" rather than in institutions, and, lacking any other convenient alternative, county and town officials complied. Almshouse children were placed in what we would today call foster homes, and were then called boarding homes, where private families were paid by the county or town to care for dependent children. By the end of the year, only four children remained in the Jones Institute, two in the Hempstead Town Almshouse, and two in the Queens County Almshouse, and these were reportedly "vicious and depraved" boys who had been placed in homes but then had been returned to the almshouses because they were "incorrigible."[10]

In their haste to comply with the new laws, county and town poor relief officials had evidently not given the boarding homes a thorough examination since volunteer visitors reported that some children were being "treated cruelly" and learning "nothing but wickedness."[11] Concerned for the county's dependent children, a small group of influential citizens succeeded in establishing the Temporary Home for Children in Hempstead in 1884, which, as its name implied, was to be "a temporary home for destitute children and such as may be committed to its care by the County Superintendents, and Town Overseers of the Poor."[12] Within a few months, town and county poor relief officials were regularly committing children to the Home, and it soon outgrew its original building. In 1888, the proceeds from a number of benefit fairs provided sufficient funds to purchase five acres of land on Willis Avenue in Mineola, where a new, larger home was constructed.[13]

In January 1899, when Nassau County came into being, there were forty-one boys and thirty-three girls living in the Temporary Home, which now included a separate school building and a children's hospital on the same grounds. Like most children's institutions at the turn of the century, the emphasis at the Temporary Home was on training the children to become useful and productive citizens. Girls were taught sewing and laundry work and did most of the housework; boys also helped with housework, but their main duties were maintaining the garden and the chicken yard. Visitors to the Temporary Home reported that the children were healthy and making "rapid progresss" [*sic*] in the Home's school, and that the management was kind, efficient, and giving the children "good care."[14]

While the Temporary Home was relatively new at the turn of the century, the two town almshouses were not, and, as the years passed, they became the targets of official complaints. Inspectors from the New York State Board of Charities began complaining about the Hempstead Town Almshouse in 1903. It seems that the recently added shower baths had been improperly installed, and that no provision had been made to drain off the water. This meant that when the shower was used, water overflowed the shower basin, collected on the floor, and leaked through to the floor below.[15] Three years later, State Board inspectors reported that the condition still had not been repaired, and now also recommended better fire escapes, repairs to buildings, and electric lights to replace the kerosene lamps that were a serious fire hazard in the wooden building, as well as the closing of the old Annex building, which had fallen into disrepair.[16]

Although the Jones Institute had installed modern bathrooms and iron fire escapes in 1902, three years later State Board inspectors began reporting that the institution lacked basic comforts and safety precautions. Like the Hempstead Town Almshouse, the Jones Institute was still using kerosene lamps and its buildings were in need of repair, but even more was needed—a better water supply, a central heating system, new furniture, a better diet for the inmates, and better record-keeping. The inspector concluded that "[u]nder present conditions . . . proper care of the inmates is impossible."[17]

Criticism increased in 1908, when the State Board's inspector complained about "the antiquated methods in vogue in Nassau County for relief of the poor," going on to say that "[t]he two almshouses at Hempstead and Oyster Bay are simply old dwelling houses used for the purpose of housing the poor, and neither are proper places." This criticism continued in 1909, when inspectors complained that no improvements had been made, and called the two institutions "among the poorest almshouses in the State."[18] The problem was at least partially solved on March 9, 1910, when the Hempstead Town Almshouse was destroyed by fire, tragically causing the death of one of the residents. As plans for reconstruction of the almshouse

The new Hempstead Town Almshouse built in 1912, on Jerusalem Avenue in Uniondale. It is now used by the Fire Marshall. Photograph by Bill DeSimone, 1999.

were debated, the Jones Institute continued to come under attack. In 1911 the State Board's inspector described the institution as "old, worn, uncomfortable, inconvenient and exceedingly dangerous in case of fire." The State Board as well as several county volunteer organizations strongly recommended that the two town almshouses be discontinued, and that service be centralized in one county almshouse. However, the Nassau County Board of Supervisors rejected the plan in 1912, and instead approved construction of a more modern Hempstead Town Almshouse. Complaints about the Jones Institute, however, continued into 1913.[19]

The new Hempstead Town Almshouse was completed and occupied on December 21, 1912. Built with the criticisms of the State Board in mind, the fireproof, two-story brick and tile building was constructed with modern plumbing and as little wood as possible. There was a central section, where the keeper and his wife lived, a right wing for men, and a left wing for women. Each wing included private rooms as well as large dormitories, sitting rooms, and porches. The State Board "congratulated" the Town on its "sanitary and convenient" building.[20]

Perhaps spurred by what had been accomplished in Hempstead, the trustees of the Jones Fund finally began to respond to the State Board's criticisms in 1913. The trustees first sold the old almshouse and farm. They then purchased a new twenty-five-acre tract of land on West John Street at Hicksville in Oyster Bay and began construction of a building that was, once again, very similar to the Hempstead Town Almshouse: a modern, fireproof, two-story Georgian-style brick and white stone building. In 1914 the building was ready for occupancy and was praised by the State Board of Charities' inspector as being "well arranged, well managed, and of ample capacity." The Jones Institute continued its tradition as a farm-home at the new site, with a twenty-acre working farm on the premises that produced sufficient potatoes, cabbage, corn, and other vegetables for the use of the residents, as well as a surplus for sale.[21]

Children's Home, Mineola, c. 1910. Postal, *NCM Collection, LISI at Hofstra.*

Shortly after the new Jones Institute building was constructed, the Temporary Home at Mineola also came under attack by the State Board of Charities. While the Home's buildings were still in good condition, its administration apparently had not kept up with the times. A routine investigation by the State Board of Charities in 1916 had graded the state of the Home's buildings and grounds a "B," or above average, but assigned a grade of "D," or substandard, for its administration and "Ideals." Specific criticisms were leveled at the Home's school, the way meals were served in the dining room, the lack of vocational training for both boys and girls, inadequate record-keeping and medical care, and the lack of any programs that would help the children develop initiative, such as allowing them to organize clubs or exercise some form of self-government. By April 1916 a number of these criticisms had been addressed. Electric lights and a fire alarm system had been installed, the one-room schoolhouse had been divided and an additional teacher had been hired, so that the primary and secondary school students could be taught separately, and more attention was now being given to the medical needs of the children. However, the problems about vocational training and development of initiative had not been addressed.[22]

The decline in the Temporary Home's standing with the State Board of Charities was accompanied by a drop in commitments. The combined effects of a slow shift in public poor relief policy away from institutions for children in favor of placement in private boarding homes, and a new public relief program instituted in Nassau County in 1915 that provided aid to widowed mothers so that they could care for their children at home (so-called widows' pensions), caused the number of children being committed to the Temporary Home to slow to a trickle.[23] An attempt was made to make up for the drop in commitments by bringing in children from other Long Island counties. However, as the Home's income dropped, it became increasingly difficult to keep the premises in adequate condition to meet the state's requirements, and in July 1919 the Home was closed. In 1921, the Home was reopened as a Cardiac Home for Children, but by 1924 it was again unoccupied. After a few more efforts to get various organizations interested in reopening the facility, the property was sold in 1925, ending the history of Nassau County's first institution for children.[24]

Meanwhile, the types of people who were residents of the town almshouses began to change. In the nineteenth century, almshouses often had been extremely unpleasant places because they acted as a kind of catch basin for every type of dependent. Entire families were relocated in almshouses when the father was ill or injured and unable to work; single mothers who had been widowed or deserted lived there with their children; and unmarried, pregnant women came to the almshouse to give birth. These populations were joined by unemployed single men and elderly, senile, physically handicapped, alcoholic, mentally ill, and chronically ill persons of both sexes, with little or no effort made to segregate the different types of residents. During economic downturns, which were endemic in the second half of the nineteenth century, overcrowding often made an unsavory situation intolerable.[25]

By the end of the nineteenth century, the emergence throughout the United States of specialized institutions for various types of needy and disabled persons contributed to a general improvement in almshouse conditions. Gradually, persons who formerly had been committed to almshouses were instead committed to the new institutions. There were now institutions for the "deaf and dumb," institutions for the blind, institutions for crippled children, institutions for the insane, institutions for the mentally impaired (referred to as "feeble-minded" in the nineteenth and early twentieth centuries), and institutions for dependent children, as well as special institutions for delinquent children and youths.[26]

The Nassau County Almshouse provides a good example of an almshouse with a mixed population. Just before it closed in 1901, the population of this facility included two epileptics, three "cripples," five "idiots," four residents who were "feeble minded," and two who were blind. After the almshouse was closed, these people were sent to the Brunswick Home in Amityville, a private institution that provided care for a wide range of "defective" people. The rest of the (presumably "healthy") residents of the almshouse were sent either to the Hempstead Town Almshouse or to the Jones Institute.[27] In 1910, Nassau County was sending its dependent population to three different institutions for deaf mutes, to the Syracuse State Institution for Feeble Minded Children, and to three different orphan asylums. The towns also made liberal use of institutions. For example, in 1920, the Town of Oyster Bay was supporting residents in the Brunswick Home, the Howard Orphan Asylum for Colored Children in New York City, the Brooklyn Home for the Blind, the Brooklyn Home for Defective Children, and a number of other private institutions.[28]

With so many recipients of county and town relief going to specialized institutions, who was left to send to the almshouses? In the early twentieth century, most of the residents of the Hempstead Town Almshouse and the Jones Institute were elderly or ailing individuals with nowhere else to go, supplemented by a small, constantly shifting population of temporary residents. Occasionally mentally or physically impaired persons were housed at the almshouse while they awaited placement in an appropriate institution. For instance, in 1915, a "finely educated" young German man, who had lost his sight and hearing when a stone fell on his head, was staying at the Jones Institute while he recovered, and in 1923 two sisters were housed at the Jones Institute until they could be transferred to the State Institution for the Feeble Minded. There was also a more or less constant presence of mothers with their babies.[29]

Ever since the first almshouses were established in the eighteenth century, it had been common for unmarried women to use them as maternity hospitals. In fact, "[m]ost public officials considered this use of the almshouse as a reasonable and necessary alternative to infanticide and abandonment." The Nassau County almshouses were no exception, and even New York State tacitly accepted this situation by specifically exempting children younger than three years of age from the laws of 1875 and 1878 which made it illegal to house children in almshouses.[30]

In 1914, the problem of caring for unmarried mothers became something of a crisis when forty illegitimate children were born in Nassau County. Prominent citizens, who formed the Nassau Cottage Association to address the problem, had very specific concerns:

> The tendency of an unmarried girl who becomes a mother is often to cast off the child and rid herself of responsibility. The child becomes a burden upon public institutions, and the mother finds the way very easy towards a life of prostitution. Thus she becomes a permanent menace to her community.

In 1915 the Association purchased a ten-room house on an acre of land in West Hempstead and opened "Nassau Cottage," a home for single mothers. By January of the following year, Nassau Cottage was caring for six "unfortunate girls," with more awaiting admission.[31]

Public care for unmarried mothers and their babies continued, however. In 1916 a temporary hospital was built adjacent to the Hempstead Town Almshouse to quarantine children stricken by a polio epidemic. By January of the following year the epidemic had ended, and the building then became the Hospital Annex where residents of the Almshouse were treated, including single mothers. A new hospital building was erected on the same site in June 1926, complete with a separate maternity ward. In the 1930s, as the Depression began to affect Long Island communities, the maternity ward was filled to overflowing with new mothers of all types, who could no longer afford private medical care.[32]

Once the care of expectant mothers had been moved to the new hospital, in 1926, the Hempstead Town Almshouse population became even more specialized. A new name reflected the institution's new focus: The Hempstead Town Almshouse was now called the Hempstead Home for the Aged and Infirm. In 1938, when the County adopted a new charter, supervision of the Home was transferred from Town officials to the County Department of Public Welfare, and the name was changed again to the Nassau County Home for the Aged and Infirm.[33]

In spite of the changes, some aspects of the Home remained the same. Now using paid help, the Home's farm continued to supply the residents with vegetables, dairy products, pork, and chicken until 1954, when the farm was taken over by the Sheriff's Department. The farm itself remained in operation until 1958, when ground was broken for an ambitious $12 million building complex dedicated to the care of the county's aged and infirm population. The first wing of the A. Holly Patterson Home for Nassau County Aged and Infirm was completed in July 1961, and the first residents made the short trip from the old almshouse to the new building the following month. The complex was completed in 1963, with three, four-story wings designed to care for a total population of 900.[34]

Today, the 1912 almshouse building remains standing, on Jerusalem Avenue in Uniondale, and is now the headquarters of the Nassau County Fire Marshall. Next door is the 1926 hospital building, now the home of the Nassau County Vocational Education and Extension Board. Now a skilled nursing facility providing accommodations for 889 residents, the A. Holly Patterson Geriatric Center is nationally recognized for its excellence in treating Alzheimer's disease, AIDS, pulmonary disease, and dementia. Seventy-two acres of former farmland are now maintained as part of the Center's grounds.[35]

Like the Hempstead Town Almshouse, the Jones Institute remains in operation today. After the Institute moved into its much more spacious building in 1914, it continued to survive, supported by income from the Jones Fund and the supplemental support it received from Nassau County. In 1935, the Social Security Act was passed, providing for the payment of Old Age Assistance to needy persons over the age of sixty-five. These payments, and later payments of Social Security benefits, helped maintain the Jones Institute into the 1970s. The working farm, partially staffed by residents of the Institute, continued to operate as late as 1963.[36]

Then, in 1971, New York State Governor Nelson Rockefeller began a campaign to limit welfare expenses, and, by 1974, the Nassau County Department of Social Services was forced by budget constraints to discontinue its contributions to the Jones Institute. Struggling to survive, the Institute sold off half of its twenty-five-acre property in the late 1970s, but even this did not provide sufficient funds to upgrade the Institute's aging building to meet state standards. In June 1980, the Trustees of the Jones Fund announced that as soon as the Institute's residents could be relocated, the home would be closed and the property sold. A proposed $2 million sale to the King Kullen Grocery Company was delayed for a year by a coalition of community groups. They protested that the sale was contrary to the provisions of the will of Samuel Jones, who had provided the original trust fund for the Jones Institute. After a series of lawsuits and appeals, the sale was finally approved on the condition that the Trustees of the Jones Fund use the proceeds of the sale to establish another home for the elderly poor. The sale was consummated in July 1981, and the current property was purchased in November 1982.[37]

The new institution, called Jones Manor On-The-Sound, is located on the grounds of the former Clarkson estate on Bayville Avenue in Bayville, a quiet, suburban community in northern Long Island. Jones Manor is located in the estate's expanded and renovated carriage house and now provides home-like care for forty-six elderly residents whose average age is eighty. The property in Bayville is much smaller and less rural than the Institute's previous properties; while there is a small garden, there is no farm, and there is a shopping center directly across the street. The location is still very pleasant, and a deck on the northern end of the building provides the residents with sweeping views of the Long Island Sound. With the guaranteed support of the Jones Fund, which is now valued at over $1 million, Jones Manor expects to continue for many years to come.[38]

Both the A. Holly Patterson Geriatric Center and Jones Manor are testaments to Nassau County's continuing commitment to provide care for its most vulnerable residents. One citizen's generosity in 1836 is still making it possible for a small group of the county's elderly residents to live out their days in comfort. In Hempstead, the preservation of the old almshouse building provides a direct link to the past, while the county's preservation of the almshouse's farmland to provide pleasant surroundings for the Geriatric Center's residents is remarkable, especially considering today's property values. When many communities have either ignored their poor or condemned them to miserable places, Nassau County stands as a model for its dedication to its more unfortunate citizens.

Notes

1. Outdoor relief is a form of relief dating back to colonial times that aided families or individuals in their own homes by providing cash payments or goods such as groceries and coal. Because of space constraints, this paper will not include a discussion of the County's outdoor relief programs. The author discusses outdoor relief as it related to the support of the County's needy children in a forthcoming article, entitled "Child Welfare in Nassau County: The First 50 Years, 1899-1949."

2. The location of this island was reported as being "off Oceanside" in Clinton E. Metz, "Sarah Ann Baldwin Barnum: A Nineteenth Century Achiever," *Long Island Forum* 57, no. 9 (September 1984): 170; as being near Far Rockaway in Jean Spellman, "The Local Visiting Committee of Nassau County," *Nassau County Historical Journal* 8, no.1 (Summer 1945): 19; and as being at Rockville Centre in *Annual Report of the [New York] State Board of Charities for the Year 1900* (Albany: James B. Lyon, 1901) (hereafter cited as NYSBC, *Annual Report* [1900], and all other NYSBC Annual Reports are similarly cited), 2:449. The island has been completely developed and it now includes the incorporated village of Island Park and two unincorporated communities, Harbor Isle and Barnum Isle.

3. Metz, "Sarah Ann Baldwin Barnum," 167, 171-73; *Annual Report of the [New York] State Board of Charities For the Year 1902* (Albany: Argus Company, 1903), 2: 611; *Thirty-fifth Annual Report of the [New York] State Board of Charities* (n.p., 1902), 528-29; *Annual Report of the [New York] State Board of Charities For the Year 1899* (Albany: James B. Lyon, 1900), 1: 697-701; *Thirty-fourth Annual Report of the [New York] State Board of Charities* (n.p., 1901), 599; NYSBC, *Annual Report* (1900), 2: 449.

Although Metz stated that the proceeds of the sale were divided between Queens County and Nassau County, it was actually only the proceeds of the sale of the livestock and personal property on Barnum's Island that were divided between the counties. All of the proceeds of the sale of the land ($40,100) were deposited into the Nassau County Building Fund. *Proceedings of the Board of Supervisors of the County of Nassau for the fiscal year 1900* (Oyster Bay: Oyster Bay Pilot, 1901), 7-8; *Proceedings of the Board of Supervisors of the County of Nassau for the fiscal year 1901* (Oyster Bay: Oyster Bay Pilot, 1902), 95 (hereafter cited as *Nassau County Proceedings, 1901*).

After the almshouse closed, the county poor were cared for temporarily at the Suffolk County Almshouse in Yaphank; this ws discontinued in June 1901 when the county began utilizing the Jones Institute (then located in Brookville) for the care of its poor. Then in June 1905, the county began assigning some of its poor to the Hempstead Town Almshouse. *Proceedings of the Board of Supervisors of the County of Nassau for the fiscal year 1899* (Roslyn: Monroe S. Wood, n.d.), 75; *Nassau County Proceedings, 1901,* 85-86; *Proceedings of the Board of Supervisors of the County of Nassau for the fiscal year 1905* (Oyster Bay: Pilot Press, 1906), 97, 456; *Proceedings of the Board of Supervisors of the County of Nassau for the fiscal year 1906* (Oyster Bay: Pilot Press, 1907), 177, 597.

For reports of visits to the Barnum's Island almshouse when it had a large population, see Minute Book of the Queens/Nassau County Local Visiting Committee, in the Nassau County Museum collection (L55.20), Long Island Studies Institute, Hofstra University, Hempstead, New York, Local Visiting Committee Records (hereafter cited as LVC Minute Book), meetings of February 29, 1876, vol. 2, and January 25, 1898, vol. 7.

4. Robert Emmet Cray, Jr., *Paupers and Poor Relief in New York City and Its Rural Environs, 1700-1830* (Philadelphia: Temple University Press, 1988), 94; *Fourteenth Annual Report of the [New York] State Board of Charities* (Albany: Weed, Parsons and Company, 1881), 151; *Sixteenth Annual Report of the [New York] State Board of Charities* (Albany: Weed, Parsons & Company, 1883), 181; NYSBC, *Annual Report* (1900), 2:450; LVC Minute Book, meeting of January 31, 1899, vol. 7; reports of Nassau County Local Visiting Committee dated January 16 and 22, [1901], in the Nassau County Museum collection, Long Island Studies Institute, Hofstra University, Local Visiting Committee Records (L55.20; hereafter cited as LVC Records), Box 1, Folder C.

5. NYSBC, *Annual Report of the [New York] State Board of Charities* (1899), 1:702-3; Reports of January 16 and 22, [1901], LVC Records, Box 1, Folder C. The powers and obligations of the State Board of Charities under the New York State Laws of 1896 are set out in *Annual Report of the [New York] State Board of Charities For the Year 1896* (Albany and New York: Wynkoop Hellenbeck Crawford Co., 1897), 8-20.

6. NYSBC, *Annual Report* (1899), 1:702-3, 706; *Thirty-eighth Annual Report of the [New York] State Board of Charities* (n.p., 1905), 521; LVC Minute Book, meeting of January 31, 1899, vol. 7; Annual Report, meeting of October 31, 1899, and Annual Report, meeting of October 30, 1900, LVC Minute Book, vol. 7. Apparently, the Annex was also used to isolate "undesirable" residents from the rest of the institution's population. In January 1901 a visitor reported that the building was occupied by "Billy Renthard (the foolish boy) and two collored [sic] men" and that "any unclean transent [sic]" also would be housed there. Reports of January 16 and 22, [1901], LVC Records, Box 1, Folder C. Mention of the keeper and matron being husband and wife can be found in NYSBC, *Fourteenth Annual Report*, 151; NYSBC, *Sixteenth Annual Report*, 179; *Thirty-sixth Annual Report of the [New York] State Board of Charities* (n.p., 1903), 433; and New York Bureau of Municipal Research, *Government of Nassau County, N.Y. Description of Organization and Functions* (Albany: J. B. Lyon Company, 1915), 62.

7. Untitled article, *Brooklyn Daily Eagle*, March 5, 1923; New York Bureau of Municipal Research, 107-8; NYSBC, *Thirty-fifth Annual Report*, 527. The Trustees were paid $2 for each meeting attended.

8. NYSBC, *Annual Report* (1899) 1: 706-8, 710; New York Bureau of Municipal Research, 107; LVC Minute Book, meetings of October 25, 1898 and January 31, 1899, vol. 7. Apparently physical separation of whites and African Americans had been practiced at the Jones Institute for some time. In 1880, visitors reported that "[t]he eastern portion of the building is occupied exclusively by colored people," who made up nearly half of the institution's population at that time. Meals were also segregated; the white residents were served first, after which the African Americans were served. NYSBC, *Fourteenth Annual Report*, 149-50. Accommodations were separate but apparently not equal. In 1894, a visitor reported: "The part of the house occupied by the colored people was clean and tidy, showing a marked improvement in these respects over the same

apartments under previous keepers." Report of visit of October 26, 1894, in LVC Records, Box 1, Folder A. Segregation continued until at least 1921, when an "old colored woman" was given a bedroom to herself because the matron felt "that this change makes the [other] women happier." LVC Minute Book, 10: 67-68.

9. The earliest directory of children's institutions in Queens County published by the State Board of Charities appeared in 1898. At that time there were only two institutions for children in what would become Nassau County, other than the Temporary Home in Mineola: St. Dominic's in New Hyde Park (established in 1897 and affiliated with The Orphan Home in Brooklyn run by the Nuns of the Order of St. Dominic), and St. John's Roman Catholic Protectory in Hicksville (established in 1890 and associated with the Roman Catholic Orphan Asylum in Brooklyn). The Nazareth Trade School in Farmingdale, also affiliated with The Orphan Home in Brooklyn, was established a few years later. *Annual Report of the [New York] State Board of Charities For the Year 1898* (New York and Albany: Wynkoop Hallenbeck Crawford Co., 1899) 2: 396-99; NYSBC, *Annual Report* (1899) 2: 510.

10. *Eighth Annual Report of the [New York] State Board of Charities* (Albany: Weed, Parsons and Company, 1875), 17-18; *Tenth Annual Report of the [New York] State Board of Charities* (n.p.: Jerome B. Parmenter, 1877), 23-25; *Eleventh Annual Report of the [New York] State Board of Charities* (n.p.: Jerome B. Parmenter, 1878), 18-20; *Twelfth Annual Report of the [New York] State Board of Charities* (Albany: Charles Van Benthuysen & Sons, 1879), 18-19. The Jones Institute, however, continued to house children until October 1880. LVC Minute Book, meetings of July 29, September 30, and December 30, 1879; March 30, April 27, August 31, and October 26, 1880, all in vol. 3. The text of the 1875 Act can be found in Grace Abbott, *The Child and the State* (Chicago: University of Chicago Press, 1938), 2: 71-72.

11. LVC Minute Book, meetings of January 27 and February 24, 1880, vol. 3.

12. Many of these concerned citizens were members of the Nassau County Local Visiting Committee. *Hempstead Inquirer,* August 8, 1884, and May 8, 1885. The work of this Committee is discussed in more detail in Spellman, "The Local Visiting Committee," and in Shackelford, "Child Welfare in Nassau County."

13. The organizers of these fairs included several members of the Local Visiting Committee. *Hempstead Inquirer,* November 23, 1888; LVC Minute Book, Annual Report for 1895, vol. 7; report dated October 1, 1892, LVC Records, Box 1, Folder C.

14. "Extracts From the Minutes of the Local Visiting Committee of Queens and Later Nassau County 1873-1932," *Local Visiting Committee, Nassau County, Constitution* (n.p., n.d.), LVC Records, Box 2, Folder A; LVC Minute Book, Annual Report for 1895 and meeting of January 31, 1899, vol. 7; report dated October 1, 1892, LVC Records, Box 1, Folder C. There were three "colored" children in the Home in October 1899, but there is no mention in the records of physical segregation. LVC Minute Book, meeting of October 31, 1899, vol. 7.

15. NYSBC, *Thirty-sixth Annual Report*, 433. The Nassau County Local Visiting Committee also complained about this condition. LVC Minute Book, 8:25.

16. NHSBC, *Thirty-eighth Annual* Report, 521; *Thirty-ninth Annual Report of the [New York] State Board of Charities* (n.p., 1906), 451. The lighting hazard is mentioned in *Thirty-fourth Annual Report of the [New York] State Board of Charities* (n.p., 1901), 597.

17. NYSBC, *Thirty-sixth Annual Report*, 434; LVC Minute Book, 8:13; NYSBC, *Thirty-eighth Annual Report*, 521; NYSBC, *Thirty-ninth Annual Report*, 451.

18. *Forty-first Annual Report of the [New York] State Board of Charities* (n.p., 1908), 295; *Forty-second Annual Report of the [New York] State Board of Charities* (n.p., 1909), 451; *Annual Report of the [New York] State Board of Charities For the Year 1909* (Albany: J.B. Lyon Company, 1910), 1: 470.

19. *Forty-fourth Annual Report of the [New York] State Board of Charities* (n.p., 1911), 496; *Annual Report of the [New York] State Board of Charities For the Year 1911* (Albany: Argus Company, 1912), 1:427; *Forty-sixth Annual Report of the [New York] State Board of Charities* (n.p., 1913), 570. The State Charities Aid Association and the Local Visiting Committee of Nassau County also supported a county-wide system. See LVC Minute Book, 8:128, 132, 136. See also, the debate on the county system in *Proceedings of the Board of Supervisors of the County of Nassau for the fiscal year 1910* (Great Neck: Record Press, n.d.), 426-81 (hereafter cited as *Nassau County Proceedings, 1910*). State recommendations about adopting a county system of poor relief began as early as 1897. *Annual Report of the [New York] State Board of Charities For the Year 1897* (New York and Albany: Wynkoop Hallenbeck Crawford Co., 1898) 1:472-73. In fact, as early as 1880, Hempstead, North Hempstead, and Oyster Bay were the only *towns* in the State of New York that maintained their own almshouses, although there were a few city almshouses. *Thirteenth Annual Report of the [New York] State Board of Charities* (Albany: Weed, Parsons and Company, 1880), 10, 15-16.

20. *Forty-seventh Annual Report of the [New York] State Board of Charities* (n.p., 1914), 445.

21. Untitled article, *Brooklyn Daily Eagle*, March 5, 1923; *Annual Report of the [New York] State Board of Charities For the Year 1916* (Albany: J.B. Lyon Company, 1917), 471; New York Bureau of Municipal Research, 107; untitled brochure from the Jones Fund/Institute vertical file in the Nassau County Museum collection at the Long Island Studies Institute, Hofstra University.

22. LVC Minute Book, meeting of April 25, 1916, vol. 9; letter from Florence VanVranken to Anna Cornwall, April 27, 1916, in LVC Records, Box 1, Folder C; Spellman, 28.

23. This program is discussed in more detail in Shackelford, "Child Welfare in Nassau County."

24. LVC Minute Book, 10:24, 59, 130, 140.

25. Michael B. Katz, *In the Shadow of the Poorhouse: A Social History of Welfare in America* (New York: Basic Books, 1986) 29-30; 1913 Annual Report, LVC Records, Box 2, Folder B.

26. Katz, *In the Shadow of the Poorhouse,* 11. The classic work on the growth of institutions in the nineteenth century is David J. Rothman, *The Discovery of the Asylum: Social Order and Disorder in the New Republic* (Boston: Little, Brown and Company, 1971).

27. NYSBC, *Thirty-fifth Annual Report*, 529-30.

28. Other institutions utilized by Oyster Bay in 1920 were the Brooklyn Industrial School, St. Malachy's Home, and the Roman Catholic Orphan Asylum. *Nassau County Proceedings, 1910*, 694-95; *Proceedings of the Board of Supervisors of the County of Nassau for the fiscal year 1920* (n.p.: Daily Review Print, n.d.), 789-801.

29. LVC Minute Book, meeting October 26, 1915, vol. 9; LVC Minute Book, meeting of January 30, 1923, 10: 109. See also LVC Minute Book, meeting of October 31, 1899, vol. 7, for mention of two "imbeciles" who had been sent from the Hempstead Town Almshouse to the Brunswick Home. For examples of mothers and babies in the almshouses, see LVC Minute Book, meetings of July 28, 1914 and October 27, 1914, vol. 9, and meetings of January 30, 1923, and April 31, 1924, 10: 108-9, 126.

30. Ruth Shackelford, "To Shield Them from Temptation: 'Child-saving' Institutions and the Children of the Underclass in San Francisco, 1850-1910" (Ph.D. diss., Harvard University, 1991), 16 n. 14; NYSBC, *Tenth Annual Report*, 23; NYSBC, *Twelfth Annual Report*, 18-19.

31. Typewritten announcement in LVC Records, Box 2, Folder A. The same information is reported in LVC Minute Book, meeting of October 26, 1915, vol. 9. The Nassau County Association, a Progressive Era "good government" organization, was instrumental in establishing the Cottage. See letter from Mary Malcolm to Members of the Local Visiting Committee, January 24, 1916, LVC Records, Box 1, Folder A.

32. LVC Minute Book, Annual Report, 1916, and meeting of January 30, 1917, vol. 9; LVC Minute Book, meetings of April 31, 1924, April 27, 1926, June 22, 1926, and July 29, 1930, 10:126, 146-47, 148, 210.

33. LVC Minute Book, Meeting of April 27, 1926, 10:146; Josef J. Hayes, *The Department of Public Welfare of Nassau County, New York, During the Years 1938-1958: A History* (n.p., n.d.), 23.

34. "History of the Patterson Home," *Patterson Patter* 5, no.7 (August, 1968): 8; *Fifteenth Annual Report of the Nassau County Department of Public Welfare for the Year Ending December 31, 1953* (n.p., n.d.), 10; *Twenty-fourth Annual Report, Nassau County Department of Public Welfare* [1961] (n.p., n.d.), third and fourth pages (not paginated); *Twenty-sixth Annual Report of the Nassau County Department of Public Welfare, 1963* (n.p., n.d.), 3, 35.

35. A. Holly Patterson Geriatric Center brochure, March 1999.

36. Brochure in the Jones Fund/Institute vertical file, Nassau County Museum Collection, Long Island Studies Institute, Hofstra University; Walter I. Trattnor, *From Poor Law to Welfare State: A History of Social Welfare in America*, 5th ed. (New York: The Free Press, 1994), 290; "Charge Cruelty at LI Aged Home," *Newsday*, April 8, 1963.

37. *The Annual Report of the New York State Department of Social Services*, Legislative Document (1973), No. 92, Publication No. 1016 (3/73), Part II, 2; brochure in the Jones Fund/Institute vertical file; "Judge Rejects Jones Institute Suit," *Newsday*, June 10, 1981; "Jones Institute Home Sale Approved," *Newsday*, July 9, 1981; "Jones Fund Buys Bayville Site for Shelter," *Newsday*, November 17, 1982.

38. Brochures in Jones Fund/Institute vertical file; "Elderly Aided in Fine Manor," *Daily News*, February 27, 1996.

Italian-American Inwood and the Making of the Modern Nassau Republican Party

Marjorie Freeman Harrison

Numerous well-informed commentators have identified the Nassau Republican Party as one, if not the single, most powerful and well-organized county political organization existing today. Without question, as a *suburban* political machine, the Nassau Republican Party is virtually without equals. Furthermore, Italian-Americans, the single largest ethnic group comprising Nassau's population, have dominated positions of Republican Party leadership and public elected posts for the past three decades. Behind these truths lies a rich history which upon examination reveals much about how Nassau has defined itself in the post-World War II era. Local political culture has changed and been changed by the needs, values, and relative voting power of the ethnic and class groups which comprise major blocks of the county's population.

There is no question that if the story of the county of Nassau is to be fully told, then the history of the Nassau GOP, beyond its impressive election statistics, must be examined in all its cultural and community dimensions. And as that history is constructed, it becomes clear that if the *national* history of postwar suburban America is to be fully comprehended, the history of this premier postwar boom county, primary both in terms of its sheer size as a postwar growth area and as a companion of New York City, must be researched and integrated into the national narrative.

Two themes that relate directly to the telling of the national story will be threaded throughout this examination of Nassau's political history. One has to do with the shaping of America's postwar political topography. The history of the national GOP has been, in this period, a tug-of-war between the forces of the right and the center, between the forces of McCarthyism versus Eisenhower moderation, between the Goldwater conservatives versus the "Rockefeller" East Coast wing, between the Gerald Ford Midwest moderates versus the Reagan Sun Belt ideologues, between the Religious Right-1994 Gingrich revolutionaries-Christian Coalition versus the congressional and gubernatorial moderates. The fairly consistent stance of the Nassau GOP as a powerful and well-positioned proponent of a relatively middle-of-the-road approach is a significant part of this parry and thrust; its story must be incorporated into the national political narrative.

One of the most exciting and yet disconcerting aspects of research on Nassau's politics is the realization that the very significant national roles of

Nassau-based politicians of the postwar period such as Nassau GOP chairman and County Executive J. Russel Sprague and Republican National Committee Chairman and Oyster Bay Congressional Representative Leonard Hall, have gone virtually unnoted by professional historians. Contemporary ideological contests within the national GOP remind us that the outcomes of political battles are seldom predetermined; the political sophistication and consistent voting-booth results that Nassau GOP politicians brought to the table in the councils of the national party made them forces to be reckoned with in the battles between the GOP's opposing wings.

A corollary to the lack of academic attention to Sprague and Hall and others is the state of scholarship on suburban politics. That body of work lags behind the contemporary reality that, for some time, the largest single block of voters in national elections has resided in the suburbs. That Nassau County's political history has not generated the kind of rich academic study that cities of comparable size have received is a measure of the task before students of suburbia. A treatment of the assumption embedded in much of the work on suburban politics may be found in my article in this volume, "Myths and Realities of Suburban Politics" (38-46).

The second thread in constructing Nassau's political history has to do with the story of people becoming Americans, the story of how thousands of families of immigrants—first, second, and third generation—through their suburban lives defined for themselves, in dialogue with the already existing communities they joined, what it meant to be an American, to be middle class, to both acculturate and yet maintain certain values and outlooks related to their national heritages. To go beyond our conventional ways of thinking about politics, attention must be paid to political engagement at the community level, an arena where people created identities, identities that were personal, familial, ethnic, economic, religious, and communal. Political culture, expressed around family dinner tables and in neighborhood activity, was of a piece with the ethnic, religious, and workplace cultures in which people participated. Both the Nassau Republican and Nassau Democratic Parties, and the movements, institutions, and groups allied with them, served as the channels through which a social alchemy linked the public with the private. The purpose of this essay is to examine one particular set of elements related to community and ethnicity in the development of political identity, with the understanding that other arenas such as the workplace, religious institutions, and racial and gender dynamics, also require thorough treatment and integration into the overall picture.

Here attention is directed toward the largest demographic group of newcomers to Nassau in the late 1940s and 1950s, the Italian-Americans, with one local community as the focus. Jews comprised another major demographic constituency of the postwar influx; African-Americans have a long history in the county. Hispanics, Asians, Russians, Eastern Europeans, people from the Caribbean, and other groups constitute proportionately smaller but increasingly significant populations. Their histories also deserve careful study.

An irony in the hidden history of Nassau is that it was a community of the poorest of the poor, the southern Italian and Albanian immigrants of Inwood in southwestern Nassau, who provided the bridge for the successful transition of the pre-World War II Protestant-dominated Nassau GOP into a modern, majority, multiethnic party. The interaction between an immigrant culture and the dominant society is at the heart of the modern story of Nassau politics, especially the consistent success of the county Republicans. The Inwood immigrants developed and defined an ethnic Italian-American culture for themselves based on community-wide networks; key local GOP leaders recognized the power of this web of connections as an organizing strategy and adapted it to enable the GOP to maintain its historic dominance even as legions of Democratic-leaning voters streamed into the county (LaValle 1996, 57).

The advent of Levittown and the burgeoning of GI-generation households throughout the county posed a major challenge for the long-dominant local GOP. The party earnestly worried about the changing electorate; in October 1947, *Newsday* carried an article entitled "G. O. P. Gazes in Alarm at Levitt-Type Homes, Leases." The fact that the party's anxiety seems a bit alarmist now reflects the wisdom of hindsight. The GOP worked hard to maintain its registration advantage, even as a secular trend throughout the state's suburbs was characterized by a generic, relative erosion of the GOP voter-affiliation edge. For here is the crucial point: it was the party's relentless community organizing, its service orientation, its strategic dispensing of patronage, its general practice of eschewing distracting ideological postures, clinging instead to a centrist course, that enabled it to retain its dominance. This was the model it learned in the 1930s, before the massive postwar influx, during its recruiting of the Inwood Italian community to its side. Inwood served as a crucial proving ground for a style of local base-building that enabled the Nassau GOP to withstand and prosper despite changing demographics, despite the loss of the County Executive post for virtually the entire decade of the 1960s, and despite, more recently, the switch to a county legislature, a move that the Nassau Democratic Party had championed for decades as the key to its hopes for breaking the GOP majority (Kelly 1993, 242; Scarrow 1983, 10-11; Carlino 1996; Levy 1993).

Compared with the volumes published about Levittown and the Gold Coast of Nassau's North Shore, Inwood is obscure. By 1900, about 200 Italian-born immigrants, living in thirty-eight households, resided along narrow streets in a densely settled neighborhood where they raised large families and kept barnyard animals and vegetable gardens in the back. By 1910, those of Italian birth or Italian background numbered about 700. Almost 40 percent were Arberesh-speaking, immigrants of Albanian descent who came from the southern Italian province of Calabria. Relegated by discriminatory housing practices to the Inwood working-class neighborhood of Crow Hill, this population of dual Italian ethnicities comprised about 25 percent of Inwood's total population and slowly began to coalesce into a coherent group. They were separated by language, Arberesh and Italian, but joined by common allegiance to the Roman Catholic Church. It is important to note that Italian immigrants brought with them not an "Italian" national identity, but an identity rooted primarily in local town and region. Italian Americanism was very much a phenomenon forged out of American residency and by the American experience itself (Renoff et al. 1989, 106-11, passim).

These immigrants faced anti-Italian sentiment that dated back to the mid-nineteenth century when the first sizable emigration of Italians to America took place. There was a particular antipathy towards Italians on the part of the Irish, who viewed the pagan and anticlerical strains of Italian religious practice as debased and debasing of the Roman Catholic faith. Italians' distinct lack of economic opportunities was revealed in the fact that a vastly disproportionate number of Italians, as compared with native born men, worked as day laborers, suffering seasonal layoffs that averaged thirteen to fifteen weeks. "Italian origin groups were . . . at the bottom of the socioeconomic ladder in Inwood. Common occupations and resultant low economic status forged bonds between Albanese and Italians; at the same time, they acted to separate Italian-born from the higher-status non-foreign population." Need, hardship, intermarriage, and the practice of *comparaggio*, godparenthood, knitted the community into "networks of reciprocity." As two elderly Inwood women said in an oral history interview: "We were all poor then but we didn't know it, because we all had the same. We helped each other like one family" (Renoff et al. 1989, 112-14).

By the 1920s, Italian-owned businesses had emerged to give the community a more solid economic base, and local political leaders were coming forward. "During the 1930s, several Inwood Albanese attained some power as local leaders in the Republican Party." It was at this juncture that the partnership between the ethnic community and the WASP-dominated county GOP began to take shape (Renoff et al. 1989, 118).

Inwood and the adjacent village of Lawrence, whose predominantly middle-class and upper-class residents provided employment opportunities for Italian tradespeople, entrepreneurs, houseworkers, and gardeners, were the home turf of the leader of the county Republican Party, G. Wilbur Doughty. A state assemblyman whose wealth derived from the local oyster trade, he consolidated the power of his party as the ruling force in Nassau politics in the pre-World War I period. Republicans successfully played the "Tammany card" in the years following Nassau's establishment as an independent county in 1898, capitalizing on voters' desire to remain free from any "entangling alliance" with the city. "Doughty's anti-New York City credentials were impeccable; he actually had gotten Inwood, his hometown, taken out of Queens and placed in Nassau" (Bookbinder 1983, 210).

An effective party builder, Doughty looked beyond the WASP constituency of his party to the growing populations such as those of nearby Inwood, which was in 1900 "the island's largest Italian enclave." He began the process of bringing ethnic voters into the GOP fold, realizing that a cross-ethnic, cross-class alliance was possible. "In contradistinction to the success Democrats enjoyed among the immigrant population in big cities like New York, on Long Island it was the Republican Party that played a similar role. Much of this could be attributed to perceptive Republican leaders like G. Wilbur Doughty, who . . . possessed the cunning to seek out and to involve natural community leaders and to appoint them to pivotal positions that also yielded a degree of financial reward." With his base in the Town of Hempstead government, Doughty, as Nassau Republican leader, could dole out patronage jobs. These jobs required little formal education but did provide stable year-round wages and a possible pathway to lower-middle class status for Inwood's working class. Breaking new ground by appointing local Italian leaders to posts such as Italian-language court interpreter, Doughty sent a signal that "was appreciated by the wider community" (LaValle 1996, 57).

The Republicans and their Inwood political collaborators were skillful in using local organizations to knit the "urban village" into the political party. The Italian American Republican Club of Inwood "was utilized extensively both to cultivate the Italian vote and to serve as a manipulator of power. . . . [It] proved a useful vehicle for both Italian and non-Italian candidates for office. That the local populace reciprocated by voting consistently Republican was verified in the results of election after election." Inwood stood out as a reliable GOP stronghold in the Five Towns communities of Lawrence, Woodmere, Hewlett, and Cedarhurst, which for years provided solid Democratic vote totals. "When the

G. Wilbur Doughty of Inwood led the Nassau County Republican Party for three decades until he died in 1930. Photograph c. 1922. *NCM Collection, LISI at Hofstra.*

This cartoon, entitled "Thunder on the Left," appeared in response to a "Tammany Invasion" when city and state Democratic leaders attended a meeting at the Garden City Hotel. It was in the *Nassau Republican* (June 1954), published by the Nassau County Republican Committee. Illustration courtesy of the *NCM Collection, LISI at Hofstra.*

votes were tabulated it was Inwood which proved the bulwark of the Republican party locally . . . The loyalty thus exhibited continued to produce government jobs, many of them of a menial nature such as public works department laborers, for Inwood's Italians." Administrative and policymaking positions such as the supervisory level job given to Peter DeSibio, in the Hempstead Town Highway Department, signified a recognition that higher level posts were expected and granted (LaGumina 1988, 186).

But the numbers of Italian-Americans living in Inwood would not necessarily have provided a sizable enough bloc to be of major political consequence. What was crucial were the organizing skills that Doughty, Inwood leader Peter DeSibio, and county Republican leader Sprague brought to bear to create the sort of solid, extremely loyal, cohesive base and disciplined voting bloc necessary for a local political empire (Levy 1993; LaGumina 1988, 186).

Ethnic political cohesiveness should not be construed as an air-tight phenomenon that resulted in all Italian-American voters consistently voting Republican, or always preferring a candidate of their own ethnic background, or always backing the same contenders in internal party battles. However, a significant degree of political unity was achieved and was due, to a very measurable extent, to the unique leadership of Peter DeSibio. Born in Inwood in 1908, he had already built himself a base within the community when he came to the attention of G. Wilbur Doughty. Coming up through the ranks of community and political leadership as a protege of Doughty's, DeSibio continued his rise in party politics after Doughty died, and his nephew, J. Russel Sprague, also of Inwood and Lawrence, became county party leader. In partnership with Sprague, he consolidated the alliance between the Protestant Republican organization and the Inwood Italians that Doughty had initiated (LaGumina 1988, 186). GOP district leader in 1938, and executive area leader in 1945, DeSibio became "the first Italian American in the county to join the party hierarchy of the Sprague machine." Soon thereafter, "he was appointed Hempstead Town Deputy Highway Commissioner, serving simultaneously as chairman of the Inwood Fire District Board. Subsequently he was appointed to the Atlantic Beach Bridge Authority, becoming its chairman" in 1973. His overlapping public and party roles gave him extraordinary political influence including control over many patronage jobs (LaGumina 1988, 186, 187; see also LaValle 1996, 57; Freedman 1994, 150-51).

For more than fifty years DeSibio led a potent political operation, recognized as a unique power by no less a figure than President Ronald Reagan. His clout, reflected in the lucrative town and private positions he held and was able to dispense, was predicated on votes.

What is most illuminating is how Peter DeSibio, coming from one of the county's smallest, poorest communities, built such a durable power base, one that "raised more money for the party" than wealthier areas and that "also rolled up the biggest pluralities" (Levy 1993). Basing his strength on "Italian fraternal groups," with links to virtually all local groups, church, civic, volunteer fire, and women's auxiliaries, and a large extended family network, DeSibio tied himself into all the concerns and activities within the area. His yearly "dinners, dances and picnics, became legendary because they raised huge sums and attracted thousands of politically-minded people, thereby further solidifying his influential position in the party until his death in 1993. Alfonse D'Amato was the most famous of numerous Italian American politicians who, under his tutelage, first learned the intricacies of political life" (LaValle 1996, 57). D'Amato was known to refer to DeSibio as "God," a man he had known since he was eight years old (Breton 1964, 199; Levy 1993; Long 1993).

Although intensely partisan and local in orientation, DeSibio extended his base beyond the confines of Inwood's Italian community. He helped black leaders gain support for the Five Towns Community Center, a social services center for Inwood's African-American residents. Jewish residents and leaders interviewed about DeSibio recalled his assistance in finding locations for temples and religious schools. It may be that his ties with Town of Hempstead Republican administrations enabled him to smooth the way if zoning variances were needed for these facilities. A long-time editor of a local weekly, whose parents had roots in the socialism of New York City's Jewish neighborhoods, recounted in an interview that privately DeSibio shared many of her progressive views, including support of women's reproductive rights (Kerner 1996; Spanierman 1996; Sprague 1995).

This solid base in Inwood, and the personal ties he developed throughout the community, contributed to DeSibio's ability to withstand any challenges to his party position and his command of patronage. A good example of this is the case of the Atlantic Beach Bridge toll. For years, state comptrollers and other politicians have argued unsuccessfully for the abolition of the Atlantic Beach Bridge Authority once its bonds, the ostensible reason for the toll, had been paid off. One of them, then-Democratic Long Beach Supervisor Hannah Komanoff, accounted for the failure of attempts to eliminate the toll booths this way: "The general feeling was that it was his [DeSibio's] bridge and we shouldn't bother to disturb him about it" (Long 1993). In the late nineties, the controversy over the bridge toll continues.

When J. Russel Sprague became county Republican leader in 1934 and then consolidated his power as Nassau's first county executive in 1938, he recognized that while the Republicans "continued their superiority at the polls . . . they were running behind in percentage and stronger efforts were needed to ensure the conversion of the hordes of new residents." Both the written record of journalists and the testimony of the Sprague family and his political contemporaries reveal that what distinguished Sprague's leadership, what he was legendary for, what gave him a uniquely cohesive power base and reliable ballot-box totals in a large, growing, and constantly changing county, was his single-minded focus on the responsibilities of the local committeeperson, the party's representative at the neighborhood level. To receive Sprague's approval, this local leader had to serve as local "Welcome Wagon," with knowledge of and involvement in all manner of local activities, from the Little League to houses of worship to the Chamber of Commerce. Sprague was thus following in the footsteps of his uncle Doughty, who had been shaped by the ward-based political organizing of the New York City Tammany machine with which he had competed. Because of Doughty's influence and involvement in Inwood, it is likely that the in-depth community organizing Sprague demanded, championed, and institutionalized throughout Nassau County had as a primary local exemplar the tight networks of overlapping relationships that characterized the life of Italian-American Inwood (Sprague 1995; Levy 1993; Smits 1974, 64, 65, passim).

What was it about the Inwood Italian-American community that made it so successful as a center of county GOP power? The solid vote that maximized the political clout of the Inwood Italian community was predicated on what scholars call "institutional completeness." When virtually every social need of residents is fulfilled within the boundaries of the ethnic community

This cartoon titled "Tammany Hula Hoopla" appeared in the *Nassau Record* (October 1958), published by the Nassau Republican Committee. Carmine DeSapio was head of Tammany Hall, Averell Harriman the incumbent governor, and Frank Hogan was the Democratic candidate for the United States Senate. Joseph Suozzi of Glen Cove was running for County Executive; A. William Larson and Walter A. Lynch were Democratic candidates for Congress. Illustration courtesy of Marjorie Freeman Harrison.

and its myriad organizations and networks, the dispersion of residents into the "native" community to find friends, jobs, homes, spouses, or to form political identity is limited, and ethnic cohesion is firmly established.

But ethnic solidarity was not carried over by these immigrants from their Old World experience. Rather, a shared cultural identity had to be created which overcame centuries of loyalty based on local village allegiances. In America, a unifying identity as "Italians" coalesced as immigrants faced conditions of economic discrimination, religious conflict within the Catholic Church, and political and cultural bigotry. Contravening the legendary *campanilismo* (strong ties to the local village) immigrants from various towns and regions came together to create and share an Italian-American identity. This ethnic identity was in part a practical tool to assist families in adjusting to their strange new world, to find a place to live, a way to earn a living, and to take advantage of opportunities in the American system crucial to their survival (Breton 1964; Renoff et al. 1989; Vecoli, 1969; Yancey 1976). The process of community building that took place in Inwood represents the efforts of thousands of family members, through extended kinship networks, and dozens of fraternal, political, religious and civic groups. All shared the goal, expressed in one way or another, of achieving security in a land where the living was not so easy.

This all-important cohesion of the community allowed it to count for more than its relatively small numbers in such a large county might indicate.

structure and committed party voters, and ticket-splitters. Overlapping contacts and daily interactions contributed to that completeness and cohesiveness in Inwood which Republican leaders like Doughty and Sprague, and Italian-American leaders like Peter DeSibio, realized were the foundation for a potent and reliable electorate (Breton 1964, 199). DeSibio activated "institutional completeness" for political purposes by totally immersing himself in all aspects of the community's life and using that web of relationships to organize and direct electoral activity. Owen Smith, a Nassau County official in the 1980s, reported that, when he visited an Inwood church, DeSibio's picture was displayed on the wall next to a portrait of the Pope and a crucifix (Smith 1999).

The cross-class, cross-ethnic political alliance delivered to each side what it needed. On the one hand, there was the well-documented need of many Inwood residents for the sort of secure jobs in the public sector that the Republicans' vaunted patronage operation could offer. Italian-Americans, like other poor immigrant groups, were predisposed to organize themselves to take advantage of the goods and services available through alliance with a powerful political machine. Particularly for those who could not, or had not, availed themselves of educational opportunities that might open up other arenas of employment, or had not developed small businesses, government positions provided sure entry into a middle-class style of life, perhaps even homeownership, an aspiration dear to many. Today many Inwood residents are employed in departments such as the Town of Hempstead Sanitation Department, the Atlantic Beach Bridge Authority, and other governmental entities (LaGumina 1988, 187; Levy 1993).

No comprehensive study of Nassau County politics and government can afford to ignore or downplay the impact of patronage as a powerful shaper of the local political environment. The size of county and town governments, the relative strengths and electoral successes of the major parties, the usefulness or hopelessness of political engagement for citizens, the weight of the overall local tax burden, and the moral climate of local politics, are among the most obvious patronage-related factors. In Nassau, ethnicity-related values affected the role of patronage as the political system evolved in the pre- and postwar periods.

The aim here is not to debate the morality or fairness of patronage but rather to analyze it from the point of view of groups that participated in it and are central to the county's modern political history. Middle-class reformers for at least a century have condemned patronage as antithetical to efficient "good government." In contrast, in general terms, Italian-American culture, drawing on the traditions and realities of the old country, particularly the poverty of southern Italy, has expressed a more pragmatic, instrumental approach toward government. (By no means, however, do all Italian-Americans or politicians of Italian-American descent subscribe to the views being outlined here.) This ethnicity-based approach is not predicated on the outlook prevalent among reformers situated in the middle- and upper-class worlds of the professions and inherited wealth (Freedman 1994, 20).

The ethnic community's attitudes toward government have several components that can be traced to Italians' historical experience with the state in regions subjected to centuries of invasion, war, and occupation. Cynicism toward the state developed also because of the severe exploitation of the peasantry by an alliance dominated by bureaucrats, land-owning aristocrats, overseers employed by landowners, and the church, which, especially in southern Italy, tended to show little sympathy for the lot of the peasants. Connected to this is the legendary anticlericalism of southern Italian peasants (Vecoli 1969, 229).

Woven into this European history was the centuries-old practice of nepotism and corruption in the operation of provincial government. Law enforcement in popular lore was predicated more on personal connections and bribery than on fair administration; making this malleable system work for oneself and one's family was a more realistic approach than believing in some objective, equitable administration (Vecoli 1969). Once immigrants arrived in New York, they found a system of party government, Democratic domination in New York City, Republican in Nassau, in which political connections and wealth shaped how things got done and for whom. Like other newcomers, they adapted themselves to this system in the interest of survival.

This instrumental, cynical view of the state and the law existed side-by-side with an intense focus on the family and its extensions through webs of kinship and godparenthood. Studying the utilitarian worldview of poor southern Italian peasants, one scholar labeled their outlook "amoral familism," the determination to use the means at hand for the survival and betterment of the family. The condescending nature of this characterization reveals a class-based perspective which sees these lower-class practices as morally degraded. Outside observers tended to ignore or downplay the dire need that fueled the allegiance of working-class immigrant groups to a machine that could deliver concrete services and jobs (Banfield 1958, passim).

One pattern that emerged directly illustrates contrasting class and ethnic attitudes toward patronage and how family members help each other obtain government jobs. In many struggling Italian immigrant families, both parents had to work long hours to maintain the family. Young immigrant children and American-born offspring were faced with loving but stern parents whose ways were rooted in the Old World, while the younger generation was already embracing American culture. Contending with the strict disciplinary prac-

embracing American culture. Contending with the strict disciplinary practices of their often-absent, remote parents, these children formed strong bonds called "sibling coalitions," alliances of brothers, sisters, cousins, and others of the same generation linked through godparent-relations. Together they made their way through school and the world of American culture, work, marriage, and parenthood. In the local political context, these networks took advantage of patronage opportunities available through the party in power. Members of "sibling coalitions" helped each other. In this sense, nepotism was a logical extension of fundamental values of kinship and friendship (Johnson 1982, 164). This kind of nepotistic "networking" can be seen as an ethnic, working-class version of the proverbial WASP "old boy" network and inherited wealth, which for generations have produced many economic, political, and social advantages for "old-stock" groups.

The question for the future is whether the ethnic-neighborhood-based political bloc will be able to maintain itself as the community continues to move away from its first-generation immigrant roots. As Inwood residents avail themselves of educational opportunities, will they turn to the political network for jobs as much as in the past? The evidence so far points to several indicators that suggest some degree of continuity.

Affordable housing and family ties continue to exercise a strong "pull" for the members of the younger Inwood generation as they establish their own families, since patronage jobs assist them in reaching and maintaining middle-class status, job security, and homeownership. On the other hand, the perhaps claustrophobic tightness of the community and the desire to locate in communities of greater prestige may serve to "push" younger family members, with sufficient economic and educational opportunities, to leave. The Democratic electoral upsets of 1999, which displaced key Republican leaders on the Nassau County Legislature as well as on the Town of Hempstead Board, may affect the availability of government jobs obtainable through patronage. If patronage does continue on a significant scale, one may wonder whether these positions will continue to offer, for those who choose to remain in their hometown of Inwood, an alternative to the pursuit of other, more independent strategies for achieving greater economic and social mobility.

The political history of Inwood takes on a special significance as the Republican party defines itself during its future partisan battles on the local, state and national levels. Popular Democrats, like Mario Cuomo in gubernatorial races and Congressional candidate Carolyn McCarthy, have demonstrated that Inwood voters share to some degree the ticket-splitting proclivities that Nassau voters are known for, that is, people do not always vote the straight party ticket. As *Newsday*'s Larry Levy has pointed out so well, suburban voters constitute the single largest swing vote in the country, was so pronounced at the 1992 Republican national convention. If the national Republican Party veers off to the right, a path the local party has generally eschewed, it will be interesting to watch how the voters of Inwood react to their political choices during Nassau's second century.

References

Alba, Richard. 1976. "Social Assimilation of American Catholic National-Origin Groups." *American Sociological Review* 41: 1,030-46.

Banfield, Edward C. 1958. *The Moral Basis of a Backward Society.* New York: Free Press.

Bell, Wendel, and Marion D. Boat. 1957. "Urban Neighborhoods and Informal Social Relations." *American Journal of Sociology* 62: 391-98.

Bookbinder, Bernie. 1983. *Long Island: People and Places—Past and Present.* New York: Harry N. Abrams, Inc.

Breton, Raymond. 1964. "Institutional Completeness of Ethnic Communities and the Personal Relations of Immigrants." *American Journal of Sociology* 70: 193-205.

Fitzpatrick, Joseph P. 1966. "The Importance of Community in the Process of Immigrant Assimilation." *International Migration Review* 1: 6-16.

Freedman, Anne. 1994. *Patronage: An American Tradition.* Chicago: Nelson-Hall Publishers.

Gans, Herbert J. 1979. "Symbolic Ethnicity: The Future of Ethnic Groups and Cultures in America." *Ethnic and Racial Studies* 2: 1-20.

——. 1982. *The Urban Villagers: Group and Class in the Life of Italian-Americans.* 2d ed. New York: The Free Press.

Jackson, Kenneth T. 1985. *Crabgrass Frontier: The Suburbanization of the United States.* New York: Oxford University Press.

Johnson, Colleen Leahy. 1982. "Sibling Solidarity: Its Origin and Functioning in Italian-American Families." *Journal of Marriage and the Family* 44: 155-68.

Kelly, Barbara M. 1993. *Expanding the American Dream: Building and Rebuilding Levittown.* Albany: State University Press of New York.

LaGumina, Salvatore J. ed. 1980. *Ethnicity in Suburbia: The Long Island Experience.* Garden City: Nassau Community College.

——. 1988, 1990. *From Steerage to Suburb: Long Island Italians.* New York: Center for Migration Studies.

LaValle, Kenneth P., ed. 1996. *Italian Americans on Long Island: Presence and Impact.* Stony Brook: Forum Italicum.

Levy, Lawrence C. 1993. "DeSibio: The Indispensable Man for Inwood." *Newsday,* December 1, p. 107.

Long, Irving. 1993. "DeSibio, GOP 'Legend,' Dies." *Newsday,* November 11, p. 6.

Mangione, Jerre, and Ben Morreale. 1992. *La Storia: Five Centuries of the Italian American Experience.* New York: HarperPerennial.

MacDonald, John S., and Leatrice MacDonald. 1964. "Chain Migration, Ethnic Neighborhood Formation and Social Networks." *Milbank Memorial Fund Quarterly.* 42: 82-97.

Renoff, Richard, Angela D. Danzi, and Joseph A. Varacalli. 1989. "The Albanese and Italian Community of Inwood, Long Island." In *Italian Americans: The Search for a Usable Past,* edited by R. N. Juliani and P. V. Cannistraro, 106-32. Staten Island: Center for Migration Studies.

Scarrow, Howard A. 1983. *Parties, Elections, and Representation in the State of New York.* New York: New York University Press.

Sirey, Aileen Riotto, and Anna Marie Valerio. "Italian-American Women: In Transition." *Ethnic Groups* 4 (1982): 177-89.

Smith, Owen. 1999. Comments in discussion following presentation of paper at the "Political Leadership" session, Nassau County Centennial Conference, Hofstra University, March 19. (An audiotape of this session is in the Long Island Studies Institute collection in the Nassau County Centennial conference files, Hofstra University.)

Smits, Edward J. 1974. *Nassau: Suburbia, U. S. A.* Garden City: Doubleday.

Teaford, Jon C. 1997. *Post-Suburbia: Government and Politics in Edge Cities.* Baltimore: Johns Hopkins University Press.

Vecoli, Rudolph J. 1964. "Contadini in Chicago: A Critique of *The Uprooted.*" *Journal of American History* 51: 404-17.

——. 1969. "Prelates and Peasants: Italian Immigrants and the Catholic Church." *Journal of Social History.* 2: 217-68.

——. 1979. "The Resurgence of American Immigration History." *American Studies International*. 17: 46-66.

Yancey, William L., Eugene P. Ericksen, and Richard N. Juliani. 1976. "Emergent Ethnicity: a Review and Reformulation." *American Sociological Review* 41: 391-403.

Yans-McLaughlin, Virginia. 1974. "A Flexible Tradition: South Italian Immigrants Confront a New Work Experience." *Journal of Social History* 7: 429-45.

Oral History Interviews

Carlino, Joseph. 1996. (Former Speaker of the New York State Assembly.) Interview by author. Tape recording, East Norwich, NY, January 15.

Donovan, Frances. 1997. (Former Nassau Republican Party official and assistant to County Executive J. Russel Sprague.) Interview by author. Tape recording, Hicksville, NY, August 23.

Kerner, Edith. 1996. (Five Towns resident and participant in Jewish cultural groups.) Interview by author. Telephone taped interview, August 12.

Spanierman, Leatrice Slote. 1996. (Former editor of the *Nassau Herald.*) Interview by author. Telephone tape interview, July 3.

Sprague, John. 1995. (Grandson of J. Russel Sprague.) Interview by author. Telephone and tape recordings, May 15, August 3, and August 10.

Executive Power: A Comparison of Styles

James Shelland

In 1936 the voters of Nassau County adopted a charter providing a form of government headed by a county executive with broad executive power. A comparison of the first four individuals elected to fill that office reveals a variable use of power reflective of personality, political philosophy, and the values and needs of a given time.

Nassau's first county executive was J. Russel Sprague, a dominant figure in the local Republican Party. Often referred to as "Boss" Sprague because of his role as powerful Republican county chairman at the same time he served as county executive, he ran an administration where party interests and governmental administration were closely intertwined. Although a politician, Sprague thought of government as a business which was natural for one who was also a director of two Nassau banks.[1] Among his first acts as county executive were moves to improve the county's fiscal situation. With this in mind he instituted a comprehensive land reassessment program and reformed the procedures whereby tax liens were disposed of and the property returned to the tax rolls.[2] One associate recalled how he meticulously reviewed departmental budgets, making cuts wherever possible.[3] In 1939 he persuaded the Board of Supervisors to approve salary cuts for all county employees, an act that was probably relatively easy at a time when jobs were scarce and strong civil service unions did not exist.[4]

Sprague made a point of reducing the heavy debt incurred by the county during the depression years.[5] He liked to talk of "even-keel" financing, by which he meant the stabilization of government expenditures so that there would be little variation in the tax rate from year to year.[6] Despite these efforts, Sprague always kept party interests in mind. Potential scandals were dealt with quietly, and he warned officials that he would refer any evidence of corruption to the District Attorney. Any sign of scandal, he once said, would only drive the independent voter over to the other party.[7]

Sprague was succeeded in 1953 by A. Holly Patterson, another member of the local Republican hierarchy. While he also served as county chairman during his tenure as county executive, he never gave party matters the same attention his predecessor had. In fact, there was considerable dissatisfaction with his leadership among party members, and a feeling that the party was drifting.[8]

Patterson, nevertheless, was like Sprague in his approach to county government. A banker by profession, he also thought of government in

County Executives

J. Russel Sprague, 1938-1952.

A. Holly Patterson, 1953-1961.

Photographs, *NCM Collection, LISI at Hofstra.*

business terms and kept in close touch with the county's financial condition. He scrutinized departmental requests carefully,[9] kept the number of governmental employees as low as possible, and resisted for several years the demands of the civil service workers for salary increases.[10] Government costs, he said, are bound to rise, but every effort should be made to minimize these increases.[11]

On the issue of charter revision Patterson was also conservative. Charter revision essentially involved replacing the Board of Supervisors, who were elected at large from the three towns and two cities making up the county, with a legislature based on equal population districts. The proposal was supported by Democrats, whose strength was concentrated in certain areas, and opposed generally by Republicans who, with their three to two majority in the county, benefitted under the existing system. "The original charter," Patterson steadfastly maintained, "prepared the county for a population growth that more than tripled in twenty years. It is adaptable to changing conditions through the amending process, which has been used 138 times."[12] He said he would make changes where necessary, but was against fundamental revision since he believed the existing arrangement provided for the necessary balance between centralized and local control.

In 1961 Eugene Nickerson, a Democrat, became county executive. His election was an upset in a county where Republicans routinely won all county-wide elections. His victory can be attributed to a weak Republican candidate and the stress placed by the Democrats on the "Boss" issue, meaning "Boss" Sprague would still be controlling the county government.

Nickerson's background was totally different from his Republican predecessors. A lawyer who was Ivy League-educated, with service as law clerk to Chief Justice Harlan Fiske Stone, he had not spent years in local political activity. Furthermore, he did not make much effort during his nine years in office to build up a strong political machine. Both he and the Democratic county chairman at the time, Jack English, were focused more on state and national politics.[13]

Nickerson brought a new approach to county government. Gone was the old emphasis on economy and limited government; instead there was an emphasis on broad social goals. As he pointed out in his 1969 annual message to the Board of Supervisors, his goals were to promote human as well as property rights, avert problems before they reached the crisis stage, show a special concern for the helpless, and recognize an obligation to future generations.[14] Such goals involved a more activist role on the part of county government than either Sprague or Patterson thought appropriate.

Changing times certainly had a lot to do with this new outlook which Nickerson brought to the county government. By 1961 the problems of suburbia had come into sharper focus. Rapidly growing welfare rolls, inadequate transportation facilities, housing shortages, pollution, and unplanned growth all called for affirmative action by local governments. The times, as Nickerson himself noted, were more reform oriented.[15] The early sixties, it might be recalled, saw the burgeoning of the civil rights movement and the pronouncement of the "Great Society" agenda by President Lyndon Johnson.

To cope with these problems Nickerson created a number of new departments and agencies, and introduced initiatives in areas ignored by the previous county executives. Among the former were a department of commerce and industry, a department of labor, a bureau of consumer affairs, an office for the aging, a vocational center for women, a drug rehabilitation center, an ombudsman, and a human rights commission. In addition, new emphases were given to the work of existing departments. The department of franchises, for example, had added to its traditional function of issuing franchises to bus companies the broader one of reviewing transportation facilities and needs so the county could plan the development of a better transportation system. The Democratic county executive even used his office to help force a settlement of a strike on the bus lines serving the county. In the case of an earlier, similar strike, Patterson only went so far as to appoint a fact-finding commission.[16]

County Executives

Eugene H. Nickerson, 1962-1970.

Ralph G. Caso, 1971-1978.

Photographs, *NCM Collection, LISI at Hofstra.*

The police department under Nickerson established a community relations bureau to promote better relations with minority groups.[17] The planning department was doubled in size to more effectively cope with the needs of a rapidly growing county. To give this department more power Nickerson lobbied the state legislature to permit county planning departments statewide the power to review local zoning decisions in areas within 500 feet of any state or county property. Under Sprague and Patterson the work of the planning department had been confined to reviewing subdivision plans.[18]

Nickerson saw to it that the department of social services instituted rehabilitation services for welfare recipients and provided more varied types of entertainment and recreation at the county home for the aged. In line with his goal of promoting human as well as property rights, the county executive introduced a number of special programs for the poor and disadvantaged, such as the construction of recreational facilities in poorer neighborhoods. He also initiated the establishment of cooperative services in communities with high proportions of people on the poverty level, for the purpose of improving their employment prospects.[19] Nickerson's concern for people of low income was probably most dramatically demonstrated by his vigorous campaign for housing powers for all counties within the state. Toward this end, he sought a state constitutional amendment giving counties the power to construct housing. Before the establishment of the State Urban Development Corporation with power to construct low-income housing regardless of local zoning restrictions, he urged the creation of a State Zoning Appeals Board with authority to set aside such regulations preventing the construction of low-income housing.[20]

Nickerson was the first Nassau county executive to promote the cause of civil rights. One of his first acts was the creation of a Civil Rights Commission to combat discrimination.[21] In 1964 he mandated that all county contracts contain a clause prohibiting discrimination in hiring, and requiring employers and labor unions to take affirmative action to prevent discrimination.[22] In 1969, largely as a result of his initiative, the Board of Supervisors enacted the first county open-housing ordinance in the country.[23]

Naturally, the expansion of governmental services under Nickerson contributed to soaring budgets and rapidly rising tax rates. Fortunately, all of the new programs did not have to be financed out of the county property tax since federal and state aid to local governments increased significantly during the sixties.

If Sprague and Patterson brought the concept of sound business practices to county government, Nickerson brought the idea of the welfare state. He could truly claim, as he did at the end of his nine years in office, that the major accomplishment of his administration was a "reorienting of government to concern itself with human beings and their problems."[24]

In 1971 Ralph Caso, a Republican and Hempstead Town Presiding Supervisor during the Nickerson years, became county executive. Unlike his Republican predecessors he did not serve simultaneously as county party chairman. But like his Democratic predecessor he saw government in broad social terms. He saw that changing conditions required new approaches in county government. "Population growth," he pointed out, "has brought great changes in Nassau County, thereby making the concerns and problems of county government greater. There is a need, therefore, for the kind of leadership Nickerson exercised."[25] Like his Democratic predecessor, Caso saw the county taking the lead among local governments in dealing with the problems brought about by social change. He continued almost all the programs and services introduced by Nickerson. To some, he gave added emphasis, such as the office of consumer affairs, the office for the aging (renamed the department of senior citizen affairs), and the office of the performing arts (renamed the department of cultural development).[26] The department of franchises, which he appropriately renamed the department of transportation, continued to devote its attention to improving the transportation facilities within the county.[27] The planning commission continued to play a role in county planning policy.[28] He continued the development of the

John F. Kennedy Civic and Cultural Center at Mitchel Field, a project started under Nickerson.[29]

Like Nickerson, Caso also felt that county government must be responsive to the needs of the poor. "We cannot," he declared at the end of his first year in office, "be impervious to the urban problems that inevitably spill over our borders."[30] He continued programs initiated by Nickerson to help the poor and socially disadvantaged, such as supporting the county Civil Service Commission's policy of providing special examinations for those who had less than average educational advantages, and continuing, with evident enthusiasm, programs directed to helping people on welfare obtain jobs.[31] He promised to keep funding anti-poverty programs even though it required county funding to do so.[32]

Caso, like Nickerson, believed in the broad use of executive power. He believed it his duty to settle labor disputes that threatened the normal life of the county, as when he initiated a suit in January 1973 to end a strike on the Long Island Rail Road.[33] Under Caso, the county took over the formerly privately owned bus lines operating in the county, a move proposed by Nickerson back in 1964, but opposed then by Caso and the other Republican members of the Board of Supervisors.[34]

On the issue of restructuring the Board of Supervisors he was more in agreement with Nickerson than with his Republican predecessor Patterson. Favoring a county legislature based on equal population districts, he said, "There are problems under the existing system because the supervisor tends to see county problems from the point of view of his town only."[35]

While there was little difference between Caso and Nickerson as to the proper role of county government, there were differences in emphasis. Caso, for example, was more determined to preserve the suburban character of the county. To the County Planning Commission he stressed the need to preserve the county's suburban character. "We are suburbia," he declared just after his re-election in 1973, "and we must keep it that way."[36] Nickerson, in contrast, was always prepared to yield to the pressures for change. In discussing the need for suburban governments to prepare for the eventual migration of the city's poor to the suburbs, he said, "The question is not whether things will change—they most certainly will—but whether you plan change to make it more palatable."[37]

These different approaches of the two county executives to the pressures for social change were most apparent in the housing issue. Caso promised to promote public housing but made it clear that he planned to limit such housing to garden-type apartments on scattered sites while Nickerson felt that Nassau's housing needs could only be met by constructing large units.[38]

Caso, in line with the traditions of his party, placed more emphasis on economy. When asked during the 1970 campaign what he considered the most serious problems of his administration he replied, "Taxes. The cost of government."[39] Among his first acts as county executive were such cost-cutting measures as tight spending reviews and an expenditure freeze. Caso also sought to impose a more rational organization on a government that had burgeoned rapidly under his predecessor. Soon after taking office he ordered a sweeping, top-to-bottom restructuring of the sprawling social services department.[40]

Another Caso concern was tax stabilization. In words reminiscent of the first county executive, he declared at the end of his second year in office that "tax stabilization remains the aim of the county administration."[41] In this respect he could cite some success, at least for his first three years in office, but after that the county tax rate rose to an even higher percentage than it had been during Nickerson's last year in office.[42] It was evident that the expanding government services were forcing an increase in taxes despite concerted efforts to hold them down.

In conclusion, the following points might be made. Sprague and Patterson, with their great concern for economy, tended to restrict governmental activity to essential services, while Nickerson and Caso, with their realization that the county had an important role to play in the solving of social problems, greatly expanded the functions of government. "Boss" Sprague, who used his office to help build up one of the most powerful political organizations in the country, was clearly the most "political." Government under both Sprague and Patterson tended to be closed and remote, while under Nickerson and Caso it became more open and accessible. Board meetings, for example, during the times of the former, were held only on Monday mornings, an obviously inconvenient time for most people. It was Nickerson who introduced the practice of evening meetings.

A number of factors explain the different approaches of Nassau's first four county executives. Personality, political philosophy, and the values and needs of the times all played a part. Sprague, who became county executive in the closing days of the Great Depression, reflected the public's desire for the most stringent economy in the delivery of services. Patterson, his attitude formed in the same years, continued in the Sprague tradition. Nickerson, coming into office at a time when the problems of suburbia had come into a sharper focus, found a public receptive to his plans for an expanded role for county government. Caso, confronted with the same problems, continued essentially in the Nickerson tradition.[43]

Notes

1. J. Russel Sprague, *Nassau County Government* (Mineola, 1940), 39. (A report of the first two years of the government under the charter).

2. *The Story of the Nassau County Charter,* anonymous pamphlet, probably written by Sprague.

3. Sprague, *Nassau County Government,* 27-28.

4. *New York Times,* July 4, 1939.

5. Forrest Corson, Republican Aide to Republican majority, Board of Supervisors, interview, Mineola, March 8, 1968; and Sprague, *Nassau County Government,* 29. All interviews cited were conducted by the author.

6. Sprague, *Nassau County Government,* 39.

7. Nassau County, Board of Supervisors, *Proceedings,* 1938 through 1952. See also *New York Times,* November 26, 1961; William Meiser, Republican Co-Chairman, Nassau County Board of Elections, interview, April 5, 1971.

8. Corson, interview; Joseph M. Margiotta, Chairman, Nassau County Republican Committee, interview, Garden City, July 10, 1969.

9. Meiser, interview.

10. Edgar Mapes, Administrative Assistant, Nassau County Comptroller's Office, interview, July 16, 1968.

11. A. Holly Patterson, President, Hempstead Bank, interview, August 19, 1968.

12. *New York Times,* December 30, 1960; Patterson, interview.

13. *Newsday,* October 19, 1970; Anonymous Nassau County Democratic Committeeman, conversation with author, meeting, Nassau County Democratic Committee, Franklin Square, October 6, 1971.

14. Eugene Nickerson, *Annual Message to the Board of Supervisors,* January 6, 1969, 2.

15. Eugene Nickerson, interview, Mineola, July 16, 1968.

16. *Long Island Press,* March 1, 1968; *Newsday,* March 12, 1953.

17. *Annual Reports, Nassau County Executive*, 1962 through 1966.

18. George Andrek, Planner, Nassau County Planning Commission, interview, Mineola, August 22, 1969.

19. Robert Gamble, Deputy Commissioner of Public Works, interview, Mineola, August 9, 1968; *Long Island Press,* November 4, 1968.

20. *New York Times,* December 6, 1970.

21. *New York Times,* December 6, 1970.

22. Eugene H. Nickerson, "A Record of Nassau County Government, January, 1962 to September, 1964."

23. James Truex, Deputy County Executive, interview, Mineola, August 26, 1969; and *Long Island Press,* August 26, 1969.

24. *New York Times,* December 6, 1970.

25. Ralph Caso, Nassau County Executive, interview, Mineola, March 1, 1973.

26. *Newsday,* January 3, 1972.

27. Ralph Caso, *State of the County Message,* February 7, 1972, 9.

28. "Executive Roundtable," WLIW Television, Garden City, March 24, 1974.

29. Nassau County, *Proposed Budget of Nassau County, New York, for the Year Ending December 31, 1974,* Message of the County Executive, November 12, 1973, 30.

The proposed Educational, Civic, and Cultural Center at Mitchel Field was to have included a coliseum, concert hall, theater, and fine arts gallery. This was never realized beyond the Coliseum which opened in 1972. See Tom Morris, "The Mitchel Field

Muddle," *Newsday,* October 9, 1971, 11-13, 15; and Howard Schneider, "A Changing Course for Long Island's Culture," *Newsday,* March 29, 1972. (Editor's note.)

30. Nassau County, County Executive, *Annual Report,* 1971, December 11, 1971, p. 1.

31. "Executive Roundtable," November 15, 1972, and January 3, 1972.

32. *Long Island Press,* April 5, 1974.

33. *Long Island Press,* January 6, 1973.

34. *Long Island Press,* March 9, 1973.

35. Caso, interview, March 1, 1973.

36. "Executive Roundtable," March 24, 1974; *New York Times,* November 11, 1973.

37. *New York Times,* December 6, 1970.

38. This impression is gathered from Nickerson's strong advocacy of public housing.

39. *Newsday,* December 28, 1970.

40. Nassau County, County Executive, *Annual Report, 1971,* 2.

41. *Long Island Press,* December 10, 1972.

42. See Tax Levies, General County Tax, Code 19, Nassau County Budgets, 1972, 1973, 1974, and 1975.

43. For additional information, see James Shelland, "The County Executive: A Case Study of the Office in Nassau County, NY" (Ph.D. dissertation, New School for Social Research, 1975); a copy is in the Hofstra University collections at the Long Island Studies Institute. See also Arturo F. Gonzales, *Eugene H. Nickerson: Statesman of a New Society* (New York: J. H. Heineman, 1964). (Editor's note.)

Reflections on Nassau County's Suburban Politics

Herbert D. Rosenbaum

Observers of suburban politics across the nation have long worked to understand the political character and significance of this no-longer-emergent and increasingly powerful way of life. But even without fully comprehending its internal dynamics, essential agreement now exists among its many scholars, observers, and practitioners on some major matters.

For the United States as a whole, suburbia has become the new linchpin of political power in a sufficient number of states to be a critical mass for the presidential election. The full consequences of this in the shaping of the nation's domestic political agenda have become quite clear during the last twenty years or so.

Within many of these same states suburbanites are tending either to be politically dominant, or to be indispensable for the formation of dominant political coalitions within both of the major parties successfully contending for power. Without doubt, the suburbs have become the "third force" in state politics as they more and more successfully contend against the still mostly Democratic central cities and the mostly Republican—and shrinking—rural sectors of interest, opinion, and organization. Here too, the suburban stamp has been firmly impressed upon the political agenda of the states.

Within suburbs, the hitherto widely accepted stereotype of suburbia as the safe haven of white, middle-class migrants from the declining central cities has had to give way to the recognition of the suburban "fringe" as a place with populations of considerable diversity along a number of social, economic, racial, and ethnic dimensions. One consequence of that is the political diversity within and between suburbs with Democrats controlling some suburban counties and Republicans others. But within each, the voting patterns and the control of local units of government are quite varied, and, as elsewhere, highly dependent on the same population characteristics that account for the historic political attachments in urban and rural communities: socio-economic status, race, ethnicity, religion, and other such determinants.

So much for what is beyond dispute about the politics of suburbia. In the face of these general agreements, however, much remains that is still debated. The primary reason for this is that suburbia is probably the most dynamic sector of the American social, economic, and political landscape. Rapid—and sometimes dramatic—change is the order of the day. What was true between 1945 and 1955 is certainly not the case in 1999, and, without fear or risk it can be safely predicted, will not be true in 2050. A considerable body of case studies, doctoral dissertations, numerous books, and a plethora of journalistic coverage, to say nothing of literary works, movies, and television programs, has by now ensured that the suburban lifestyle, ethos, or "culture" is firmly ensconced in the landscape of American twentieth-century consciousness. Nassau County is the nearly proverbial prototype of suburban life, and its centennial provides an opportunity to apply some scholarly magnifying glasses to the many features of the county whose very physical existence constitutes the vaunted escape from the life and politics of the dreaded "city."

The political bargain at the heart of the unification of New York City was made possible by permitting the eastern towns of Queens County to be separated from it and emerge as the new Nassau in 1899. Perhaps we should resist here the temptation to regard that moment as an early example of an emerging urban-suburban conflict. While the urban character of the new city is beyond dispute, the towns of Hempstead, North Hempstead, and Oyster Bay did not an entire suburb make, even though the tentacles of the Long Island Rail Road were already reaching out to the thinly populated territories. So, now the question is whether the magnifying glasses turned upon the political life of suburban Nassau County show promise of contributing to the growth of an overarching appreciation of suburban politics as a special type, comparable to what we know about the politics of cities and of rural areas.

Nassau County's political history demonstrates the central importance of a single individual in shaping not only the Republican Party, but the very structure of the county's government as well. That person is, of course, J. Russel Sprague. It was he whose political acumen made possible the enlargement of the party beyond its old Protestant base to include different elements of the county's rapidly growing and diversifying population; whose management of the party's organization—which he headed for a long and critical time in the county's growth—caused him to recruit such talented leaders as J. Leonard Hall, and whose managerial skill resulted in the creation of the office of county executive, which he also occupied in the critical years of the Depression, World War II, and through the early birth pangs of the postwar period of explosive population growth. Even though no political leader can ever be solely credited for all that occurred during his or her tenure, it is difficult to imagine the present Nassau County Republican Party organization, the cadre of its leaders down to the present time, and the shape of the county's government without J. Russel Sprague's forceful, ingenious, and far-reaching presence. It is therefore inevitable that, in the observance of the county's centennial, its politics should be analyzed, and by that token unavoidable that J. Russel Sprague receive his just due.

Inwood and the Republican Party

Marjorie Freeman Harrison's essay, "Italian-American Inwood and the Making of the Modern Nassau Republican Party," explores a number of vital connections between the behavior of political and community leaders and the county's ascendant Republican Party. To begin with, she describes the importance of familial connections in the accession to power of J. Russel Sprague: he inherited the position from his father-in-law.

Secondly, she well describes the function of personal friendship between elites as a prime method of linking social prestige to political power. Peter DeSibio, the Italian-American leader, achieved political prominence by ensuring his own followers access to some of the advantages of becoming Republicans.

Thirdly, she shows the fashioning of a new Italian-American identity out of the highly diverse and localized loyalties of immigrants, and out of the social-economic pressures of their new immigrant status.

Lastly, and in the view of this writer most importantly, she demonstrates the political efficacy of using patronage as a reward for political loyalty and as a binding force of organizational maintenance. The distribution of governmental jobs and contracts to DeSibio and his followers served concretely and symbolically as tried and true methods of political socialization of the followers, and as securing the continued organizational control of the favor-dispensing leadership.

In sum, by concentrating its attention on one small community, this paper touches on some of the most critical aspects of the methods by which Nassau's Republican Party has remained dominant down to this very day, and by which the flood of immigrants since the turn of the century have become a mainstay of that power. One hopes that Ms. Harrison will continue her fruitful labors.

Leonard Hall

Owen T. Smith provides significant details of Leonard Hall's rise to prominence and, by doing so, demonstrates the dramatic change in the politics of the county from small-town to metropolitan politics, and the shift to national significance of its rising political influence.[1]

It is significant to note the somewhat surprising report of the influence of the Ku Klux Klan in Republican politics of Oyster Bay and the county in the 1920s. Leonard Hall, however, rose in local politics without joining and indeed by opposing the Klan.

Furthermore, Hall was willing to challenge established party leadership, pre-empting the usual pro forma nomination for county treasurer. Smith's characterization of how his victory was overturned by the county leader,

Wilbur Doughty, speaks volumes about Nassau's style of party leadership: "That's how boss politics worked," he writes.

In the midst of the intricacy of intra-party maneuvering, Hall continued to rise to a congressional seat, a judgeship, the chairmanship of the Republican National Committee, and a campaign for the Republican nomination for the governorship against Nelson Rockefeller. This despite J. Russel Sprague's continued behind-the-scenes opposition to Mr. Hall's rise even as he publicly supported him.

Leonard Hall's talents as a man of energy, ambition, and far-sighted political acumen were nationally recognized, but he remained at heart a locally oriented politician who drew sustenance from his life-long intimate association with his Oyster Bay community. He liked to call himself "a country politician."

Appropriately for the Nassau conference, Smith focused on the rise of this talented and ambitious avatar of Nassau Republicanism, and the glimpse into the backroom maneuvers by which roles of leadership are allocated. Smith does not discuss the public policies Mr. Hall pursued in Nassau County, in the state legislature, in the United States Congress, or as a head of the Republican National Committee. Nor do we learn what the line of policy cleavage was between his own aspirations for the governorship and that of Nelson Rockefeller. These await the larger work that Owen Smith is preparing on Hall.

County Executives

James Shelland discusses the first four leaders to occupy the office of county executive in "Executive Power: A Comparison of Styles." J. Russel Sprague, who helped create the office of county executive, assumed its duties during the Depression when fiscal discipline was widely lauded, while Patterson came into office during the great post-war population boom as the demand for governmental services grew exponentially. Beyond that, Sprague, as head of a powerful political organization and with a forceful manner, stands in contrast to Mr. Patterson's relative disinterest in that organization and his less forceful demeanor.

A great deal of the difference between County Executive Eugene Nickerson and his precursors is to be understood in terms of the great shift in the national political context from the Eisenhower period of 1953-1961 to the Kennedy-Johnson era of 1961-1969. Expansion of governmental activity was clearly the hallmark of the latter era, and the growth of public sector services occurred practically everywhere in the country. Racial equality, civil rights, and economic justice were very high on the policy agendas of nearly all governmental units, led by the initiatives of congress and the president.

That context also goes far toward explaining the administration of Ralph Caso who followed Nickerson in the office of the county executive. As James Shelland points out, Caso, though a Republican, differed more from his Republican predecessors than from his immediate Democratic one. He too favored social services and he, like Nickerson, expounded the virtues of a county legislature over the regnant Board of Supervisors, preferring "open and accessible" government to the more closed-door methods of the Board. In short, he was hardly cast in the mold of Sprague and Patterson. Apart from the difference of his social origins and his strikingly different personal temperament, Caso was also shaped in a political era in which expanded governmental services were taken more for granted than in earlier times. A confirming aside underlining this point is this: years after he left office, and in a failed attempt to re-start his political career, Ralph Caso's differences with the party of his origins caused him to change his enrollment and become a registered Democrat.

Conclusions

The politics of governmental administration in Nassau County are powerfully tied to the maintenance of political party organization and discipline. The major instrument of that is and has always been the uses and abuses of political patronage. In a 1974 documentary film titled *Papa Joe,* exploring the career of Republican Party chairman Joseph Margiotta, it was asserted by *New York Times* reporter Frank Lynn that 75 percent of the approximately 1,800 men and women constituting the rank and file of the Republican County Committee hold appointive jobs in one of the hundreds of governmental institutions and offices of the county, the towns, the villages, and the special districts.[2] This means of controlling a powerful party organization explains—at least in considerable part—the continued hold the Republican party has exercised in the county.

It is important to ask what is specifically suburban about Nassau County's government officials and political leaders. The events described here might have occurred almost anywhere, regardless of the setting. It is worthwhile to speculate on this question because of the continuing spread of the so-called "suburban way of life." In fact, *two* major sets of influences shaped the way in which the politics of suburbia, and especially that of Nassau County, were conducted in the period under discussion.

The major distinctions of American suburban life are its dynamic character derived primarily from the startling increases in population over the last five and a half decades since 1945, and the changed and changing composition of those populations. These changes imposed the necessity for the adaptive responses on the part of political leaders, their organizations, and the institutions they manage.

The second consideration by which we can understand the people and events in Nassau's history, is the larger context of the politics of New York State and of the United States during the period ranging from the early decades of the twentieth century to the 1970s. The impact of this context on Nassau County was unmistakable at several of the major junctures of that long historic era.

These two criteria allow us to draw the following conclusions:

J. Russel Sprague successfully adapted his Republican party organization to the changes indicated by including representatives of the in-migrating populations in its organizational leadership by rewarding them with public employment and contracts. Without depending entirely on patronage for his party's electoral victories, it proved effective when the changing character of the population offered many new opportunities for the inclusion of newcomers. The pattern laid down by Mr. Sprague continues to this day, as can be seen by observing the rise of the many current other-than-"native" Republican leaders.

As party leader, Sprague responded to the Great Depression's stringencies in changing Nassau County's rural-style government by imposing a powerful elective County Executive on the old Board of Supervisors. His banker's-eye view of the role of government matched the exigencies of the time.[3]

On the other hand, the changes in sheer numbers and composition of the new population severely limited the policy of cooptation. Democrat Eugene Nickerson's response to his somewhat surprising 1961 election as county executive showed that in-migrating Democrats had grown strong enough electorally to achieve occasional county-wide victories.

Nickerson's approach to his office was in keeping with his party's orientation and with the age of John F. Kennedy's New Frontier and Lyndon Johnson's Great Society programs. His expansive view of government was in tune with the national mood of that era and with the liberal Republican Governor Nelson Rockefeller's inclinations. That Nickerson was twice more elected—once in the Johnson presidential landslide of 1964, and again, in 1967, by a narrower margin over North Hempstead Supervisor (and later Judge) Sol Wachtler, is, however, an unmistakable indication that the basic composition of the formerly solid Republican electorate was undergoing seismic shifts.[4] In short, it means that by the mid-1960s sufficient numbers of Democrats had settled in Nassau County to make their occasional electoral victory possible, a change which has since resulted in significant alterations of the county's political landscape.

While Republicans continue to maintain a powerfully-led, effective organization buttressed by the many secure patronage positions of their leaders and the more conservative inclination of its electorate, they have not been able to prevent the election to office of Democratic county legislators, town supervisors and councilmen, judges, assemblymen and assemblywomen, and members of the United States Congress. Yet, even Nickerson's nine-year regime did not permit him to build a Democratic party organization the equal of the still-powerful Republicans. That response was barred by the continued Republican occupancy of most executive and legislative public offices of the county, the towns, and the villages. That Nickerson was succeeded after 1970 only by Republican county executives points both to the effectiveness of the adaptive Republican party, as well as to the shift in the national politics in that era, but may not be considered sufficient evidence of the party's success. The differences between the newly elected Ralph Caso and his Republican predecessors point to Caso's greater readiness to respond to a shift in the demands placed upon county government.

The restructuring of county and town government was one of the Democratic Party's long-standing objectives and a significant point of Republican resistance to change. After several failed attempts to change the arrangement through charter revision campaigns, the effort finally resulted in the imposition by a federal court of a nineteen-member district-based county legislature. With that in place, Democrats were enabled to elect between five and six legislators from districts where their supporters prevailed. The local elections of 1999 confirmed Democratic hopes for the efficacy of the altered system of representation. By electing four additional legislators to the five incumbents, the Democrats constitute a ten to nine majority in 2000. Efforts to require towns to adopt similar, district-based systems for the town councils appear also on the verge of succeeding by way of judicial decisions. The Town of Hempstead has now been ordered to change. That, too, is highly likely to place Democratic council members in what was once an uncontestable Republican stronghold.[5]

Leonard Hall's rise to national prominence may also be understood as a sign of the increasing political importance of suburban politics. The Eisenhower era was, after all, a time during which the suburbs came to prominence as the likely future point of pivotal change in the national policy agenda and in the potential end of Democratic party dominance in the nation and the states.

In short, the great changes in the suburban life of Nassau County significantly affected the political balance of power between the major parties, changed— and continue to change—its political institutions, altered the demands upon its governments, and gave rise to new and different types of political leaders suited to the new circumstances of life in suburbia.[6]

Notes

This essay is expanded from comments prepared originally for the conference by the moderator of the session on Political Leadership and hence refers specifically to presentations by Marjorie Freeman Harrison, Owen Smith, and James Shelland. The articles by Harrison and Shelland precede this essay.

1. Owen Smith spoke at the session on Political Leadership on "Leonard Hall: A Country Politician." A draft of his paper and his presentation are included in the audiotape of the session in the conference files of the Long Island Studies Institute at Hofstra University's West Campus.

2. *Papa Joe* was produced in 1974 by Arthur Mokin and shown on Channel 13, WNET. The twenty-seven minute film was shown at the conference and can be viewed on videotape at the Long Island Studies Institute, Hofstra University. See also Frank Lynn, "Nassau Republicans March to Beat of Powerful Drumming by Margiotta," *New York Times,* December 8, 1972.

3. J. Russel Sprague explained the benefits of the new county charter in a county-produced film, *Nassau County and its Government,* portions of which were shown at the conference. A videotape copy of the thirty-minute film is in the Nassau County Museum collection in the Long Island Studies Institute at Hofstra University. See also Peter L. Van Santvoord, "The Nassau County Charter," honors paper, Hofstra College 1960 (copy in the Nassau County Museum Collection in the Long Island Studies Institute). (Editor's note.)

4. CBS television produced a thirty-nine minute documentary, *Campaign American Style,* on the 1967 Nickerson-Wachtler election campaign. The videotape, which was shown at the conference, is in Hofstra University's Media Services in Monroe Hall.

5. In the November 1999 elections, Democrats won a majority of seats on the county legislature and three seats on the Hempstead Town Board. See also the article below in this volume (137-42), "The Creation of the Nassau County Legislature," by John B. Kiernan. (Editor's note.)

6. For additional information on Nassau County politics, see Herbert Rosenbaum, "The Political Consequences of Suburban Growth: A Case Study of Nassau County, New York" (Ph.D. dissertation, Columbia University, 1967); and Dennis Stephen Ippolito, "Political Perspectives and Party Leadership: A Case Study of Nassau County, New York" (Ph.D. dissertation, University of Virginia, 1967). Copies of these dissertations are in Hofstra University's Special Collections at the Long Island Studies Institute. (Editor's note.)

Preserving Nassau County's Heritage in Museums and Parks

Mildred Murphy DeRiggi

This article examines the changing sense of the governmental mission from the relatively simple task envisioned by the founders of Nassau County, that of providing the political and economic basis needed to continue a mostly rural way of life, to the expanded role of county government adopted in mid-twentieth century to meet the challenges of economic change and rapidly increasing population. When farms and great estates were being replaced by housing developments and malls, residents looked to county government to preserve environmentally sensitive land and to provide open space and facilities for recreation. They also called on Nassau County governmental leaders to take a leading role in preserving the history of a way of life that was fast fading. Still maintaining this vision of the mission of county government, Nassau County today maintains 5,598 acres of park land in more than thirty facilities.[1] (See Appendix for listing of individual parks pp. 133-35.) Its museum system is one of the most extensive of any county, indeed of many states in the country. As Nassau County enters its second century of life, the role of its government is far more complex than that which existed in its early years.

Nassau County came into being in response to a particular governmental problem. When Greater New York City was formed in 1898, it incorporated as a borough only the western half of Queens County. Tensions had existed for decades, between the more industrially developed western section of Queens and the more rural eastern part of the county, over issues such as the location of the Queens County Courthouse and the comparative burden of governmental costs. There were political motives as well in the call for a new county. It was, however, the awkward situation of the Towns of Hempstead, North Hempstead, and Oyster Bay, as part of the County of Queens but not part of the Borough, that prompted a group of concerned residents to go to the Allen Hotel in Mineola on January 22, 1898 to draw up plans for the creation of a new county.[2]

For the founders of Nassau County, the mission of government was simply to provide basic services to the residents to insure a continuation of life style that provided most hard-working individuals and families with employment and the opportunity to own land and to prosper. Home rule would also distance the people of Nassau from the problems, urban complexities, and rumored political corruption of the neighboring City of New York.

Nassau County came into existence on January 1, 1899. The first Nassau County Board of Supervisors that met on January 3, 1899 consisted of the elected Supervisors of the Towns of Hempstead, North Hempstead, and Oyster Bay.[3] It was reassuring that the towns already boasted long histories. When the City of Glen Cove assumed independence from the Town of Oyster Bay in 1918 and the City of Long Beach separated from the Town of Hempstead in 1922, each sent a Supervisor to the expanded Board.[4]

On January 1, 1938 Nassau County began a new form of government, becoming the first chartered county in the State of New York (under the amendment to Article III, Section 26, of the New York State Constitution). The most important feature of this new government was the creation of the Office of County Executive. The first official elected to this post was the Honorable J. Russel Sprague. As a member of the Nassau County Board of Supervisors from 1930, Sprague, a powerful Republican leader, had led the way toward adopting a charter form of government.[5]

Nassau County attracted workers as a center for defense industries in World War II, and, following the end of hostilities, the growth in population accelerated. On December 4, 1944, the County Board of Supervisors, with the encouragement of County Executive Sprague, took a major step in providing recreation for the county's growing population by establishing the Nassau County Park at Salisbury, today known as Eisenhower Park. The park area had originally been developed as the Salisbury Golf Club. Nassau County acquired 820 acres by foreclosing unpaid tax liens, and additional land was condemned and purchased to form an administrative unit.

County Executive Sprague described his vision of the future when he foresaw a "public park which one day will be to Nassau County what Central Park is today to New York City." With its 930 acres, Eisenhower Park is actually larger than Central Park.[6] In the mid-nineteenth century, when population grew and expanded northward in New York City, a number of civic leaders and planners had wanted to preserve an open area within the city where residents could enjoy nature and relax. A century later, Nassau County leaders acted from similar motives when they created their park in the exact geographical center of the county in East Meadow. Nassau County's park also contains ballfields, picnic areas, playgrounds, a scenic pond, open meadows, and an area for concerts. When the park land was obtained from the Salisbury Golf Club, there were two eighteen-hole golf courses in playing condition. Nassau County redesigned the courses, adding another eighteen-hole course and a large facility for dining. This emphasis on golf gives Nassau County's park a clearly suburban focus.

Even before the creation of the park at Salisbury, Nassau County had acquired excess parcels of land in connection with drainage, highway, and sewage projects. The largest parcel, containing seventy acres, controlled drainage along six miles of a creek in Seaford. This became Tackapausha Preserve, named in honor of the seventeenth-century leader of the Native Americans on western Long Island. Trails were marked throughout the preserve, and the first Nassau County museum opened in May 1947 to provide information on the natural history of the region through exhibits and programs featuring animals native to the area.[7]

The policy of converting drainage systems into recreational areas was heralded in a 1959 article in the *Long Island Daily Press* under the headline "Nobody Wants Land; Plan Parks." Drainage properties were developed as parks, including: Saddle Rock Park (ten acres); Manhasset Valley Park (eighteen acres); Milburn Pond, Freeport (ten acres); Wall's Pond (also known as Hall's Pond), there West Hempstead (six acres); Baxter's Pond, Port Washington (five acres); Herricks Pond (six acres); and Silver Lake Pond, Baldwin (nine acres).[8]

The remarkable growth of population in Nassau County, symbolized by the development of Levittown, led to increasing demands for recreational facilities. In 1965 Nassau County opened Cantiague Park, its first major park since the facility at Salisbury, which became the site of the first county swimming pool and the first artificial ice skating rink. Christopher Morley Park in North Hills, also with more than one hundred acres, opened soon after Cantiague Park. In the summer of 1963 Nassau County had opened its first boat launching ramp at Milburn Creek in Baldwin.[9]

Demographic changes and the rapid development of open land prompted a movement to preserve some of the remaining estates in order to retain their natural beauty and architectural achievements for the enjoyment of future generations. Nassau County residents have benefited from generous gifts of land and timely purchases, which today comprise a system of preserves administered by the Department of Recreation and Parks.

Muttontown Preserve is a magnificent area in the middle of Nassau County just west of Route 106. The preserve, encompassing 522 acres, is divided into two sections by Muttontown Road. The northern part, with an entrance on Northern Boulevard, is the estate known as *Chelsea.* This estate of almost one hundred acres was acquired by Benjamin and Alexandra Moore about 1920. Benjamin Moore was a descendant of the author Clement Moore and the name *Chelsea* commemorates the section of New York City where the Moore family lived and held property. The poetic association and a snowy vista make *Chelsea* an ideal site for a holiday recitation of *The Night Before Christmas.* The mansion has elements of Chinese design, inspired by a trip taken by the Moores. Mrs. Moore (later Mrs. McKay), gave the property to the County of Nassau. The building now houses the offices of the Nassau County Office of Cultural Development, which provides changing art exhibits and cultural events in the building's public areas.[10]

The 240–acre estate of Charles Hudson comprises the remainder of the northern section of Muttontown Preserve. Hudson, who died in 1921, built a palatial mansion called *Knollwood* in 1907. Of later owners, the most interesting (although he never actually lived there) was King Zog I of Albania. In 1955 Lansdell Christie bought the property and had the mansion, by then badly vandalized, torn down.[11]

The major portion of the southern Muttontown Preserve was once part of the estate of Bronson Winthrop. It was later purchased by Lansdell Christie. His widow, Helen Christie, sold the house and its 183 acres to Nassau County in 1969 for $2,244,180. The Christie house, known as Nassau Hall, is now the headquarters of the Friends for Long Island's Heritage and the Theodore Roosevelt Association.[12]

On the North Shore of Nassau County at Glen Cove is Welwyn Preserve, the former Harold Pratt estate, with stands of towering pine and oak trees, meadows, and a rocky beach bordering Long Island Sound. The preserve boasts a wide variety of wildlife, including the red-tailed hawk, osprey, and the great-horned owl with a wing-spread of six feet. The Pratt mansion is home to the privately-run Holocaust Museum of Nassau County.

Nassau County also owns and maintains as a preserve the grounds of the former Frick Estate in Roslyn, where the privately-run Nassau County Museum of Art houses its permanent collection. The Museum also features concerts, classes, and changing exhibits.

In addition to recreational parks and preserves, Nassau County supports a system of museums that endeavor to interpret and maintain its heritage. The creation of this museum system owes much to two County Historians, Jesse Merritt and the present Historian, Edward J. Smits, and to the Nassau County Historical Society. In 1915 the Nassau County Historical and Genealogical Society had been formed but soon became inactive. In 1936 a group of individuals met to reorganize the Society and began efforts to collect books and manuscripts that related to the history of Nassau County. The collection was originally stored at Adelphi College.[13]

In 1938, when the new County Courthouse was being built on the old Mineola Fairgrounds, Jesse Merritt wrote a column in the Society's *Journal* suggesting that space in the old Courthouse be set aside for a museum depicting the county's history. Members of the Nassau County Historical Society continued to promote the idea of a county museum. In 1944, when plans were being made for the Nassau County Park at Salisbury, they suggested that a museum be developed at the site. In the middle of the park lands was a brick house then owned by Max Staller. This estate was purchased by Nassau County in 1955 for $98,500 to become the Nassau County Historical Museum, later known simply as the Museum in the Park. Here the collection of the Nassau County Historical Society, along with additional donations to the Nassau County Museum, was stored and organized under the direction of a young Hofstra graduate, Edward Smits, who began his career with Nassau County in 1955.[14]

In 1985 Nassau County and Hofstra University entered into an agreement creating the Long Island Studies Institute. The Nassau County collections of books, manuscripts, photographs, newspapers, maps, periodicals, microfilm, and ephemera were moved from the Museum in the Park to Hofstra University. At the Long Island Studies Institute, now located on the West Campus of Hofstra at 619 Fulton Avenue, Hempstead, the Nassau County Collection as well as Hofstra Special Collections are available to the public. This partnership between the Nassau County Division of Museum Services and Hofstra University has resulted in the creation of a major research center for the study of Long Island history.[15]

The history depicted in Nassau County's museums covers a long span of time. The earliest ages are studied at Garvies Point Museum and Preserve. Nassau County acquired the sixty-two-acre preserve at Glen Cove overlooking Hempstead Harbor in 1963. The unique features of the site had long been known to local residents familiar with the multi-colored layers of glacial clay exposed in the cliffs along the beach, and who marveled at the extensive middens or shell heaps in the area, reminders of the Native Americans who once inhabited the region.

Garvies Point Museum, which opened July 4, 1967, is a facility devoted to archaeological and geological studies. An archaeological dig on the site uncovered objects dating from 3,500 years ago. More than 10,000 students each year take part in school programs on nature studies and Native American life. During the summer of 1999 half a dozen donated large tulip tree trunks rested on the ground in front of the facility to be used in a program to construct dugout canoes employing methods used by Native Americans.[16]

Not long after Europeans settled in what is now Nassau County, they began to build mills, and Long Island became a milling center. One of the earliest restoration projects undertaken by Nassau County concerned a grist mill in the Village of Saddle Rock on the Great Neck peninsula. Records for the mill date from 1702, and for many years it was operated by members of the Udall family. The mill was left by a Udall descendant, Louise Udall Eldridge, to the Nassau County Historical Society, which deeded it to Nassau County in 1955. Nassau County restored the mill to its c. 1845 appearance and opened it to the public in September 1961. It is one of the few intact tidal mills remaining in the country. In addition to the Saddle Rock Grist Mill,

Nassau County is restoring a grist mill in Roslyn. The Roslyn Grist Mill, which dates to 1730, is a rare commercial building of Dutch construction.[17]

In the 1960s, Nassau County embarked on a very ambitious project, becoming the first county in the United States to construct a restoration village as a source for the study of living history. Several events came together to make this happen.

In the early 1960s, Town of Oyster Bay Supervisor John Burns suggested the acquisition of a 160-acre parcel of land in Old Bethpage to use as a land bank. At the same time, a number of historically significant buildings became threatened by the demands of development. Aware of the work at Old Sturbridge Village in Massachusetts, County Historian Edward J. Smits suggested to Nassau County that the construction of a restoration village would provide both a way to preserve the structures and enable visitors to better understand rural life in nineteenth-century Long Island. The Restoration, which eventually contained more than two hundred acres, opened to the public in June 1970. Visitors to Old Bethpage Village Restoration have witnessed a recreation of the everyday routines of farm families and local tradesmen in the nineteenth century. Young visitors, who might spend hours in the malls and on computers, can step back in time to watch the actual creation of cloth: from the shearing of a sheep, to the carding and spinning of wool, and, finally, to the weaving of fabric in intricate patterns.[18]

The dramatic era of Long Island's Gold Coast is brought to life at another major historic site, the Sands Point Preserve. Originally an estate built by Howard Gould at the beginning of the twentieth century, Sands Point contains several dramatic buildings. Castlegould is an imposing, turreted building, the design of which was influenced by Kilkenny Castle in Ireland. Originally this was used for stables and as a support building for the estate. Today it is used for special exhibits, administrative offices, and to store the large collection of artifacts belonging to Nassau County.

Hempstead House, a large Tudor-style castle, overlooks Hempstead Harbor and houses the Buten Collection, the most extensive collection of Wedgewood in America. Although Gould originally intended Hempstead House to be his residence, he never lived there. In 1917 Daniel Guggenheim purchased the estate. When Daniel's son, Captain Harry F. Guggenheim, came to Sands Point, he built his own Norman-style mansion overlooking the Harbor. Known as *Falaise* the mansion appears now in the same elegant style as when the Guggenheims lived there. It was through the will of Harry Guggenheim and a gift from the federal parks program that Nassau County acquired the 208-acre preserve in 1971. The Guggenheims were great patrons of the development of aviation. Charles A. Lindbergh, a close friend and frequent visitor of the Guggenheims, was the honored guest when Sands Point was dedicated.[19]

Hempstead House at Sands Point Preserve. *NCM Collection, LISI at Hofstra.*

Nassau County has other important historic sites, including Cedarmere, the country home of the nineteenth century's eminent poet and newspaper editor, William Cullen Bryant. Bryant wrote many of his poems in his Roslyn home overlooking Hempstead Harbor. The house and grounds are open seasonally as restoration efforts continue.

Nassau County's African American Museum began as a storefront in Hempstead in 1970. It now is located in an attractive building at 110 North Franklin Street and offers lectures, changing exhibits, and special events. Plans are being made for the installation of a permanent exhibit tracing the history of African American people on Long Island.[20]

As Nassau County embarks on a new century and prepares for a new millennium, plans are underway for a museum complex at the former Mitchel Field Army Air Corps base, including a Children's Museum, a Science Museum, and a Firematics Museum. At the center of this plan is the new Cradle of Aviation Museum. In 1978, plans were drawn to use two hangers at Mitchel Field for the development of the Cradle of Aviation Museum. Since then an important collection of aircraft has been assembled, from an early Curtiss Jenny biplane owned by Charles P. Lindbergh to a Republic P-47 and a full-size lunar module. A dedicated group of volunteers has been restoring the air and space craft. At the same time that the powerful aviation firms of Republic, Grumman, and Sperry were disappearing from Long Island, the Nassau County Board of Supervisors, with the recommendation of County Executive Thomas Gulotta, approved the bonds that would enable the creation of a state-of-the-art facility. In addition to the exhibits, the Cradle of Aviation will feature a seven-story I-MAX theater and theme restaurants.[21]

These plans are more than fitting. Nassau County residents had assisted at the birth of the aviation industry. They had later built the planes of World

War I, World War II, the Korean War, Vietnam War, and recent overseas conflicts. At Grumman they had helped to put a Lunar Module on the moon. The Nassau County government, representing the present generation of residents, would provide a facility to preserve this heritage of achievement and to instruct and educate future generations. Implicit in this commitment is the same sense of governmental mission that characterized the decisions that guided the creation of the Nassau County system of museums, parks, and preserves more than a half century ago.

Appendix: Nassau County Parks and Preserves

Parks and Preserves in Use	**Acreage**	**Date(s) of Acquisition**[22]
African American, Hempstead	0.5	
Bailey Arboretum, Lattingtown	42.0	1968; P
Baxter Pond Park, Port Washington	5.4	1944; .7 acres, 1975; D
Bay Park, Bay Park	96.0	1947; S
Bayswater Park, Inwood	0.4	1963; T
Bayville Bridge Park, Bayville	0.5	1940; R
Cammanns Pond Park, Merrick	7.8	1961; D
Cantiague Park, Hicksville	127.0	1961; G
Carle Place Memorial Park, Carle Place	0.3	1931; R
Cedar Creek Park North, Seaford	68.0	1943; G, P
Cedar Creek Park, South, Seaford	191.0	1941; 55 acres, 1964; G, P
Cedarmere, Roslyn Harbor	7.0	1975; P
Centennial Park, Roosevelt	1.9	1938; .3 acres, 1970; G, P
Christopher Morley Park, North Hills	98.4	1961; P
Cow Meadow Park, Freeport	171.2	1970; G
Cradle of Aviation, Garden City	1.49	
Dock Hill Park, Sea Cliff	0.2	R
Doxey Brook Park, Hewlett	0.5	1963; D
East Williston Park	2.6	1953; D
Eisenhower Park, East Meadow	930.0	1944; P
Elderfields, Flower Hill	4.0	1996
Flower Hill Park, Flower Hill	10.0	1957; D
Garvies Point Preserve, Glen Cove	62.3	1963 - 1.9 acres 1970; P, G
Grant Park, Hewlett	34.8	1955; P, G, Po 1962-1965, 30.8 acres
Grist Mill Pond Park & Museum, Saddle Rock	18.2	1955; 8.2 acres, 1973; P, D
Halls Pond, West Hempstead	11.0	1956; 1 acre, 1965; D, P 2.5 acres 1970 (10 yr. lic.)
Herricks Pond Park, Williston Park	2.4	
Hempstead Harbor Beach, Port Washington	60.0	1962; G, R
Herricks Park, Garden City Park	2.4	1947; D
Hewlett House	1.0	1997
Inwood Park, Inwood	16.1	1956; 4.0 acres, 1964; G
Jericho Historic Preserve, Jericho	21.2	1974; P
Leeds Pond Preserve, Plandome Manor	35.0	1970; P
Lofts Pond, Baldwin	14.4	1963; 2.0 acres, 1966; G

Manhasset Valley Park, Manhasset	26.6	1947; D, P 1949-1968, 31.3 acres
Massapequa Preserve, Massapequa	423.0	1984; P
Milburn Creek Park, Baldwin	24.3	1961; .3 acres, 1962; D, P
Milburn Pond Park, Baldwin	7.8	1956; D
Mill Neck Creek Preserve, Bayville	56.9	1969; 25.9 acres, 1972; C
Mill Pond (Jones Pond), Wantagh	54.0	1984; P
Mitchel Park, Uniondale	67.0	1965; P
Muttontown Park & Preserve, Muttontown[23]	549.9	1964, 11.5 acres; C, P
Nassau Beach, Lido Beach	121.3	1967; 34.29 acres 1966; G
Northern Boulevard Park, Manhasset	.3	1957; R
North Woodmere Park, North Woodmere	150.0	1965; G
Old Bethpage Restoration, Old Bethpage	209.3	1963; 160.5 acres; P, G 1964-1968, 48.7 acres
Plandome Park, Plandome Hgts.	4.5	1958; D
Polaris Field, Levittown	3.0	1938 and 1949; T
Roosevelt Park, Roosevelt	27.0	1984; P
Roosevelt South Park, Roosevelt	73.0	1984; P
Roslyn Grist Mill, Roslyn	.3	1976; H
Sands Point Park & Preserve, Sands Point[24]	216.0	1971, Guggenheim Estate, 800 acres; P
Silver Lake Park, Baldwin	9.2	1946; D
Stannard's Brook Park, Port Washington	3.0	1944; D
Syosset Memorial	0.5	
Tackapausha Preserve, Seaford	77.4	1939; 20.9 acres, 1955; D
Tackapausha Natural History Museum, Seaford	5.6	1962; .6 acres, 1966; G
Tackapausha Pond Park, Seaford	8.5	1939; D
Tanglewood Preserve, Lynbrook	11.4	1962; 1.0 acres, 1963-1964; G, D
Terrell Avenue Park, Oceanside	.8	1938; D
Tiffany Creek, Oyster Bay	197.0	1992; + 40.0 acres easement
Wantagh Park, Wantagh	111.3	1961; 13.0 acres, 1963; P, R, G
Wantagh Railroad Museum	2.8	
Washington Avenue Park, Seaford	4.0	1941-1942; D
Welwyn (Pratt Estate), Glen Cove	204.3	1975; P
Whitney Pond Park, Manhasset	24.0	1947; 5.0 acres, 1964; D
Willis Avenue Park, Albertson	.2	1958; R
William Cullen Bryant Preserve, Roslyn Harbor	141.0	1969; 3.9 acres, 1975; P

Parks and Preserves in Landbank	**Acreage**	**Date of Acquisition**
Battle Row Park, Old Bethpage	44.1	1965; P
Boorman's Island, Hewlett Harbor	12.0	1942; T
Hempstead Harbor Park, Port Washington	230.0	1962; P, G, R
Manetto Hills Park, Plainview	145.0	1966; 45.5 acres, 1968; G
Meadowbrook Park, East Meadow	65.7	1967; 26.0 acres, 1970; P
Merrick Preserve, Bellmore	24.5	1967; 22.0 acres, 1969; G
Silver Point Park, Atlantic Beach	119.6	1968; P
Stillwell Woods and Preserve, Woodbury	287.0	1973; P

Total County-owned Land for Park Use 5,597.8 acres

Legend for Acquisition Status

C—Acquired for conservation and open space
D—Acquired for drainage purposes
G—Acquired for general purposes
H—Acquired for historic purposes
P—Acquired for park and recreational purposes
Po—Acquired for police purposes
R—Acquired for road widenings, new roads, and bridge construction
S—Acquired for sanitary sewer purposes
T—Acquired in tax foreclosure
W—Acquired for waterway

Notes

1. Harold Hecken, Director of Budget, Management, and Planning, Nassau County Department of Recreation and Parks, "Nassau County Parks, Preserves and Historic Sites," October 5, 1999. The information in the Appendix has been updated and modified from the county's listing.

2. Original minutes of the January 22, 1898 meeting at the Allen Hotel, Mineola are in the Nassau County Museum Collection at the Long Island Studies Institute, Hofstra University (hereafter cited as NCMC-LISI). See "'Boss' Platt's Role in Creating Nassau County" in this volume (47-54).

3. Original minutes of the first Nassau County Board of Supervisors meeting, January 3, 1898 are in the NCMC-LISI (L68.4.3). Present were: William H. Jones, Oyster Bay Supervisor; Augustus Denton, North Hempstead Supervisor; and Smith Cox, Hempstead Supervisor.

4. Ward Dickson was elected the first Supervisor of Glen Cove. Long Beach became a city on June 1, 1922 and Wilfred M. Thompson was elected its first Supervisor. Robert Reed Coles and Peter Luyster Van Santvoord, *A History of Glen Cove* (Glen Cove: Privately printed, 1967), 62; Henry Isham Hazelton, *The Boroughs of Brooklyn and Queens, Counties of Nassau and Suffolk, Long Island, New York 1609-1924,* 6 vols. (New York: Lewis Historical Publishing, 1925), 2: 886.

5. *Proceedings of the Board of Supervisors of the County of Nassau for the Fiscal Year 1938* (Roosevelt, NY: Roosevelt Press), 9-11; "J. Russel Sprague Obituary," *New York Times,* April 19, 1969, 43. See also Peter Luyster Van Santvoord, "The Nassau County Charter," Senior Honors Essay, Hofstra University, 1960 (photocopy in the NCMC-LISI).

6. J. Russel Sprague, "Statement of County Executive J. Russel Sprague at Board of Supervisors' Meeting Monday, December 29, 1952," typescript (NCMC-LISI), 1-4; "Board Approves Salisbury Plans," *Nassau Daily Review-Star,* December 5, 1944.

7. Robert R. Gamble, Nassau County Deputy Commissioner of Public Works for Recreation and Parks, "Planning Recreation in Nassau County," typescript, 1965 (NCMC-LISI), 1.

8. "Nobody Wants Land; Plan Parks," *Long Island Daily Press,* July 12, 1959.

9. Cantiague Park is in Hicksville, south of the Northern State Parkway, between Kuhl Avenue and Cantiague Road. Nassau County condemned the 118-acre property,

that was formerly known as the Press Wireless land. The county paid $704,000 for the 100-acre former North Hills estate of Nettie G. Ryan that would become Christopher Morley Park. "Park Land Owner Gets $3.8 Million," *Newsday,* August 30, 1963; *Newsday,* August 15, 1961; Gamble, "Planning Recreation," 3.

10. Richard Winsche, "Muttontown Preserve: Preliminary Historical Summary," Research report for Nassau County Division of Museum Services, typescript, 1-4. Copy in the NCMC-LISI.

11. Winsche, "Muttontown Preserve," 2.

12. Winsche, "Muttontown Preserve," 3.

13. The collection moved to Hofstra College in 1950. Arthur L. Hodges, "The History of the Nassau County Historical Society," *Nassau County Historical Society Journal* 26: (1965): 1-31.

14. Edward J. Smits, "Nassau County Establishes a Museum System," *Nassau County Historical Society Journal* 37 (1982): 1-27. The former museum building in Eisenhower Park now houses the Women's Sports Foundation.

15. "LI History Center at Hofstra OKd," *Newsday,* March 26, 1985.

16. Gamble, "Planning Recreation," 4.

17. Smits, "Nassau County Establishes a Museum System," 5-6.

18. Smits, "Old Bethpage Village Restoration: A Perspective on its Twentieth Anniversary," *Nassau County Historical Society Journal* 44 (1989): 1-19.

19. "County Preserve Plans in Progress," *Manhasset Mail,* December 13, 1970; Robert Weddle, "2 Mansions Stars of New LI Park," *Long Island Press,* April 8, 1973.

20. "News Release from County Executive Eugene H. Nickerson," September 15, 1970, typescript in NCMC-LISI.

21. Groundbreaking for the new Cradle of Aviation facility took place on May 1, 1997. Bruce Lambert, "The Other 'Cradle of Aviation' Unveils Museum," *New York Times,* May 2, 1997, B-4.

22. Many parks were acquired in several acquisitions with different reasons given for each acquisition. Also, some parks were acquired in one acquisition but several reasons were given. The acquisition status is based on the map titles and/or resolutions of the Board of Supervisors for each acquisition. The initials used for acquisition status are explained at the end of the Appendix. See note 1 above for source of data on the parks.

23. Between 1965-1968, 37.5 acres were acquired and from 1969-1973, co-ownership of 50 acres (the total of the McKay Estate is 99 acres). In 1968-1969, the Christie Estate of 424.2 acres was added to Muttontown Park and Preserve; in 1971, 7.2 acres of Church property and in 1974, the Hammond Estate of 19.5 acres were acquired.

24. Sands Point Preserve grew with 127.8 acres from the United State Department of the Interior in 1971 and 7.4 acres donated by Van De Maele in 1979.

Mrs. Daniel Guggenheim had donated a portion of her estate (including Hempstead House and Castlegould) to the Institute of Aeronautical Sciences. The federal government purchased it in 1946 for use as a Naval Training Devices Center. It became surplus property in 1967, and the United States government turned it over to Nassau County in 1971. For additional information, see Richard A. Winsche and Gary R. Hammond, "The Evolution of the Gould/Guggenheim Estate at Sands Point," in *Long Island: The Suburban Experience,* edited by Barbara M. Kelly (Interlaken, NY: Heart of the Lakes Publishing, 1990), 39-49.

The Creation of the Nassau County Legislature

John B. Kiernan

The most dramatic change in the way Nassau County has been governed since the county charter/county executive form of government was adopted in the 1930s, was the creation of a Nassau County Legislature pursuant to Local Law 11 of 1994, approved by the voters of Nassau County in a countywide referendum in November 1994.[1]

The creation of the nineteen member, single member district legislature followed a federal court decision by Judge Arthur Spatt on April 14, 1993. In his decision Judge Spatt ruled that the then six person Board of Supervisors, with a weighted voting system, did not meet the constitutional criteria of one person, one vote. In other words, Judge Spatt said that each county resident did not enjoy equal representation in county legislative matters and that the weight or influence of each vote cast in elections for members of the Board of Supervisors was not equal.

The decision of Judge Spatt concluded a lawsuit, *Jackson v Nassau* County Board of Supervisors, which had been filed by eight residents of Nassau County, primarily from minority neighborhoods. One of their arguments was that although the minority communities had significant numbers of residents, mostly concentrated within the Town of Hempstead, the sheer size of the town, where the town supervisors ran on a townwide basis for their county legislative seat, i.e., the Board of Supervisors, resulted in a system in which the voting influence of the minority communities were subsumed by the rest of the town. The effect, they argued, was that there was no minority voice or influence in the legislative branch of county government.

Consequently, on June 30, 1993, Judge Spatt issued an order directing the existing Board of Supervisors to remedy the constitutional infirmity in the county government through the appointment of a Charter Revision Commission. This mechanism was authorized in the existing county charter and the formal title given to the commission in the charter was the Commission on Government Revision.

Judge Spatt further mandated that the members of the Commission be a diverse body of individuals reflective of the ethnic and political diversity of Nassau County. He also established a strict timetable for the Commission and the Board to follow and established guidelines for public participation throughout the process. The purpose of the Commission was to explore the form, powers, and structure of this new legislature and to make recommendations to the Board regarding it and other areas of the county government.

The Commission was required to prepare and submit a preliminary report to Judge Spatt on or before April 1, 1994. It was further required to submit a report and districting plan to the Board of Supervisors and Judge Spatt on or before June 1, 1994. The Court gave the Board a deadline of June 15, 1994, to enact a local law that would put a referendum to the voters, so that it could be voted on later in the year. The Commission met all of its deadlines, the Board did not.

The Commission had seventeen members, who were recommended by County Executive Thomas Gulotta and unanimously approved by the Board of Supervisors in mid-August of 1993. Among them were four women, three African Americans, one Latino, five Democrats, ten Republicans, one Conservative, and one Independent. These people, who were not paid for their efforts, worked tirelessly, giving hundreds of hours of time.[2]

Following Judge Spatt's directive, the Commission held eleven public hearings in three separate stages at various locations in the county. Residents were given the opportunity to speak on any issue involving the county government. The work of the Commission was subject to the provisions of the state's open meetings law, which meant that every work session of the Commission was open to the public. There were twenty-four public work sessions in addition to the public hearings. The recommendations of the Commission, with the exception of the establishment of exact boundaries of the nineteen districts, were finally approved by the Board on September 8, 1994, and approved by the voters 149,573 to 82,043 on November 8, 1994.

As a former member of the Board of Supervisors and then as a commissioner of a major county department who had to deal with the old Board and now deals with the new legislature, I can state that there is a world of difference between a Board of six people, who primarily were involved in the workings of their town or city, and a nineteen-member legislature, whose members are primarily concerned about a single district with a population of about 67,000 people. For one thing, county public works projects now receive a much higher level of scrutiny. The legislators naturally are concerned about improvements in their own districts. While the town supervisors were able to boast about town park projects, town road projects, and town senior citizen programs because they were directly responsible for them, the legislators now want to secure county projects for their constituents. As a result, the interest level and involvement is much greater than in the past.

While villages always have been important to our county, and have made their views known, they now wield more influence on the county legislators. A village having 10,000, 15,000, or 20,000 residents comprises a major portion of a legislative district, whereas in a town the size of Hempstead,

Oyster Bay, or North Hempstead, a village of that size was only a fraction of the individual supervisor's "county district." On a similar note, the supervisors previously could boast about their town budgets, town tax cuts, and so forth, but now the individual legislator is much more involved in the county budget process. And, as noted above, there is also a greater level of involvement or interest in county programs whether they be parks, senior citizens, and so forth, because the legislators do not have their "own" programs to look out for back at town or city hall.[3]

The process mandated by Judge Spatt also intended to give minorities a greater representation and voice in county government. That goal was realized. For the first time we have two African-American legislators in county government. We have more women involved in the county—there are five women legislators. The Commission also recommended the creation of a Council on Minority Affairs. This agency now exists and has become involved in many areas, including the county budget process. As a department head, I now receive minority impact statements and recommendations from the Council.

The county budget process also has changed significantly. The county's budget recommendation formerly was sent to the Board of Supervisors in mid-November for adoption on the third Monday of December. Now it is released in mid-September for adoption on or before October 30th—that is, before election day. The process involves more public hearings and the Office of Legislative Budget Review, independent of the legislature's own finance committee, issues a public report on the proposed county budget. Moreover, the county comptroller now has a formal role in the budget process. The comptroller is required to render an opinion on the estimates contained in the county executive's proposed budget related to non-real property tax revenues. There is also a requirement that the comptroller issue a mid-year financial report relating to any projected surplus or deficit.

The legislature was given a mandate to establish a working committee structure. These committees now meet regularly and review proposed legislative items. Under the old system, pre-calendar meetings were held and, for the most part, the work was done by staff personnel. Supervisors did not usually attend these meetings, primarily because of their other responsibilities.

Some critics or observers will say that the new system is slower or more costly. Those criticisms are true. It does take more time to get projects through the system. On the other hand, there is greater participation now, and more public discussion than ever before. I suppose you can call the additional time and cost the price of democracy. As John Fitzgerald Kennedy once said, "A democracy is the most difficult kind of government to operate. It represents the last flowering, really, of the human experience."

There will be problems and difficulties to overcome in implementing the legislature. But this is a dynamic process and just as some of our great county officials had to make changes about sixty years ago, I am confident that our new system of governing Nassau County can be improved and can flourish as we continue in our second century as the County of Nassau.

Questions and Answers

Q. Was the Commission aware of the New York City's Board of Estimate case and were there any parallels drawn in the situations?

A. We were very much aware of the city case and the fact that part of the reasoning and the decision actually was the reasoning that had been given in the Board of Estimate case. Judge Spatt was very much aware of that proceeding. Of course, I think the city charter change preceded us by about four or five years. If I'm not mistaken, I think it was 1989 that it went through. We were aware of it. We had people come in and suggest everything from five districts to forty-three or fifty-three. I think one of the plans was 25,000 people which meant you would have had two county legislators from the Village of Hempstead. The fact of the matter is Judge Spatt had made it very clear that we had to come up with a one-man or one-person/one vote system and he also made it very clear that he expected significant minority representation and he had final approval of this plan—significant minority representation in a way that was somewhat proportional to the census figures. When you look at it, I think two districts out of nineteen comes out to be somewhere around 11 percent and that roughly tracks what the minority population was in the county at the time that we had the 1992 census numbers.[4]

Q. Is there a conflict now between town projects and county? Or is it an adding-on?

A. It's not an adding on of another level of government because we always had a county government. I could tell you from personal experience that intially the county legislators were much more receptive to capital project proposals than perhaps the old Board of Supervisors would have been just because of the natural process of wanting to do improvements within your area and show the people that are sending you to represent them that you're doing something that is positive. So I think that, initially anyway, the county capital project process opened up more than it would have if it had still been the Board of Supervisors.

Q. Have we actually had better representation county-wide, or has there just been better representaton of little blocks within the county? Has the overall county mission and development actually been diminished rather than strengthened by this?

A. I can tell you from personal experience, I ran for town supervisor five times. In those five elections, I don't think five people ever asked me how I voted on a county matter. For instance, they asked me what we were doing in Manorhaven Park or they wanted to know what we were doing with the town senior citizens. They thought of you not as a county legislator but as a town official. And I'm not saying that we didn't pay attention to what we did, but the fact of the matter is, I think, in the mind of the voter, the county government was the county executive and the town government was the town supervisors and the town board. Now there are nineteen more people involved and their whole being is county government not town government. There is a greater awareness. But we're only in the fourth year of the legislature. It would be interesting to come back in twenty-five years and maybe revisit this and see whether it worked out for the good. The men and women who are involved are extremely sincere and hard-working on both sides of the aisle, but they're only in their second term.

Q. The rationale for the revisions for the legislature was the exclusion of minority populations and voters from the process. Earlier today we heard from a speaker discussing the Republican party in Nassau County [Marjorie Freeman Harrison]—that they went out of their way to include newcomers, Jews, Italians, and others who were coming into the county, as a way of maintaining their control over the county. Did the Republican Party in Nassau County actively exclude the black population from its deliberation? Was there something different between the way they dealt with the black population as opposed to the Irish, Jewish, or Italian newcomers? In other words, was there an active problem that this was being addressed?

A. I've been a member of the executive committee of the Nassau County Republican Committee since March 1976, and quite the contrary, I've never seen any, there was never any active strategy or movement or plan to exclude anybody. And I can remember both under Chairman Joseph Margiotta when I was first supervisor, and then Chairman Joseph Mondello, that there were frequent meetings with the black clergy, both in my town (North Hempstead) and other towns. Ironically, the one thing that the Democratic Party thought they would have a lock on was the two minority districts that were created. It was a sure "slam-dunk" that they started with two, they thought. Funny thing happened. A black woman named Darlene Harris was elected in the first district both times. She's a black Republican. And the leading vote-getter in the 1997 town election in the Town of Hempstead is the black councilman Curtis Fisher. He received the highest number of votes cast in that election. The first time I ran for office, the current director of the county's council on minority affairs, Briding Newell, ran for the state assembly, a black woman. That's almost twenty years ago on the Republican line, so, I don't think there was ever any plan. I've never seen any evidence of it and I've never heard anything like that from any of the leaders that I've been involved with in my almost twenty-five years as a member of the executive committee.

Notes

1. John B. Kiernan chaired the Commission on Government Revision whose role in creating the new county legislature he discusses in this essay. For background, including prior efforts to change the system, see Edward J. Smits, "Legislative Reorganization in Nassau County, New York," in *Contested Terrain: Power, Politics, and Participation in Suburbia,* edited by Marc L. Silver and Martin Melkonian (Westport, CT: Greenwood Press, 1995), a paper presented at a 1993 Hofstra University conference. (Editor's note.)

2. Members of the Commission were: the Hon. John B. Kiernan, Chair; John L. Kearse, Vice Chair; Members: Hon. Pauline C. Balkin; Roger H. Corbin; Roger Fay; Margarita Grasing; Neal Lewis, Esq.; Dennis M. Libutti; Hon. Barbara Patton; Hon. Henderson W. Morrison; Stuart Rabinowitz, Esq.; Clifford M. Riccio; Edward T. Robinson III, Esq.; Denise Harvey Sher, Esq.; Dr. James M. Shuart; Salvatore Spano, Esq.; Jeffrey L. Stadler, Esq.; Lousette James Turner; and Melvyn I. Weiss, Esq. Before the Commission completed its work, one member (Libutti) died and two resigned, Judge Morrison because of poor health and Ms. Sher because she was appointed a judge. The Staff of the Commission were: Francis X. Moroney, Esq., Executive Director; Mary W. Bossart, Esq., Special Assistant for Administration; Marlene Kastleman, Director of Communication; and Annette Debnam, Secretary/Administrative Assistant. Commission Consultants were: James P. Marlin, Esq., of Mudge Rose Guthrie Alexander & Ferdon, Esqs.; Luther Blake, Ph.D.; Vincent Bruy; Ze Ming Cheng; and Frank Lewis.

3. Under the previous governing system, each of the members of the Board of Supervisors had also been a supervisor in one of the three towns or two cities. In Glen Cove, the supervisor actually served as the mayor. In Long Beach there was no formal city government role because Long Beach has a city manager form of government. However, the Long Beach Supervisor was given an office in City Hall and additional compensation from the city. The weighted voting system was roughly based on population but not strictly based on population because the two Hempstead Supervisors, representing more than half of the county's voters, could not enact any item without another supervisor's vote.

4. In the November 1995 elections, two African Americans were elected to the county legislature. The same pattern has followed in 1997 and 1999. Farrell T. Jones, an African American who was appointed as Commissioner of Human Relations by Democrat Eugene Nickerson, stated in the panel discussion that Joseph Carlino, the Republican county leader in the late 1950s and early 1960s, was always trying to recruit him and other Blacks for "visible" government positions. (Editor's note.)

The Hempstead Plains: A Capital Field for Military Exercises, 1700-1898

James M. McKenna

"Officers from New York have been making observations on the Plains, and at East Meadow with a view to an Encampment. It is likely that the Plains will be selected, and the work of digging wells, and laying out the ground, be soon begun. The Plains are a capital field for military exercises, and one or more regiments would contribute considerably to the trade of this village."[1] So wrote John H. Hentz the editor of the *Queens County Sentinel* on August 29, 1861—and how right he was.

From the time of their first discovery by English settlers in 1643, the Hempstead Plains had attracted military leaders as a place to train their men in the skills of war. Early militia companies trained on the Plains in the 1600s, and the Plains were used for the gathering and training of Queens County troops sent to fight in the French and Indian Wars. During the colonial era militia companies from New York used the Plains to train in the summer in order to avoid illnesses that plagued the city in the warmer months. One account mentions Lord Cornbury, Governor of the New York Colony (1702–1708), reviewing his troops on the Hempstead Plains, with several French-allied Indian leaders by his side, in order to intimidate the native chiefs.[2]

At the dawn of the American Revolution the Hempstead Plains were a focal point for encampments of American militia, and, after the American defeat at Brooklyn Heights, the British and American Provincial regiments found the Plains an ideal location for military drills, reviews, and encampments. The Plains became a natural spot for the mustering of the Loyal Queens County Militia under the command of Colonel Archibald Hamilton. The Plains were chosen as the summer encampment location for both the Sixteenth "Queens Own" Light Dragoons and the Seventeenth Light Dragoons. Fox hunting on the Plains also was a popular pastime enjoyed by homesick British officers during their stay in Hempstead.

After the American Revolution, the Hempstead Plains were once again home to sheep and cattle more than tents and muskets. Occasionally a militia company from New York City might encamp upon the Plains during the summer or early fall. In early September 1836 the Veteran Corps of Artillery, Jefferson Guards, and Napoleon Cadets of New York visited the Hempstead Plains for an encampment and target practice.[3] This visit to the area of neatly uniformed and well drilled volunteer soldiers prompted several local citizens to form a uniformed volunteer company of their own, the Hempstead Light Guards. This company, along with other volunteer companies and the local common militia, would drill upon the Plains each fall as required by the New York State Militia Law of the period.

Within two decades the Hempstead Plains would take on more importance as a military encampment locale. In 1861 the American Civil War began when eleven southern states seceded from the United States of America. After President Lincoln's call for northern men to defend the Union, camps had to be established to train these young men to become soldiers. Accordingly, camps were set up on Staten Island, on the Union Course in present-day Woodhaven, Queens, and on the Hempstead Plains near Mineola. New York State military officers determined the site of the encampment by August 29, 1861, and immediately began the task of preparing the area for a large-scale military camp. Twelve wells had to be dug for the incoming soldiers and the area was marked off to indicate the camp's boundaries. The camp was at first named in honor of General Thomas W. Sherman, the commanding officer of the regiments assigned to train on the Plains, but was later renamed Camp Winfield Scott in honor of the Union Army's overall Commander and a veteran officer of every American conflict since the War of 1812.

The camp was to be occupied by the Third New Hampshire Infantry Regiment and the Eighth Maine Infantry Regiment, as well as several other New England and New York regiments. The Third New Hampshire, one thousand men strong, arrived on September 4, having traveled by train, steamboat, and again by train, via the Long Island Rail Road, from Hunter's Point to Mineola. The regiment disembarked the train at Mineola and marched the short distance to the site of the encampment. The camp was situated south of Old Country Road traversing present-day Washington Avenue. The regimental officers were impressed by the expanse of the Plains and immediately began to set up quarters.

The Camp was "laid out in streets, one street for each company, tents upon each side facing inward, with four men for each tent. The officers' tents . . . at the head of, and facing the company streets."[4] Colonel Enoch Q. Fellows led the Third New Hampshire and issued his first order at Camp Sherman (shortly to be referred to as Camp Winfield Scott) on the very next day, September 5, 1861: "This regiment being the first to occupy this camp ground it is hoped we will set a good example to others soon to arrive and become the model regiment of the command. Beginning tomorrow, the 6th, the following will be the routine duty: Reveille at 5, company drill 5:30 to 7, breakfast 7, guard mounting 8, surgeon's call 8:30, squad drill 9 to 11, dinner 12, company drill 2 to 4, battalion drill 4:30, dress parade 5:30, supper 6, tattoo 9, taps 9:30."[5] On September 5, the men of the Third New Hampshire went about rearranging some of their tents and digging their "sinks" or toilets. On September 7 some trouble in Mineola was recorded when "the Co. E boys went to the village (Mineola) and broke up a rum shop, destroying several casks of liquor."[6]

Generally life was quite peaceful and routine within the camp, though it was "drill, drill, drill, every day. The usual camp scenes: visitors of both sexes, of vendors of fruits and vegetables, of receiving mail, etc."[7] Many citizens from both Mineola and Hempstead did become frequent visitors to Camp Scott. The soldiers as well were given passes to visit both villages, and the famous Third New Hampshire's Regimental Band visited Mineola and Hempstead to entertain the patriotic citizenry. The ladies of Hempstead were so impressed by these soldiers from the Old Granite State that they sewed a flag for the Third New Hampshire. Unfortunately the flag was not presented to the troops while on Long Island, but had to be presented to them at their regimental camp in Washington, D.C. because of the regiment's quick departure from the region.

The Eighth Maine arrived at Camp Scott on the evening of Thursday, September 12, 1861. The Maine Regiment, seven hundred men in all, many of whom were over six feet tall, wore the soon to be replaced gray uniform popular with many northern militia companies. Unfortunately for the Maine boys, gray was also the regulation uniform color of the new Confederate Army, thus creating confusion among the troops on the battlefield. The boys from Maine were not as disciplined as their fellow New Englanders and on the day of their arrival three men of the Eighth Maine visited Mineola and returned to camp quite intoxicated. Newly appointed Brigade Commander General Egbert L. Viele, a known strict military disciplinarian, sent the Camp's patrol guard to destroy "every drop of the liquor in Mineola," which, it is recorded, they did.[8]

Camp Scott did not become the encampment originally planned for, with more than ten regiments of New England troops. In fact, its life ended shortly after it began when, on Saturday, September 14, 1861, the Third New Hampshire and Eighth Maine received their orders from General Winfield Scott to "Come here [to Washington] with all your command without delay, leaving the smallest guard necessary to protect your camp."[9] These were the days after the humiliating Union defeat at Bull Run and our nation's capital was often in danger of near certain capture by the rebel military. Both regiments took leave of the camp that very day by way of the Long Island Rail Road to Hunters Point, their point of entry eleven days earlier. By the next morning they were in Philadelphia on the way to the front. By September 23, "the encampment was entirely broken up."[10] The guard of the Third New Hampshire and Eighth Maine Regiments had struck their tents and rejoined their regiments in Washington along with their horses, ambulances, and other equipment.

The local community was quite impressed by the spectacle of a military camp on the Plains, *The Hempstead Inquirer* noting that, "From the short time this corps has been training they show their ability to become proficient in military tactics, and the men are doing credit to themselves and to their officers for the promptness with which the orders are executed."[11]

The Hempstead Plains reverted back to their pastoral beauty and peace-time grazing lands after the soldiers left. Over the next several decades the Plains would take a dramatic turn with the purchase of more than seven thousand of their acres in 1869 by A.T. Stewart for his planned community of Garden City.

In 1898, the United States found itself in a war with Spain shortly after the Battleship *Maine* exploded in Cuba's Havana Harbor on February 15 of that year. The United States began to mobilize its military forces, but also needed to rely on the individual state's militias or National Guard forces. New York set about organizing its forces for training shortly after the April 11 declaration of war. Many of the New York troops were sent to the Hempstead Plains for training at Camp Black, named in honor of New York Governor Frank S. Black. Initial troops from Company H, Seventy-first Regiment began guard duty at the camp on April 29, 1898. The *Long Island Farmer* reported:

> At 9 o'clock Monday morning there were ten tents on the edge of Hempstead Plains. All the rest of the expanse looked as usual. At 5 o'clock in the afternoon a city of white had arisen on the level tract, and for miles around the country was alive with the citizen soldiers of New York State. Eight thousand stalwart, determined young men have taken possession of Hempstead Plains, and for several weeks, at least, they are to keep it. The drudgery of camp life has no terrors for them. The idea that life at Camp Black is to be anything like that they have experienced in past years at the annual Peekskill encampments has vanished. General Orders No. 1 issued by Gen. Roe late Sunday afternoon, made it plain that there is nothing in the nature of a joke about this affair, and the men are ready for the work which they realize is in store for them.[12]

Camp Black was a major addition to the Hempstead Plains and remained in place through September 28, 1898. The camp was located at what is now the Roosevelt Field Shopping Mall, being situated on the east side of Clinton Road, south of Old Country Road and north of the Central Line of the Long Island Rail Road.[13] Establishing a camp for more than eight thousand men was no easy task as was reported by the *Farmer*:

> Gen. Roe got to work without a moment's delay. On Sunday he had made arrangements with every farmer within a radius of five miles to get out all of his rolling stock for the transportation of luggage from the railroad track to the camp, a distance of nearly half a mile. On early trains a great stock of tents and poles and bales of hay had arrived. The camp had been all carefully surveyed and the space to be allowed to each tent marked out. The farmers, their sons, and hired men dumped a roll of canvas, a set of poles, guy ropes, and stakes on each plot, and by ten o'clock this work was almost done. A bale of hay was placed beside each tent. It was all the protection from the dampness of the ground that the men were to get.[14]

By 10:00 a.m. the soldiers began arriving into camp, the first to arrive being the Forty-first Separate Company of Syracuse. Over the next several hours men from all over New York State began to occupy the Plains, including the famous Fourteenth Regiment of Brooklyn and the Sixty-ninth Regiment, "The Fighting Irish Regiment." The *Farmer* described the scene:

> The troops marched across the plains some to the music of drums and fifes others to the inspiriting blare of the bugle. Behind each regiment and separate company came the wagon trains each vehicle piled high with bags and boxes. As each organization reached its section of the camp ranks were broken and the men were ordered to get to work and provide for their comfort. After an impromptu meal the men set to work with a will to erect their tents. The hospital tent of the Seventy-first Regiment was the first up but after it had been erected it was discovered that the energetic young doctors had failed to attach the Red Cross flag to the flagpole. An agile young man shinned up the pole and nailed the emblem in place. It was the first flag to wave in Camp Black.[15]

The rigors of army life are best described in a book written by Charles Johnson Post, *The Little War of Private Post.* Post, a member of the Seventy-first New York, describes in wonderfully detailed prose his experiences at Camp Black. He writes:

> I had a uniform—cerulean-blue pants with a broad, deep blue stripe down the sides, and they fitted reasonably well. But my blouse! I had always thought that a "blouse" was specifically an article of feminine apparel, a sort of loose shirtwaist with a snappy, come-hither effect. But in that man's army, a blouse was anything worn outside a shirt and inside an overcoat, and instantly provocative of a sergeant's acute anguish if it wasn't buttoned. Also, it was supposed to fit

Like so many soldiers' complaints decades earlier, during the Civil War, Post lamented the lack of proper fitting attire. He wrote,

> They were short on blouses when mine was issued; that is, short of normal blouses for normal men. So my blouse was left over from some outsized predecessor, a mere fragment of whose clothing would

> have outfitted me inside and out, with a Sunday suit left over. The turned-back sleeves reached my elbows; the blouse folded around me so that its buttons were at all times under my arms, and it reached to my knees like a frock coat. But my choice was this, or not marching at all in the parade that would start us into the real war, at Camp Black out on Hempstead Plains, Long Island. So I took the blouse, crept into it, and marched, undoubtedly passing as some sort of regimental mascot.

Quickly Private Post adapted to his life in this sea of white tents, even with his misfitting blouse,

> At Camp Black we raw recruits were separated, the sheep from the goats. The goats were those who had not yet had any part of a uniform issued to them. They drilled as an awkward squad in their wrinkled, slept-in civilian jackets, trousers, and derby hats. The tents were already up when we arrived; one bale of straw to a tent, and bedding for the four men to that tent. It was April [actually early May] and the ground was wet and soggy with spring. I had roughed it a bit in the open and knew enough to put my poncho rubber-side-down next to the sod. Some men didn't. But with the blanket over the straw, it made a fine bed, soft and warm.[16]

The lives of the men of Camp Black weren't only work and drill, with no play. *Leslie's Weekly* reported: "The forms of amusement in camp at night are many. In some tents they sing, in others play cards, in others talk. It all depends upon the kind of men who have been thrown together."[17] By early June many of the New York troops proceeded south to Tampa, Florida, to prepare for transport to the seat of the war, Cuba. On June 20, 1898, Private Post and the men of the Seventy-first New York landed on Cuba to put their training to the test. By July 17, the fighting in Cuba was over, the Americans having accepted the surrender of Spanish forces on the island.

As the twentieth century dawned on Long Island, the Plains once again became a peaceful prairie, gradually adding airfields to the landscape as decades passed. The Plains were to host other military camps throughout the first half of the twentieth century, one of which, Camp Mills, was established on the Plains east of Garden City shortly after the United States declared war on Germany in 1917. The camp was named after Major General Albert L. Mills, Chief of the Division of Militia Affairs for the War Department. Camp Mills became the training encampment of the 42nd Infantry Division, also known as the "Rainbow Division." The Rainbow Division was made up of Infantry Regiments and Field Artillery from all over the country, including, once again, the old Fighting Sixty-ninth of New York, now designated the 165th Infantry.

The Plains were a capital field for military exercises and performed that duty well for almost three hundred years. Today the Plains are just a fragment

Soldiers at Camp Black, 1898. *NCM Collection, LISI at Hofstra.*

of their former expanse, preserved in small plots on Mitchel Field (near Nassau Community College, north and south of Charles Lindbergh Boulevard) and in Eisenhower Park. However, the military heritage of the Plains lives on in the establishment of the Cradle of Aviation Museum located at the former Mitchel Field Army Air Corps Base and in the re-creation of Camp Winfield Scott at Old Bethpage Village Restoration.[18]

Notes

1. *Queens County Sentinel,* August 29, 1861.
2. Bernice Schultz Marshall, *Colonial Hempstead: Long Island. Life Under the Dutch and English,* 1937; reprint, 2d ed. (Port Washington, NY: Ira J. Friedman, 1962), 102.
3. Harrison Hunt, "Soldiers in Peace and Citizens in War: The Hempstead Light Guards Militia, 1836-1847," *Nassau County Historical Society Journal* 45 (1990): 30-31.
4. Elbridge J. Copp, *Reminiscences of the War of the Rebellion* (Nashua, NH: Telegraph Publishing, 1911), 22.
5. D. Eldredge, *The Third New Hampshire and All About It* (Boston, 1893), 23.
6. Eldredge, *Third New Hampshire,* 23.
7. Eldredge, *Third New Hampshire,* 25.
8. Copp, *Reminiscences,* 29.
9. Eldredge, *Third New Hampshire,* 26.
10. *Queens County Sentinel,* September 26, 1861.
11. *Hempstead Inquirer,* September 14, 1861.
12. *Long Island Farmer,* May 6, 1898.
13. Vincent F. Seyfried, *The Long Island Rail Road, A Comprehensive History—Part 6,* (Garden City: Privately printed, 1975), 222.
14. *Long Island Farmer,* May 6, 1898.
15. *Long Island Farmer,* May 6, 1898.
16. Charles Johnson Post, *The Little War of Private Post,* (Boston: Little, Brown, 1960), 8-10.
17. *Leslie's Weekly,* June 9, 1898.
18. A New York State Education Department historical marker on Eleventh Street in Garden City commemorates Camp Scott. The historical marker at the corner of Washington Avenue states: "Site of Camp Winfield Scott, established August 1861. A Civil War Army Camp of Instruction. Commanded by Gen. Thomas W. Sherman."

When Nassau Supplied Brooklyn's Water

Richard A. Winsche

When the City of Brooklyn was incorporated, on March 24, 1834, its population was slightly more than 23,000 persons. At that time its source of water supply consisted of a series of wells located within Kings County. By 1850, Brooklyn's population had risen to almost 131,000, and its existing water supply was proving inadequate. Consideration was then given to proposals to sink additional wells and raise the water to a reservoir elevated forty or fifty feet above the highest buildings, but no action was taken on these proposals.[1]

That same year William Burden, who was a member of the Water Committee of the Brooklyn Common Council, prepared plans for a supply of water to be obtained from Jamaica Creek, the first stream of any importance east of the city. He proposed constructing steam engines and stand pipes at the stream to send the water through iron pipes to Flatbush. This appears to have been the first suggestion of using the streams on Long Island, or more specifically in Queens County (which then included the present Nassau County area), as a source of water for the City of Brooklyn.[2]

Burden's plan received support from two distinguished engineers, William J. McAlpine and John B. Jervis, who respectively had charge of building the Albany and the New York Water Works. Their report considered the streams on the south side of Long Island to be the only water source of permanent value available to the city.[3] They proposed placing dams on the four streams nearest to Brooklyn, from which they estimated a daily supply of ten million gallons of water could be obtained. The water would then be sent through a conduit to a reservoir on Mt. Prospect, which would have a capacity of sixty million gallons. Seventy-five miles of distributing pipe would be required and the cost of this work was estimated at $3,500,000.[4] After much consideration this plan was placed before the voters who defeated it at a special election held on July 11, 1853.[5]

In response to the municipality's failure to provide an adequate water supply, private water companies began to organize. On April 16, 1852, the Williamsburg Water Company was incorporated and, in June 1853, it became the Long Island Water Company. On April 12, 1855, another private company was chartered under the name of the Nassau Water Company, and was given authority to purchase all the holdings of the Long Island Water Company.[6] By 1858 the Nassau Water Company had acquired ownership of Jamaica (or Baiseley's) Pond in Queens County, and Brookfield Pond, Clear

Stream Pond, Valley Stream Pond, Rockville Pond, and Hempstead Pond, all of which were located in what later became Nassau County.

In 1854, the City of Brooklyn obtained a new charter incorporating the village of Williamsburg and the Town of Bushwick into the city, thereby increasing its population to more than 200,000 persons. Realizing that the water from the wells in the denser populated portions of the city was becoming impure and could not meet the needs of this increased population, Brooklyn took action by subscribing $1.3 million to the stock of the Nassau Water Company on June 4, 1856. The next year the City of Brooklyn issued bonds in the amount of $2.9 million to complete the purchase of the Nassau Water Company, which ceased to exist.[7]

By that time the City of Brooklyn had decided to construct its primary reservoir at Ridgewood, with a conduit running to it from the Jamaica Pond. During the fall of 1858 this work was completed and water was pumped into the Ridgewood reservoir, and from there into the mains supplying the city. This system had a pumping capacity of fifteen million gallons a day into the reservoir which held an average of 154 million gallons of water, sufficient to supply the city for a ten-day period.[8]

By 1870 Brooklyn's population had grown to more than 400,000 persons. For this reason it was recommended that a storage reservoir be constructed in the valley of the Hempstead stream. That area, situated south of the Village of Hempstead, had originally been the site of three mill ponds. Purchased at a cost of $110,982, the grounds of this reservoir contained 557 acres with an estimated water surface, when full, of 253 acres.[9] On February 18, 1871, permission was given to construct this reservoir at a cost not to exceed $1.4 million.[10]

When William McAlpine had studied this area some twenty years earlier, he noted that rainfall sank into the pervious sand there building up a vast underground reservoir of water. He determined that any retaining dam should not exceed eight feet in height, but the Brooklyn Water Commissioners felt that a higher dam would impound more water. They decided on a twenty-two foot dam, which, in theory, would have formed a reservoir more than two miles long and twenty feet deep, capable of impounding one billion gallons of water. They did not take into consideration, as had McAlpine, that a twenty-two foot dam would collect water until it was twenty feet higher than the water table. The pressure of this water would then reverse the flow and it would seep down into the pervious sand. In other words, the water would seep out as fast as it ran in and as a consequence this reservoir could never be filled to such a height. After several years work and the expenditure of much of the appropriated money, this project was completed. Tests were then made and when the gates were closed, the reservoir started to fill at the expected rate of six million gallons a day. As the water rose higher, however, the flow decreased alarmingly. It then became apparent that this reservoir could never be filled beyond one-third of its estimated capacity. Had this project been successful it probably would have solved all of Brooklyn's future water needs.[11]

As a result of this disastrous project Brooklyn's Water Commission was abolished and the responsibility for providing an adequate supply of water was placed with the Department of City Works. The population had grown to almost 600,000 persons by 1880 and, with the opening of the Brooklyn Bridge on May 24, 1883, continued to climb until by 1890 there were more than 800,000 residents. It became apparent that the City of Brooklyn would be forced to extend its system of conduits east from Rockville Centre. For this reason field crews began making surveys out to Massapequa, near the Suffolk County line.[12]

Up to this point the City of Brooklyn had negotiated with individual property owners in order to expand its water system into the Queens-Nassau area, acquiring more than three hundred separate parcels of land in this manner between 1853 and 1887. To simplify this process and guarantee access to waters in Queens County, Brooklyn Assemblyman Thomas F. Magner introduced a bill in the state legislature in 1887. This bill would have given the City of Brooklyn the right of eminent domain in acquiring any lands in Queens and Suffolk Counties that it might require to extend its water system. Under the terms of this bill the city could then simply have taken what it wanted, with compensation later being set by a referee.[13]

That bill failed to pass and in March 1888 a similar bill was introduced by Assemblyman Magner.[14] At this point several Queens County newspapers, notably the *Queens County Sentinel* and the *Hempstead Inquirer,* came out strongly in opposition. The latter newspaper stated that Brooklyn was "sapping, as it were, the very life-blood of Queens County. . . . And Long Island is not blessed with much more than enough to supply her own needs."[15] In addition to the local newspapers, the Queens County Board of Supervisors was also opposed to this bill and they arranged to have former Assemblyman James S. Allen argue against its enactment. On April 5, 1888, he debated the issue with Brooklyn Corporation Council Almet Jenks.[16] Despite his efforts the bill ultimately passed, largely because of Brooklyn's stronger political backing.

Queens County officials did not give up their fight and, in March 1890, they had Assemblyman Henry C. Johnson introduce still another bill in the state legislature. That bill would have prevented the City of Brooklyn from pumping more than fifty million gallons of water a day from Queens County except by permission of the Board of Supervisors. It also called for the placing of meters to determine the quantity of water consumed.[17] As with

Milburn Pumping Station, North Brookside Avenue, Freeport. Postcard, c.1910, courtesy of the *NCM Collection, LISI at Hofstra.*

previous bills entered to protect Queens County, the Brooklyn legislators managed to defeat this.

In July 1888, Commissioner of City Works John P. Adams urged the Brooklyn mayor and aldermen to approve the extension of the water system from Rockville Centre east to Massapequa. He stated that Brooklyn's existing water supply would soon be exhausted and that it would take at least three years to build this extension.[18] No action was taken on this proposal until June 18, 1889, when the project was approved with the backing of Mayor Alfred C. Chapin.[19] In addition to the extension of the system some ten miles east to Massapequa Pond, the plan called for the acquisition of all ponds of importance along the route of the line. Near Milburn Stream, about two miles east of Rockville Centre, there would be built a strong reservoir with a capacity of 400 million gallons, which was thought to be sufficient to meet all future needs. To force the water along this line a large pumping station would be erected at Milburn (at the western border of the Village of Freeport) from which the water would be pumped into the reservoir to a height of thirty feet. The conduit running from the Milburn Pumping Station to the one at Ridgewood would be constructed of iron, while that connecting Milburn with Massapequa would be brick. According to Robert Van Burne, the chief engineer, this conduit could be relied upon to carry 75 million gallons of water daily. To cover the cost of this construction, the alderman and mayor approved an appropriation of $4.5 million.[20]

By July 1889, the City Works Department had selected Brooklynite Frank Freeman to be the architect for the Milburn Pumping Station. Freeman was then only twenty-eight years old, but was known as a master of the

Romanesque Revival style. Among the many Brooklyn buildings he later designed were the Hotel Margaret, the Brooklyn Fire Headquarters (now listed on the National Register of Historic Places), the Eagle Warehouse and Storage building, and the Brooklyn Savings Bank.[21]

In the late winter of 1890 work began on the reservoir and conduits in the area of the proposed Milburn Pumping Station, and in March a local newspaper reported that several hundred Italian laborers were working in that locality.[22] By early September it was announced that these men were busy constructing the brick conduit from the Milburn Pumping Station through the Village of Freeport. To lay the bricks properly, however, it was necessary to have pumps, with a capacity of 5,000 gallons a minute, operating night and day to remove the water from the work area. Unfortunately, this constant pumping was also lowering the water level in all the neighboring wells, causing great concern to the local residents.[23]

By December 1891 work on this system had been virtually completed and it was decided to test the equipment. It was then reported that "one of the new pumps at Milburn Station was started on December 12th, sending a large volume of water through the new conduit. The pump and engine worked well, but the water never reached Brooklyn, because the connection at Rockville Centre was not completed and the water flooded out the workmen. The remark that came over the telephone made the air blue."[24] Following this test the pumping station went into full-time operation and by the next

Brooklyn Water Works conduit under construction, c.1908, looking east from Brookside Avenue. Photograph courtesy of the *NCM Collection, LISI at Hofstra* .

week it was noted that "water from the Milburn stream is being pumped to Brooklyn night and day."[25] By 1907 it was estimated that 85 percent of the 145 million gallons of water being supplied to Brooklyn was coming from this system.[26]

When Kings County and the City of Brooklyn became a borough of the Greater City of New York in 1898, Brooklyn's water supply became the responsibility of the Board of Water Supply of the City of New York. By 1905 that department had begun work on a new Catskill aqueduct at upstate Ashokan. Fearing that additional sources of water might be needed before that aqueduct was completed, the Board began to investigate the possibility of further extending the Ridgewood system to Quogue, in eastern Suffolk County.[27] This extension was never necessary, as by 1917 the Catskill system had been completed and was supplying most of the water needed in Brooklyn and New York City. The Ridgewood system was then held in reserve, but was seldom used.[28]

By the early 1920s the City of New York was paying Nassau County $80,000 a year in taxes on the water system property it owned within the county. In an effort to lessen that amount city officials proposed that the state build an east-west highway over the route of their pipeline. Enlisting the aid of Nassau Assemblyman Thomas A. McWhinney, a bill calling for the construction of this highway was presented to the state legislature and subsequently approved. Because of delays in appropriating the money for the project, this road, which was named the Sunrise Highway, was not completed and dedicated until June 8, 1929.[29]

In addition to this roadway, the City of New York dedicated 2,200 acres of water supply lands in Nassau County to the Long Island State Park Commission in 1925. These lands would later comprise the backbone of the Southern State, Meadowbrook, Wantagh, and Bethpage State Parkways, and became the sites of Valley Stream, Hempstead Lake, and Massapequa State Parks. The dedication of these areas was in the form of a permanent surface easement for state park and parkway purposes. The City of New York reserved the right to continue to pump water as needed and required that the donated watershed areas be protected by the Long Island State Park Commission.[30]

Through the years New York City's dependence on the old Brooklyn water supply system continually lessened, until it was only used in emergencies. In 1959 the City Department of Water Supply, Gas and Electricity turned 856 acres of this land over to the city's Bureau of Real Estate to sell.[31] Upon learning of this, Nassau County officials offered $5 million to buy all the city's water supply property in their county. This offer was made contingent upon proposed legislation that would insure the protection of surface easement rights then held by the Long Island State Park Commission for park and parkway purposes.[32] In making the offer Nassau County officials stated it would relieve the city of taxes of over $100,000 a year on an assessed valuation of approximately $2 million plus annual maintenance costs of about $500,000.[33] No action was taken on this offer, which was renewed in 1961, 1963, and 1965. In 1965 the City of New York announced that it was abandoning its plans to sell these properties as a severe drought, which lowered the water level in upstate city reservoirs, was forcing them to again put this system into use.[34]

In the years that followed, however, improvements in New York City's water supplies finally made the Ridgewood system obsolete. On April 1, 1977, therefore, the County of Nassau took possession of the Milburn Pumping Station when New York City vested title to it in anticipation of the sale of its properties.[35] In 1979, a tentative agreement was reached between these parties regarding the sale of much of the water system property. Finally, on July 1, 1981, the County of Nassau became the absolute owner of some 1,750 acres of watershed land upon payment of $6.7 million to the City.[36] Five years later, on June 3, 1986, the County purchased the remainder of the Brooklyn water system property, thereby ending an unwanted chapter in its history.[37]

In summation, Brooklyn's chronic water shortages reshaped the physical appearance of Long Island. Further, Brooklyn's exploitation was bitterly resented by the residents of Long Island, especially those persons living in south shore communities. As the water table of these communities was lowered, mills were unable to operate, and even their oyster industry almost ceased to exist. Although Queens County officials attempted to block further encroachment by Brooklyn, all of their efforts failed and this water system became a monument to one municipality's dominance over another. While this water system ceased activity, except during the drought of 1965-1966, vestiges of it can still be seen along the south shore of Nassau County. However, the Milburn Pumping Station, which was sold to private owners in 1986, serves as a reminder of rural Long Island's importance to Brooklyn and New York City.

Notes

1. Henry R. Stiles, *The Civil, Political, Professional and Ecclesiastical History and Commercial and Industrial Record of the County of Kings and the City of Brooklyn, N.Y. From 1683 to 1884,* 2 vols. (New York: W. W. Munsell, 1884), 1: 584.

2. Stiles, *Civil,* 1: 584.

3. Henry R. Stiles, *A History of the City of Brooklyn,* 3 vols. (Brooklyn: Published by subscription, 1870), 3: 590.

4. Jacob Judd, "Water for Brooklyn," *New York History* 47, no. 4 (October 1966): 367.

5. Stiles, *Civil,* 1: 585.
6. Stiles, *Civil,* 1: 586.
7. Stiles, *History,* 3: 592-94.
8. Stiles, *History,* 3: 595.
9. W. W. Munsell, *History of Queens County, New York, With Illustrations, Portraits & Sketches of Prominent Families and Individuals* (New York: W. W. Munsell & Co., 1882), 151.
10. Stiles, *Civil,* 1: 588.
11. Preston R. Bassett, "Mill River," *Nassau County Historical Society Journal* 25, no. 2 (Spring 1964): 12-13.
12. Stiles, *Civil,* 1: 590.
13. *Brooklyn Daily Eagle,* February 24, 1888, 2; February 28, 1888, 4.
14. *Brooklyn Daily Eagle,* March 28, 1888, 2.
15. *Hempstead Inquirer,* March 9, 1888, 4.
16. *Queens County Sentinel,* March 29, 1888, 2; *Brooklyn Daily Eagle,* April 6, 1888, 1.
17. *Long Island Democrat,* March 11, 1890, 2.
18. *Queens County Sentinel,* July 19, 1888, 2.
19. *Brooklyn Daily Eagle,* June 29, 1889, 1.
20. *Brooklyn Daily Eagle,* June 29, 1889, 1.
21. Donald Martin Reynolds, *The Architecture of New York City: Histories and Views of Important Structures, Sites and Symbols* (New York: Macmillan, 1984), 322.
22. *Hempstead Inquirer,* March 7, 1890, 2.
23. *South Side Observer,* September 5, 1890, 3.
24. *South Side Observer,* December 18, 1891, 3.
25. *South Side Observer,* December 25, 1891, 3.
26. New York City Board of Water Supply, *Long Island Sources: Reports, Resolutions, Authorizations, Surveys and Designs Showing Sources and Manner of Obtaining from Suffolk County, Long Island an Additional Supply of Water for the City of New York* (New York: Board of Water Supply of the City of New York, 1912), 1: 56.
27. New York City Board of Water Supply, *Long Island Sources,* 58.
28. Avendt Group, Inc., *Study of Potential Uses for the Sunrise Highway Aqueduct System* (Annapolis, MD: Avendt Group, Inc., 1989), 1.
29. *Nassau Daily Review,* March 19, 1921, p. 1; June 10, 1929, 1.
30. Chester Blakelock, "History of Long Island State Parks," in *Long Island: A History of Two Great Counties,* edited by Paul Bailey, 2 vols. (New York: Lewis Publishing Co., 1949), 2: 274, 278.
31. *New York Herald Tribune,* March 23, 1959, 17.
32. *New York Times,* March 23, 1959, 24.
33. *Newsday,* March 23, 1959, 7.
34. *New York Journal-American,* June 23, 1965, 12.
35. Nassau County Deeds, Vestment Deed no. 11987/76.
36. *Newsday,* July 2, 1981, 9.
37. *Newsday,* June 4, 1986, 9.

The Naming of Nassau County

Dorothy Horton McGee

The Nassau family, whose name the county bears, can be traced back to the eleventh century in Germany. Drutwin (d. 1076) and his brother Dudo, the Count of Laurenburg, constructed a castle near the present town of Nassau, on a hill overlooking the Lahn River. A descendant of Drutwin, named Walram (d. 1198), adopted the title, Count of Nassau.[1]

The grandson of a later Count, John of Nassau-Dillenberg, was William, Count of Nassau, Prince of Orange, who as William I, The Silent, was the founder of the Dutch Republic.[2] William I was born in Nassau, in western Germany, in 1533. He inherited the principality of Orange in southeastern France, as well as possessions in the Netherlands, from his first cousin, Réné of Orange-Chalons, who had died at the siege of St. Dizier in 1544.[3] Charles V's son and heir, Philip II of Spain, on leaving the Netherlands for Spain in 1559, appointed William I, Prince of Orange, Count of Nassau, to the posts of Stadholder (governor) of Holland, Zeeland, and Utrecht. William I, founder of the house of Orange-Nassau established in 1558, was instrumental in the Revolt of the Netherlands against Spain, begun in 1568 and lasting until 1648.[4]

After the assassination of William I at Delft in July 1584, he was succeeded by his son, Maurice of Nassau, then seventeen years old. Maurice served from 1584 to 1625. He was succeeded by his brother, Frederick Henry, from 1625 to 1647. Both sons were renowned as generals.

In addition to this historical background, various uses have been made of "Nassau" as a place name. Following Henry Hudson's voyage of 1609 to the northern hemisphere of the New World, which provided the Netherlands with a claim to New Netherland, a navigator named Adriaen Block sailed to New Netherland in 1614. Exploring the Atlantic coast eastward from Manhattan by sail, Block named a large body of water, Bay of Nassau (now Narragansett Sound).[5]

In 1614, too, a fort named Nassau was built by Dutch traders on Castle Island opposite present-day Albany.

In 1664, as is well known, the Duke of York's English fleet captured New Netherland, which had been granted to the Royal Duke of York by his brother, King Charles II of England. The Dutch/Nassau influence was, however, not over.

On King Charles II's death, the Duke of York, as James II, became King of England. His sister, Mary, married William II, Prince of Orange (1647-

1650), who had succeeded his father, Frederick Henry, of the house of Orange-Nassau. The posthumous son of William II and Mary Stuart, William III, Prince of Orange (1672-1702), married his Stuart cousin, Mary, daughter of James II of England. After James II was overthrown, William III and Mary became joint sovereigns of England in 1689.[6]

In the Royal Colony of New York, as New Netherland was renamed following the English takeover from the Dutch, the Royal Duke's laws were promulgated in 1665. Long Island was pronounced part of the north riding of Yorkshire. In a letter of November 1665 to the Duke of York, Richard Nicolls, Governor, stated: "I gave the name of Albania to the territory lying west of Hudson's River, and to Long Island the name of Yorkshire, as to this place, the name of New York, to comprehend all the titles of your Royal Highness."[7]

Not for some eighteen years was the act to divide the province and dependencies into shires and counties passed, on November 1, 1683. There were then twelve counties. Although the act does not say so, it was to perpetuate the titles of the British royal family that the names were selected and adopted. King's County was named for King Charles II, the Duke's brother; Queens, for Queen Catharine of Braganza, the Royal Duke's sister-in-law; and Suffolk, for the Dukedom of Suffolk.[8]

In April 1693, the Colonial Assembly approved an act renaming Long Island the Island of Nassau. This was to honor Dutch William, Prince of Orange and King of England.[9] Used for many years in deeds, the name did not become popular and eventually became obsolete.

Unsuccessful Efforts to Divide Queens County

By 1869 the division of Queens County was "one of the principal themes of discussion of the inhabitants of the eastern towns," according to the *Hempstead Inquirer*. On February 1, 1869, a meeting at Mineola was held for the purpose of forming a new county out of the three eastern towns of Queens and the Town of Huntington in Suffolk County (Huntington included Babylon until 1872). The Honorable William T. McCoun called the meeting to order. Mr. Gideon Frost of Glen Cove offered the following resolution: "That we deem it expedient to divide the County of Queens on the basis of the eastern towns, and receive any proposition on the part of the towns of Suffolk County which they may make."[10]

The motion was approved unanimously. A committee was then appointed by the chairman to take the matter in hand and present the question to the State Legislature. Those selected were William T. McCoun, George S. Downing, Oyster Bay; Charles R. Street, Huntington; John A. Searing, Mineola; and Ebenezer Kellum, Hempstead.

Assemblyman William Conant of Suffolk County introduced the bill for a new county in the State Legislature, "to be called the county of Nassau."[11] The Assembly passed the measure, but the Senate did not concur. A complication of the unsuccessful bill was the location of a new Queens County courthouse.

Another movement to divide Queens County came in the Centennial year of the United States—1876. An Executive Committee meeting on the possible division of the County was held at Mineola on January 14, 1876. A draft of a "division bill," as amended, was referred back to a sub-committee with instructions to forward it to Assemblyman Townsend D. Cock for immediate introduction in the Legislature. When the subject of a name for the new county arose, only two names were considered—Ocean and Nassau. Ocean won by a vote of nine to three.

At a succeeding meeting, including Huntington and Babylon, each speaker insisted he was for division under any names and was willing to accept the majority opinion. On motion, the adoption of Nassau was approved "without a dissenting vote."[12] Assemblyman Cock, who was at the meeting, said that he would introduce the new Nassau County Bill, with Huntington and Babylon included, in the Legislature and secure a hearing for the committee.[13]

The newspaper commented on the change of name from Ocean to Nassau:

> This change, we believe, will be well received. To our mind Nassau is a far better appellation than Ocean. We are not of those who believe that there is nothing in a name, although we are free to admit that a rose by any other would smell as sweet. There is a fitness sometimes in names that cannot be ignored. Since Nassau was, in 1693, by an act of the Colonial Assembly, made the name of Long Island, it is proper in this Centennial year. When we are making a retrospect of the past, we should go back and take it up and give it to the new county. Nassau by all means.[14]

The Committee on Civil Divisions reported adversely on the Cock Bill to erect Nassau County and the bill was defeated.[15] The bill was reintroduced in 1877, but Assemblyman Elbert Floyd-Jones was the only representative from Queens and Suffolk to vote in favor of the new county. The vote was 42 in favor and 56 opposed.[16]

Formation of Nassau County in 1898

The Consolidation of the City of New York indirectly brought about final official action on the new county government. Approved by Governor Frank Black, Greater New York City was initiated as of January 1, 1898, and included the three western towns of Queens County.

A meeting of those interested in the affairs of the towns of Hempstead, North Hempstead, and Oyster Bay was called by P. Halstead Scudder of Glen Head. Held at Allen's Hall, Mineola, on the afternoon of January 22, 1898, the meeting was "to consider the situation and determine upon some definite future course of action." P. Halstead Scudder acted as temporary chairman and called the meeting to order. The purpose, he declared, "was not political, but to secure a better form of government. . . . Under the new conditions, the three eastern towns would be at the absolute mercy of the dominant element in New York . . . The dangers confronting the eastern towns are numerous."[17]

Of the five solutions proposed by Mr. Scudder, the erection of a new county, comprised of the three eastern towns, was considered the "wisest and best plan and the one most feasible to have adopted." John B. C. Tappen of Glen Cove made the following motion, as recorded in the *Hempstead Inquirer:* "Resolved, That it is the sense of this meeting that Hempstead, North Hempstead and Oyster Bay withdraw from the county of Queens, and that a new county, to include said towns, be formed." The resolution was overwhelmingly adopted, there being only a few noes.[18]

James H. Ludlam of Oyster Bay moved a preamble and resolutions which were approved. The Supervisors of the eastern towns were to request a sum up to $250 from their respective town boards to defray related expenses, and the chairman was to appoint a committee to take "general charge of matters, select a name for the county, prepare a bill, etc."[19]

The committee members appointed were: P. Halstead Scudder of Oyster Bay, chairman; General James B. Pearsall and James H. Ludlam, Oyster Bay; William G. Miller and Lott Van deWater, Jr., Hempstead; Dr. S. H. Bogart and Wilbur H. Lewis, North Hempstead. The names suggested for the county were: Matinecock, Norfolk, Bryant, and Nassau.[20]

Proposals for Matinecock, Norfolk, and Bryant

For the new county's name, Edward N. Townsend of Hempstead, formerly of Oyster Bay, nominated Matinecock, an American Indian word of Eastern Algonquian language origin. (The Delawares of the south coastal area, including western Long Island, spoke an eastern Algonquian language dialect, Munsee.)[21] Matinecock was certainly the historic name, dating from the prehistoric period before the Europeans came. The Matinecock lands extended from Newtown to the Nissequogue River along the northern half of the island.

The word Matinecock appears on the post-European contact records. The meaning has been given as "at the place to search, or to look around from" and "at the hilly land."[22] Initiating the Town of Oyster Bay, the "First Purchase" of Matinecock land was made in 1653 from Asiapum, alias Mohanes, by three New Englanders and seven joint purchasers.[23] Edward

N. Townsend who proposed the name Matinecock, was a descendant of Samuel Townsend, builder of the Townsend Homestead, known as Raynham Hall, owned by the Town of Oyster Bay. The extent of his interest in the Matinecocks is not known, but it must have been considerable for Edward Townsend and his wife named their youngest child Mohanes Henry Townsend.[24]

The name Norfolk was nominated by John B. C. Tappen of Glen Cove for the new county on Long Island—so that Norfolk and Suffolk Counties would be contiguous, as Norfolk and Suffolk Counties were in Massachusetts and in England.[25]

William G. Miller, part owner of the Freeport construction firm of Miller and Randall, suggested the name Bryant for the new county. The name was intended to honor William Cullen Bryant (1794-1878) who had had a country place at Roslyn, "Cedarmere," on the east shore of Hempstead Harbor. He was one of the most eminent residents of the area, and his poetry was very popular in the nineteenth century. Bryant had been a supporter of the new county, as were the "people in Roslyn and its neighborhood," he wrote.[26]

Nassau

Nassau was nominated by Archer B. Wallace, son of Assemblyman George Wallace. With a connection to both the Dutch and English provinces, as outlined previously, Nassau was a logical choice.

The final committee meeting about the new county, chaired by P. Halstead Scudder of Glen Head, was held at Pettit's Hotel in Jamaica on February 5, 1898. The committee named the county-to-be Nassau, citing the Colonial Assembly Act of April 10, 1693, designating Long Island as the Island of Nassau. A draft bill was presented for immediate introduction to the State Legislature. Assemblyman George Wallace, from the Third Election District of Queens, introduced the bill February 17, 1898. The bill passed the Assembly and the Senate, sponsored by State Senator Theodore Koehler, as Chapter 588, Laws of 1898.

There was opposition, however, at the meeting of the Queens County Board of Supervisors. Supervisor Ott of the Fifth Ward introduced resolutions opposing the Nassau County Bill, then "in the hands of the Governor, and empowering the Board to attend the hearing before the Governor . . . and oppose the signing of the bill." These resolutions were opposed spiritedly by the Supervisors of the eastern towns but were passed. Board of Supervisors' Counsel, Townsend Scudder, was then directed to go to Albany to oppose the bill.[27]

Members of the Board attended the hearing on the Nassau County Bill before the Governor. At the hearing, however, was a delegation headed by Benjamin D. Hicks in support of dividing Queens County. Townsend Scud-

Nassau County Seal. *NCM Collection, LISI at Hofstra.*

der, for the Supervisors' majority, spoke in opposition to the new county. He "contended that Nassau County would have no public property and that the timing was wrong because of the [Spanish-American] war." Allegedly, he took up almost all the allotted time, leaving Hicks only a chance for a few words.[28]

According to the *Brooklyn Daily Eagle,* the Governor stated that he was "inclined to look upon the measure favorably and to sign the bill," although he had not fully made up his mind. But sign he did, on April 27, 1898, the Nassau County bill, which would become effective January 1, 1899."[29]

P. Halstead Scudder, who called the January 1898 meeting, outlined the choices, chaired the appointed committee that named the county, and proposed the draft bill, may well be called the "Father of Nassau County." (His photograph is on p. 54.) Scudder worked successfully to achieve the new county, "free from entangling alliance with the great city of New York."[30]

Mineola was voted the new county seat at the 1898 November elections. At the Nassau County Board of Supervisors' organizational meeting held in Mineola on January 3, 1899, the first resolution passed was the adoption of a county coat-of-arms, seal, and flag. Townsend Scudder, counsel of the Queens Board and legal advisor to Nassau County, suggested that the "seal and colors of the county flag be based on the House of Nassau." Scudder was influenced by "the fact of the Dutch settlement on Long Island, and the name Nassau, which was given to the Island." The crown on the Lion rampant was replaced by a bushy head of hair. The county bill specified "seven billets" or blocks, but they are on a slant rather than vertical as in the House of Nassau's coat of arms. The billets possibly indicated the seven elected officials in Nassau County. Colors were specified as well: "azure" or blue, and gold (in French, "*or*") for the lion, and an orange flag with the seal. In the 1930s, a version of the coat of arms in error had only six billets and the six billet version of the seal is over the entrance to the new county courthouse.[31]

Notes

1. *The Encyclopedia Britannica* 11th ed., 29 vols. (New York: Encyclopedia Britannica Company, 1911), 19: 250-51.

2. *Encyclopedia Britannica,* 19: 250-51, 28: 672-74; Suzanne Cornelisse, *The Dutch Royal Family* (Amsterdam: De Bezige Bij, 1963?), 6-7.

3. *Encyclopedia Britannica,* 20: 146-47; Cornelisse, *Dutch Royal Family,* 8-9. Réné of Nassau-Chalons had succeeded his uncle Philibert, Prince of Orange-Chalons (1502-1530), who had no children, as ruler of the principality. Réné was the son of Philibert's sister, Claudia, and her husband, Henry, Count of Nassau. Henry was a counsellor of Charles V, son of Philip the Fair of Habsburg, Emperor of Germany, King of Spain.

4. William L. Langer, ed. *An Encyclopedia of World History* (Boston: Houghton Mifflin and Company, 1968), 474-76. The house of Orange-Nassau, later Royal, is ongoing in the Kingdom of the Netherlands.

5. E. B. O'Callaghan, ed., *History of New Netherland; or New York Under the Dutch,* 2 vols., 1846-1848 (Reprint; Spartanburg, SC: Reprint Company, 1966), 1: 35, 73. During the stadholdership of Maurice of Nassau, Prince of Orange, in 1623 Fort Nassau was constructed on the South (Delaware) River. This followed the chartering of the Dutch West India Company in 1621.

6. King James II was overthrown with the overt aid of his son-in-law, William III of Orange-Nassau.

7. Morton Pennypacker, *The Duke's Laws: Their Antecedents, Implications and Importance* (New York: New York University School of Law, 1944), 35; E. B. O'Callaghan, ed., *Documents Relative to the Colonial History of the State of New York,* 10 vols. (Albany: Weed, Parsons and Company, Printers; 1853), 3:105. When the Dutch briefly recaptured New Netherland (1673-1674), New York City was renamed New Orange. Orange was for the Royal Duke's nephew, the Prince of Orange.

8. Pennypacker, *Duke's Laws,* 34-35.

9. As a contrast in geography but exhibiting the English connection, in the Bahamas, when Governor Nicholas Trott rebuilt Charles Towne in 1695, he named it "Nassau" after King William III of England, Prince of Orange-Nassau. Fort Nassau was also constructed at that period.

10. *Hempstead Inquirer,* February 5, 1869, 2.

11. The Assembly vote in favor was 77-11. *Journal of the Assembly of the State of New York at their Ninety-second Session* (Albany: Argus Company, 1869), 1: 331, 2: 1,769.

12. *Hempstead Inquirer,* February 25, 1876, 2.

13. *Journal of the Assembly of the State of New York at their Ninety-ninth Session* (Albany: Weed, Parsons & Co., 1876), 1: 330 (cited hereafter as *Assembly Journal,* 1876); Paul Bailey, ed., *Long Island, A History of Two Great Counties Nassau and Suffolk,* 3 vols. (New York: Lewis Historical Publishing Co., 1949), 2: 215-16.

14. *Hempstead Inquirer,* February 25, 1876, 2.

As Richard A. Winsche indicates in the preceding article, the name Nassau was used by the Nassau Water Company, incorporated under that name in 1855. The first hospital in what would become Nassau County adopted the name Nassau Hospital when it was organized in 1896. See article in this volume by Dr. Thomas I. Palmieri, "History of Hospitals in Nassau County." (Editor's note.)

15. *Assembly Journal,* 1876, 1: 1,036. Townsend Cock had received petitions in favor from 500 citizens from North Hempstead and 85 from Oyster Bay which he referred to the appropriate committee. Samuel B. Gardiner of Suffolk presented "two remonstrances" from 1,195 citizens of Suffolk County opposing the new county. *Assembly Journal,* 1876, 1: 369-70, 424, 518.

16. *Hempstead Inquirer,* May 25, 1877, 2. See also *Hempstead Inquirer,* February 2-March 2, 1877; March 16, 1877; May 18, 1877.

17. *Hempstead Inquirer,* January 21, 1898, 2; January 28, 1898, 2-3.

18. *Hempstead Inquirer,* January 28, 1898, 3.

19. *Hempstead Inquirer,* January 28, 1898, 3.

20. Bailey, *Long Island,* 2: 217; Edward J. Smits, *Nassau, Suburbia, USA 1899 to 1974* (Syosset: Friends of the Nassau County Museum, 1974), 39-42.

21. Bailey, *Long Island,* 2: 217; Bruce G. Trigger, ed., *Handbook of North American Indians, Northeast,* 20 vols. (Washington: Smithsonian Institution, 1978), 15: 214-15.

22. William Wallace Tooker, *The Indian Place-Names on Long Island and Islands Adjacent*, 1911 (Reprint, Port Washington, NY: Kennikat Press, 1975), 115-17.

23. *Oyster Bay Town Records,* ed. John Cox, Jr., 8 vols. (New York: Tobias A. Wright, 1916), 1: frontispiece.

24. Information on Mohanes Townsend from family descendant.

25. There was another possible reason for the choice of Norfolk. The Wrights and the Townsends—and probably others—emigrated in the seventeenth century to the new country from Norfolk County, England. Justin Winsor, ed., *The Memorial History of Boston, 1630-1880,* 4 vols. (Boston: James R. Osgood and Company, 1880), 1:131; *Encyclopedia Britannica,* 17: 352 ff.

26. Poet Bryant had three residences, a New York townhouse, Cedarmere in Roslyn in the proposed new county area, and the family homestead in Cummington, Massachusetts. *Hempstead Inquirer,* April 29, 1898; Jeffrey A. Kroessler, "The Greater City and Queens County," *Long Island Historical Journal* 11 (Fall 1998): 11-12.

27. *East Norwich Enterprise,* April 30, 1898.

28. Townsend Scudder was the younger brother of P. Halstead Scudder. Josephine C. Frost, ed., *Underhill Genealogy: Descendants of Capt. John Underhill,* 6 vols. (Privately printed, 1932), 3: 617.

29. *Brooklyn Daily Eagle,* April 28, 1898, 4.

30. See *Nassau County Sentinel,* January 20 and 27, 1898; *Hempstead Inquirer,* January 28, 1898, 3; Edward J. Smits, "The Creation of Nassau County," *Long Island Historical Journal* 1 (Spring 1989): 179.

31. Edward J. Smits, *The Nassau County Seal* (Mineola: County of Nassau, 1970), 3, 5, 10-11.

On the creation of Nassau County, see also: Geoffrey Mohan, "Nassau's Difficult Birth," in *Long Island: Our Story,* by Newsday (Melville, NY: Newsday, 1998), 232-35; Edward J. Smits, "Creating a New County: Nassau," *Long Island Historical Journal* 11 (Spring 1999): 129-44; and "'Boss' Platt's Role in Creating Nassau County" earlier in this book, 47-54. (Editor's note.)

Changes and Transformations

Left: Samuel Velsor on farm equipment, c. 1910. Three generations of Velsors operated a farm for more than a century on the west side of Old Westbury Road in Old Westbury (north of I. U. Willets Road and south of today's Long Island Expressway). *NCM Collection, LISI at Hofstra. Right*: Hofstra University built its ten-story Library (center) and thirteen-story Residence Towers in 1966-1968. Photograph by Buckley Chin, 1989, courtesy of Hofstra's University Relations.

Left: Omni building at 333 Earle Ovington Boulevard, Mitchel Field, Garden City. Photograph courtesy Reckson Associates Reality Corporation. *Right:* EAB Plaza, on Hempstead Turnpike in Uniondale, was designed by the Spector Group in 1984. Photograph courtesy of the Spector Group and the Society for the Preservation of Long Island Antiquities.

An Ecodeterminist View of Nassau's Growth

Edward J. Smits

Although Nassau County's growth into one of the most vibrant suburban areas of the United States occurred in the twentieth century, its natural environment and ecology have influenced its development pattern from the time of colonial settlement. The unique physical geography of this central portion of Long Island attracted its first settlers from New England in the 1640s even before Niew Amsterdam began its rise into the great metropolis that would eventually dominate and stimulate growth of a wide hinterland.

Nassau's ecosystem has particularly affected its pattern of twentieth century suburban growth compared to other areas of the megalopolis that now stretches along the northeastern seaboard of the United States as a continuous urban and suburban complex from southern New Hampshire to northern Virginia. As with other suburbs within the megalopolis, Nassau was affected by the common determinants of suburban growth including the decline of farming, the impact of transportation changes, the burgeoning urban population seeking better housing and recreation, and the economic base of jobs and business opportunities of New York City.[1] However, Nassau possessed an ecosystem that provided an environmental influence which differentiated it from the other fringe counties of New York and determined its growth into one of the premier suburbs of the country.

Bordered by the great expanse of Long Island Sound and its picturesque inlets and harbors on the north, the county also possessed a south shore with sandy, endless Atlantic Ocean barrier beaches protecting miles of bays rich in marine life. Long Island's division into two great natural areas is most evident in Nassau. Deposits of ancient glacial movements created the north shore's rolling hills and scenic woodlands overlooking the silvery Sound. The same glaciers left an out-wash plain that provided a fertile, level landscape to the marshlands of the south shore bay.

These two very different environments were separated by a unique physical phenomenon—a great extent of grassy plains land. Stretching four miles from north to south and some sixteen miles long across central Nassau, the Hempstead Plains was acclaimed by colonist Daniel Denton in 1670 as growing "very fine grass that makes exceeding good Hay, and is very good pasture" with "neither stick nor stone to hinder the Horse heels, or endanger them in their races."[2] This feature initiated local ecotourism as early colonists flocked to the site for horse racing and awarded as a prize the earliest marked piece of American silver, a small porringer inscribed "Wunn at Hempstead plains, 1668." Royal Governor Lovelace ordered trials of speed there with the purpose of improving and encouraging a good breed of horse. As later discussion will attest, from that time American thoroughbred horse racing has been centered here.

Throughout the next two hundred years, growth of the area was slow, and it remained a quiet agricultural scene with small maritime villages along its shores. As transportation improved in the 1800s with the extension of the Long Island Rail Road and steamboats traversing the Sound, the special maritime recreational activities on both shores began to draw seasonal visitors.

From colonial times wealthy New Yorkers, including Governor Thomas Dongan in the 1680s, had established manorial estates in the area. Travel improvements by the early 1800s increased the accessibility of the picturesque north shore. In 1842 William Cullen Bryant purchased an estate on the water at Roslyn Harbor. Cedarmere became a popular weekend visit spot for prominent Americans since Bryant, as editor of the *New York Post* and civic leader, was one of the country's foremost citizens. After the Civil War the establishment of country estates accelerated along the north shore. In 1885 Theodore Roosevelt built Sagamore Hill at Cove Neck initiating an enclave of Roosevelt family estates that was duplicated in other areas by extended families. After Roosevelt's ascension to the presidency in 1901, the media attention of the country was focused on the quiet hamlet of Oyster Bay. Roosevelt enthused about his life there, the endless recreational activities and closeness to nature, exclaiming "there could be no healthier place to bring up children."[3]

Wealthy titans of industry and finance acquired farms and established grand estates duplicating the manorial homes of Europe. From Great Neck to Oyster Bay along the shore and inland to Old Westbury and Syosset up to the edge of the plains, the verdant field and woodlands were transformed into Long Island's Gold Coast. The crowning development welcoming the new century was Clarence Mackay's imposing 650 acre estate on Harbor Hill overlooking Roslyn. Its elaborate landscaping, gardens, and buildings, including a gymnasium, swimming pool, and even a Turkish bath, provided a veritable recreational paradise. The *New York Herald* proclaimed "nowhere else certainly in America, probably in the world, are to be found so many great landed estates."[4]

The essential element of this movement was the enormous recreational appeal and possibilities of the area. Long Island Sound and its protected harbors provided ideal sailing waters and organized racing had begun there in the 1840s. By the 1890s the Manhasset Bay Yacht Club, the famed Seawanhaka Corinthian Yacht Club on Centre Island, and others were leaders in the international sport of yacht racing.

The Seawanhaka Corinthian Yacht Club on Centre Island opened in 1892. Korten photograph, c. 1910, *NCM Collection, LISI at Hofstra.*

Before the turn of the century golf had also taken hold in the county with the Meadow Brook Club opening in 1895 and the Garden City Golf Club hosting the U. S. Open in 1902. The exclusive country club with its manicured golf course became the center of estate social and recreational life. By 1930 there were thirty-six golf clubs in the county and the greatest players of the day, including Bobby Jones, Walter Hagen, Gene Sarazen, and Sam Snead, played in national tournaments on local links.

The historic interest in equestrian activities was shared by the Gold Coasters and Nassau became an international center of polo and horse racing. The Meadow Brook Club built its first polo field in 1884 and its famous robins-egg-blue grandstands hosted many international championships. Its team won the trophy in 1909 and at its height in the 1920s the sport was a favorite of the young generation of estate owners. Meadow Brook then had eight fields while some twenty-two others were located at clubs and private estates in the county. The nation's trend-setting publication, *Country Life in America,* reported that "everyone rode, hunted, or played polo."

August Belmont, Jr., and William C. Whitney led a group to build a grand new racetrack for the sport of kings. More than five hundred laborers were employed to transform some 650 acres in Elmont on the edge of the plains into Belmont Park which opened in 1905 with some two thousand stalls and room for nine thousand spectators. It soon became another international sports center and the grandstand was expanded to seat twenty thousand. The Belmont Stakes became one of the country's premier races and the stables of local millionaires held the most American racing records by mid-century.

Crowds of spectators also came to the plains land to view a new form of racing with early automobiles. Races along Merrick Road, then the finest highway in the East, were held by the Automobile Club of America in the early 1900s. From 1904 to 1910 the Vanderbilt Cup races across the center of the county attracted the greatest number of spectators of any sport in the country up to that time. William K. Vanderbilt desired to advance American prestige in the new world of motorcars and his cup races attracted a "frenzied, jovial exodus, 200,000 strong from New York alone, by ferry, train, auto, wagon and bike" that eventually created such danger they were stopped.[5]

The multitude of sport and recreational activities earned Nassau the designation "playground of New York" and local promoters contended "no other area in the country is so ideally adapted to the promotion of every conceivable form of amusement. It already holds first rank in golfing, tennis, horse racing, yachting, polo." Russel Doubleday expressed this appeal of the north shore enthusing over its "beauty and great variety of scenes, of topography" but also as a "center of fashionable life" and "all sports."[6]

While the northern section of the county was being reshaped by the Gold Coast, the south shore was also under change. All along the shore from the Pavilion Hotel in Woodsburgh to the bay front of Massapequa, a maritime resort business was growing. Each south shore village had small hotels, boarding houses, and resort cottages for city residents to enjoy summer vacations on the shore. A major land development, begun in 1907, created Long Beach as a major resort city on a strip of barrier beach.[7]

The Great South Bay was a sportsman's paradise with baymen guides available for fishing and duck hunting parties. Vacationers could enjoy swimming and bathing in the bay and overnight trips to the barrier beach at High Hill. On one warm July day in 1899, the railroad brought fifteen hundred people to Freeport.[8] As rail service improved after 1910, when through service by an East River tunnel to Pennsylvania Station reduced travel time, local real estate developers began to promote year round residency. Middle class residents were attracted to these waterfront communities and land prices zoomed in the late 1920s in a feverish burst of real estate auctions and sales. Movie magnate William Fox and local lawyer George Morton Levy planned Biltmore Shores on more than five hundred acres in Massapequa offering building plots for $1,980 and "a vast park, schools, golf, tennis, yachting and riding clubs . . . happy combination of green lands and salt sea."[9]

The burgeoning growth of the south shore villages strained the existing road systems and the state government began extensive road improvements including construction of Sunrise Highway and creation of the Long Island State Park Commission in 1924. Local Assemblyman F. Trubee Davison introduced the legislation for a system of state parks on Long Island so that the average man could "enjoy the natural outdoor things." Dynamic, young state planner Robert Moses proposed a far reaching development of public

West Bath House and Beach at Jones Beach State Park, c. 1935. Albertype photograph, *NCM Collection, LISI at Hofstra.*

beach and park facilities on the island and initiated construction of parkways both on the north and south shores to enable motorists to travel easily to the new facilities.

His grandest plan was the creation of a great public beach on the ocean front barrier island. The first referendum to turn over Town of Hempstead lands for such a development was defeated 12,106 to 4,200 due to residents' fears that the facility would attract city "rabble." Undeterred, Moses solicited the aid of county Republican boss G. Wilbur Doughty and the voters resoundingly approved a resubmittal of the proposal in 1926. Under Moses' vigorous leadership the Long Island State Park Commission developed a whole string of parks along Nassau's south shore on former City of Brooklyn watershed property. Nothing on the scale of Jones Beach had ever been done in the United States but Moses had the full support of Governor Alfred E. Smith and J. Russel Sprague who succeeded Doughty as Nassau Republican leader and first County Executive.[10]

The extensive recreational and sport activities fostered by Gold Coast residents and the middle class facilities of the south shore developed by the 1930s were a major influence on the initial suburban growth of Nassau as its population more than doubled from 126,120 in 1920 to 406,748 in 1940. The growth of recreation as a critical element in daily life was recognized by scholar Ralph H. Gabriel who pointed out in 1921 that "there is a phase in development of Long Island life that is full of significance for one who desires to understand Americans of the present. We are today a people of games, sports and out-of-doors pleasures. . . . Play has come to be an important part of Long Island life."[11]

While the recreational activities on the north and south shores were influencing Nassau's initial suburban growth, an equally eventful activity began on its central area. The New York Aeronautic Society had purchased an airplane from Glenn Curtiss in 1909. With members of the group he visited the Hempstead Plains and chose an area east of Mineola as a "nice flat place" to fly. Early on the morning of July 7, 1909 he took off and circled over the field for half an hour, thus winning the Scientific American prize for the first sustained flight of more than twenty-five kilometers. Aviation had come to the plains and would grow from that short flight into a giant industry.[12] Several airfields were established there and fearless aviators, men and women, flocked to the Moisant School becoming America's earliest pilots, including its first licensed woman pilot, Harriet Quimby. In 1910, aviators from around the world participated in a great International Aerial Tournament at Belmont Park focusing national attention on this wondrous new daredevil sport.

Nassau became a hotbed of aviation experimentation, record flights, and aircraft construction in local shops and garages. The area east of Garden City exploded into a maze of military and aviation installations in World War I. Mitchel Field remained after the war and by the early 1930s developed, with permanent brick hangars and military housing, into the region's principal Army Air Corps base. A center of technical and safety experimentation, the field was the site of the first blind flight using only instruments, flown by Jimmy Doolittle. Nearby Roosevelt Field became the busiest civilian airfield in the country and its weekend air shows drew thousands of spectators. Aviation was a great sport but it entered a new era of public interest after May 19, 1927 when Charles Lindbergh made the first successful non-stop solo flight across the Atlantic Ocean, leaving from Roosevelt Field for his Paris destination.[13]

An infant industry was growing, and by the late 1930s Grumman Aircraft Engineering Corporation and the Republic Aviation had established large factories in Bethpage and Farmingdale at the plains' eastern edge. With the approach of World War II, the industry expanded with dozens of related subcontractors and manufacturers. At the height of the war more than 90,000 men and women were employed in Nassau war plants producing the Army and Navy aircraft vital to the free world's victory. After World War II, the experienced engineers and technicians turned their talents to space flight and in 1962 Grumman was chosen to build the Project Apollo Lunar Module. The entire world celebrated on July 20, 1969 when Apollo 11 landed a man on the moon. Nassau's aerospace industry had progressed in two generations from training America's first aviators to constructing the spaceship to the moon. The industry continued as a backbone of the Long Island economy through the 1980s when consolidation and diminished military aircraft needs led to severe retrenchment and eventual closure of production lines in the mid-1990s.

Nassau's unique Hempstead Plains provided an ideal environment for the early years of aviation experimentation and a site for the following industry that not only made major contributions to the development of aviation but also provided a considerable economic base for a major population shift after World War II. These plains also supplied the key resource, open land, for a great tide of population and housing development that swept over Nassau County making it the fastest growing postwar suburb in the United States.

Between 1945 and 1960, Nassau's population rose by fifty thousand residents annually, surging from 456,748 to 1,300,171. The vast growth touched every community, but the most dramatic change was in the central plains area. On May 27, 1947 a headline in the daily tabloid *Newsday* proclaimed "2,000 $60 RENTALS DUE IN L.I. PROJECT." A revolutionary new mass-produced development was underway by builders Levitt and Sons. There was an overwhelming demand for housing and within a year the homes were offered for sale, additional vacant farm land of the plains was acquired, and by 1948 some 17,447 homes were completed. The growth spread over the plains developing not only Levittown but Uniondale, East Meadow, and portions of villages from Elmont eastward to Farmingdale. The county's older villages and south shore communities from Wantagh to Massapequa also received intensive development. Postwar Nassau real estate promotion used the same recreational and environmental appeals that attracted the first wave of suburban growth in the 1920s. A 1960 *New York Suburbs* realty magazine fostered Nassau village facilities as "of a resort area . . . with beaches and water sports . . . boating, fishing, bathing . . . natural landscape undisturbed . . . superb scenery."[14]

In addition to the system of state parks developed by Robert Moses, local government also devoted significant resources to park, recreational, and conservation programs. County Executive J. Russel Sprague foresaw the postwar expansion and proposed a major county park in 1944 on the old Salisbury Golf Course in East Meadow which was delinquent in tax payments. He urged that the 820 acre parcel be dedicated as a public park since "our county would not be complete without envisioning county-owned recreational facilities."[15] His proposal did not meet universal approval; as one letter to the editor commented: "It's a joke. We are surrounded by water and beaches and every backyard is a park. I'm sure I'm not going to pack a lunch and run out to Salisbury to eat it are you?"[16] Sprague persevered and today Salisbury, now Eisenhower Park, is one of the heaviest used Long Island facilities. County park development continued through the 1960s and 1970s with some additional five thousand acres of nature preserves, regional parks, and historic estates and preserves. Local villages and towns also greatly extended their facilities in the postwar years. Open space and recreation land presently comprises some 20 percent of Nassau's land area of 183,700 acres, and, combined with the 21,100 acres of estates, clearly represents the strong impact of recreation and environment on Nassau's land use and lifestyle.[17]

Changing recreational and sports interests have affected such activities in the last quarter of the twentieth century. With the decline of the great estates, polo has almost disappeared as has harness racing, which had a wildly popular period at Roosevelt Raceway in Westbury in the 1950s and 1960s. However, expanded league field sports, particularly for youth and young adults, in baseball, football, soccer, and lacrosse have dramatically increased participation. Golf has gained widespread popularity and new individual activities such as running and walking are reshaping leisure activities. *Newsday's* 1999 *Long Island Fun Book* delineates the county's changing and complex recreation resources including outdoor and waterside activities, golf, skating, and numerous organized team, spectator, and physically challenged sports. Visitation to Jones Beach tripled after World War II to more than ten million annually and the county's exceptional marine environment became one of the most active water sports and recreational resources in the nation. A whole maritime economy of marinas, shipyards, repair shops, bait and tackle stores, and restaurants grew along the county's shorelines. Preservation of the south shore bays, ocean fishing, and sound ecological conditions of Long Island Sound have been strong public issues in the last decade and will continue to be a challenge for the future to retain this special inheritance.

Nassau County has developed almost all its residential land to present zoning levels. New population patterns and the maturation of its infrastructure will affect future growth. The early twentieth century growth of the county centered on its extensive Gold Coast (which remains as an extensive green belt), and the marine environment of its north and south shores. Its unique ecological feature, the Hempstead Plains, provided a vital economic resource enabling growth of an aviation industry and vacant land for post-World War II population expansion. The large airfields in its center have become the major regional core center, Nassau's Hub, with educational, commercial, cultural, and recreational facilities.

Although the *Great Gatsby* lifestyle has disappeared, recreation, sports, and play are still major elements of county life. Nassau County continues its leadership and national prominence in this aspect of American culture, as evidenced by the new aquatic center in Eisenhower Park, the largest in the country and the U. S. Open golf tournament, which returns again to Nassau in 2002 at Bethpage State Park's premier Black Course. Nassau County's ecology and its concomitant recreational resources have been major determinants of its growth and development in the last century and will continue to influence its future in the new millennium.

Notes

1. Jean Gottmann, *Megalopolis* (New York: Twentieth Century Fund, 1961), 318-19.

2. Daniel Denton, *A Brief Description of New York,* 1670. (Reprint; New York: William Gowans, 1845), 28. (Sections dealing with Long Island are reprinted in "Daniel Denton's Long Island, 1670," in *The Roots and Heritage of Hempstead Town,* edited by Natalie A. Naylor [Interlaken, NY: Heart of the Lakes Publishing, 1994], 192-96. Editor's note.)

3. Theodore Roosevelt, *Theodore Roosevelt, An Autobiography* (New York: Macmillan, 1913), 342.

4. *New York Herald,* January 10, 1918, 3.

5. Peter Helck, *The Checkered Flag* (New York: C. Scribner's Sons, 1961), 43-63.

6. Russel Doubleday, *Long Island* (New York: Doubleday, Doran & Co., 1939), 5.

7. See the article in this volume by Roberta Fiore and Liz Coffin Allerhand, "Sand Bar to City: William H. Reynolds and the Planned Community of Long Beach, 1906-1922," 265-81. (Editor's note.)

8. *South Side Observer,* July 7, 1899, 2.

9. *Biltmore Shores* (Massapequa: Frankel Sales and Development Co., 1927), folder.

10. Robert Caro, *The Power Broker* (New York: Vintage Books, 1975), 209-23. See also *Robert Moses: Single-Minded Genius,* edited by Joann P. Krieg (Interlaken, NY: Heart of the Lakes Publishing, 1989).

11. Ralph H. Gabriel, *The Evolution of Long Island* (New Haven: Yale University Press, 1921), 166.

12. Preston A. Bassett, *Long Island, Cradle of Aviation* (Amityville: Long Island Forum, 1950), passim.

13. Joshua Stoff, Curator of Nassau County's Cradle of Aviation Museum, has written several books on Long Island and America's aviation history, including: *The Aerospace Heritage of Long Island* (Interlaken, NY: Heart of the Lakes Publishing, 1989); *From Airship to Spaceship: Long Island In Aviation and Spaceflight* (Interlaken, NY: Empire State Books, 1991); *Picture History of Early Aviation, 1903-1913* (New York: Dover, 1996); *Picture History of World War II American Aircraft Production* (New York: Dover, 1993); *Roosevelt Field: World's Premier Airport* (Terre Haute, IN: Sunshine House, 1992); *The Thunder Factory: An Illustrated History of the Republic Aviation Corporation* (Osceola, WI: Motorbooks International, 1990); and (with Charles R. Pellegrino), *Chariots for Apollo: The Making of the Lunar Module* (New York: Atheneum, 1985). See also George Dade and Frank Strnad, *Picture History of Aviation on Long Island, 1908-1938* (New York: Dover, 1989). Editor's note.

14. *New York Suburbs* (New York: Mega Publishers, 1960), 49-57.

15. *Newsday,* April 22, 1944, 4.

16. *Newsday,* April 10, 1947, 28.

17. *Nassau County Comprehensive Plan* (Mineola: County of Nassau, 1998), Appendix B-2. (See also Mildred Murphy DeRiggi, "Preserving Nassau County's Heritage in Museums and Parks," pp. 126-36 in this book. Editor's note.)

Public Education in the Bellmores, 1850–1950

Kenneth M. Foreman

The Bellmores, actually Bellmore and North Bellmore, are two unincorporated communities situated in the southeast part of Long Island's Town of Hempstead. They are bounded on the east by Wantagh, on the south by East Bay, on the west by Merrick, and on the north by East Meadow. Over a hundred-year period these two communities have moved to the forefront of progressive school districts by repeatedly accepting change and adapting their common school structure, always in the interests of better education.

By 1850 the original thirteen Hempstead common school districts, established under the 1812 New York State legislature, had been reorganized into twenty-four by the Town's Superintendent of Schools. District 4 encompassed the northern half of the Bellmores and North Merrick; District 7 covered the southern half of the Bellmores and Merrick.

In 1901 Merrick became School District 25 following intensive negotiation by a committee of its citizens with District 7's trustees, and the intervention of District Superintendent Dr. James S. Cooley. The western boundary of District 7 then became Wynsom Avenue, and later, in 1922, Cedar Swamp Creek. In 1921 North Merrick became District 29, with no resistance from the District 4 school board (governing what had been Smithville South, but changed in that year to North Bellmore), and with the concurrence of the District Superintendent.

Facilities

There is a theory that among the complex determinants of successful education, the schoolhouse remains one of the most important factors. Especially since the late nineteenth century, leading American educators have encouraged the public to view public school facilities as special, easily identifiable, and deserving of their lavish support because of the link between youth and future society.[1] Therefore, we review initially the development of Bellmore's school facilities.

In 1850, the one-room school building that had served District 4 since 1820 was located at Newbridge Road and Broad Street. Until 1890, typically two teachers taught a basic elementary education to an average of fifty pupils who attended regularly out of a student body twice that number. However, the overcrowding, caused by a steadily increasing student body, and the recommendation of the District Supervisor of Education convinced the trustees to authorize the construction of a new two-room building nearby on the east side of Newbridge Road in about 1900.

New legislation was passed in Albany in 1907, requiring school attendance between the ages of eight and sixteen and a minimum of 130 days instruction. Perhaps stimulated by these new educational standards, in that year the trustees belatedly petitioned and gained state approval for a Union Free School District (UFSD) designation.[2] The newly installed UFSD 4 Board of Education obtained public acceptance to finance a two-story Georgian-style school building costing $18,000. This 1908 frame building, constructed by local residents Charles Johnson and A. Frisch, immediately provided four main floor classrooms and a second story auditorium. After 1912, the upper story was partitioned into four more classrooms. The large cities of New York State had already instituted programs before 1900 for masonry construction of schools when, in the early 1920s the State Education Department issued statewide school construction guidelines requiring schools to be fire resistant.[3] Faced with an obsolete facility only sixteen years old and raising health and safety issues, District 4's School Board moved forward, with only mild community resistance in 1924, to erect a new eight-classroom red brick building, featuring a castellated roof line above the entrance at the Newbridge Road school grounds site. This facility, with further additions in 1927, is currently still an active center of a now multi-school system district.

District 7's school in 1850 was an 1836 vintage former chicken coop on Merrick Road near Hewlett Avenue. Pupils were crowded into this intolerable situation until 1888 when the trustees authorized construction of a two-room, clapboard-frame building still standing on Orange Street near Newbridge Road in Bellmore. Real estate development frenzy and rapid student population growth that forced the school building expansion in District 4, similarly also affected District 7, even after the transfer in 1901 of sixty-seven Merrick pupils to the new District 25. A new two-story, six classroom, frame building was approved and erected in 1908 on the east side of Bedford Avenue, north of Merrick Road in Bellmore. The building was a large square with many windows, three chimneys, and a square bell tower above the entrance. For a few years, further student growth was accommodated by a modest addition to this facility at a cost of $8,000. In 1922, however, the School Board was rudely awakened to the changing schoolhouse standards that no longer allowed them to follow prior action. They found it necessary to finance and gain Albany's approval for a new building of fireproof construction and of a form unmistakenly dedicated and impressive for the job of educating the next generation. The two-story, flat roofed, red brick building on Winthrop Avenue was dedicated in 1924 after costing $180,000.[4] It provided ten classrooms and an auditorium on the north end.

Further additions providing ten more classrooms started in 1927 and were dedicated in 1930, after an expenditure of another $250,000; these sufficed to meet District 7's elementary education requirements until 1950.

Student Body

Prior to 1870, both Bellmores were primarily rural agricultural communities. The traditional seasonal demands on the time of the average farmer's children prevented their continuous attendance for the full school term even if children's predilection to be truant was not the cause. Education was held in high regard, yet only about half of the 80 to 120 enrolled girls and boys of District 4 were present on any one school day.

In District 7, after 1870, the newly installed railroad made the hamlet accessible to Brooklyn business and professional people who became residents and commuters. Their children could attend school with regularity, and the parents were supportive of a full elementary preparation to enable going on to secondary education. At the turn of the century large farms were being sub-divided into private home sites in School Districts 4 and 7. A good public education system was important for those families in the market for homes. The rural public school had offered its pupils only a rudimentary education, but it had promoted moral and social community values. In both districts, the interaction of children of different ages in daily contact in the single classroom and with the same teacher formed a heterogenous group sharing common interests, experiences, and traditions. But pragmatic solutions to changing public desires, as the community began a transition to suburbia, carried the danger of undermining the sterner moral code of the formerly rural environment. Compounding this situation was the overcrowding due to the rapid and accelerating increase in student enrollment as sales of new single family housing blossomed. After 1915, enhanced mobility from wider use of autos and road improvement programs made the 1920s an era of the first great suburban growth.

The total student enrollment in District 4 reached 160 in the year Nassau County was formed. District 7 enrolled 100 pupils in 1899 but lost 60 of them when Merrick's District 25 was formed in 1901. By 1913, District 4 enrolled 275 youngsters and this grew over five times to 875 in 1931, or an average of almost 18 percent per year. Statistics for 1915 indicate an average of 69 percent of the total enrollment of 349 were in daily attendance.[5] District 7's rate of increase from 80 in 1913 to a 1931 high water mark of 700 can be judged by the related rate of increase in its eighth grade graduating classes from ten in 1922 to fifty in 1930, or more than a 60 percent increase per year. More importantly, average daily attendance increased from about 58 percent in 1900 to 73 percent in 1915, as the compulsory education regulations were enforced more vigorously and viewed more sympathetically by parents.[6]

Elementary School Faculty

Teachers of country elementary schools in the 1800s were more like tradespeople than professionals. They contracted individually with school trustees on a yearly basis, and frequently moved from one district to another offering them a higher salary. Usually the better paying districts were closer to the city, or larger. Teachers, at best, had only high school training, but this background sufficed to teach the three Rs. In some cases, like Thomas D. Smith and Anthony Waring, teachers were over-qualified. Waring of District 4, and Smith of District 7, were country lawyers. After teaching school between 1865 and 1867, Smith went on to be a land surveyor and was politically active enough to become a Town supervisor.

Between 1850 and 1890 each district hired two teachers, usually male, who were recruited from the nearby communities. But in 1895, District 4 hired Miss Carrie Fish as principal, and Minnie MacDonald for the primary grade pupils; MacDonald bicycled in from Massapequa most of the school year.[7] A few years later, in 1899, Miss Fish moved up to head the District 7 school (built in 1888), and a Miss Shephard taught the higher grades.

With the formation of Nassau County, new civic pride raised the aspirations of the school trustees, and they started to seek graduates of the normal schools.[8] While the principals were men, women who had attended such schools as New Paltz, Oneonta, and Albany State were interviewed to fill teaching positions. However, even these professionally trained educators continued to move on after two to five years, either to another school for higher pay or a career change.

Principal Frank Hyle of District 7 was one of those exceptions who had a long connection with the community. First hired in 1920, succeeding New Paltz alumni Corodon Norton, Hyle had the satisfaction of directing the rapid growth of the District during the 1920s and into the 1930s, in both facilities and faculty (from five in 1921 to twenty-three in 1931). Earlier, in 1904, District 4, being somewhat larger in student enrollment, was able to entice Dr. George Newton (of Freeport) as principal and teacher. In 1906, a quiet, young-looking new teacher from upstate New York, Wellington C. Mepham, was contacted and hired as principal by the District. Two years later he moved on to Merrick's District. But his influence on the quality of education in the Bellmores proved pervasive for three decades after he became Second District Superintendent in 1912. Meanwhile, Indiana Normal (of Pennsylvania) graduate, Raymond Hilton, was hired in 1908 as principal and teacher where he remained until 1921, when William Schermerhorn became District 4 principal. He was followed by Dr. Edward McCleary in 1934. During the two decades after 1910, District 4's teaching staff grew from five to twenty-six. The war years interrupted the careers of many capable educators including Dr. McCleary who had been brought to the Bellmores in the 1930s. Upon their return to civilian life they faced an unprecedented challenge because of the explosive population growth into and beyond the 1950s. They also inherited better working and contract representation conditions, and more cosmopolitan education boards that generally were sympathetic and supportive for the huge task ahead.

A 1917 state survey concluded that teachers' salaries for 1915 were in the $400 to $700 per year range in the Town of Hempstead. District 4's principal, Ray Hilton, was hired in 1908 at a $650 annual rate, but by 1918 his salary had increased by annual increments to $1,150. Teachers with less experience were hired at $450 per year in 1908 and $500 in 1918. An experienced teacher, Katti Torance, had been hired by District 4 for $550 per year in 1914, which grew to $650 per year in 1918. However, the survey found that experience alone appeared not to change the conventional $25 or $50 per year trustees' incremental salary policy. The "creeping growth" of salaries continued into the "roaring" twenties. District 7's principal Corodon Norton earned $1,560 per year in 1920, and his teachers' annual salaries ranged between $900 and $1,080. Norton's successor, Frank Hyle, received $1,800 for his first year, in 1921, and his four teachers who taught at two grade levels each earned $1,200. Hyle entered District 7 with twenty years experience and retired in 1941, having doubled his salary in the interim. When Hyle left, the faculty numbered twenty-three whose salaries ranged from $1,200 to $1,800 depending on their grade level assignment and special skills, such as piano playing. Hyle was succeeded by H. Curtis Herge at a salary of $3,400; Herge previously had been with the Bayville UFSD and brought with him several new ideas to interest the trustees, including enrichment of curriculum and deliberate male teacher recruitment to give upper-grade school boys role models. He appears to have ingratiated himself with the taxpayers because he was offered a four-year contract renewal after his first year. Dana Smith became the next Supervisory Principal in 1947. He supervised the District's accommodation to the second, and unprecedentedly greater, pupil growth period into the 1950s.

Secondary School Education

Since the inception of public schooling in the Bellmores, secondary education was the unmentioned and forgotten provision for the districts' eighth grade graduates. State law in 1853 allowed public high schools to be built in the larger villages and cities that could afford the expense. By the turn of the century, Bellmore parents could arrange to pay for their qualified children in non-resident status openings in high schools of Freeport, Baldwin, Hempstead, and Amityville.

This improvisation was challenged in 1916 by a number of District 4 parents led by local lawyer Francis Deckel. The School Board rejected Mr.

Deckel's request for high school tuition reimbursement in July 1916. Board President Thornton ruled that state law didn't require any more than a common school education be provided. Mr. Deckel appealed and filed for a special taxpayers' meeting to provide the District's graduates with grades 9 to 12 education. The mid-December meeting resulted in an indefinite tabling of the proposition. Deckel persisted in a letter campaign to the State Commissioner of Education, where, surprisingly, he obtained a supportive reaction. Albany directed District 4's Board to confer with Superintendent Mepham on details. The Board continued to resist this action and their appeals were rejected until finally in November 1917, Principal Hilton was instructed to list students entitled to attend high school. Parents of three students already attending Baldwin High School were notified to send their tuition bills to the District Clerk; Mr. Deckel received a $50 tuition reimbursement.

The consequences of being made legally and morally responsible for high school education spilled beyond the boundaries of District 4. It cost District 7, typically, $480 a year for twelve graduates attending Baldwin High School in 1923; the two Karp sisters (of Bellmore) cost the District $100 for attending Amityville High School. These stop-gap measures ceased in 1934 when the Baldwin High School class openings became filled with Baldwin residents' children. By that year more than 125 graduates of District 7 alone were commuting to Baldwin High School. The two Bellmore districts started urgently to examine their options. Superintendent W. C. Mepham helpfully called attention to a 1917 state law encouraging formation of a Central High School District (CHSD) for neighboring districts too small to maintain small high schools alone. The law had been further strengthened in 1925 with provisions to use state money for transportation and 25 percent of building costs and operations, if the cooperating districts would forego civic pride. Because the two adjacent Merrick districts faced identical problems, Mepham suggested they could also become CHSD components.

On September 25, 1934, the issue of a CHSD was discussed in a joint meeting of the four districts and passed by a vote of 712 to 67. Commissioner Frank Graves officially established CHSD 3 on November 1, 1934, encompassing an area of 14.5 square miles and a population of 15,000. Architect Fred P. Wiedersum was selected to design the building, and, at a special meeting, an overwhelming vote approved the purchase of twenty-one acres in North Bellmore at a cost of $49,800 and the budgeting of $810,00 for the high school building. The site of the school was on the north side of Camp Avenue, east of Cedar Swamp Creek, and almost centrally located to the four districts. Wiedersum's clean modern design with the gym on one end and the 850-seat auditorium on the east end, was a fitting setting in which to

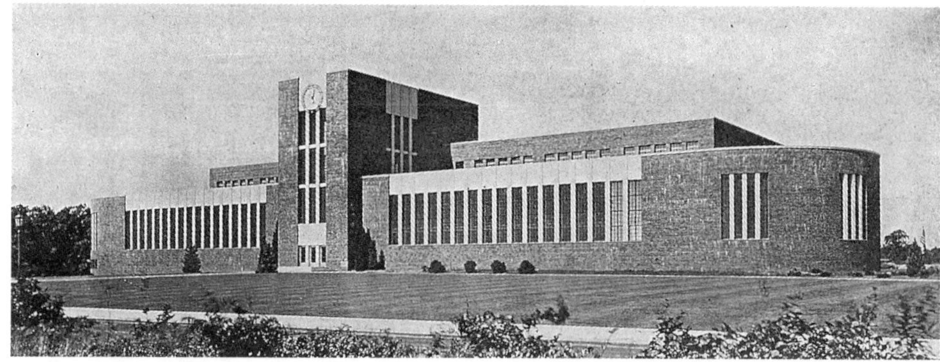

Wellington C. Mepham High School Building for CHSD 3 was completed in 1937. Photograph courtesy of the Historical Society of the Bellmores.

develop the CHSD innovative approach and motivate students (see illustration).

Sanford Calhoun of Troy, New York, and previously Supervising Principal of Sag Harbor's high school for five years, was hired at a $5,000 salary to head the CHSD. Calhoun had a Master's degree in educational administration from Columbia University's Teachers College. With an initial staff of five teachers and a student body of 150 freshmen, classes were begun in September 1935 in six classrooms of the 1908 vintage Bellmore school building. In January 1936, ninety-seven more students entered the high school. The new high school building was dedicated in September 1937 for 741 students and a faculty of seventeen, including a nurse and dental hygienist. The home district distribution of the students was 26.5 percent North Bellmore, 25.6 percent Bellmore, 22.2 percent Merrick, 15 percent North Merrick, and the balance of 9.8 percent from neighboring districts.

The initial staff came from as near as Wantagh, Long Island, and from nine states as far away as California and Florida It included fourteen men and twenty-four women, but excluded married women.[9] The 1936-1937 budget for operations was $100,438. By 1941, there were already 1,100 students, forty-five faculty members, forty-three classrooms in use, and a $215,000 budget. The average salary of the thirty-eight teachers in the 1938-1939 school year was $2,000. Physical Education instructor, Frank Gardner, was the highest paid, at $3,000, which was in consideration of his sports coaching duties. Garner produced many championship wrestling teams, which helped Mepham's early reputation and student morale. The course of study included English, Social Studies, Music, Art, Language, Mathematics, Science, Biology, Commercial (business subjects), Home Economics, and Industrial Arts.

The Mepham graduate of 1940 was mindful of the high (12 percent) unemployment situation ahead. At the second commencement exercise in

1940, with the overall theme "The Socially Competent Individual," one student speaker defined this as, "one who has learned to employ [his] best abilities in the highest interests of his fellow man." Regarding the objective of the secondary school, several graduating students' recommendations were pragmatic, "preparation and training for economic security . . . provide a basis for physical and mental health, and . . . produce a base for cultural and spiritual development." From these responses, it would appear that moral values of the rural past had not been compromised by the change in student body homogeneity. New student relationships developed based on the high school culture of academics and sports instead of on local community identity.

The outbreak of war caused many dislocations in the CHSD operation. After two years of wartime service in the Air Force, Mr. Calhoun returned, together with several other former Mepham teachers, to continue the implementation of the CHSD approach to public education. By 1950, the CHSD budget of $446,900 exceeded the combined budgets of the Bellmores, and thought was being given to extending the CHSD responsibility for the seventh and eighth grades of the CHSD 3 component districts by means of junior high school facilities.

Conclusion

From a rural area of the 1850s which provided the barest of an elementary education, with inadequately trained teachers and in dismal, crowded facilities, to 1950, the Bellmores had moved to the forefront of progressive school districts. In making the transition to a suburban community, two pivotal changes stand out in the one hundred year period briefly reviewed.

The first, beginning shortly after the formation of Nassau County, and taking two decades to complete, was the steady upgrading of the caliber and professionalism of the teaching corps, and provision of state-of-the-art school houses. The district trustees were important in accomplishing this movement. Like many other Town of Hempstead school boards of small districts, Bellmore's trustees had to find ways of paying the cost of implementing state mandated measures, while remaining responsive to local expectations for quality education. Lobbying for more state aid became an increasingly sought-after option.

The second outstanding public education development in the Bellmores was the initiation, in 1917, of secondary education opportunities. The recognition and acceptance by the Boards of Education (with state prodding) of the right of elementary school graduates to higher education ultimately led to the innovative centralized high school approach. Without relinquishing local district board representation and control, a cooperative educator/community relationship took hold in the mid-1930s, and continues to be demonstrated with an economical and high-performance-yielding educational environment.

Notes

The author acknowledges with thanks information provided by John Dinkelmeyer, Grace Hickey, and Mary Ann Agiato, and access to unpublished school records now retained in the Archives of the Historical Society of the Bellmores. Tom Saltzman of the Town of Hempstead's Town Clerk's Office also was helpful in making available the Town's School Records. All information not specifically cited is from these records.

1. William W. Cutler III, "Cathedral of Culture: the Schoolhouse in American Educational Thought and Practice Since 1820," *History of Education Quarterly* 29, no. 1 (Spring 1989): 1.

2. The New York State Legislature had first authorized the formation and designation of Union Free School Districts in 1853.

3. Cutler, "Cathedral of Culture," 8-9.

4. Kenneth M. Foreman, "Bellmore's Brick School House," *Long Island Forum* 60 (Fall 1997): 36-41.

5. University of the State of New York, *Report of a Survey of Public Education in Nassau County, New York, Bulletin*, no. 652 (December 1, 1917): 5-242. Available at the Long Island Studies Institute, Hofstra University (Nassau County Museum Collection, 379.2).

6. "Commissioners' Reports—Nassau County," Department of Public Instruction, Forty-sixth Annual Report for the Year ending July 31, 1899 (Albany: James B. Lyon, 1900), 361-63. Available at the Long Island Studies Institute, Hofstra University (Nassau County Museum Collection, 379.747).

7. Carrie Fish of East Meadow had attended Albany State Normal School, and her name appears on District 4's teacher records as far back as 1875. Her career in education continued in teaching and supervisory positions for the smaller Long Island school districts such as Plainview, up through the mid-1910s. Elbert Fish, a relative, also was active as a trustee of the Bellmore school district during this time.

8. Normal schools initially offered a two or three-year course of study and teacher training. Albany State was the first in New York State, established in 1844. Beginning in 1938, these normal schools preparing elementary teachers developed into four-year teachers colleges; later they became liberal arts colleges.

9. This policy was, presumably, a response to high unemployment conditions among (male) teachers, who were also head of a family, during the 1930s Depression. However, married female teachers were hired during these years for elementary school positions in the Bellmore districts, continuing a practice of the 1920s. But single female elementary teachers were hired under contracts that became invalidated if the teacher married during the contract period. These restrictions gradually disappeared in the 1940s.

From Orchard Street to Sunrise Highway: The Establishment of Jewish Communities in Nassau County, 1897-1999

Martha Kreisel

On September 12, 1654, the first Jewish services in North America were held in secret by the founders of New York Jewry. This was the modest beginning of the oldest existing Jewish congregation in North America, Congregation Shearith Israel—the Spanish and Portuguese Synagogue of New York. In 1656 the congregants acquired the ground for a Jewish cemetery and in 1673 public services were held in a rented room on Beaver Street in New Amsterdam.[1]

Long Island had been traveled by Jewish merchants from New York City as far back as the 1660s, but no permanent record was left by these early settlers. The Island, which was to remain for another two centuries "rural with an economy based on agriculture and the water," was separated from New York City by life-style as much as by its 118 actual miles. The Jewish peddlers who traveled through Nassau and Suffolk counties carrying their packs had a demanding occupation. The forty mile trip from Jamaica to Setauket had to be made from after sundown on Saturday to sundown on Friday night so that the Sabbath could be observed.[2]

> The pack itself has been described as enormous; it could have weighed close to two hundred pounds and made of striped mattress ticking, and filled with small soft, unbreakable items—ribbons, needles, pins, and the like. . . . It could take hours to unpack, have a farmer's or bayman's wife sort through to choose her purchases, then repack. Often [the peddler] carried two suitcases, one in each hand for balance.[3]

Although no Jewish community was established in these early years of what was to become Nassau, and no Jewish cemeteries purchased, nor organized religious service conducted in the eighteenth and early nineteenth centuries, there was a handful of Jews scattered throughout the county. Between 1840 and 1870, German Jews arriving in America peddled their way out to the principal Long Island trading villages of Jericho, Lynbrook, Hempstead, Glen Cove, Rockville Centre, and Port Washington, where some chose to settle. By the 1870s and 1880s the eastern European Jews who had arrived in New York City began to move east from the city to establish the first major Jewish settlement on Long Island, in Sag Harbor. In the late 1880s,

Adolph Levy, a Russian immigrant began peddling among the clam diggers in the waterfront shacks from Baldwin to Massapequa. Eventually Levy would make a Seaford hotel his base, until he bought the hotel and could host other traveling salesman. At the turn of the century Levy moved to Freeport and opened a men's clothing store.[4] By the 1890s, German-Jewish vacationers who spent summers in the seaside villages on the Rockaway Peninsula, and the peddlers who saw opportunities in rural Queens villages, helped to establish early permanent Jewish settlements in Nassau County.[5]

As the peddlers moved east onto Long Island, communities like Glen Cove could offer the prospects of jobs. By 1868, Samuel Sandman, who was in the real estate business, became the first Jew to settle in Glen Cove. He was soon followed by Benjamin Cohen and Barney Friedman who ran a general store and arrived in the 1870s. In the 1880s the Glen Cove Jewish community was increased by the arrival of Isaac and Esther Bessel who ran a horse farm. These early Jewish families held services in local homes for almost twenty years, using a Torah that the Bessels owned. It is still in use today. By the year 1897, the Jewish community of Glen Cove had grown large enough to be able to establish a synagogue, *Tifereth Israel,* the earliest one in Nassau County, and only the second on Long Island.[6] In 1900 the Jewish community bought a building called the "opera house" and used it as a synagogue until 1925. The "opera house" on Continental Place was razed in 1926 and a new synagogue was erected in its place. The 1927 building still stands in downtown Glen Cove. In 1955 construction was begun on a new building on Landing Road.[7]

With the first large wave of immigration from Europe in the 1880s and 1890s, Glen Cove's Jewish population increased. "The newcomers sold men's wear, and jewelry, Jacob Feinberg was the baker and Smith Levine and Harry Lifshitz were the shochetim or ritual slaughterers. They provided the chickens for the community and traveled to New York City at least twice a week to bring back meat in their ice wagons."[8] After encountering anti-Semitism in Hicksville, Bernard Singer moved to Glen Cove. He peddled sewing supplies from a cart and then from a horse and wagon. In 1901 he opened Singer's Department Store on School Street, later moving it to Glen Street. The store survived almost a century.[9]

As the Jewish peddlers, factory workers, and storekeepers moved into Nassau and established the early communities, so did the Guggenheims and Kahns come to the shores of Nassau for the summer ocean breezes, and stayed to build the mansions on the Island's Gold Coast. Great Neck and other North Shore communities also began to attract Jewish families at the turn of the century. Abram Wolf, a tailor, was the first Jew to settle in Great Neck. He may have been brought to Great Neck in 1875 by W. R. Grace, the shipping magnate. Wolf later went into the real estate and insurance business.[10] But "it took another twenty-one years for another Jew to join Wolf in Great Neck. He was Morris Lefkowitz, a wagoneer, who later built Belgrave Motors."[11]

By the 1920s Great Neck had become home for many wealthy Jewish manufacturers and celebrities, among them Eddie Cantor and Groucho Marx, even though some in the Great Neck village openly barred Jewish homeowners until the 1930s. In the early years, in order to attend services on the High Holidays, the Jews of Great Neck had to travel to Brooklyn or the Bronx and stay overnight. Finally, in 1928, Temple Beth-el was founded by Jews as a Reform synagogue. Since it was the only synagogue in the community, people of diverse background joined. This arrangement proved difficult, and in 1940 Temple Israel, with a more conservative religious orientation, was formed.[12] Throughout the years there would be other Nassau County Jewish communities where synagogues were organized by congregants of varying Jewish backgrounds. Compromises were made in the services to accommodate Orthodox, Conservative, and Reform worshipers, but many of these alliances failed. Splinter groups formed their own congregations to adhere to their style of Judaism.

Although they came from different backgrounds, practicing different Jewish customs, many of the initial experiences in the formation of Jewish communities in the suburbs of New York had common beginnings. Many of the early congregations could barely call upon the ten Jewish men needed to hold a service and had no formal place to worship. As the numbers of Jewish families in Nassau increased, they began to meet in their own homes, storefronts, real estate offices, converted barns and taverns, local churches, and firehouses. Many early congregations had to meet each week in a different location. Some worshipers had to bring their own chairs to services, and many early congregations had a portable ark by which a Torah could be carried from location to location. Jewish men from several neighboring towns often walked many miles to attend one prayer service. Services were led by student or intern Rabbis who were often only called to officiate the services on Shabbat or the High Holidays. Many of them stayed on to become permanent Rabbis for the newly organized communities.

Shaaray Tefila of Lawrence, one of the oldest Orthodox congregations in Nassau County, was founded in 1909. It actually had its beginnings in Far Rockaway, but by 1925 a new building was built in Lawrence.[13] Temple Israel, a Reform congregation also in Lawrence had a similar beginning. It actually was founded in 1908 in Far Rockaway and its first permanent home was built in 1911. In 1930 the building was sold and the congregation moved across the city line into Nassau. Membership stood at about one thousand families for many years.[14]

Barnett Salke, who had moved to Hempstead during the Civil War was one of its earliest Jewish settlers. By the turn-of-the-century there were a few Jewish storekeepers in Hempstead. "But it wasn't until 1901 that Adolphe Rosenthal brought [this handful of storekeepers] together at a meeting in Rockville Centre to discuss starting a congregation. The initial attempt failed because of an inability to round-up the necessary minyan" of ten men.[15] Like other contemporaries, they had to travel to New York or Brooklyn to worship for the High Holidays.

Finally, in 1908 Jewish men from Hempstead, Freeport, and Rockville Centre held services in various locations in the village of Hempstead. By 1914 a plot of land was purchased on Center Street by the Hempstead Hebrew Congregation, but it was not until 1919 that enough money could be raised to construct a synagogue. The congregation outgrew the building; in 1944 funds were raised to purchase the Onderdonk property on West Fulton Avenue. Additional funds were raised in 1948 to purchase the adjoining Allaire property. The Greek-revival synagogue was dedicated in 1950. By the 1970s the demographics of Hempstead had changed with many of the Jewish families moving away. The synagogue was sold for use as a Korean Methodist Church, and the few remaining families moved their place of worship to a private home.[16]

Also, before the turn of the century, Jewish families had moved into Farmingdale and formed the Farmingdale Hebrew Association, holding services there in the home of Jacob Kranzler at the southwest corner of Main and Front Streets. In 1899 Aaron Stern, another Jewish resident of Farmingdale, opened his pickle processing plant, which would become known as Stern's Pickle Products, an establishment that would continue in operation until the 1980s.[17]

Permanent Jewish communities were being established in Long Beach and the Five Towns as summer residents began to stay year-round. Large numbers of Jewish families moved to Long Island as the draftees trained in Camps Yaphank and Upton were called for duty in World War I. After their return from service, many chose to remain on the Island.[18]

The first quarter of the twentieth-century in Nassau was also a time of social turmoil. It was a time of subtle and not-so-subtle anti-Semitism. "Galvanized by the great waves of immigrants from Europe . . . a new generation of Klansmen sprung up in Georgia in 1915 and spread to the North. . . . Historians estimate [that in the late 1920s] one out of seven to eight Long Island residents was a Klan member"[19] spreading their message of hatred that "Jews and Catholics were a danger to the nation."[20] On August 14, 1924, Ernest Louis, a Jewish druggist in Freeport, received threats from local Klansmen, and when he refused to leave, was kidnapped and released in Hicksville. A month later Louis sold his business and moved from New York.[21]

According to Bernard Postal, "as late as 1915, Long Beach . . . was dotted with clubs and hotels that refused to admit Jews. Most golf and country clubs, or resorts on Long Island . . . were not open to Jews." It was not uncommon in the 1930s to see Nazi Bundist parades and rallies in villages and streets of the county. "Zoning ordinances were invoked in efforts to bar the construction of synagogues in some Long Island . . . communities in the 1940s and 1950s and it took a while before Jewish home buyers broke through unwritten restrictions" in towns such as Garden City.[22]

In the 1950s the congregants of the Community Synagogue in the village of Sands Point had to take the village to court in order to establish its home at an historic estate. Finally in 1956 "the State Court of Appeals ordered the village to grant the synagogue the necessary permit to establish a house of worship at the Chimneys, former estate of Fleischman Yeast heiress Bettie Holmes."[23]

The beginning of what Jacob Marcus has called the "Voluntary Suburban Ghetto," came at the end of World War I. American Jews have always been joined by a consciousness of a common past and tradition—a sense of kinship. They moved out to the suburbs, and congregated together to "create voluntary physical and psychological havens," by the pull of Jewish communality and Zionism, and to insure their survival as Jews and the survival of Jewish practices.[24] "The rise of Nazi anti-Semitism and its American imitators welded all Jews together, if only through resentment, shock, and despair. Intense Jewish sympathies and loyalties were engendered by Zionism, which recommended itself increasingly as an effective defense against the burgeoning anti-Semitic threat."[25]

The era of the Depression brought its own problems. When the Merrick Jewish Centre was started in 1928 dues were $28 per family. Members caught by the Depression had their dues waived during those difficult years. The congregation voted to help some of the less fortunate members and by 1932 outstanding dues were forgiven. Rockville Centre's Central Synagogue of Nassau County was somewhat typical of the pre-World War II congregations. Efforts were begun in 1940 to start a synagogue fund, but as the war began, fund-raising efforts were slowed as members gave money to war bonds appeals. Even their Rabbi left the county to serve as a military chaplain. By 1944, the Rabbi returned to the Synagogue and the congregation swelled with the families of the returning veterans.[26]

The largest movement of Jewish families to Nassau County came at the end of World War II. Thousands of New York City veterans, many newly married and unable to find housing in the city, streamed into the new low-cost housing developments that were springing up all over Nassau County. What

Jewish Population in Nassau County, 1900-1998

	Jewish Population	Total Nassau County Population	Jewish % of Total County Population
1900	1,000	55,448	1.8
1910	1,500	83,930	1.8
1920	3,000	126,120	2.4
1930	6,000	303,053	1.9
1940	17,300	406,748	3.7
1950	155,000	672,765	23.0
1960	345,000	1,300,171	26.5
1970	372,000	1,428,838	26.0
1980	395,000	1,321,582	29.8
1990	311,000	1,287,348	24.0
1998	207,000	1,302,220	15.8

Source: *Long Island Almanac* (Ronkonkoma: Long Island Business, 1997); U.S. Census Bureau, "County Population Estimates for July 1, 1998"; Bethamie Horowitz *New York Jewish Population Study* (New York: United Jewish Appeal 1995); and Council of Jewish Federations, unpublished data (for 1998)

had been potato fields, peach orchards, or land fills, soon became instant Jewish communities. At first the new congregations met in taverns and firehouses, schools, churches, and Masonic halls. But as the communities became more established there was a rush to build new synagogues. William Levitt even donated land in Levittown for the community to build Levittown's Israel Community Center. In the older communities synagogue expansions were needed to accommodate the newcomers. "A second wave of Jewish migration from New York in the early 1950s carried the Jewish population to the North Shore, the far edges of Nassau County and into the western part of Suffolk County." As Jewish families prospered, they began to leave the smaller, mass-designed developments for custom-built homes in the more affluent communities of the Five Towns and the North Shore communities.[27]

"By the 1960s a new trend had set in. Nassau County had run out of land for large scale housing developments but garden and cooperative apartments were beginning to sprout. Older families that had roots on Long Island and preferred to stay in the suburbs eagerly became renters once again. The concept of an apartment in the sun in the beach areas also attracted former Jewish home owners to the new high rise apartments in Long Beach. . . . At the same time, communities that were once heavily Jewish, became less so.

Rockville Centre, which developed into a major Catholic community . . . lost much of its Jewish population. As Jewish families with grown children departed for the city, suburban apartments, or Florida and Arizona and were replaced by non-Jews, synagogue membership on Long Island which once numbered 80 percent of the total Jewish population began to fall off."[28]

The rise to power of the Ayatollah Koumenei in the late 1960s forced Iranian Jews to flee their homeland and many moved to Great Neck to join other Sephardic Jews who were then holding services in the Great Neck Synagogue.[29] The new immigrants have brought to Nassau County, as did the immigrants of the last century, a new blend of Jewish customs and traditions. In September 1998, more than two hundred Iraqi Jews were celebrating the official opening of the Babylonian Jewish Center in Great Neck. Its mission is to strive to create an environment in which to preserve the traditions of their subtly distinct style of Jewish worship.[30]

"In 1963 there were 109 congregations in Nassau County, all with full-time rabbis and their own buildings. In the 1970s there were 130," and today the number is down to approximately 115, a reflection of the overall population trends of the county.[31]

For many synagogues on Long Island the 1980s and 1990s were times of retrenchment and struggle. The region's Jewish population has been declining, and some congregations are faced with the prospect of closing or merging with others. Baby Boomer families had less children than their parents. Many are about to retire and are moving away, as did the previous generations who have died or retired to warmer climates. But the cycle continues with a new-found exodus of Orthodox families with many children who are leaving New York City to live in areas such as the Five Towns.[32] Older congregations in need of revitalization have courted these families, set up housing assistance for them and, in several synagogues, reorganized their services to meet the more traditional practices of these new members.

More than 340 years ago a handful of Jewish refugees found a grudging haven in New Amsterdam. More than one hundred years ago the immigrant, low-income, embattled Jews of New York began to move eastward to Nassau and in that time have established themselves into a well-educated, middle-class community.[33] The children and grandchildren of Eastern European immigrants now live and worship with the children of Russian, Iraqi, and Israeli Jews in more than one hundred synagogues in Nassau County. This brief study provides only a sampling of the rich history of the establishment of Jewish communities in Nassau County. There is much more work that can be done; in a sense it is a work in progress.

Notes

1. Bernard Postal, *Jewish Landmarks in New York: An Informal History* (New York: Hill and Wang, 1964), 18.

2. Helene Gerard, "Yankees in Yarmulkes: Small-Town Jewish Life in Eastern Long Island," *American Jewish Archives* 38, no. 1 (1986): 25.

3. Gerard, "Yankees in Yarmulkes," 27.

4. Bernard Postal and Lionel Koppman, *American Jewish Landmarks: A Travel Guide and History,* 2 vols. (New York: Fleet Press, 1977), 1: 297-98.

5. Postal, *Jewish Landmarks,* 48.

6. Stuart Vincent, "Long Island's Founding Jews: Although far apart, Sag Harbor and Glen Cove both had early Jewish communities," in Newsday, *Long Island Our Story* (Melville: Newsday, 1998), 229; also at http://www.lihistory.com/6/hs629a.htm web site.

7. Postal and Koppman, *American Jewish Landmarks,* 299.

8. *"That I May Dwell Among Them": A Synagogue History of Nassau County* (New York: Conference of Jewish Organizations of Nassau County, 1991), 46.

9. Vincent, "Long Island's Founding Jews," 229.

10. Postal and Koppman, *American Jewish Landmarks,* 1: 298, 300.

11. *"That I May Dwell Among Them,"* 57.

12. *"That I May Dwell Among Them,"* 57-59.

13. *"That I May Dwell Among Them,"* 82.

14. *"That I May Dwell Among Them,"* 78.

15. *"That I May Dwell Among Them,"* 65.

16. *"That I May Dwell Among Them,"* 66-67.

17. *"That I May Dwell Among Them,"* 39.

18. Postal, *Jewish Landmarks,* 50.

19. David Behrens, "The KKK Flares up on LI: In the early 1920s, white robes and burning crosses are seen in many villages," in Newsday, *Long Island Our Story,* 293; also at http://www.lihistory.com/history/7/hs725a.htm web site.

20. Behrens, "KKK," 1.

21. "KKK," *Newsday,* May 6, 1965, 2.

22. Postal, *Jewish Landmarks,* 57.

23. Stuart Vincent, "The House That Faith Built: Synagogue to be Finished Years After Court Battle," *Newsday,* May 21, 1995, 4.

24. Jacob Marcus, *Studies in American Jewish History* (Cincinnati: Hebrew Union College Press, 1969), 204, 207.

25. Marcus, *Studies in American Jewish History,* 204.

26. *"That I May Dwell Among Them,"* 139.

27. Postal and Koppman, *American Jewish Landmarks,* 301, 302.

28. Postal and Koppman, *American Jewish Landmarks,* 302.

29. *"That I May Dwell Among Them,"* 57.

30. Joy Alter Hubel, "New Home for an Ancient Culture," *The Long Island Jewish Week,* September 25, 1998, 22.

31. Postal and Koppman, *American Jewish Landmarks,* 302.

32. Stuart Vincent, "LI Jewish Population Drops: Shift to Sun Belt forces synagogues to adapt to survive," *Newsday,* August 16, 1992, 6.

33. Postal, *Jewish Landmarks,* 94.

Additional Works Consulted

Behrens, David. "Growing Up With Subtle Anti-Semitism." *Newsday,* May 10, 1998, sec. A, p. 41. Reprinted in Newsday, *Long Island: Our Story,* 298. Melville: Newsday, 1998.

Blumenstein, Rebecca. "Jews Leaving LI." *Newsday,* October 16, 1993, 6.

Bookbinder, Bernie. *Long Island: People and Places, Past and Present.* New York: Harry N. Abrams, 1983.

D'Antonio, Michael. "Orthodox Jews: The Lure of Long Island." *Newsday,* August 12, 1986, sec. 2, pp. 4-5.

Dobkin, William S. "No Delancey Street for These Immigrants." *Newsday,* April 4, 1989, 61.

Eisenberg, Carol. "Plan for Great Neck Synagogue Opposed." *Newsday,* September 15, 1989, 29.

——. "Rift Over Plains for Synagogue." *Newsday,* October 1, 1989, 1.

Fried, Heidi. "Early Jewish Settlements in Nassau County: The Communities, the People, The Synagogues." Master's essay, Hofstra University, 1988. Copy in Hofstra University's Special Collections, Long Island Studies Institute.

——. "Early Jewish Settlement in Nassau County," *Nassau County Historical Society Journal* 44 (1989): 21-33.

——. "Kosher Style Judaism Meets the Mikvah: A Conflict of Values in the Five Towns," Senior paper, SUNY Purchase, 1986. Copy in the Hofstra University vertical file (Jews), Long Island Studies Institute.

Gerard, Helene. "Yankees in Yarmulkes: Small-Town Jewish Life in Eastern Long Island." *American Jewish Archives* 38, no. 1 (1986): 22-56.

"KKK." *Newsday,* May 6, 1965, 2.

Mondello, Lynn Marie. "Continuing the Family Tradition." *Newsday,* December 4, 1994, sec. A, p. 89.

Nelson, Soraya Sarhaddi. "Melting Pot Housed Under One Roof: Glen Cove Synagogue Provides a Second Home for Diverse Worshipers." *Newsday,* April 20, 1997, sec. E, p. 13.

Powell, Amy. "1st Jews Came to Long Island Three Hundred Years Ago." *Long Island Sunday Press,* February 13, 1955.

Singer, Cathy. "Immigrants' Influx Changed L. I. Persian-Jews' Life Style." *New York Times,* March 21, 1993, Long Island sec., 14, p. 8

——. "Iranian Immigrants Blend Old and New." *New York Times,* March 21, 1993, Long Island sec., 14, p. 1.

Smith, Andrew. "Great Neck: A Jewel in a Gold Coast Setting." *Newsday,* http://www.lihistory.com/history/spectown/hist0029.htm.

Vincent, Stuart. "Keeping the Faith: Reflections on the History—and the Future—of the Synagogues Founded by Long Island's First Jewish Settlers." *Newsday,* August 25, 1992, 48.

The American Welfare State and the Growth of Suburbia: Nassau County, A Case Study

Hugh A. Wilson

Scholarly explanations of the explosive post-war suburban population growth have emphasized four models: self-selection,[1] consumer preference,[2] a spillover of urban populations to the urban fringe,[3] or the result of explicit governmental policy.[4] While we do not denigrate the demographic, economic, and ecological factors in contributing to the growth of postwar suburbia, we will attempt in this essay to offer what we consider a more compelling explanation of suburban growth, using Nassau County as an exemplar of this growth. We argue that the growth of the postwar suburbs was an integral part of the postwar expansion of the American welfare state.

Demographic, economic, and ecological explanations of suburban growth as articulated in the first three explanations imply individual or group agency. The assumption undergirding these explanations is that private entrepreneurs, seeing the pent up need for postwar housing, undertook economic risks in a market economy to meet the need by providing a range of housing types for economically self-sufficient families. Some of the demand for postwar housing *could* have been met in the marketplace but the results would have been vastly different from the results of federal interventionist strategies utilized as part of the American welfare state. Without these strategies, large segments of the population would have been excluded from the suburban move, resulting in a greatly reduced suburban population featuring a sharper upper class and upper middle class tint. The fourth explanation for suburban growth, i.e. as the result of explicit federal policies, while a more accurate analysis, is limited as it sees suburban growth arising solely from federal housing and highway policies and subsidies over a particular time frame.

The postwar suburbs grew out of a web of federal legislative, administrative, and budgetary initiatives that sought to expand the American version of the welfare state. A paler version of European welfare states, the American welfare state seeks to provide economic security for individuals and families through governmental intervention in a market economy in order to remedy the inequitable distribution of resources and goods. These federal interventions were not isolated, temporal policies but part of the creation and maintenance of the American welfare state which saw its first wave arising from the New Deal, its second wave of institutionalization during the era between 1944 and 1963, and the third wave resulting from the Great Society.[5]

The New Deal ushered in the American welfare state by initiating expansive federal intervention in the American economy to provide economic security for families. This was done by guarantees to workers of their right to unionize, the adoption of minimum wage laws, regulation of banks and protection of deposits for individuals, subsidies for farmers, and enactment of the Social Security Act of 1935 which ensured income support for the elderly and the unemployed.

Essential to the modern suburb's growth was the liberal reformulation of banking and mortgage policies in the New Deal era. This reformulation created: a national market for mortgages thus allowing a more dependable flow of mortgage capital; the insurance of bank deposits by individual depositors against bank failure; the provision of federal protection against default of individual mortgages, and changing the structure of mortgages from economically stressful high-down-payment, short-term balloon mortgages (three to five years) with high interest rates, to low-down-payment, long-term amortizing (twenty years) single mortgages at below market interest rates. These New Deal policies altered the housing market by removing substantial risks from the industry's players and set the standards for all mortgages, government insured or conventional, during the next forty years.[6]

The second wave of the American welfare state occurred between 1944 and 1963 when the national government sought to further moderate the effects of the marketplace by federal intervention to expand housing opportunities (GI Bill, 1944; Housing Acts of 1949-1961); educational opportunities (GI Bill, 1944; Korean GI Bill, 1952; and National Defense Education Act of 1958); health care (Hill-Burton Act of 1946 and Health Professions Educational Assistance Act of 1963); and employment for American families. This second wave was not a formal, coherent, comprehensive one but was informal, ad hoc, incremental, and somewhat redistributive. During this second wave, the federal government used direct funding, tax subsidies, and federal guidelines to manipulate the private and state sectors to provide education, homeownership, health care, and employment to its citizens. In short, it offered economic security.[7]

An important ripple effect of federal intervention in these specific sectors was the numerous collateral professions and occupations that were aided by these welfare state initiatives. A by-product of this involvement was that private entrepreneurs and organizations, which formerly provided their own stakes and assumed the risks inherent in the market place, now had both stakes and risks assumed by a wide array of governmental agencies. As W. Andrew Achenbaum concludes, "The federal government increasingly functioned as a broker, mediator, and senior partner in all spheres of economic life after 1945."[8]

The third wave of the American welfare state occurred with the passage of the Great Society's legislative agenda when the federal government became a guarantor of health care for the elderly (Medicare) and the poor (Medicaid) in 1965. The Great Society also expanded educational opportunities, employment training, and was responsible for historic anti-discrimination and anti-poverty legislation between 1964 and 1968.[9]

We will analyze three key components of the postwar welfare state (the second wave) which contributed significantly to the growth of postwar suburbia and the economic security of suburbanites. These components of the American welfare state are: housing, education, and labor or employment policies. These three policies are, of course, instructive rather than exhaustive.

Housing

Homeownership has been one of the key ingredients of the suburban value system, along with such cultural emphases as the nuclear family and child-centeredness, good schools, and small government. Postwar suburban homeownership arose from the several housing initiatives enacted by Congress—Title III of the 1944 GI Bill and the Housing Acts of 1949 through 1961.

The Servicemen's Readjustment Act of 1944 (GI Bill) was the first federal attempt to provide for the postwar needs of an important segment of the American population. Fearful of an economic depression after the war, as well as the potential volatility of twelve million unemployed demobilized military veterans, the political and social elites, along with veterans' groups, pushed the GI Bill through Congress.[10] The GI Bill of 1944 provided preferential treatment for World War II veterans in education, health care, employment, unemployment insurance, and housing through direct subsidies to the tune of $14.5 billion.[11]

In the area of housing, the GI Bill provided low cost, long-term guaranteed loans with no down payments for the purchase of homes. The Veterans Administration (VA) greatly facilitated this risk-free policy by notifying builders prior to construction whether their projects were eligible for VA mortgages which smoothed the way for access to construction loans.[12] In addition to subsidized loans under the GI Bill, Congress, through various other postwar housing legislation between 1949 and 1961, sought to provide support for a needy housing industry, revitalize downtown areas, provide public housing, and most importantly, provide funding for the housing needs of the approximately five million families who were either doubled up with other families or living in transient housing.[13] Towards this end, Congress allocated more than $50 billion between 1949-1954 and provided tax subsidies for homeowners in 1951 and 1961.[14] Fueled by Federal Housing

Administration (FHA) and VA mortgages and tax subsidies, the United States averaged 1.5 million housing starts per year during the 1950s. This federal housing policy evolved into a suburban housing policy as approximately 90 percent of this housing was built in the suburbs.[15]

Nassau County's housing expansion occurred within the context of a federally subsidized suburban housing policy. A prime example of this was the creation of Levittown. William Levitt, one of the nation's big builders, was privy to the federal government's new practice of providing easy access of credit and loans to large builders while freezing out small builders. As a favored builder, Levitt received "FHA commitments to finance 4000 homes before clearing land." These advances usually covered "up to 95 percent of the value of the house."[16] Levitt's customers, virtually all GIs, were eligible for no down payment, low cost federally guaranteed VA loans, which assured Levitt of buyers with easily approved mortgages. Bankers' loans to GIs were federally guaranteed so it was no surprise that bankers were quite willing to set up one-day approvals for Levittown loans. Levittown, in short, was a largely *risk-free proposition* for builders, bankers, and buyers as the federal government assumed virtually all the risks.

Levittown was just one slice of the federal homeownership pie in Nassau County. New communities sprang up in central Nassau during the 1950s while older ones expanded with the aid of VA loans and FHA loans that required modest down payments and long amortization.[17] During the early

Levittown in the 1950s, looking east with Hempstead Turnpike in center and Division Avenue running off to the left. *NCM Collection, LISI at Hofstra.*

fifties in Nassau County, VA loans were apparently quite prevalent as one study found that 67.4 percent of applications for homeowner loans were for VA approved loans. There were also indications that FHA mortgages were used for home purchasing in some upscale communities, such as Garden City.[18] Like other suburban homeowners, Nassau homeowners were further subsidized by federal tax policies which allowed mortgage interest tax deductions on owner occupied housing which defrayed "a fifth or more of the costs of homeownership and virtually subsidized the new suburban houses."[19] Along with tax deductions there was also the 1951 capital gains tax benefit for a "homeowner who sells his home and purchases another of equal or higher price within one year."[20] This capital gains benefit was estimated to increase national housing demand and consumption by 30-42 percent.[21] Congress, in 1961, further expanded homeowner tax benefits to energize the housing industry.

Nassau's federally subsidized building boom lasted until 1960. It fueled a mass movement of families from New York City and its environs to Nassau County, increasing the population from 406,748 in 1940, to 672,765 in 1950 and 1,300,171 in 1960.[22] This federally subsidized mass movement to Nassau, and other suburbs in the nation, was akin to the great mass movement westward after the Civil War, financed by federal homestead policies and federal subsidies of railroads.[23]

Homeownership in Nassau County, as in other suburbs, was also responsible for the creation, expansion, and economic support of several industries, e.g., lumber, furniture, public utilities, consumer durables, real estate brokers, automobile dealers, repairmen, and road building.

The population explosion in Nassau County further resulted in a public school population, which rose from 69,575 students in 1947 to 294,246 by the end of the housing boom and a peak of 331,810 students in 1967.[24] The increased number of students led to expanded school construction. To provide for this construction, Nassau County school districts, between 1950 and 1954, assumed $234,272,000 in bonded indebtedness. By 1960, the debt had reached $394 million.[25] Between 1950 and 1955 Nassau County received more than $97 million from New York State in four state-aid categories to help in moderating this economic burden. The federal government was also a contributor, providing over $8 million to Long Island to defray postwar public education expenses.[26] The local, state, and federal funding for school construction increased the numbers of teachers and teacher training programs at local colleges, and provided work for the construction industry in Nassau County.

Thus, the federal government's housing policy not only provided subsidized homeownership for Nassau residents but also became a labor market policy by directly and indirectly providing employment in various sectors to meet the growth of Nassau County's population.

Higher Education

Both the 1944 and the 1952 Korean GI Bills helped to expand access to college for working-class men and women as well as expand those universities they attended. The GI Bill of 1944, and subsequent amendments, provided up to $500 per year for four years of tuition for veterans, plus stipends for books, dependents, and housing. (Harvard's tuition during the immediate postwar era was $400 per year.)[27] The Korean GI Bill cut back on some of the stipends, such as money for books. More than 2.2 million World War II GIs received a college education in 2,000 colleges at a cost of $5.5 billion to the United States Treasury.[28] The Korean GI Bill educated 2.3 million veterans.[29] In addition, the Housing Act of 1950 created the College Housing Loan Program, which, by 1963, had provided $2 billion in funding for 40 percent of all new college dormitories built in the nation.[30]

Nassau County colleges participated actively in this federal largesse to U.S. veterans. For example, the enrollment at Adelphi University, a women's college prior to admission of men in 1947, was 1,100. The September 1947 admission of men as a result of the GI Bill added 804 men, 700 of whom were veterans at a tuition of $450 per person. By September 1948, there were 1,100 men at Adelphi, 800 of whom were veterans. Existing departments expanded by hiring new faculty while new departments were created.[31] Other Nassau County universities also benefitted from this new burst in government support for higher education. Hofstra University (then Hofstra College) went from 500 students in 1945 to approximately 5,000 in 1955 and its faculty grew from twenty-five members to approximately 150 in 1955.[32] With Hofstra's help, Farmingdale restructured its curriculum in 1947 and hired new staff to accommodate over two hundred veterans.[33] Long Island University President David Steinberg also saw the GI Bill as vital to C.W. Post's growth: "We were built by the GI Bill."[34]

The National Defense Education Act of 1958 (NDEA), passed in response to the Soviet Union's perceived leadership over America in the sciences, provided low interest, long term student loans for academically superior high school students who were interested in careers in modern languages, science, mathematics, and engineering or those who wanted to become high school teachers or guidance counselors. In response to this Cold War legislation, Adelphi University began hiring more scientists. Adelphi also received approximately $1 million in grants from the National Science Foundation and the Atomic Energy Commission during the summers of 1958 to 1964 for summer training of high school science teachers, geared towards "helping America in staying ahead of Russia," as Congressman Steven Derourian stated in 1958.[35]

The federal subsidy of the Long Island defense industry (see below) also contributed to the expansion of Nassau County colleges. For example, of Sperry's 18,000 workers in 1959, approximately 2,000 were in Nassau colleges pursuing science degrees. Fully 80 percent of Adelphi's majors in Physics and Mathematics were employed in the federally subsidized Long Island defense industry.[36]

These increases were also fueled by the College Housing Loan Program which aided funding for construction of new dormitories at some Nassau colleges. For example, Adelphi University received approximately $4 million in federal loans between 1958 and 1964 for building a number of dormitories.[37]

The various government subsidies for higher education affected Nassau County in several ways. They opened up educational opportunities to new arrivals who formerly had no hope of higher education. This education, combined with federally subsidized homeownership, created a new middle class and imbued their children with middle class aspirations, including a college education. These subsidies also created employment for construction workers and related professions. As universities expanded new faculty were hired, especially in the sciences and languages. There was also an increased need for pink-collar employees to staff these expansions. As George DeWan stated in *Newsday*'s 1998 history of Long Island, the GI Bill "changed the face of college campuses, on Long Island and across the nation."[38]

Labor Market Policy

America's labor market policy after World War II was not to create jobs directly by government through nationalization of industries, or the creation of labor exchanges, but to subsidize with substantial federal funds, the key economic sectors that drove the economy, including housing, highway construction, and hospital construction. We have discussed housing subsidies and their impact on Nassau County. An equally important subsidy for Nassau County was that of the defense-related industry. The subsidy of aviation became entangled in both labor market policies and Cold War policies.

In 1944, a year before the end of World War II, the national aviation industry had built 96,000 planes. By 1947, this number had declined to 1,800 planes, rendering the aviation industry moribund and hundreds of thousands of workers unemployed. To revive the industry, the United States government poured approximately $7 billion into the industry in 1947 and 1948. By 1948-1949, 90 percent of the aviation industry's business was in military contracts, geared towards contesting the might of the Soviet Union in the aviation field.[39]

In 1950, the militarization of the United States federal budget and the United States economy were formalized through a national security memorandum, NSC-68, which called for substantial increases in defense spending to offset the perceived Soviet threat. The understanding among defense and economic policymakers at the federal level was that this unprecedented peacetime spending could be absorbed by the American economy without damage, i.e., without inflation. The 1950s and 1960s saw defense budgets ranging from \$40 to \$50 billion annually. This varied from a high of 65 percent of the entire federal budget in 1952 and a low of 47.8 percent of the federal budget in 1962.[40]

It was within this context of the creation of the national security state that Nassau County's postwar economy benefitted. Originally, Nassau's defense industry grew out of the funding of several aviation and defense related plants during World War II by various branches of the military. Prior to World War II, approximately 5,000 employees worked in the aviation industry on Long Island. During the war the number exploded to 90,000 employees. The three major defense companies during the war were Grumman Corporation with 25,000 workers, Republic Aviation with 24,000 workers, and Sperry with 22,000 workers.[41] The end of the war and the military cancellation of its contracts decimated the aviation industry on Long Island.[42]

However, the Cold War between the United States and the Soviet Union, and the Korean War, revived the sagging fortunes of the aviation industry on Long Island[43] and contributed greatly to the dynamism of the Long Island economy. In 1947, Fairchild Engine and Airplane Corporation in Farmingdale was contracted by the War Department to build atomic powered engines. By 1948, when Levitt was selling his homes in Levittown, Grumman was "the prime contractor for Navy airplanes for the 1949 fiscal year. Eighty percent of its business was comprised of Navy contracts." By 1950, Republic Aviation was devoting the "major portion of its time and efforts to the production and development" of Air Force contracts.[44]

The dependence on federal contracts by the Long Island aviation and defense related industries continued during the 1950s at a time when Nassau County's population was expanding. In 1954, 75 percent of manufacturing jobs in Nassau County were defense related. By 1964, 70 percent of all manufacturing jobs in Nassau County were still defense related.[45] As Pearl Kamer, the economist for the Long Island Regional Planning Board, stated in a 1971 report, "the Long Island Economy crested and fell with the volume of government aerospace contracts."[46]

Once again we must look at the ancillary economic benefits that flowed from this federal largesse: more homes needed (builders and construction workers), more FHA mortgages issued (bankers), more schools needed (teachers and construction workers), more housing equipment needed (furniture stores, electric appliance stores), more food consumed (supermarkets and restaurants).

Conclusion

The expansion of the American welfare state between the New Deal and the Great Society—1944–1963—greatly facilitated the growth of the postwar suburbs. The United States government's policies to ensure economic security through federal intervention in the economy included ensuring homeownership, expanding access to higher education, and subsidizing and stimulating strategic economic sectors to provide employment for most of its citizens.

This explosive growth resulted from a federal housing policy that provided access to homes for people who would probably have been shut out of the housing market; an educational policy that provided access and subsidies to education for people who might never have gone to college; a labor market policy that provided employment directly through subsidies to Nassau's universities, housing industry, and defense industry, and, indirectly, to collateral professions and industries. These policies were instrumental in determining the contours and the substance of Nassau County's growth during the late 1940s and the 1950s.

The irony of this is that builders, Congresspersons, veterans' groups, and other free market advocates, who all feared that general governmental intrusion in the postwar economy would usher in socialism or communism, nevertheless, actively sought intervention in specific sectors of the economy that would benefit their interests.[47] Their vigorous attempts resulted in expanding the postwar American welfare state and brought to fruition one of its shining examples, the Nassau County postwar suburb.

Notes

1. Wendell Bell, "Social Choice, Life Styles, and Suburban Residence," in *The Suburban Community,* edited by William Dobriner (New York: G. P. Putnam's Sons, 1958), 225-47; Sylvia F. Fava, "Contrasts in Neighboring: New York City and a Suburban County," in Dobriner, *Suburban Community,* 122-31; Claude S. Fischer and Robert Max Jackson, "Suburbs, Network, and Attitudes," in *The Changing Face of the Suburbs,* edited by Barry Schwartz (Chicago: University of Chicago Press, 1976), 279-307.

2. V. Ostrom, C. M. Tiebout, and R. Warren, "The Organization of Government in Metropolitan Areas: A Theoretical Inquiry," *American Political Science Review* 60 (December 1961): 831-42.

3. Herbert Gans, *The Levittowners* (New York: Vintage Books, 1967); Norval D. Glenn, "Suburbanization in the United States Since World War II," in *The Urbanization*

of the Suburbs, edited by Louis Masotti and Jeffrey K. Hadden (Beverly Hills, CA: Sage Publications, 1973), 51-78.

4. Charles Abrams, *The City Is the Frontier* (New York: Harper & Row, 1965); Barry Checkoway, "Large Builders, Federal Housing Programmes, and Postwar Suburbanization," *International Journal of Urban and Regional Research* 4 (March 1980): 21-45.

5. Almost all scholars examining the American welfare state perceive it as occurring in two stages, the New Deal and the Great Society. The years between these two stages are seen as either fallow years or characterized by welfare capitalism, i.e., fringe benefits for individuals and families advanced through collective bargaining. See Bruce S. Jansson, *The Reluctant Welfare State: American Social Welfare Policies—Past, Present and Future* (Pacific Grove, CA: Brooks/Cole Publishing, 1997); Christopher Howard, "The Hidden Side of the American Welfare State," *Political Science Quarterly* 108 (Fall 1993): 403-36; Theodore J. Lowi, "The Welfare State: Ethical Foundations and Constitutional Remedies," *Political Science Quarterly* 101 (1986 Centennial Year): 197-220; Norman Furniss and Timothy Tilton, *The Case for the Welfare State: From Social Security to Social Equality* (Bloomington: Indiana University Press, 1977).

Our research indicates that these so-called fallow years evidenced extensive federal legislative, executive, and budgetary activities that properly constitute a separate second wave. See Hugh A. Wilson, "Between F.D.R. and L.B.J.: The Lost Years of the American Welfare State" (paper presented at the annual meeting of the Northeastern Political Science Association, Boston, MA, November 1998).

6. James H. Boykin, *Financing Real Estate* (Lexington, MA: Lexington Books, 1979); J. Paul Mitchell, "Historical Overview of Federal Policy: Encouraging Homeownership," in *Federal Housing Policy and Programs: Past and Present*, edited by J. Paul Mitchell (New Brunswick, NJ: Center for Urban Policy Research, Rutgers, SUNJ, 1995), 39-46; J. Paul Mitchell "Historical Context for Housing Policy," in Mitchell, *Federal Housing Policy,* 6.

7. Wilson, "Between F.D.R. and L.B.J."

8. W. Andrew Achenbaum, *Social Security: Visions and Revisions* (London: Cambridge University Press, 1986), 42.

9. Jansson, *The Reluctant Welfare State;* Lowi, "The Welfare State"; Furniss and Tilton, *The Case for the Welfare State;* John E. Schwarz, *America's Hidden Success: A Reassessment of Twenty Years of Public Policy* (New York: W. W. Norton and Co., 1983).

10. Theodore R. Mosch, *The G.I. Bill: A Breakthrough in Educational and Social Policy in the United States* (Hicksville, NY: Exposition Press, 1975); Keith W. Olson, *The G.I. Bill, the Veterans, and the Colleges* (Lexington: University of Kentucky Press, 1974); Michael J. Bennett, *When Dreams Come True: The GI Bill and the Making of Modern America* (Washington, DC: Brassey's, 1996).

11. Olson, *The G.I. Bill,* 10.

12. United States President's Commission on Veterans' Pension, "Objectives and Historical Development of Veterans' Loan Benefits," in Mitchell, *Federal Housing Policy,* 114.

13. Checkoway, "Large Builders," 22; Martin Meyerson, Barbara Terrett, and William L. C. Wheaton, *Housing, People, and Cities* (New York: McGraw-Hill Book Company, 1962), 246.

14. Checkoway, "Large Builders," 31-34.

15. Mitchell, "The Historical Context for Housing Policy," in Mitchell, *Federal Housing Policy,* 9.

16. Checkoway, "Large Builders," 27.

17. Edward J. Smits, *Suburbia, U.S.A.: The First Seventy-five Years of Nassau County, New York, 1899-1974* (Syosset, NY: Friends of the Nassau County Museum, 1974), 197-99; David Behrens, "The New Frontier," in *Long Island: Our Story* by Newsday (Melville, NY: Newsday, 1998), 323.

18. William A. Nielander and James R. Thomen, *Quality and Stability of New Homeowners in Nassau County, Long Island, N.Y.* (Garden City, NY: The Long Island Association Industrial Bureau, July 23, 1951), 6; Walter S. Ross, *People's Banker: The Story of Arthur T. Roth and the Franklin National Bank* (New Canaan, CT: Keats Publishing, 1987), 82-83.

19. Checkoway, "Large Builders," 34.

20. Mitchell, "Historical Overview," in Mitchell, *Federal Housing Policy,* 46.

21. Richard E. Slitor, "Rationale of the Present Tax Benefits for Homeowners," in Mitchell, *Federal Housing Policy,* 173.

22. Smits, *Nassau,* 198; Nassau County Planning Commission, *Aspects: An Analysis of Social, Economic and Housing Characteristics of Nassau County, N.Y.*, Part 5; Origins of the Population (Mineola, NY, July 1963).

23. Nassau's housing boom was facilitated not only by federally guaranteed loans and mortgages but by road systems. The Southern State and Northern State Parkways, built in the 1920s and 1930s for leisure activities, were pressed into service as commuter lanes allowing people to live further and further away from their places of work. This was reinforced by the Long Island Expressway built in the 1950s. See Robert Caro, *The Power Broker: Robert Moses and the Fall of New York* (New York: Vintage Books, 1975), 953; Smits, *Nassau,* 153; George DeWan, "The Master Builder," in *Long Island,* by Newsday, 289; Behrens, "New Frontier," 321.

24. Smits, *Nassau,* 210; New York State Division of the Budget, Office of Statistical Coordination, *New York State Statistical Yearbook 1967.* (Albany, February 1968), Table H-8, p. 99; 1968-69, Table I-4, p 165.

25. Lewis Wilson, "Population and Schools," in Hofstra College, *The Problems of Growth in Nassau and Western Suffolk: A Planning Forum* (Hempstead: Trustees of Hofstra College, [1955]), 26; Smits, *Nassau,* 210.

26. George L. Hubbell, Jr., "Aid for Education," in Hofstra College, *The Problems of Growth,* 29-30.

27. Olson, *The G.I. Bill,* 62; Bennett, *When Dreams Come True*, 18.

28. Olson, *The G.I. Bill,* 59.

29. Mosch, *The G.I. Bill,* 84.

30. Nathan M. Pusey, "The Carnegie Study of the Federal Government and Higher Education," in *Higher Education and the Federal Government: Programs and Problems* (Washington, DC: American Council on Education, 1963), 23.

31. Chester Barrows, "Adelphi Since 1946," unpublished manuscript, Adelphi University Special Collections, 1-14.

32. *Hofstra College Twentieth Anniversary* (promotional brochure), unpaginated (Hempstead, NY: Trustees of Hofstra College, October 12, 1955).

33. John Cranford Adams, "Reflections of Hofstra," unpublished manuscript, Hofstra University Archives, 84.

34. George DeWan, "The Hunger for Learning," in *Long Island,* by Newsday, 326.

35. Barrows, "Adelphi," 119.

36. Barrows, "Adelphi," 145.

37. Barrows, "Adelphi," 93.

38. DeWan, "Hunger for Learning," 326.

39. Daniel Yergin, *Shattered Peace: The Origins of the Cold War and the National Security State* (Boston, MA: Houghton-Mifflin, 1977), 337-42.

40. James T. Patterson, *Grand Expectations: The United States, 1945-1974* (New York: Oxford University Press, 1996), 176-78; United States Bureau of the Census, *Historical Statistics of the United States, Colonial Times to 1970, Bicentennial Issue, Part 1* (Washington, DC: Government Printing Office, 1975), Series Y, 457-65.

41. George DeWan, "The Wings of War," in *Long Island,* by Newsday, 307-11; Joshua Stoff, *The Aerospace Heritage of Long Island* (Interlaken, NY: Heart of the Lakes Publishing, 1989), 51.

42. Smits, *Nassau,* 117; DeWan, "Wings of War," 311; Bernice Marshall, "The Rest of the Story, 1929-1961" (A Sequel), in 2d ed., *Long Island's Story,* by Jacqueline Overton (Port Washington: Ira J. Friedman, Inc., 1961); 10.

43. Stoff, *The Aerospace Heritage,* 68; Marshall, "Rest of the Story," 11; William N. Leonard, "Industrial Growth," in Hofstra College, *The Problems of Growth,* 9-10.

44. Raymond V. DiScala, *The Development of the Aerospace Industry on Long Island.* Vol. 3, *A Chronology, 1833-1965,* edited by William K. Kaiser (Hempstead: Hofstra University Yearbook of Business, Series 5, 1968), 74, 76.

45. Leonard, "Industrial Growth," 10; Pearl M. Kamer, *Nassau-Suffolk's Changing Manufacturing Base: A Case Study of a Suburban Labor Market,* Nassau-Suffolk Regional Planning Board Research Monograph Series No. 1 (Hauppauge: Nassau-Suffolk Regional Planning Board, November 1977), 14.

46. Pearl M. Kamer, *The Long Island Economy: Anatomy of Change* (Hauppauge: Nassau-Suffolk Regional Planning Board, December, 1971), 20.

47. Gwendolyn Wright, *Building the Dream: A Social History of Housing in America* (New York: Pantheon Books, 1981), 240-45; Geoffrey Mohan, "Suburban Pioneers," in *Long Island,* by Newsday, 416; Brian J. O'Connell, "The Federal Role in the Suburban Boom" in *Suburbia Re-examined,* edited by Barbara M. Kelly (New York: Greenwood Press, 1989), 184.

Health Care

Left: The 1904 fundraising fair for the Nassau Hospital in Mineola was held at Harbor Hill, the home of Clarence H. and Katherine Duer Mackay in Roslyn. *Right*: North Shore Hospital, Manhasset, aerial view by Skyviews, 1964. *NCM, LISI at Hofstra.*

The Nassau County Medical Center on Hempstead Turnpike in East Meadow, c. 1990. Photograph courtesy of Urbahn Associates and the Society for the Preservation of Long Island Antiquities.

History of Hospitals in Nassau County

Thomas Joseph Palmieri, M. D.

At the turn of the twentieth century there were no hospitals in Nassau and Suffolk counties. People avoided hospitals, which were looked upon as places to go to die. Rural doctors were notified by post cards from patients when they were needed. Upon receipt of these post cards, the rural physicians would then visit using a horse and buggy.

In 1896, three years before the birth of Nassau County, a group of physicians and local residents started the first medical dispensary in Nassau County located in West Hempstead. This was Nassau Hospital which would later become Winthrop Hospital. At the same time, but further east in Amityville in Suffolk County, Brunswick Hospital Center was starting, not as a medical facility but rather, as an institution to treat mental illness.[1]

Let us look at what was happening in medicine and science throughout the world at the same time as hospitals were developing in Nassau County: in 1896, in Wurtzburg, Germany, William Roentgen published his first paper depicting an x-ray of his wife's hand; and the germ theory of disease, as popularized by Louis Pasteur, was also in its infancy.

Two births and eight deaths were recorded during Nassau Hospital's first year of operation, and in 1897, ninety-one patients were admitted and twenty-four operations were carried out. By coincidence, a war was going on in the Caribbean which led to further publicity for the infant Nassau Hospital.

In 1898, the Spanish-American War was underway in Cuba. Long Islander Theodore Roosevelt, who had been Assistant Secretary of the Navy, resigned to assemble the First United States Volunteer Cavalry Regiment known as the Rough Riders and was commissioned a lieutenant colonel in the United States Army. Roosevelt led his troops in battle up Kettle Hill in the San Juan Heights near Santiago, Cuba, on July 1, 1898. When the war ended, the soldiers were quarantined in Cuba for thirty days and then returned by ship to Montauk. Many of the returning soldiers were suffering from various infectious diseases such as malaria and typhoid fever. During those times, most casualties of war were from infections and other illnesses rather than from direct enemy weapons. The seriously ill and wounded soldiers had already expired and those soldiers with extremity injuries had amputations done at the time of their injuries.

After being at Camp Wykoff in Montauk for another period of quarantine, the soldiers were transported by rail to Nassau Hospital. If a soldier

Nassau Hospital in Mineola, 1913. Korten photograph, *NCM Collections, LISI at Hofstra.*

could make the trip by ship from Cuba to Montauk and then by freight train to Mineola, he must have been in fairly good health so that his chances of survival were excellent. The closest hospital to Montauk was Nassau Hospital, thus it took care of fifty veterans of this Spanish-American conflict.

In 1899, Nassau Hospital admitted 223 patients, averaging four patients a day. In 1900, Nassau Hospital moved to an area adjacent to a horse and buggy trail which became Old Country Road. It was located a few hundred yards from the Mineola station of the Long Island Rail Road.

Also in 1900, Nassau Hospital opened the first school for nurses. This school was founded and funded by private citizens and later merged with the nursing program at Molloy College.

Nassau Hospital participated in many other medical "firsts." It provided the first ambulance service, consisting of a horse and buggy. The only way people were able to summon an ambulance at that time would be on foot since telephone service was extremely rare. In 1914, the ambulance became motorized.

In 1910, surgery was done under what we would now consider poor sanitary conditions. Surgeons operated without gloves or masks nor did they put on any protective gowns. This was because the knowledge of bacteria and other infecting organisms was hardly known. The operative field was sprayed with carbolic acid in order to reduce the chances of infection. No antibiotics were available at that time since they had not yet been discovered.

By 1920, as physicians learned that bacteria were the cause of various types of infections, masks and surgical gowns began to be used. The antibiotic sulfa was developed in 1935 and was then available for the treatment of infections. Penicillin, the most practical antibiotic, was developed during World War II.

The early hospitals were overcrowded, with patients placed close to each other. This practice followed the tradition of military hospitals of that period. It was, therefore, not unusual for infections to spread from one patient to another especially since the cause of infections was not known and physicians did not wash their hands between treatment of patients. Hospital rooms consisted of large wards accommodating up to forty patients. Eventually, beds were situated further apart so as to prevent contamination from patient to patient.

In 1900, it was not unusual for a traveling physician to do surgery on a kitchen table at a patient's home. If the patient did not develop an infection, he would go on to have a slow recovery. At the time, medical education was primarily by local apprenticeships. A "doctor boy" would follow his physician educator around for three to five years and learn his profession directly from the teaching physician. Occasionally, an apprentice would travel into New York City in order to hear a lecture. Somewhat more formal training in medicine occurred overseas in Europe.

New hospitals were started in various ways. Following the tradition in Europe during the Middle Ages, hospitals were frequently founded and operated by various religious groups. The same thing happened on Long Island. In 1905, the Catholic Diocese of Brooklyn (which included all of Long Island) started the Brooklyn Home for crippled and "defective" children in Port Jefferson. This was primarily a hospital to treat children with birth defects or psychiatric problems. This hospital later became St. Charles Hospital. In 1913, Mercy Hospital started as a sanitarium in Hempstead. In 1937, St. Francis Hospital was founded by a group of Catholic Franciscan nuns who initially went door-to-door begging for monies to start and run their hospital.[2]

The population on Long Island doubled after World War II. As a result, many new hospitals developed. In 1953, North Shore Hospital opened in Manhasset and in 1954 the Long Island Jewish Medical Center opened in New Hyde Park. Long Island Jewish Hospital, incidentally, was the first hospital in Nassau County to offer accredited residency programs for the training of young physicians. It also was the first hospital on Long Island to be affiliated with a medical school, namely, the State University of New York (SUNY) Downstate Medical Center in Brooklyn (now the Health Science

Center). This was the beginning of the establishment of physician training in Nassau County, eliminating the need to go "off island."

In 1980, the State University of New York at Stony Brook opened the first medical school in Nassau or Suffolk. The first medical school on Long Island, however, was in Brooklyn, namely, the State University of New York which traced its existence to the early 1900s and was known at that time as the Long Island College of Medicine.

Basic medical research has occurred in various institutions in Nassau County. The Cold Spring Harbor Laboratory in Cold Spring Harbor carries on research in molecular genetics. In Suffolk County, the Brookhaven National Laboratory in Upton has probed the atom's core and Plum Island is a government animal disease research center. Each of the major hospitals on Long Island is affiliated with a medical school. Regional hospital research has also developed and kept pace with research being done at pure research institutions. As evidence of this, Long Island has its share of Nobel laureates, with four at Brookhaven National Laboratory, three at Cold Spring Harbor Laboratory, and one at the State University of New York in Brooklyn.

Nassau County established Meadowbrook Hospital in East Meadow in 1935 which expanded over the years; this view is c. 1950. The hospital's 17-story tower on Hempstead Turnpike was completed in 1973 and it was renamed the Nassau County Medical Center in 1974. Fairchild photograph, *NCM Collection, LISI at Hofstra.*

In the late 1990s, hospital care has again metamorphosed. With the advent of managed care, the hospitals have been forced to merge and mate in order to cut costs and streamline care. North Shore Hospital has merged with the Long Island Jewish Medical Center forming the North Shore Long Island Jewish Healthcare System. This system now consists of eighteen institutions. Winthrop-University Hospital, formerly Nassau Hospital, has affiliated with the South Nassau Communities Hospital. The Catholic hospitals have also formed a joint affiliation.

All sorts of changes in medical care are occurring. Hospitals and physicians now compete for their share of patients in various types of commercial entities. Listening to the radio or reading our newspapers, we note that various hospitals and physicians are now advertising in order to garner as many patients as possible. Hopefully, "quick care" and "short care" as advocated by various health maintenance organizations will equilibrate with traditional care, and personal individualized patient care will continue into the twenty-first century.

Notes

1. Kings County (Brooklyn) and New York City had established farms for their poor and mentally ill residents in King's Park and Central Islip in Suffolk County, in 1885 and 1889 respectively. New York State took these over in 1895 as hospitals for the mentally ill. See Bill Bleyer, "Caring For The Mentally Ill," in *Long Island: Our Story* by Newsday (Melville, NY: Newsday, 1998), 249. (Editor's note.)

2. On the history of St. Francis, see Sr. Lois Van Delft, "Women of Faith: The Spiritual Legacy of the Founders of St. Francis Hospital," in *Long Island Women: Activists and Innovators,* edited by Natalie A. Naylor and Maureen O. Murphy (Interlaken, NY: Empire State Brooks, 1998), 146-53. (Editor's note.)

Bibliography

Hall, Courtney R. "Doctors and the Rise of Civilization in Long Island." *Medical Times,* November 1939, 523 ff.

Hazelton, Henry I., "Nassau Hospital." In *The Boroughs of Brooklyn and Queens, Counties of Nassau and Suffolk, Long Island, New York 1609-1924,* 2: 928-30. New York: Lewis Historical Publishing Company, 1925.

Lewi, Maurice J. "Licensing of Physicians in New York State, An Eyewitness Account." *History of Medicine in New York State,* January 15, 1955, 251 ff.

Walsh, James J. *History of Medicine in New York, Three Centuries of Medical Progress.* Vol. 4. New York: National Americana Society, 1919.

Trauma Care in Nassau County
The Past 100 Years

L. D. George Angus, M.D. and Dina Fahmy, M.D.

Governor Frank S. Black signed the bill creating Nassau County out of the towns of Hempstead, North Hempstead, and Oyster Bay on April 27, 1898. At the time, Nassau Hospital, founded two years earlier, was the only voluntary non-profit hospital from Queens to Montauk. The population of Nassau County in those early days was about 47,000.[1]

The care of the trauma patient during that period was not at all organized. There are sporadic reports of injury described in the *Hempstead Inquirer* and the *New York Times,* but there was no organized system in place for handling the severely injured. Nor were there standards or guidelines for physicians in those days. There are, however, occasional case reports by physicians in the medical literature describing the management of specific injuries and even though they were limited by the technology of the times, doctors clearly did their best and used a common sense approach in dealing with the injured. During those early years roads were poor or nonexistent, and quite often the injured were cared for by families who claimed to have their own "cures."[2] Telephone communication was not widespread but was emerging.

Prior to the opening of Nassau Hospital, the injured were often taken to hospitals in Queens—particularly St. John's, St. Mary's, and Flushing Hospital—by whatever means possible but most often via horse drawn ambulances.[3] Around the same period, there was a concerted effort—primarily by the Red Cross—to teach and certify interested individuals to provide first aid to the injured; and that effort continues until today with our EMS system.

According to the first report of the surgical activity of Nassau Hospital (1896-1897), the institution admitted ninety-one patients, performed twenty-seven operations, and reported two births and eight deaths in that year.[4] In the second year of the hospital's operation, in 1899, 225 patients were admitted including fifty soldiers from Camp Black, which was located in the approximate area of what was to become Roosevelt Field in Garden City.[5] The soldiers were veterans of the Spanish-American War and Nassau Hospital was certainly proud of the fact that forty-nine of the seriously ill recovered, which was extraordinary in those days. Indeed, the horror and inadequacy of medical care in dealing with infection and gangrene was one of the most fearful aspects of medicine not only for the soldiers of the time but also for anyone sustaining significant trauma. By 1900, the population in Nassau had increased to 55,448 and the small house in West Hempstead purchased from Abner Bedell could no longer sustain the high patient load.[6] During the early period of Nassau County, the Long Island Rail Road was a constant source of injury to both workers and pedestrians alike, and accounted for much of the patient trauma. The lack of adequate safety measures was a contributing factor in those injuries.

As the population of Nassau County increased, there were three catastrophes in the early twentieth century that were directly responsible for stimulating public awareness of the need for more hospital beds. They included the poliomyelitis epidemic of 1916 where the mortality rate was as high as 20 percent, the world influenza epidemic of 1918, and the grim blizzard of 1920, which resulted in the Town of Hempstead being isolated for six weeks making it impossible to move the seriously ill and injured to a hospital.[7] The blizzard resulted in a large number of residents sustaining frostbite. Many had to be transported to the city due to the limited number of hospital beds. Furthermore, the cost of hospitalization (as high as $5 per day) was considered exceedingly high by the local residents. The great majority of the patients with frostbite were indigent and the majority of admissions were for surgical procedures. Following these catastrophes, the Nassau County Medical Society proposed the establishment of a county facility for the treatment of the sick and injured who could not afford private hospital care. In 1923, there were only 120 medical/surgical beds in all of Nassau County divided among Nassau Hospital (71 beds), Glen Cove Hospital (19 beds), Mercy Hospital in Rockville Centre (23 beds), and a small sanitarium also in Rockville Centre, housing the remainder of the beds.[8] It was in this environment that the Nassau County Medical Center was constructed in an East Meadow potato field and opened on July 15, 1935. Today, there are more than 5,000 hospital beds in Nassau County.[9]

As Nassau's population increased, so did the incidence of trauma. However, it was still not organized into a specialty and was still being handled by a handful of physicians and surgeons as part of their hospital responsibility. During the ten years from 1929 to 1938, accidental deaths in Nassau County totaled 2,171.[10] A high of 253 deaths due to injury were reported in 1937 and by this time trauma was the fourth cause of death in the county. In 1939, the Department of Health in its first annual report published its data on Nassau's health and for the year 1938-1939, there were 180 deaths classified as due to external violence or accidental deaths. Approximately 5 percent of all deaths in Nassau County were due to accidents and the death rate was 46.1 per 100,000 population.[11] Currently, surrounding trauma centers admit 1,200 to 1,300 patients per year as a result of severe trauma. For the period 1995-1997, the county had 3,874 patients sustaining significant injury requiring in-patient hospital care with an overall mortality of about 3 percent.[12] The number of assaults, however, have increased as well as the number of penetrating injuries. From its rural beginning, Nassau County is becoming a true metropolis. Injuries of all types are becoming a real public health issue in the county, and the Department of Health closely monitors these.

There are a number of committees, such as the Regional Emergency Medical Advisory Committee (REMAC) as well as the Nassau Committee on Trauma, which monitor injuries in the county along with the quality of trauma care being rendered by health care professionals. As a result of an increasing population and increasing trauma, selected Nassau hospitals were designated by the State of New York in 1990 either as a Regional, also known as a level 1, or as an Area trauma center, also referred to as a level 2, trauma center. Each trauma center is now required to collect a set of clinical data on each trauma patient treated in the region. In addition, they are also required to undergo a survey periodically in order to ensure that they remain compliant with the New York State Appropriateness Review Standards for trauma centers. A Regional trauma center is defined as an institution capable of providing definitive treatment to the full range of trauma patients including a commitment to trauma research and education. Such a facility has 24-hour availability of specialists in both surgical and non-surgical fields, and is capable of treating at least 1,000 severely injured patients per year. The minimum number should not be less than 400 patients per year for that designation.

An Area trauma center, on the other hand, is capable of providing definitive treatment to most trauma patients. Although emergency medicine specialists and general surgeons are available 24-hours per day, other medical specialists are available on an on-call basis. The minimum number of severely injured treated at an Area trauma center should not be less than 250 per year. There are currently three Regional and two Area trauma centers in Nassau County. The three Regional centers include Nassau County Medical Center, Winthrop, and North Shore University Hospital. The Area centers include Mercy Hospital and South Nassau Communities Hospital. Trauma care in the county is now one of the best in the country, and that was clearly exemplified on a cold, rainy night on January 25, 1990 at 9:42 pm, when an Avianca Airlines Boeing 707 from Colombia, bound for Kennedy Airport, crashed in Cove Neck, on Long Island's north shore, killing seventy-three and injuring eighty-five. Hospital disaster and trauma teams throughout the county were activated. Helicopters transported the most seriously injured to our trauma centers and other area hospitals. While the crash victims were recovering, Nassau County Medical Center and other area hospitals received accolades from around the county, the state, and the nation. New York's Governor Mario Cuomo and State Health Commissioner Dr. David Axelrod visited our trauma centers to applaud the dedication and commitment of the hospital workers in Nassau County. The *Congressional Record* commended the Nassau County Medical Center, among other area hospitals, for bearing the brunt of the burden in the heroic effort to save the lives of crash victims. Eighty-five people survived this incident.[13]

There were no burn centers in Nassau until 1948 when Dr. Leonard R. Rubin pioneered burn care in Nassau County. The Burn Center originally occupied a multiple-bedded room in the Meadowbrook Hospital where adult and pediatric burn patients were admitted. The opening of the dynamic care building and the renaming of the hospital as the Nassau County Medical Center in 1974 brought the opening of the Burn Center, with a capacity of eighteen beds. Dr. Rubin directed the Burn Center until 1978 when Dr. Vincent Digregorio was appointed. In 1981, Dr. Roger Simpson assumed the position of Director and continues in that position at the present time. The bed capacity remains eighteen, including facilities for adults and children. Approximately 250 patients are admitted yearly to the Burn Center and more than 500 surgical procedures are performed annually. It is the only Burn Center in Nassau County and one of the best in the nation.

Although trauma care was slowly becoming a specialty and more organized in the county, the Emergency Medical System (EMS) was not fully developed until 1973 with the passage of the Emergency Medical Services System Act in the United States Congress. EMS is crucial to getting treatment to the injured or critically ill patient. It provides specialized transportation for a vast number of Nassau residents with critical trauma, severe burns, heart attack, spinal injury, critical poisoning, and critically ill new-borns. While in transit to the hospital, monitoring and emergency care can be initiated using established protocols while in constant communication with a physician. Currently, the system functions smoothly through the close cooperation of the Police Department, the Fire Department, and sixteen local hospitals. The training of professional and para-professional personnel in emergency medical care is another important function of this program. A vast number of highly trained Emergency Medical Technicians have been produced as a result of this program and over 100,000 lay persons have been trained in cardiopulmonary resuscitation. EMS has also established the Advanced Life Support Motor Skills Academy at the Nassau County Medical Center which provides hands-on teaching instruction for each advanced life support skill. This program translates into more people reaching the hospital alive than ever before. There has been a significant increase in the chances of survival following major trauma or heart attack in Nassau County making it one of the top five EMS systems in the United States.

Nassau County has come a long way in caring for its injured since 1899 and it is now at the forefront of trauma care. As we enter the new millennium and use the latest in technology to provide the best for our injured, we must remember that in Nassau County we have one of the most highly skilled and dedicated teams of health care professionals in the country. It is that team that will continue to demonstrate excellence and leadership in the field of trauma surgery and ensure that the injured of Nassau County continue to receive the best that modern medicine and technology can offer.

Notes

1. *Hempstead Inquirer,* May 6, 1898. Nassau Hospital was the predecessor of today's Winthrop-University Hospital.
2. P. E. Sammis, "Early Long Island Docs—Dedicated, Compassionate," *Long Island Press,* February 22, 1976.
3. "Run down by an ambulance," *New York Times,* October 2, 1896.
4. *Hempstead Inquirer,* May 5, 1898.
5. Winthrop-University Hospital, *Historical Highlights,* Winthrop Hospital Publication. January 16, 1998.
6. "Nassau Historical Notes," *Nassau County Historical Society Journal* 24, no. 1 (Winter 1963): 22.
7. M. Pochedly and C. Pochedly, "Building Meadowbrook Hospital," *New York State Journal of Medicine,* November 1976, 2,074-76.
8. G. S. Smith, "A History of Nassau County Medical Center," *Nassau County Medical Center Proceedings,* 50th Anniversary Commemorative issue, 13, no. 1, Fall 1985.
9. *Hospital Statistics and Service Utilization Report,* Nassau-Suffolk Hospital Council Inc., February 1999.
10. *Nassau Health in 1939,* Department of Health, First Annual Report, December 31, 1939.
11. *Nassau Health in 1939.*
12. *Injury Facts for New York State,* New York State Department of Health, Bureau of Injury Prevention, 1997.
13. G. Ignacio, "The Sixtieth Anniversary of Nassau County Medical Center: The Last Ten Years," *Nassau County Medical Center Proceedings* 23, no. 1, Summer 1996.

Surgery in Nassau County in the Twentieth Century

Stanley D. Berliner, M.D.

In 1900, a Long Island farmer with a hernia could choose to get fitted for a truss, which was usually hand crafted out of leather, or he could have surgery, which meant a hospital stay of two weeks and a failure rate of 35 percent.

The chances of that Long Island farmer's wife developing breast cancer was very real and the consequences of her not seeking treatment dire. Even today, 18 percent of untreated breast cancer patients will survive just five years and only 3.6 percent will live for ten years.[1] The breast, which is the most common site of cancer in women, ranked number one as the cause of death from cancer in women until 1985. It is only exceeded today by lung cancer.

In 1900 travel to New York City, where more appropriate care was available, was a major undertaking. The Long Island Rail Road was one possibility or it might require a boat trip on the Long Island Sound or an arduous horse and buggy ride. Thus the situation for the farmer and his wife was indeed serious.

It was two decades before the inadequacies of hernia surgery were properly addressed. In 1920 William Downes, a New York surgeon, voiced his discontent with the high failure rate of the procedures developed by Eduardo Bassini of Italy and William Halsted of Baltimore. Downes modified the Bassini operation first described in 1884 and vastly improved the failure rates.[2] However, this did not improve the situation for the residents of Nassau County. In 1920 there were only 120 hospital beds available in the county, and the majority of these were devoted to managing patients with medical, not surgical, problems. The 1916 polio epidemic with a 20 percent mortality, and the massive 1919 influenza epidemic affected Nassau County as well as other areas.

In 1921 the Queens-Nassau Medical Society split into two bodies. Two years later the Nassau County Medical Society published a report documenting the lack of hospital beds. This inadequacy was highlighted during the blizzard of 1920 during which time the Town of Hempstead was isolated for six weeks making it impossible to transfer critically ill patients to New York City. The Medical Society began to campaign for a county hospital, and in 1935 the 200 bed Meadowbrook Hospital was built in an East Meadow potato field. By way of contrast, today the North Shore-Long Island Jewish Health System Hospitals alone have more than four thousand beds devoted to providing Nassau County residents with the most modern and sophisticated medical and surgical care.

By the 1970s an adult hernia patient was usually admitted to the hospital on the day prior to surgery and discharged on the first or second postoperative day. Today same-day surgery is the norm. Patients with a hernia are admitted to the ambulatory section of the hospital or to an ambulatory center. Surgery is performed on the morning of admission and the patient is discharged to the quiet and comfort of his own home several hours later. He may resume work without heavy lifting within the week, and the chances of his hernia recurring are in the 1 percent range.

Breast cancer is a serious situation in Long Island with prevalence rates among the highest in the country. In the 1970s, the probability of a woman developing breast cancer was estimated at one in thirteen; in 1980 it was one in eleven; and in 1996 the frequency was one in eight. There is investigative work in process to establish the cause of this heightened incidence of frequency.

During the five year period between 1972 and 1978, a review of 15,000 consecutive general surgical operations performed at the Long Island Jewish Medical Center in New Hyde Park revealed that inguinal hernia operations in adults comprised 15.4 percent of the total; pediatric and adolescent hernias comprised 14.6 percent; and breast surgery comprised 14.4 percent of the total.[3] In 1998 the hernia figures have not changed, although today the operation is done in an ambulatory setting rather than an in-patient environment. The statistics for breast operations have changed dramatically. During the three year period from 1996 through 1998, 4,223 general surgical operations were performed at the Day Op Center of Long Island in Mineola. Of these, 1,268 were herniorrhaphies, which is an incidence of 30 percent. During that same period, breast biopsies made up 61 percent of the general surgical procedures performed at that institution.[4]

At the turn of the century, radical breast cancer surgery was available only at select hospitals in New York City. This involved removal of the breast, the underlying muscles, and the lymph glands under the arm.[5] The operation was extensive but the results were gratifying. For fifty years, this Halsted radical mastectomy was the procedure of choice. During the past quarter of a century surgeons have become more discriminating, and less radical operations combined with radiation and/or chemotherapy have yielded equally good results.

Chemotherapy, which traditionally had been reserved for treatment after surgery, now appears promising when used prior to operation. In some cases the tumor disappeared completely, and in the majority of the remaining cases the cancer was reduced sufficiently in size so as to allow for simple local excision rather than requiring more radical surgery.

Nassau County has conducted screening programs consisting of physical examination and mammography of women with no symptoms. Both are necessary for a maximum yield, which is as high as six cancers detected per thousand women. About 80 percent of these women have no involvement of the axillary lymph glands compared to 45 percent of breast cancer patients found during the course of usual medical practice. Despite the steady increase in incidence, overall breast cancer deaths have not increased. This relative decrease in mortality reflects the detection of an increasing percentage of early disease. Between 1960 and 1963 the five-year survival rates were 63 percent in white women and 46 percent in black women. Between 1981 and 1987 the figures were 78 percent and 63 percent respectively.[6]

We have progressed enormously in ninety-nine years from the Long Island farmer having to face a 35 percent failure rate after a hernia operation, or his wife who may have had an undetected and therefore untreated breast cancer. Hernia and breast surgery, the two most common general surgical procedures, as well as all other operations are now readily available in Nassau County at facilities rated among the most outstanding in the nation and by well trained, highly qualified surgeons.

Notes

1. H. J. G. Bloom, et al., "Natural History of Untreated Breast Cancer (1805-1933): Comparison of Treated and Untreated Cases According to Histologic Grade of Malignancy," *British Medical Journal* 5299 (1962): 213.

2. W. A. Downes, "Management of Direct Inguinal Hernia," *Archives of Surgery* 1 (1920): 53-73.

3. S. D. Berliner, "Adult Inguinal Hernia: Pathophysiology and Repair," *Surgery Annual* 15 (1983): 307-29; and S. D. Berliner, "An Approach to Groin Hernia," *Surgical Clinics of North America* 64 (1984): 197-213.

4. The Day-Op Center of Long Island, Mineola 1999, with permission.

5. S. Halsted, "The Results of Operations for the Cure of Cancer of the Breast Performed at the Johns Hopkins Hospital from June 1889 to January 1894," *Annals of Surgery* 20 (1894): 497.

6. S. Schwartz, *Principles of Surgery,* 7th ed. (New York: McGraw Hill, 1999), 554.

The History of Orthopedics in Nassau County

Adrian R. Coren, M. D.

While 1929 brought an end to an era in many institutions, it marked the birth of orthopedics at Winthrop-University Hospital (then Nassau Hospital) in Mineola, Long Island. The precursor of this department has much to do with Dr. William L. Sneed, a consultant orthopedic surgeon in New York City, who visited Winthrop Hospital on a weekly basis. Dr. Sneed brought with him to Winthrop a young orthopedic surgeon named Otho Hudson who was to play a defining role in the history of orthopedics in Nassau County.

No account of this history can be written without paying tribute to this young surgeon, Dr. Hudson. After graduation from the University of Kentucky, Dr. Hudson completed a surgical residency at the Henry Ford Hospital in Detroit, Michigan (1926-1929), and spent one year (1929) at the prestigious Hospital for Ruptured and Crippled in New York City. In 1930 he opened his office to the practice of orthopedic surgery in the Professional Building in Hempstead, not far from Winthrop Hospital, whose staff he joined.

At the time of his appearance on the scene, hospitals were approved for surgical training only. It was not until 1944 that a separate list of "Approved Orthopedic Residencies" was published by the American Medical Association (AMA). At the time, orthopedic training centers were few and included: the Mayo Clinic in Minnesota, Western Reserve University Hospital in Ohio, Harvard University Hospital in Boston, the Campbell Clinic in Memphis, and Hospital for Ruptured and Crippled in New York City.

The role of an orthopedist, as we see it today, differs greatly from what existed in Dr. Hudson's pre-antibiotic era. Patients then were treated by closed manipulation and traction, and open long bone surgery was fraught with danger of infection. Internal fixation materials were unreliable, and children's orthopedic deformities were treated with braces, subcutaneous tenotomies, manipulations, and casts.

The only formally trained orthopedist in the area was Dr. Hudson, who was the ultimate itinerant consultant. His travels took him to Long Island Beach Memorial Hospital, South Nassau Communities Hospital, the Tuberculosis Sanitarium in Plainview, and Mercy Hospital. From there he motored to Brunswick Home in Amityville, and to Mather General Hospital and St. Charles Hospital in Port Jefferson. He also made trips to Huntington Hospital, Southampton Hospital, and Greenport Hospital. These trips would take as long as three weeks before he could return to his home base in Winthrop

Hospital where he established a Department of Orthopedics in 1934. His next milestone was the establishment of an Orthopedic Residency at Nassau County Medical Center (NCMC), then Meadowbrook Hospital, in 1935, the year of its opening.

Prior to 1946, orthopedists frequently achieved their "Specialist" rating through preceptorship and through compensation classification. The "preceptorship" concept was soon formally discouraged. Most trauma treatment before World War II was done by general surgeons with interest in fracture care. Dr. Carl Freese, Dr. Richard Bartels, and Dr. Julius Felicetti were general surgeons who, through their association with Dr. Hudson, were classified as orthopedists.

The first formally Long Island-trained orthopedist was Dr. J. Ostrowski who graduated from the Nassau program in 1947. The second graduate, Dr. Armand Prisco (who recently retired), accompanied the "Chief" (Dr. Hudson), on his itinerant rounds in surgery in 1948 and 1949. Though his methods of treatment suited the circumstances of his early career, they rapidly became obsolete in the post-war period with universally accepted internal fixation, antibiotics, and an invasive orthopedic philosophy. Gradually the insular environment created by this bright, dedicated, somewhat rigid pioneer was diffused and the mantle of leadership passed to individuals trained at other centers.

St. Charles Hospital was where his personally trained associate Dr. Julius Felicetti, and then his residency-trained Dr. Joseph Consoli, accounted for much of the pediatric component of the Nassau orthopedic program. His trauma center at NCMC became a fully independent residency under Dr. A. Potenza and then Dr. Adrian Coren in 1974. The Winthrop program was eventually headed by Drs. Walter Trenkle and Sherwood Greiner.

Total hip replacements were done at several institutions in Nassau County and Suffolk County, including NCMC and the Central General Hospital, by the writer. The total joint replacements were done at Huntington Hospital and Southside Hospital in Bay Shore. The contribution of Winthrop Hospital was the concept of Grand Round presentations of the case prior to and following surgery. This, and the supervision by the presiding orthopedist at these clinics, led to a degree of stability and training for the local orthopedists and residents.

Scoliosis clinics were established at Nassau County Medical Center by Dr. Leonard Weiss and at Huntington Hospital by Dr. Andrew Lawrence, the latter Hudson-trained. This included Risser scoliosis treatment as well as Harrington Rod fixation treatment involving open surgery and metallic fixation and fusion.

Dr. Richard Gilberti, one of Dr. Hudson's associates, developed a bipolar hip procedure in 1976. This concept is still in use and many variations have been developed throughout the orthopedic community worldwide.

Total knee replacements were performed in the early 1970s by Dr. A. Coren at Central General Hospital and by Dr. Richard Laskin at Nassau County Medical Center and South Shore Community Hospital. Dr. Jorge Cerruti, a Hudson Resident, performed his procedures for total knee surgery, for the most part, at Mercy Hospital in Rockville Centre and at Winthrop Hospital.

Arthroscopy was pioneered on Long Island by Dr. Joseph Dashefsky at Central General and Massapequa General Hospital. Dr. Paul Yerys, also Hudson-trained, did his procedures at Winthrop Hospital and Hempstead General as well as Mercy Hospital. By the mid-1970s, Dr. Yerys developed his own Anterior Cruciate Ligament (ACL) two-stage replacement procedure for the knees, an innovative procedure at the time.

Sports Medicine as a specialty was early considered by Dr. R. Linden (Hudson-trained) and Dr. Patrick DeRosa, one of my NCMC residents, as a major part of their practices.

Fracture care with AO plating and internal fixation was done by Dr. Eric Jorgensen (Hudson-trained) and Dr. Ralph Hirshorn at South Nassau Hospital. Dr. Hirshorn developed his own compression plating system at South Nassau Hospital.

With the establishment of the State University of New York Hospital at Stony Brook, residences of both institutions were transferred to the directorship of Dr. Roger Dee. Both the NCMC and Winthrop residences are now affiliates of the University program with residents rotating through both institutions under the Chiefship of Dr. Lawrence Hirst.

With the advent of mega-hospitals and more rigidly supervised programs, one may be assured that orthopedic training and orthopedic procedures on Long Island will change to keep pace.

Author's Source Note

Many of the anecdotes of Dr. O. Hudson's experiences are from his own and his residents' communications. Dr. Jorge Cerruti's biography (May 20, 1993) was particularly heart warming and helpful. Many of the events, changes in services, and innovative surgical procedures have occurred since my professional career began on Long Island in 1948 and thus are based on my own observations.

Pediatric Care in Nassau County

Jack David Gorvoy, M.D.

To attempt to record the growth of pediatric care in Nassau County over the past one hundred years would be to undertake an imprecise task. Since the American Academy of Pediatrics was founded only in 1930, to be followed by the establishment of the American Board of Pediatrics in 1935, any historical compilation of pediatric growth prior to that time would be, at best, anecdotal if not inaccurate.

Nassau was a county of general practitioners in the years prior to 1930. A landmark in its medical progress was the dedication of the Meadowbrook Hospital in East Meadow, New York, in 1935. Dr. Alexander McKae, the first superintendent, exercised his credo of excellent patient care, good hospital food, and cleanliness. The Meadowbrook Hospital had the good fortune of having Dr. Minor C. Hill as the first Director of Pediatrics. Dr. Hill was a graduate of Princeton University and Johns Hopkins Medical School, and had the distinction of having been the first pediatric resident at Bellevue Hospital in New York City under the distinguished pediatric professor, Dr. Emmet Holt, Sr. Dr. Hill initiated three services at Meadowbrook, a regular pediatric division, a nursery, and a contagious disease unit. His classic Sunday morning rounds would be made in a morning coat and striped trousers with his staff following behind him in the same attire. Most of the members of the pediatric staff were general practitioners with more than an average interest in pediatrics. There were very few pediatric specialists on Long Island, and many Nassau families would visit New York City for their pediatric needs rather than rely on the sparse care offered in their vicinity. Even in New York, there was only one pediatric surgeon prior to 1940, and none on Long Island.

The newborn service was small because most babies were born at home. Prior to World War II, most infants and children were treated by the general practitioner. After the war, and with the influx of young families from Brooklyn and Queens, there were increasing demands for pediatric services.

The contagious disease service was extremely active. During the well-documented epidemic of poliomyelitis during the first summer for the Meadowbrook Hospital, the well-organized care for these patients was exemplary. By 1963, poliomyelitis became essentially a disease of the past with the introduction of immunization for this dreaded disease during the late 1950s. Before the discovery of sulfonamide drugs and penicillin, pneumococcal pneumonia would be treated with anti-serum. The Meadowbrook

Hospital was designated as one of the stations in Nassau County to serum-type for this infection.

During the depths of the depression, when poverty was at its peak, the Nassau County Medical Society made efforts to care for the out-patient needs of the indigent patients. The well-baby clinics in Nassau County were started in 1938. Visits to these clinics required authorization from a private doctor. This type of clearance was soon remedied in order to have the hospital's doctors residency program approved.

In the early 1930s, intravenous therapy was introduced in Nassau County, and facilities for determining blood electrolytes became available. This adjunctive therapy for the high incidence of diarrheal disease and their complications became a major contribution to pediatric care. Intravenous fluids would be administered on a mass basis in the pediatric clinic for lack of bed space for admissions. When exchange transfusions were introduced in 1946, various hospitals in Nassau became active in these procedures.

In 1965, Dr. Irving Olshin, a former resident in Pediatrics (1956-1957) at Long Island Jewish Medical Center (L.I.J.M.C.), was appointed Director of Pediatrics at Meadowbrook Hospital. A cystic fibrosis center was established at L.I.J.M.C. in 1960, and at present is recognized as the largest Cystic Fibrosis Center in the New York metropolitan and the Long Island areas. The program was initiated by the writer of this paper, who at present remains the director of the Schneider Children's Hospital Cystic Fibrosis Diagnostic, Research and Treatment Center, located in New Hyde Park, New York.

In 1973, the Meadowbrook Hospital became the Nassau County Medical Center, now well recognized for the quality of its care. To enlarge the scope and expertise in medical care for the expanding population on Long Island, the Stony Brook Medical School was created. By 1974, the first class of eighteen students graduated from Stony Brook, and in 1980 the University Hospital of Stony Brook admitted its first patient. At present there are four hundred medical students enrolled in the Stony Brook Medical School, among whom are many who intend to carry on and extend the history of pediatric care in Nassau County.

Note

The history of pediatric care has not been previously recorded. This brief account is based on the author's personal knowledge and on I. M. Frodkin, "Meadowbrook in Retrospect," *Nassau County Medical Center Proceedings* 3, no. 2, 1977.

A History of Heart Surgery on Long Island

B. George Wisoff, M. D.

Heart surgery in our area required the development of sophisticated diagnostic and treatment facilities in addition to the recruitment of physicians with adequate drive and knowledge to succeed in this new medical field.

The heart was the last of the major organs amenable to surgery. Technical problems (bleeding and motion) in addition to physiological demands (circulatory and respiratory) made the surgical approach to the heart risky and usually fatal. The technical demands and the physiological support problems have been partially solved only in the last half of this century. This has led to the remarkable expansion of effective and fairly safe procedures on the heart and great vessels. Diagnostic sophistication and scientific development in a multitude of fields have supplied the basic underpinnings for surgical success. Long Island hospitals, and in particular Nassau County hospitals, were early participants and contributors in this new medical field.

St. Francis Hospital

St. Francis was established by the Catholic Diocese in 1922 as a summer camp for inner city children. In 1937 it became a sanitarium for children with cardiac diseases, mainly those with rheumatic fever. Dr. Leo Taran was the medical director. Diagnostic cardiac work led to the ability to perform closed heart procedures (those not involving use of heart-lung machines) in 1954. The hospital later was opened to adults, and open-heart surgery (with use of a heart-lung machine) was first successfully done on Long Island in 1956. In 1959 the hospital expanded to a full-care institution in addition to the cardiology specialty. In the 1970s St. Francis recruited full-time physicians. Dr. William Noble managed the diagnostic and medical aspects of cardiology and Dr. Norman Thompson led the surgical department. A dedicated pediatric surgeon, Dr. Paul Damus, joined the group. The DeMatteis Rehabilitation Center was a major addition for cardiac care. St. Francis has become one of the highest volume cardiac diagnostic and procedure institutions in the country.[1]

Long Island Jewish Hospital

Long Island Jewish was opened as a general hospital by the Federation of Jewish Philanthropies in 1954. A residency training program, the only one on Long Island, was set up for the education and certification of cardiac and thoracic surgeons. This was originally directed by a visiting surgeon, Dr.

At left: Shumacher Potato Farm, 1940s, the future site of the Long Island Jewish Hospital. *Below*: Long Island Jewish Hospital, 1954. Photographs courtesy of the Public Affairs Department, Long Island Jewish Medical Center.

Philip Crastnopol. Dr. Walter Phillips was then recruited from South Africa to direct the program. In 1969 Dr. B. George Wisoff took over and expanded the teaching, research, and clinical programs. Subsequent to 1980, the surgical division has been directed by Drs. George Greene, Dennis Tyras, and Michael Graver. The impetus for new diagnostic and surgical modalities was provided by the research and development in cardiology led by Dr. Ephraim Glassman and Dr. Robert Hamby. In 1969 this led to the first direct coronary surgery in the New York area.[2] Pediatric research and care was managed by Dr. Norman Gootman.

North Shore Hospital

North Shore began in 1950, and cardiac surgery was instituted in 1968. The cardiac program was run by Drs. Arthur Beil, Martin Kaplitt, and Anthony Tortoloni, and is now under the supervision of Dr. Michael Hall. Early procedures to clear coronary obstructions with pressurized gas were performed by Kaplitt.[3] The Grumann Corporation contributed to the development of an open heart machine and intra-operative angiography (x-rays of the coronaries) were utilized.[4]

Winthrop-University Hospital

Winthrop was opened as Nassau Hospital in 1896. In the 1970s a heart program was established by Drs. Manucher Mohtashami, George Hines and others. With the arrival of Dr. William Scott the program enlarged to a major service in the Long Island area. Dr. Scott expanded the use of heart-assist devices which allowed minimally invasive access (small incision) for surgery. In addition, he utilized left ventricular assist devices (support for the failing heart) to allow for recovery or transplantation.

Meadowbrook Hospital

Meadowbrook, now Nassau County Medical Center, performed heart surgery early in its history. With the expansion of successful programs in the neighboring voluntary hospitals, the transport of patients requiring urgent and elective procedures led to the eclipse of the procedures at Nassau County Medical Center.

Other Institutions

Stony Brook University Hospital established a program for cardiac surgery that has become very active. It is the only such service east of Nassau County. Other hospitals, such as Southside and Good Samaritan have diagnostic facilities, but refer patients to surgical centers for operative care. There has been a recent agglomeration of hospitals such as North Shore and Long Island Jewish entered into with the hope of more efficient and superior care than which had been possible in smaller facilities.

Diagnostic and interventional cardiology provides the basic impetus for heart surgery. Dedicated pediatric programs have led to various procedures for correction or palliation of congenital heart malformations. St. Francis performs the largest number of adult interventional procedures in the country, e. g., coronary clot lysis, angioplasty, and stents.

All the surgical programs now rank in the top levels of New York State's coronary bypass surgery.[5] A high proportion of coronary surgery is now performed on an urgent or emergency basis, which has led to a decrease in heart damage from obstructed coronary arteries. Valve replacements and repairs have become routine. The volume of adult surgery has continued to grow, coincident with our aging population as well as the more aggressive approach to the management of life threatening heart disease.

Academic affiliations, important for access to teaching and research institutions, were established with Stony Brook, New York University,

Cornell, Columbia, and Einstein medical schools. The universities use our local programs for clinical training of undergraduate and postgraduate medical students. The only free standing residency teaching program for heart surgery has remained at Long Island Jewish Hospital. Basic research is done at Cold Spring Harbor in addition to our hospital based laboratories. Outstanding academic work was performed in pediatric circulation (Dr. Norman Gootman)[6] and adult heart function (Dr. Robert Hamby).[7] The American Heart Association, Long Island Chapter, has been a strong supporter of local research. Heart arrhythmia specialists are now in the forefront of sudden death prevention.

Rehabilitation and public health concerns are becoming more prominent. Institutions such as St. Francis' DeMatteis Center, in addition to our physicians, are providing diagnostic procedures leading to early diagnosis and surgical management of heart disease. Postoperative rehabilitation is available through all the Nassau hospitals and cardiologists.

Heart transplants are not available locally. There is no major academic institution that can provide the large investment in diagnostic and therapeutic modalities needed for this procedure. However, the close affiliations and availability of temporary support (such as the left ventricular assist device at Winthrop) have allowed safe transport to transplant programs in Manhattan.

Notes

1. On the history of St. Francis Hospital, see also Sr. Lois Van Delft, "Women of Faith: The Spiritual Legacy of the Founders of St. Francis Hospital," in *Long Island Women: Activists and Innovators,* edited by Natalie A. Naylor and Maureen O. Murphy (Interlaken, NY: Empire State Books, 1998), 146-53. (Editor's note.)

2. B. G. Wisoff, M. L. Hartstein, A. Aintablian, and R. I. Hamby, "Risk of Coronary Surgery; Two Hundred Consecutive Patients with No Hospital Deaths," *Journal of Thoracic and Cardiovascular Surgery* 69, no. 5 (May 1975): 669-73.

3. M. J. Kaplitt and G. Robinson, "Coronary Gas Endarterectomy," *American Heart Journal* 81, no.1 (January 1971): 136-40.

4. M. J. Kaplitt, S. L. Frantz, A. R. Beil, H. L. Stein, and S. J. Gulotta, "Analysis of Intraoperative Coronary Angiography in Aortocoronary Bypass Grafts," *Circulation* 50, no. 2 Suppl. (August 1974): 141-48.

5. New York State Department of Health, *Coronary Artery Bypass Surgery in New York State, 1994-1996,* October 1998, 14-15.

6. N. Gootman, P. M. Gootman, L. A. Crane, and B. J. Buckley, "Integrated Cardiovascular Responses to Combined Somatic and Visceral Afferent Stimulation in Newborn Piglets," *Biology of the Neonate* 36, no. 1-2 (1979): 70-77.

7. R. I. Hamby, A. Aintablian, M. Handler, C. Voleti, D. Weisz, J. W. Garvey, and G. Wisoff, "Aortocorony Saphenous Vein Bypass Grafts: Long Term Patency, Morphology and Blood Flow in Patients with Patent Grafts Early after Surgery," *Circulation* 60, no. 4 (October 1979): 901-9.

The Origins of Airplane Manufacturing in Farmingdale, New York: 1917–1928

Roy Douglas

The first years of airplane manufacturing in Farmingdale in Nassau County have not received the recognition they deserve. Farmingdale was actually an important center for the manufacture of planes, plane engines, and avionics, all of which paved the way for the development of other, vital developments in aircraft. In particular, the work of three men, Sydney Breese, Lawrence Sperry, and Sherman Fairchild, established Farmingdale as a center for, even, one might say, a "cradle" of aviation.

Aviation began in Farmingdale during World War I with a plane that couldn't fly! The United States Army wanted a "non-flying ground trainer," which would familiarize pilots-in-training with the difficulties of controlling unstable aircraft and "facilitate the transition between primary trainers and secure types."[1] Workers in the Breese Aircraft Company factory, located on Eastern Parkway, along the Main Line of the Long Island Rail Road, built three hundred of these short-winged "Penguins" in 1918.[2] Sydney Breese's underpowered trainer had neither brakes nor steering wheel, which, as one pilot recalled, created difficulties:

> I found that it was very difficult to keep a straight course when tearing across a field at the rate of about forty miles an hour. It was comical to see how the clumsy contraption behaved, turning circles, . . . rolling over on its wing, and behaving in every way like a drunken sailor trying to walk a chalk line.[3]

The Breese Penguin, powered by a 2-cylinder 28 horsepower Charles Lanier Lawrance engine, was obsolete even before it was produced, and was never really a part of United States pilot training during World War I. It is said that fewer than two hundred of the Farmingdale-produced Penguins were actually assembled because the Army used Thomas-Morse biplane trainers instead.[4]

The manufacture of airplanes and airplane instruments in Farmingdale originated with the Lawrence Sperry Airplane Company in May 1917.[5] Son of legendery Sperry Gyroscope founder, Elmer Sperry, Lawrence incorporated his company with $50,000 in capital after experimenting with unmanned aerial torpedoes near Amityville and Copiague in 1916 and early 1917.[6] At that time the factory was located in the former Bausch Picture Frame Company factory at Rose and Richard Streets in the Village of Farmingdale.[7]

Lawrence Sperry was an important pioneer in American aviation. In 1914, he was honored by the French government for developing the gyro-stablizer auto pilot, which freed pilots from constantly handling the controls, and greatly improved in-flight stability.[8] Other aviation "firsts" developed by Sperry, in association with his father, included turn and bank instruments, and retractable landing gear in a monoplane. Lawrence Sperry was the first pilot to fly at night over water in America (fifty miles from Moriches to Amityville on September 2, 1916) and the first to use landing lights. He improved the magnetic compass, developed an optional drift set, and experimented with night flying over land to demonstrate the usefulness of Sperry-built searchlights as beacons in helping pilots locate landing fields after sunset.[9] Jimmy Doolittle acknowledged that virtually all the cockpit instruments used on his historic September 24, 1929 "blind-flight" from Mitchel Field "had been conceived, invented, or developed by Lawrence Sperry."

The intrepid Sperry, who was motivated toward aviation as a youngster after seeing Henri Farman fly at the First Mineola Air Meet in 1908, developed one of the first seat-pack parachutes in America, which he tested himself in a dangerous jump over Dayton, Ohio.[10] Lawrence Sperry's employees manufactured three very different types of historic aircraft in Farmingdale in the six years between 1917 and 1923. He first built airplanes in his factory on Rose Street in the Village of Farmingdale.[11] There his sixty workers built fifteen Navy Amphibian Triplanes, eighteen Messengers, three Verville-Sperry R-3 racers, and worked on his innovative aerial torpedoes.[12]

Before Lawrence Sperry began manufacturing airplanes in Farmingdale, he already had been conducting highly original research and development on unmanned "aerial torpedoes" at the Sperry hanger on the east side of Unqua Place below Lower Ocean Avenue in Amityville next door to the Unqua Corinthian Yacht Club, and at the flying field he rented about two miles east on South Road in Copiague along the Great South Bay shoreline.[13] Working for the United States Navy, Sperry experimented first with N-9 Curtiss seaplanes.[14] Subsequently, the Curtiss Aircraft Company produced five "flying bombs," using Lawrence Sperry's gyro-stabilizer.[15] Sperry modified the preset aerial torpedoes "under close marine guard at Sperry Field, near Copiague, L.I.," by equipping the aircraft with skids, and made dangerous test flights, launched by catapults, off the ice of the Great South Bay.[16] This was extremely treacherous work. Lawrence had several serious mishaps, breaking his nose and his pelvis in separate accidents while experimenting with the unpredictable aerial torpedoes. While perfecting the Curtiss-Sperry flying bomb on test flights, he strapped himself to the underside of the fuselage. As Preston R. Bassett noted, "As it was too expensive to lose an airplane every time it was tested. Sperry would ride out as a passenger on the missile until it had reached its target over the ocean, he would then take over the controls and fly it back."[17] Commander Benjamin B. McCormick, inspector of naval ordinance, watched these tests. As he observed: "The Curtiss flying bomb slammed down on the ice, a complete wreck. Only the engine, the radiator and Lawrence Sperry came out undamaged."[18]

On March 6, 1918, from a flying field on the Great South Bay near Copiague, after adding a distance responsive air log, and launching the torpedo from an inclined track with rails, and a turntable (to allow the flying bomb to take off into the wind),[19] Lawrence Sperry succeeded in directing an unmanned "flying bomb" one thousand yards onto his target in the Great South Bay.[20] Rear Admiral Fahrney, who watched Sperry's historic test, said:

> It was "the first entirely successful flight of an automatic missile in this country if not in the world." The fact that an unmanned plane was under the control of automatic equipment from the catapult launch, through a smooth stabilized flight until the automatic distance gear ordered it to descend to the water is unique in aviation history and up to that day had no parallel in world achievement. [21]

Toward the end of World War I, Sperry conceived of a naval amphibian, which would improve on the Curtiss flying boat. He wanted an amphibian that would be able to handle rough ocean seas, and have wheels that could be folded out of the way, using a crank and cable system.[22] The result was a Farmingdale-built 48-foot wingspan triplane pushed by a 370 horsepower, 12-cylinder Liberty engine.[23] As usual, Lawrence tested the plane himself. As William Davenport describes the scene in his biography of Sperry, *Gyro:*

> As Navy officials and two hundred Sperry employees stood on the shore of the Great South Bay, Lawrence and a Navy co-pilot took off, flew over Fire Island, and landed in the Atlantic amid heavy ocean swells that would have swamped any previous plane. Then he took off again, churning through the furrows of the ocean, rising up in a geyser of salt spray, triumphantly aloft. Above Farmingdale, he cranked down his retractable landing gear and made a perfect landing on the field of the Lawrence Sperry Aircraft Company. The employees . . . pulled their boss and the Navy pilot out of the cockpit and carried them around the field on their shoulders. . . .The Sperry amphibian was a success and production began on a fifteen-plane order.[24]

Sperry was both fearless and reckless. For example, he is said to have looped the loop with the bulky triplane amphibian off Mastic Beach.[25] As Joshua Stoff has noted in *The Aerospace Heritage of Long Island,* Sperry's triplane amphibian "was remarkably fast for its day."[26] In 1982, the United States Postal Service honored Lawrence and Elmer Sperry with an airmail stamp, which highlighted the triplane amphibian.[27]

Sperry Amphibian Triplane, c. 1918. *NCM Collection, LISI at Hofstra.*

Sperry's workers assembled forty-two "Messengers" for the United States Army in Farmingdale; eighteen in his Rose Street Shop, and twenty-four in the eastern half of the Raymond Engineering building on Fulton Street in South Farmingdale (where Victor Page also built automobiles), which he occupied in August 1921.[28] The Sperry Messenger was the fulfillment of two dreams. Lawrence wanted an "aerial flivver," a small plane, which the average auto owner could buy and fly. As he said, the aerial flivver would provide "motorists of the air" with "no traffic jams, no jaywalkers, no poor road surfaces. . . . No officious cops to bawl you out," and "no constable to enforce freak speed laws to finance the village government."[29]

Brigadier General William "Billy" Mitchell, Assistant Chief of the United States Army Air Force, also wanted a small, inexpensive, single-engine plane that could be used to train pilots in pursuit maneuvers, and which could take-off and land easily "from roads and unimproved fields for communications duties."[30] Alfred Verville designed the Messenger, which General Mitchell named (also calling it the "motorcycle of the air").[31] The ultralight 500-pound, seventeen and a half foot long, twenty-foot wing-spanned Messenger was powered by a 3-cylinder, 64-horsepower Lawrence radial engine. It flew ninety-five miles-per-hour and traveled thirty miles on a gallon of gasoline.[32] This is the $5,000 plane Sperry commuted in between his Garden City home and the fifteen acre flying field alongside his South Farmingdale factory. It is also the "baby" plane he landed on the steps of the United States Capitol when annoyed that Assistant Secretary of the Navy

Lawrence Sperry fueling his Sperry M-1 Messenger, 1922. *NCM Collection, LISI at Hofstra.*

Theodore Roosevelt, Jr. wasn't paying him promptly for the Naval Amphibian Triplanes.[33] Sperry earned great fame with the Messenger after the United States Army awarded him an $84,000 contract in April 1920 to experiment with three Messengers as MAT's or, Messenger aerial torpedoes. Sperry ingeniously equipped the three M-1's with radio controls, and successfully directed them, from Mitchel Field, unmanned, to targets 30, 60, and 90 miles in the Atlantic off Long Island on June 29, 1922, winning a $40,000 bonus, which he distributed among his employees.[34] As Thomas Hughes wrote in 1971: "Generally speaking, Sperry's work in the flying bomb, or guided missile, field is not appreciated or understood by historians."[35]

Lawrence Sperry's craftsmen fabricated three low-wing, cantilever Verville-Sperry racing airplanes in his factory on Rose Street for the United States Army in 1922. The R-3 was designed by Alfred Verville, at the request of General Mitchell, who wanted a sleek, fast, maneuverable fighter for the Army, which wouldn't have the "squirrel-cage" exterior struts and wires.[36] Alfred Verville, who had assisted Glenn Curtiss design the Jenny, didn't trust Sperry to stick to his design. Thus we read that, "Verville was at the Lawrence Sperry Aircraft factory every day watching every move Lawrence made, afraid that this pragmatic 'flying fool' might modify his specifications by a single millimeter."[37]

The Verville-Sperry racer featured the first retractable wheels in a monoplane.[38] The R-3, powered by a Wright H-2 350 horsepower motor, held the world's speed record for twenty minutes in the 1924 Pulitzer race at Dayton, Ohio, reaching a top speed of 216 miles-per-hour.[39] The streamlined R-3 utilized steel tubing and was covered with aluminum in front of the cockpit, and doped fabric behind.[40] Joshua Stoff has noted that the R-3's "presaged fighters of the 1930s."[41]

Lawrence Sperry was flying a Messenger when it fell into the English Channel where he drowned in December 1923. He had taken the Messenger to Britain on the liner *Mauretania* to demonstrate how "practical his aerial 'flivver' was for election purposes."[42] Before he died, Sperry had begun testing Messengers to hook-up with other aircraft. With his untimely passing, the Lawrence Sperry Aircraft Company also died. Farmingdale mourned the loss of their innovative industrialist. The village board named a street in his honor, Sperry Place, just west of the Farmingdale Long Island Rail Road station.[43] Airplane manufacture in Farmingdale, however, did not expire with Lawrence Sperry's death.

Sherman Fairchild had successfully developed aerial cameras and an aerial photography business in the early 1920s.[44] When his pilots and photographers in Canada complained about the cold, the noise, and the fumes of the open-cockpit aircraft they were using, Fairchild decided to start his own airplane manufacturing company and build his own planes with heated enclosed cabins especially designed for aerial photography.[45] Fairchild was similar to Robert Moses in that Moses never drove a car, and Fairchild never piloted an airplane.[46] Fairchild hired Norman McQueen to design the Fairchild Cabin high-wing, large-windowed, folding-wing monoplane. Fairchild leased the idle Sperry plant in South Farmingdale, where Bob Simon supervised the production of Fairchild's FC-1, which was powered by a Curtiss OX-5 engine. The FC-1 was successfully test flown from Curtiss Field on June 14, 1926 by famed Fairchild test pilot Dick Depew.[47] The FC-1 flew for thirty minutes at a top speed of 97 miles-per-hour, after having been trucked from Farmingdale to Curtiss Field with its wings folded. In August 1926 it was flown around America by pilot "Johnnie" Johnson in the arduous 2,600 mile Ford Reliability tour. The weaker OX-5 was soon replaced with a more powerful Wright J-4 engine, and the FC-1 became the FC-1A.[48] Kent Mitchell, an historian of Fairchild aircraft, has said that the 44-foot wing-spanned FC-1 was the first aircraft "with predictable flying characteristics."[49]

Sherman Fairchild and Bob Simon expanded the Sperry facility in South Farmingdale in 1927, by contracting with the Truscan Steel Company to build additional factory buildings within six weeks, to permit Fairchild to produce FC-2s and Caminez engines.[50] The FC-2s were equipped with 220 horsepower Wright J-5 Whirlwind engines.[51] The larger engine allowed the fuselage to be widened to carry more passengers, baggage, or equipment. In the summer of 1927, Fairchild took orders for about 100 FCs.[52] The FC-2s were rugged and dependable aircraft that they could fly almost anywhere on wheels, skis, or pontoons.[53] Realizing in mid-1927 that the South Farmingdale factory in Nassau County was too small for the automobile type assembly line production he was planning, Fairchild drew up plans for modern airplane and airplane engine factories, and a larger flying field to be located in East Farmingdale, on both sides of Conklin Street, in Suffolk County, just east of Route 110.[54]

Fairchild's Farmingdale FC-2s helped the Canadians map and administer large parts of their vast nation, delivered the first American international air mail from Key West, Florida to Havana, Cuba; and accompanied Lindbergh on his 1927 tour of America after his historic transatlantic flight. A Fairchild FC-2 helped rescue German pilots in the *Bremen,* who had been the first to fly the Atlantic east to west from Ireland to Nova Scotia. Pilots and photographers in an FC-2 also explored New Guinea.[55] Perhaps the three most famous FC-2s built in Farmingdale were the *City of New York,* the *Stars and Stripes,* and the Bell Labs *Flying Telephone Booth.*

Powered by a 400 horsepower Pratt &Whitney "Wasp" engine, the *City of New York* flew around the world (it was shipped across the Atlantic and the Pacific) in 23 days 15 hours and 21 minutes (then a world record) by John H. Mears and Capt. Charles B. Collyer. The FC-2W was the first U.S. aircraft to traverse Stalin's Soviet Russia.[56]

The *Stars and Stripes* was one of three planes taken by Commander Richard Byrd to explore and photograph Antarctica in 1929. The Farmingdale-built *Stars and Stripes,* an FC-2W2 , flew 146 hours in extremely frigid and windy conditions mapping Antarctica. It was left there and was flown another 41 hours when Byrd returned in 1933! Aviation historian Jim Boss believes the *Stars and Stripes* and the Bell Labs aircraft were begun in South Farmingdale, but completed in the new East Farmingdale factory.[57]

The FC-2W Bell Labs *Flying Telephone Booth* was the first aircraft to be delivered from Fairchild's new East Farmingdale factory in Suffolk County in May 1928.[58] This aircraft pioneered in air-to-ground radio experiments showing the usefulness of two-way radios that "soon made possible regularly scheduled air transportation."[59]

In addition to assembling 369 airplanes in Farmingdale, Sherman Fairchild's workers also created pontoons and constructed airplane engines.[60] In 1925, he hired Harold F. Caminez from the United States Army Bureau of Engine Design at McCook Field in Dayton, Ohio, to supervise the production of cam-drive airplane engines. His simpler, lighter "Cam" engine utilized a double-lobed camshaft instead of a crank shaft. While first test-flown from the South Farmingdale field on April 12, 1926 in a World War I Avro 504 by Dick Depew,[61] the Caminez engine was never really success-

The *Stars and Stripes* was built in Farmingdale for Richard Byrd's 1929 Antaractica expedition. *NCM Collection, LISI at Hofstra.*

ful. It vibrated a great deal, and was very rough-running, as was shown in the Ford Reliability Tour of 1928.[62] Caminez left Fairchild Engine Company in 1929, and was replaced by Walter F. Davis, who developed Ranger inverted in-line air-cooled engines in East Farmingdale, which powered P-19 and P-26 training aircraft during World War II.[63] Bill Stockert, a long-time Farmingdale resident, supervised the 50-hour tests of the first Caminez engine. He recalled that the "Cam" ran hot and vibrated a great deal because it fired on every second revolution rather than every fourth, as had been customary on earlier engines.[64]

Thus, after looking at airplane manufacturing in Farmingdale, Nassau County, between 1917 and 1928, from Sidney Breese and his Penguins, to Lawrence Sperry and his Naval Amphibians, Aerial Torpedoes, Sperry Messengers, and Verville-Sperry racers, to the versatile Fairchild utility monoplanes, it is evident that Farmingdale is truly one of America's "cradles of aviation." The work Breese, Sperry, and Fairchild did between these years in establishing Farmingdale as an important center for the manufacture of airplanes, airplane engines, and avionics set the stage for the future development of the Republic P-47, F-84, and F-105, and the Fairchild-Republic A-10 in Farmingdale. The economic stimulus generated by these industries provided a major economic underpinning for the rapid suburbanization of Nassau and Suffolk Counties after World War II.

Notes

Acknowledgements: This research was done with the generous assistance and cooperation of: the Long Island Room of the Queensborough Public Library; Rebecca Looney, Joshua Stoff, and Tom Gwynne of the Cradle of Aviation Museum; Mildred

Murphy DeRiggi and Gary Hammond of the Division of Museum Services of Nassau County; Professor Natalie Naylor, Dr. Barbara Kelly, and the staff of the Long Island Studies Institute at Hofstra University; the staff of the Reference Room in the Farmingdale Public Library; William J. Johnston, Historian of the Village of Farmingdale; Richard Baldwin, a volunteer at the Suffolk County Historical Society Library; the staffs of the Suffolk County Clerk's Office in Riverhead and the Nassau County Clerk's Office in Mineola; and Lynn McDonald of the Republic Airport Historical Society, who produced the slides shown at the Conference on the Centennial of Nassau County at Hofstra University on March 19, 1999.

1. Robert Casari, *U.S. Military Aircraft: 1908 to 1917: Part II: The World War Production Program* (Chillicothe, OH, 1974), 43; Mark Munzel, "The Penguin Flies (almost)," *Turn And Bank,* January/February, 1999, 5; Joshua Stoff, *The Aerospace Heritage of Long Island* (Interlaken, NY: Heart of the Lakes Publishing, 1989), 26; "Sydney Breese, Engineer and Designer Dies at 90," *New York Times*, February 9, 1974, 32.

2. Casari, *U.S. Military Aircraft,* 43; Stoff, *Aerospace Heritage,* 26-27; See "Farmingdale" social notes on Breese Aircraft Company in the *Amityville Record,* February 8, 1918, February 22, 1918, March 8, 1918, and June 7, 1918.

3. Dana C. Winslow, *With the French Flying Corps* (New York: Scribners, 1917), 215.

4. Casari, *U.S. Military Aircraft,* 44, 48; Munzel, "The Penguin Flies (almost)," 5; On Charles L. Lawrance, see: Harry W. Havemeyer, *Along the Great South Bay* (Mattituck, NY: Amereon House, 1996), 321-22, 330-31.

5. "Lawrence Sperry, American," *Farmingdale Post,* December 21, 1923; Stoff, *Aerospace Heritage,* 26; Edward J. Thompson, *Farmingdale Train Restoration Project: A Commemorative History of 150 Years of Long Island Railroad Train Service to Farmingdale, NY: 1841-1991* (Farmingdale: Farmingdale Train Station Restoration Committee, 1991), 21.

6. *Farmingdale Post,* February 16, 1924; William Davenport, *Gyro: The Life and Times of Lawrence Sperry* (New York: Scribners, 1978), 139; Thomas Parke Hughes, *Elmer Sperry: Inventor and Engineer* (Baltimore: The Johns Hopkins Press, 1971), 232.

7. Junior Historical Society, *Farmingdale's Story: Farms to Flights* (Farmingdale: Howitt School, 1956), 107; Charles L. Keller, "The First Guided Missile Program: The Aerial Torpedo," *Sperry Engineering Review* 14, no. 1 (March 1961): 11-18.

8. George C. Dade and Frank Strnad, *Picture History of Aviation on Long Island: 1908-1938* (New York: Dover Publications, 1989), 31; Joshua Stoff, *Picture History of Early Aviation, 1908-1913* (New York: Dover Publications, 1996), 88; Davenport, *Gyro,* 111-12.

Peter Cooper Hewitt, the inventor who first encouraged Elmer and Lawrence Sperry to develop aerial torpedoes, partially funded Lawrence Sperry's testing of the gyro-stabilizer in airplanes near Amityville and Copiague, after his initial experimental flights at the Brooklyn Navy Yard, and at the Bayside Yacht Club. See Rear Admiral Delmar S. Fahrney USN (Ret.) and Robert Strobell, "America's First Pilotless Aircraft," *Aero Digest* 69 (1954): 28-30; *Young Men in Aeronautics, A Twenty-Year Progress Report of the Lawrence B. Sperry Award* (New York: Institute of the Aerospace

Sciences, 1957), 19; "Jervis House on Sperry Field Burned, *Amityville Record,* February 25, 1921, 1; Hughes, *Elmer Sperry,* 262.

9. *Young Men in Aeronautics,* 21; Stoff, *Picture History of Early Aviation,* 88; and Davenport, *Gyro,* 111-12.

10. Davenport, *Gyro,* ix, 1-15; Elmer A. Sperry, Jr., *Notes . . .* (Np: Privately printed, 1969), 15 (a copy is in the Nassau County Museum Collection, Long Island Studies Institute at Hofstra University).

11. Junior Historical Society, *Farmingdale's Story,* 107; Stoff, *Aerospace Heritage,* 43, 99; Preston R. Bassett, "Aviation on Long Island," in *Long Island: A History of Two Great Counties: Nassau and Suffolk,* ed. Paul Bailey (New York: Lewis Historical Publishing Company, 1949), 2: 433, 435.

12. Davenport, *Gyro,* 235. According to Charles L. Keller, Sperry's Amityville hanger was erected in the spring of 1916. He rented the Copiague field and its three hangers in the early summer of 1917. See Keller, "First Guided Missile," 12-13. There is a debate as to where Sperry did his historic work on the flying bomb. In fact, Lawrence Sperry made aviation history in both Amityville and Copiague.

13. Lt. Col. H. F. Smith, "The World's First Cruise Missiles," *Air Force Magazine,* October 1977, 42-44; Fahrney and Strobell, "America's First Pilotless Aircraft," 28; R. J. Seese, "Flying Bomb: The Story of America's First Guided Missile Program," *Air Classics* 19, no. 8 (August 1988): 70-80; Davenport, *Gyro,* 187-88; E. Belcher Hyde, *Atlas of the Ocean Shore of Suffolk County, Long Island: Westerly Section* (New York: E. Belcher Hyde, 1915), Plate no. 16.

14. Smith, "World's First Cruise Missiles"; Seese, "Flying Bombs," 82.

15. Davenport, *Gyro,* 188-89.

16. "Aerial Torpedo Explained: Steered 100 Miles Accurately by Gyroscope Compass, 10,000 Would Win A War," *Brooklyn Daily Eagle,* December 8, 1926, 7; Davenport, *Gyro,* 189.

17. Davenport, *Gyro,* 189; Preston R. Bassett, *The Life and Times of Preston R. Bassett* (Ridgefield, CT: Privately printed, 1976), 73-74. This is a collection of reprinted articles in a ring binder which is in the Nassau County Museum Collection, Long Island Studies Institute at Hofstra University.

18. Davenport, *Gyro,* 189.

19. Fahrney and Strobell, "America's First Pilotless Aircraft," 29; Dade and Strnad, *Picture History of Aviation,* 46; Davenport, *Gyro,* 189.

20. Smith, "World's First Cruise Missile," 43; Davenport, *Gyro,* 190; Fahrney and Strobell, "America's First Pilotless Aircraft," 29; George DeWan, "A Missile Flies Over the Bay," in *Long Island: Our Story* by Newsday (Melville: Newsday, 1998), 270.

21. Fahrney and Strobell, "America's First Pilotless Aircraft," 29; Davenport, *Gyro,* 190.

22. Davenport, *Gyro,* 214-15.

23. *Aircraft Yearbook:1921* (Boston: Small & Maynard Co., 1921), 27.

24. Davenport, *Gyro,* 222.

25. *Amityville Record,* October 19, 1917; *Farmingdale Post,* December 21, 1923.

26. Stoff, *Aerospace Heritage,* 99.

27. *Scott 1999 Specialized Catalogue of United States Stamps* (Sidney, OH: Scott Publishing Company, 1999), 217. The Naval Amphibian is shown on the Sperry 39-cent

airmail stamp, AP 87; Alfred Verville and the R-3 Army racer are illustrated on the 33-cent AP 86 stamp.

28. Stoff, *Aerospace Heritage,* 43; Ward Phillips, "Mr Sperry's Might Midget," *Air Classics* 15, no. 5 (May 1979): 23; "Farmingdale," *Amityville Record,* September 5, 1921.

29. Davenport, *Gyro,* 181, 218.

30. Davenport, *Gyro,* 215; Phillips, "Mr. Sperry's Mighty Midget," 17.

31. Dade and Strnad, *Picture History of Aviation,* 73; Phillips, "Mr. Sperry's Mighty Midget," 17, 73.

32. Dade and Strnad, *Picture History of Aviation,* 73; Stoff, *Aerospace Heritage,* 99; Davenport, *Gyro,* 215.

33. Dade and Strnad, *Picture History of Aviation,* 73; Stoff, *Aerospace Heritage,* 99; Davenport, *Gyro,* 193, 222-24.

34. Davenport, *Gyro,* 215, 217; Hughes, *Elmer Sperry,* 272; Phillips, "Mr. Sperry's Mighty Midget," 17.

35. Hughes, *Elmer Sperry,* 274; See also: "Sperry Aerial Torpedo Deadly, "*New York Sun,* December 8, 1926; "Deadly Air Torpedo: Ready at War's End," *New York Times,* December 8, 1926; and "Aerial Torpedo Explained," *Brooklyn Daily Eagle,* December 8, 1926.

36. Davenport, *Gyro,* 237.

37. "Alfred V. Verville, Airplane Designer," *New York Times* obituary, March 14, 1970, 31; Davenport, *Gyro,* 235.

38. Stoff, *Aerospace Heritage,* 43.

39. Davenport, *Gyro,* 235; Alfred V. Verville obituary, *New York Times,* March 14, 1970, 31; William R. Bassett recalls in "Aviation On Long Island" (433), that the Sperry-Verville speed record was beaten by "a Curtiss racer built at Garden City."

40. William J. Kaiser, *The Development of the Aerospace Industry on Long Island: 1904-1964* (Hempstead, NY: Hofstra University, 1968), 1: 30.

41. Stoff, *Aerospace Heritage,* 99.

42. "Sperry Believed Drowned in English Channel; Wreck of Baby Plane Found, Flier Missing," *New York Times,* December 14, 1923, 1.

43. *Amityville Record,* September 23, 1924; Davenport, *Gyro,* 280; Phillips, "Mr. Sperry's Mighty Midget," 20.

44. Kent A. Mitchell, *Fairchild Aircraft: 1926-1987* (Santa Ana, CA: Narkiewicz/Thompson, 1997), 6; *Yesterday, Today, and Tomorrow: Fifty Years of Fairchild Aviation* (Hagerstown, MD: Fairchild-Hiller Corp., 1970), 4.

45. Mitchell, *Fairchild Aircraft,* 6, 8.

46. Mitchell, *Fairchild Aircraft,* 5.

47. Mitchell, *Fairchild Aircraft,* 6, 8-9; Theron K. Rinehart, Fairchild-Republic Company historian and archivist, letter to Jim Boss, a volunteer at the Cradle of Aviation Museum, February 21, 1977, in Cradle of Aviation Museum files.

48. Mitchell, *Fairchild Aircraft,* 9-10; *Yesterday, Today, and Tomorrow,* 9.

49. Mitchell, *Fairchild Aircraft,* 8.

50. Mitchell, *Fairchild Aircraft,* 10.

51. *Yesterday, Today, and Tomorrow,* 9.

52. Mitchell, *Fairchild Aircraft,* 11, 14.

53. Mitchell, *Fairchild Aircraft,* 6; Fairchild built a seaplane hangar on property he purchased June 15, 1918 between Bayview Avenue and Ketcham's Creek in Amityville. See the deed in Liber 1355, 386 at the Suffolk County Clerk's Office in Riverhead.

54. Dade and Strnad, *Picture History of Aviation,* 122; Roy Douglas. "From Farmland to Aviation Center," *Long Island Forum* 53 (Summer 1990): 81-88.

55. *Yesterday, Today, and Tomorrow,* 11-12; George Kirchmann, "Fitzmaurice Flying Field," *The [Oyster Bay Historical Society] Freeholder* 3, no. 1 (Summer 1998): 3.

56. Dade and Strnad, *Picture History of Aviation,* 120; *Yesterday, Today, and Tomorrow,* 11 and map on 12-13.

57. Dade and Strnad, *Picture History of Aviation,* 120; Stoff, *Aerospace Heritage,* 97; *Yesterday, Today, and Tomorrow,* 14, 16; and Long Island-Republic Airport Historical Society Vice-President Lynn McDonald conversation with the author, March 7, 1999.

58. See photograph caption in Long Island-Republic Airport Historical Society exhibition Republic Airport Terminal Building, East Farmingdale, New York.

59. *Yesterday, Today, and Tomorrow,* 12.

60. Stoff, *Aerospace Heritage,* 46; *Aviation,* May 17, 1926; "Fairchild Builds New Factory," *Aviation,* April 11, 1927, 732; "Fairchild Increases Manufacturing Facilities," *Aviation,* August 15, 1927, 375.

61. Dade and Strnad, *Picture History of Aviation,* 100; Mitchell, *Fairchild Aircraft,* 51.

62. Bill Stockert taped interview with Long Island-Republic Airport Historical Society, 1991; Mitchell, *Fairchild Aircraft,* 51.

63. Mitchell, *Fairchild Aircraft,* 58.

64. Stockert interview, 1991.

From Long Island to the Moon: The Project Apollo Lunar Module

Thomas J. Kelly

Project Apollo, the manned exploration of the Moon, was one of the most audacious feats of human exploration and one of the outstanding engineering projects of the twentieth century.* This historic program was recently brought alive again to a new generation by the book and movie *Apollo 13* and the HBO TV series *From the Earth to the Moon.* It was my good fortune to be in engineering at Grumman during the 1960s and to play a key role from beginning to completion of the world's first manned lunar landing spacecraft, the Lunar Module, or, LM. I'm pleased to be able to share some of those experiences with you today. I'll first give a little background on how the United States decided to send men to the Moon and how Grumman got involved. Then I'll describe the Apollo mission and the Lunar Module, and review some of the achievements of the Apollo program.

How did this country get into sending men to the moon? It was really part of the space race with the Soviet Union. It was a Cold War competition. The Russians' launch of Sputnik in October 1957 greatly enhanced Soviet prestige. It really shook this country up. The United States responded by forming the National Aeronautics Space Administration (NASA). This was formed from a predecessor organization called the National Advisory Committee for Aeronautics.

The United States created its own space program, and also made efforts to improve science and mathematics education. There was a lot of soul searching as to whether we were teaching our children the right things in science and math. But then Yuri Gagarin's first manned orbital flight in April 1961 boosted the Soviet lead in space and extended the superpower competition to manned space exploration.

While trying to catch up to Soviets in a manned Earth orbit with project Mercury, the United States space planners devised several possible future space missions, including a spectacular space mission to demonstrate to the world American technological superiority: manned exploration of the moon.

---

* Thomas J. Kelly, "Father of the Lunar Module," gave a slide presentation at the conference discussing Project Apollo which he headed at Grumman. The session was transcribed and edited from an audiotape and this article includes questions and answers following the talk. The author reviewed and revised the transcription.

To provide the necessary technical and operational experience with space-walks or extra vehicular activities (EVA), and multi-person flight crews, the Earth orbital Gemini program was approved as an interim, setting the stage for Project Apollo.

The American humiliation by Cuba at the Bay of Pigs in April 1961, together with Gargarin's successful flight, was used by the Soviets to project an image of advancing, progressive Communism destined for world domination. To offset Soviet successes, President John F. Kennedy determined that America should adopt the most ambitious, demanding, and spectacular space program offered by his advisors: manned exploration of the Moon. He proposed this in an address before a joint session of Congress on May 25, 1961:

> I believe that this nation should commit itself to achieving the goal, before this decade is out, of landing a man on the Moon and returning him safely to Earth. No single space project in this period will be more impressive to mankind, or more important in the long-range exploration of space; and none will be so difficult or expensive to accomplish.

In this very famous statement he said the goal, very simply, was to get the men to the moon and bring them back safely, and he set the time table within the decade. This program was approved unanimously by Congress, despite NASA Administrator James Webb's estimate of a total cost of $20 to $40 billion. That was 1961 dollars, so you have to multiply that times five or six to get the equivalent cost today. It went through, basically, without any objection.

That's how the United States got into it, as a Cold War activity. How did Grumman get into it? Prior to Sputnik and NASA, Grumman in the mid-1950s was mainly a designer and builder of tactical Naval aircraft. They built some very famous ones, of course, in World War II: the Wildcat, the Hellcat, and the Avenger, which played a very major role in the war in the Pacific. After World War II, Grumman was producing airplanes primarily for the Navy. They had converted to jet airplanes with the F9F Panthers series and that's basically what they were doing. However, after Sputnik, Grumman formed a Space Sciences Group in 1958 to begin competing for the space projects that were being put out for industry bids by the newly created NASA.

In 1960, Grumman won a major space contract to design and develop the orbiting astronomical observatory, or OAO. This was a forerunner of today's Hubble space telescope. Winning the OAO competition established Grumman as a major contender in the newly developing field of space technology.

In 1960, I began looking into the emerging Apollo program for Grumman's Space Sciences Group. After President Kennedy's announcement, aerospace industry interest was at a fever pitch in anticipation of NASA competitions for contractors to build the rocket boosters, spacecraft, and other hardware that would be required to get to the moon. Shortly before the request for proposal from the government was released in July 1961, Grumman senior management decided that Apollo was too big for Grumman to be the prime contractor and that we should, instead, seek a major subcontractor role on the team of a larger prime contractor. Needless to say, I was pretty disappointed. That was the decision, and that's the way it went. We joined the General Electric Company's team with responsibility for the crew compartment of the command module. The GE proposal was unsuccessful. In November 1961, NASA selected North American Aviation as the Apollo Spacecraft contractor.

During the GE proposal effort, we at Grumman studied a specific approach to perform the Apollo mission called Lunar Orbit Rendezvous (LOR). After losing the bid, we continued to study this technique and advocated it to NASA as the best mission plan for Apollo. It had the advantage of requiring the least total booster and spacecraft weight and needed only a single Earth launch per mission. Some of the competitive approaches required two or three launches. It also led to the development of two specialized spacecraft. The Command Module, designed primarily by the requirements of re-entry through the Earth's atmosphere, had to be smooth, dense, and heavily insulated. In contrast, the Lunar Module, designed primarily for lunar landing and liftoff, could be light, spindly, and angular. These were two totally conflicting sets of technical requirements, which were best satisfied with two different spacecraft.

The only disadvantage to this LOR approach was that you had to complete a rendezvous maneuver in lunar orbit, part of which would be outside of the Earth's view. The rendezvous would occur when the Lunar Module rose from the moon's surface and had to find the Command Module that would be orbiting, waiting for it. This one drawback made everybody pretty nervous, but all the other advantages overcame their reservations.

When LOR was selected by NASA, Grumman proceeded with in-house studies of the newly defined spacecraft that would be needed: the Lunar Module (LM). The LM design, development, and test was within Grumman's capabilities, and Grumman management agreed to bid as the prime contractor. Our proposal was successful. In November 1962, we were selected by NASA to be prime contractor for the Apollo Lunar Module.

About the Apollo mission and the LM: The lunar configuration at liftoff had a three stage booster stack on the pad. The crew was in the Command Module way up at the top of that stack. This vehicle on the launch pad at Cape Kennedy weighed six million pounds and it was 330 feet tall. It would get seven and a half million pounds of thrust from five F-l rocket engines. At liftoff the lunar module was stowed inside what was called the Spacecraft/LM Adapter, which was a hollow, almost cylindrical, structure that housed the LM. The launch escape tower was on the very top of the stack. Its function was to pull the command module and the crew to safety rapidly in case the whole thing blew up on liftoff. Fortunately, nothing like that ever happened.

The Saturn booster was a three-stage booster rocket. It had liquid oxygen and kerosene fuel in the lower stage, called the S-1, and liquid hydrogen and oxygen in the second stage, called the S-2, and the third, the S-IVB. The S-1 and the S-2 stages were burned out and jettisoned on the way to Earth orbit. The S-IVB, however, went into Earth orbit with the spacecraft and was restarted to inject the combined spacecraft on an escape trajectory towards the moon.

To quickly explain how the mission was conducted, this is how an LOR mission was accomplished. As the combined spacecraft were coasting toward the moon, having been put into escape velocity by the S-IVB booster stage, the Command and Service Modules, which could maneuver in space, came free of the Spacecraft/LM Adapter (SLA). They turned around and docked with the Lunar Module and extracted the Lunar Module from the SLA, which was then jettisoned along with the S-IVB stage.

During translunar coast, mid-course trajectory corrections were made with the Service Propulsion System, which was a liquid rocket engine in the Service Module, a cylindrical module just below the conical Command Module. Lunar orbit injection was accomplished with the Service Propulsion System. The crew was able to transfer from the Command Module into the Lunar Module through a pressurized tunnel connecting the two vehicles. There were three astronauts in the crew. Two of them would go down to the surface of the moon in the LM, the third one minded the mothership, the Command and Service Modules, as they orbited the moon, waiting for the lunar explorers to return. The LM landed on the moon and provided the home base for the astronauts while they were on the surface. The upper stage lifted off at completion of the lunar surface mission, ascended to lunar orbit, rendezvoused and docked with the Command and Service Modules. At that point, they were back in lunar orbit again. The crew returned to the Command Module via the connecting tunnel. They jettisoned the LM Ascent Stage, no longer needed, and were ejected into a trans-Earth trajectory by the Service Propulsion System. They had a long two-and-a-half day coast back towards Earth, making mid-course corrections with the Service Propulsion System engine. The very last thing they did before re-entering the Earth's atmosphere was to jettison the Service Module. The Command Module alone re-entered the Earth's atmosphere and made a parachute descent to the ocean for a naval recovery of the crew. That's the basic mission, and as you see, our Lunar Module, our proud product of Grumman on Long Island, never came back. It was used and discarded during the mission. In fact, it could not come back because it had none of the heavy duty thermal protection that would keep it from burning up when it re-entered the Earth's atmosphere.

The lunar module was a two-stage vehicle. The upper stage we call the Ascent Stage because that ascended from the lunar surface. That was the inhabited part of the LM, with the triangular windows at the front. The crew stood in front of the windows and flew the LM standing up, like driving a delivery van. A waist belt, tethers, and foot restraints kept them anchored in position. Since their eyes were close to the windows they had a wide view of the approaching landing site. When on the Moon, the astronauts depressurized the cabin and opened LM's forward hatch. In spacesuits and wearing their life support backpacks, they crawled backward out of the cabin onto the "front porch" platform, and then down the ladder on the landing gear leg of the Descent Stage to reach the lunar surface. The Descent Stage contained mainly tanks of rocket fuel and oxidizer, and also other expendables: water and oxygen. It also contained the landing gear which was vital to safely completing the mission. It had a rocket engine that was throttle-able so you could adjust the amount of thrust coming from it, enabling the LM to make a very smooth landing. In fact, the astronauts always set it down so gently that it hardly ever stroked the energy absorbing capability of those large landing gear struts. The ascent rocket engine was much smaller and simpler, with fixed thrust and position.

The LM was manufactured and assembled at Grumman in Bethpage, where it was usually surrounded by steel platforms and scaffolding during assembly and extensive ground testing. In some of the last assembly steps Grumman applied the external thermal insulation blankets, which were covered with an outer thin aluminum sheet. This was intended as micro-meteoroid protection, because the moon, lacking any atmosphere, is subjected to natural micro-meteoroid bombardment from space. The completed LM in Bethpage was removed from the assembly fixture and the Descent Stage was mated to the Ascent Stage. The stages were then separated and individually shipped down to Cape Kennedy for pre-launch testing and installation in the SLA and the booster.

At the peak of the program in 1969, we were firing a lunar mission every three to four months, so there was a lot of activity at the Cape. The spacecraft were readied and checked out in the vehicle assembly building prior to installation in the launch vehicle stack.

The Spacecraft/LM Adapter was a hollow protective structure that housed the LM during launch. The LM was lowered into the Adapter and attached by the upper portion of the landing gear struts. Then the Service Module was lowered to mount atop the SLA, which would hide the LM from view.

Long Islanders building the Lunar Module at Grumman, 1972. *NCM Collection, LISI at Hofstra.*

When the LM got out into lunar orbit and separated from the Command Module prior to descending to the lunar surface, one of the first things done when the two vehicles were free of each other was to have the Lunar Module pirouette in front of the Command Module window. This was necessary so the Command Module pilot could take a good close look at it and see if everything looked OK before they ventured off on their descent to the moon.

Six Lunar Module Descent Stages are on the Moon today. Those six very successful missions far exceeded President Kennedy's requirement to get somebody there and get them back. The astronauts did a great deal of very extensive exploration, especially on the last three missions where they were able to stay longer. They could stay for three full days on the last three lunar missions. And they also had the benefit of the Lunar Roving Vehicle, which was an electric-powered car that they could drive around the lunar surface. That greatly increased their ability to explore various portions of the surface. Apollo 15 Commander Dave Scott was photographed in front of a mountain called Hadley Ridge, a very rugged terrain. On the later missions they got progressively more daring and headed for challenging areas that the geologists thought would be the most interesting from a scientific standpoint, as far as determining clues to the past history and formation of the Moon. Apollo 15 was the first extended-stay mission, and they went into some very challenging terrain.

After the lunar surface mission was over and redocking with the Command Module was underway, it was only the Ascent Stage of the Lunar Module that was returning. The pilots really enjoyed flying this light-weight Ascent Stage on the way back to rendezvous for the docking operation. They said it handled like a sports car, very quick and maneuverable.

Here's the total score on the LM (see table). There were six successful landings and explorations; there was one abort, that was Apollo 13 where the LM saved the day by acting as a life boat and getting the crew back alive; there were two lunar fly-bys; and there were two Earth-orbital flights of the Command Module and the LM separately. LM had an unmanned Earth-orbital flight and then its first manned Earth-orbital flight as Apollo 9. There were twelve flight LMs built, two of which were unmanned. Ten were flown in space, one of which was unmanned, and two of them are now in museums—one at the Smithsonian Institute's National Air and Space Museum in Washington, D.C., the other at Johnson's Space Center in Houston.[1] It was a very successful program, far exceeding the initial requirements of President Kennedy.

Apollo/LM Flight Missions

Mission	Crew	Dates	Mission Area
Apollo 5	Unmanned	Jan. 22, 1968	Earth orbit
Apollo 9	McDivitt, Scott, Schweickart	Mar. 3, 1969	Earth orbit
Apollo 10	Stafford, Young, Cernan	May 18, 1969	Lunar orbit
Apollo 11	Armstrong, Collins, Aldrin	Jul. 20, 1969*	Sea of Tranquility
Apollo 12	Conrad, Gordon, Bean	Nov. 19, 1969*	Ocean of Storms
Apollo 13	Lovell, Swigert, Haise	Apr. 11, 1970	Translunar abort
Apollo 14	Shepard, Roosa, Mitchell	Feb. 5, 1971*	Fra Mauro
Apollo 15	Scott, Worden, Irwin	Jul. 30, 1971*	Hadley-Apennine
Apollo 16	Young, Mattingly, Duke	Apr. 21, 1972*	Descarte
Apollo 17	Cernan, Evans, Schmitt	Dec. 11, 1972*	Taurus-Littrow

*Landing date; other dates are dates of launch.

In summary, the Apollo program opened the frontiers of the universe to human exploration and provided much new scientific knowledge about the Moon. It met and exceeded President Kennedy's challenge resulting in two landings in the decade of the 1960s, and six total landings.

It was the engineering achievement of the century, and freely re-established American technical supremacy over the Soviets. It also demonstrated the courage and capability of a free society. I don't know if you remember back to those days, but the Russians conducted their space program in absolute secrecy. They never revealed that a mission was planned or being carried out until it was successfully completed, and only then would they talk about it. If it was unsuccessful, you never heard about it. We didn't operate that way at all. Every American mission in the entire manned space program was conducted in the relentless glare of world-wide TV. If there had been any disasters the world would have known about them, and the world knew in advance what we were trying to do. We were calling our shots freely and openly.

The Apollo program was made possible by a unique combination of circumstances. America was confident and had belief in its capabilities under President Kennedy. The country was willing to challenge the Soviets in every arena of competition. Fortunately, the technology was ready for the application that the politicians chose and the program enjoyed broad support by the American people.

The legacy of Apollo is apparent today. It set NASA on the path of unmanned and manned space exploration. It forever changed our view of mankind's place in the universe. We now see, based on actual observation from space craft, many galaxies and worlds in the expanding cosmos. We realize the statistical likelihood that millions of worlds with intelligent life like our own must exist in this boundless universe.

In addition, we have reaped many practical benefits from space. Worldwide communications have translated us into a global village with instant knowledge of all activities throughout the world. Greatly improved have been weather forecasting, climate predictions, understanding the Earth's environment, and the realization of long-term problems such as global warming. We have achieved and now understand improved means of protecting and preserving Mother Earth.

Apollo has also lead to enhanced understanding of the origins of the Earth, the Moon, and the solar system. Exploration of the solar system by Pioneer, Vanguard, and other satellites and robots has extended mankind's reach and understanding of our closest neighbors in space. Improved instruments and techniques, such as the Hubble space telescope, are flooding space scientists and cosmologists with new observations and data to test theories of the origin and future of our universe.

The Apollo Program accelerated space exploration and changed our view of where we are and where our world fits in the cosmos. I'm proud to have played a part with my Grumman colleagues in adding this great endeavor to Long Island's aerospace heritage.[2]

Questions and Answers

Q. You say that the Apollo mission plan, that the proposal that Grumman and NASA came up with only needed one launch. How many other programs only needed one launch?

A. I was referring to the difference between the Lunar Orbit Rendezvous approach to the mission versus another approach called Earth Orbit Rendezvous. Earth Orbit Rendezvous consisted of having two launches from the Earth, assembling the combined spacecraft in Earth orbit, and then launching the whole thing towards the Moon, landing it on the Moon, and bringing it back. The reason you had to have two launches is you were launching a much greater weight of material and propellant because you were bringing so much stuff back with you from the Moon, and it's very expensive in terms of mission performance to do that. So that's what the multiple launches meant.

Q. Talk a little bit about the creative process. The moment that you sat down with a blank piece of paper and a pencil, how did the design for the Lunar Module take shape?

A. We had a lot of fun with the early days of the LM. The first year was very exciting because we were doing things nobody had ever done before or even thought about doing before, and we just had a field day trying to think about how would you do this? and how would you do that? what would it look like? We soon realized that you didn't have to worry about how anything looked on the LM because it was going to be different from any of our preconceptions anyhow. It didn't have to be aerodynamically contoured, it did have to be extremely lightweight, so you had to do everything in the lightest possible fashion. So you ended up with a spindly-looking creature like you saw in the photographs. It was a lot of fun getting there.

Q. Could you comment on Grumman's reaction to the film *Apollo 13?*

A. Well, I'll give you my reaction. It was a kind of bitter-sweet reaction. I thought it was a great movie. It captured the excitement and the drama of that amazing rescue in space, and it got, I think, a whole new generation of people to understand and appreciate what had gone on in the Apollo program. The only bad part was they went out of their way to make a slam at Grumman; completely unnecessary. We were sad about that because Grumman was really the hero of that whole Apollo 13 and why Hollywood chose to portray them that way, I'll never understand.

Thomas J Kelly, with model of the Lunar Module, c. 1969. Photograph courtesy of the Cradle of Aviation Museum.

Q. In retrospect, what portion of the mission gave you the most fear?

A. Well, I would have to say the landing. That was the part we could never adequately simulate on the ground. There was just no way to simulate that one-six gravity really reliably. So that was the worry. I worried about the ascent, too, because if it doesn't work there you're really in trouble. With the ascent part of the mission, it was over in a fraction of a second. I mean, you hit that button and it either went or it didn't, and if it went, everything was great. The landing was more protracted. After the first couple of landings, however, we realized that the astronauts were very skillful from their simulator training and their vast pilot experience, and they were able to overcome local obstacles and set the vehicle down gently. I used to say they set it down like a crate of eggs and never disturbed a thing.

Notes

1. A thirteenth Lunar Module which was to be used on the Apollo 18 mission that was canceled was not completed. This Lunar Module is to be on display at Nassau County's Cradle of Aviation Museum at Mitchel Field, scheduled to open in the year 2000. (Editor's note.)

2. On the building of the Lunar Module, see also Charles Pellegrino and Joshua Stoff, *Chariots for Apollo: The Making of the Lunar Module* (New York: Atheneum, 1985); and Michael Dorman, "A Giant Step for L.I.," in *Long Island: Our Story,* by Newsday (Melville: Newsday, 1998), 351-54. (Editor's note.)

Theodore Roosevelt in the Local Arena

Natalie A. Naylor

Nearly a century after he became President of the United States, Theodore Roosevelt is still the most famous resident of Nassau County. He had been born in New York City and lived in the governor's mansion in Albany and the White House in Washington, D.C., but Sagamore Hill, in Oyster Bay Cove, was the only home he ever owned in New York.[1] Roosevelt's national career is familiar, and he is still a subject of interest to historians and biographers.[2]

One of Roosevelt's lines most quoted by later politicians was, "It is not the critic who counts. . . . The credit belongs to the man who is actually in the arena."[3] I have adapted the last phrase in my title. TR was involved in the local arena of Nassau County as an involved citizen as well as a national political leader.

Despite the voluminous literature on TR, no one has focused on his local public activities in Nassau County. Of course, Roosevelt's priority was on his national responsibilities, even after his presidency and especially when he tried to make a comeback in the 1912 Bull Moose campaign, but he was also active in the local arena. He was certainly the leading citizen in the new county during its first two decades.

The Roosevelt family summered in Oyster Bay when Theodore was young and he developed there a love of natural history. In 1879, while attending Harvard College, he published a pamphlet, *Notes on Some of the Birds of Oyster Bay, Long Island.* Roosevelt continued his interest in natural history and in 1915, founded and was first president of the Long Island Bird Club.[4]

Roosevelt became famous because of his exploits leading the Rough Riders during the Spanish-American War in 1898. The Rough Riders returned to Camp Wikoff in Montauk. There, and while on leave in Oyster Bay, Roosevelt met with Republican and Independent party leaders about a nomination for governor. Right after the Rough Riders were mustered out of service, Roosevelt met with the New York State Republican boss, United States Senator Thomas C. Platt, to discuss the governorship. One obstacle arose a few days before the party convention in Saratoga. State law required residence in the state for five years preceding nomination. Roosevelt's political opponents publicized an affidavit he had filed in March 1898, while Assistant Secretary of the Navy, naming Washington as his legal residence. When his personal property taxes substantially increased in Oyster Bay in

1897, he had changed his legal address, first to his sister's house in New York City, which he leased, and then to Washington. TR maintained that he had planned to pay his Oyster Bay taxes after he was informed he would lose his right to vote, but it had not been done. Elihu Root addressed the convention on the issue focusing on the definition of residence, and despite the legal cloud, Roosevelt became the Republican Party's nominee for Governor on September 25, receiving more than three-quarters of the votes.[5]

A few days earlier, on September 21, Roosevelt delivered his first address after returning from Cuba to his Oyster Bay and Long Island neighbors at a "Peace Jubilee and Roosevelt Reception." The town was festooned with flags and red, white, and blue bunting, and the honored guests included several of the Rough Riders and Long Island officials. After the band played "Hail to the Chief," Roosevelt declared, "Next to the greeting that my own regiment gave me, I could appreciate nothing so much as this greeting from you, my fellow townsmen." He said he had determined that his first speech would be to his neighbors. After describing the experiences of the Rough Riders in Cuba, he was presented with a sword by his Oyster Bay neighbors.[6]

The Democratic gubernatorial candidate in 1898 was Judge Augustus Van Wyck of Brooklyn, but Roosevelt campaigned primarily against the Tammany boss, Richard Croker. Van Wyck had refused to renominate a judge who would not appoint a Tammany candidate as court clerk. A local newspaper headline proclaimed, "Colonel Roosevelt Lashes Croker All Up and Down Long Island." Not all the newspapers were impressed. His train stopped for five minutes in Freeport at 9 a.m. on Wednesday morning November 2, where he addressed about two hundred people a week before the election. The *Hempstead Inquirer* reported that he "spoke about Richard Croker in a very uncomplimentary manner. . . . He did not make a very favorable impression by his mud-slinging in this village." On the same day, Roosevelt also spoke in Valley Stream, Rockville Centre, Mineola, and Hicksville, as well as at a total of seven stops in Queens and Suffolk County.[7] Roosevelt won a narrow victory in the state (with a margin of less than 18,000 or only 1.3 percent of the votes); he carried Nassau County with a plurality of 1,262 votes.[8]

While governor, Roosevelt delivered a Fourth of July speech in Oyster Bay and spoke at the Queens County Fair in Mineola in September 1899. Though the county was predominantly Republican, local papers were not uncritical of Roosevelt as governor. The *Hempstead Inquirer* reported in September 1899, "Governor Roosevelt is making a round of the State visiting and speaking at the county fairs." They observed that "Republican papers are calling on the Governor to do less talking and more visiting," criticized him for trying to "gloss over the enormity of the canal frauds," and compared him unfavorably to former Democratic Governor Samuel J. Tilden.[9]

Roosevelt had not been directly involved in the formation of Nassau County in 1898. When the organizational meeting for the county was held in January 1898, he was in Washington, serving as Assistant Secretary of the Navy. But when he became New York governor, he appointed William Youngs his confidential secretary. In October 1898, at Nassau's Republican nominating convention, Youngs had supported the losing county candidates. The effect of Roosevelt's naming Youngs to a position in Albany was to help "unite the Nassau Republicans by removing one of the sources of friction."[10]

The local *Oyster Bay Guardian* had been urging a Roosevelt nomination for president as early as October 1899. It noted the enthusiastic cheering he received when he rode at the head of the parade honoring Admiral George Dewey, and added that he had been politicking for the nomination at soldiers' reunions and county fairs.[11] William McKinley, however, was renominated for president with Roosevelt as the vice-presidential candidate.

One of the first concerns facing the new Nassau County Board of Supervisors in 1899 was to erect a court house. Land was donated by the Garden City Company early in 1899, construction bonds sold, plans adopted, and a contract awarded. Governor Roosevelt was invited to speak at the laying of the cornerstone on Friday afternoon, July 13, 1900, just three weeks after being nominated for vice president of the United States. Some 2,500 attended the courthouse ceremonies and heard Roosevelt speak on civic duty. He urged citizens to "insist that every public servant shall show the same qualities of honesty and uprightness as in private and business relations." He reminded his listeners, "Free government is not a gift that can be handed out by the celestial powers, but only by hard work under self-government and we must preserve it."[12]

Robert Gaston Herbert's 1937 WPA mural in the courthouse of TR speaking at the cornerstone laying in 1900. *NCM Collection, LISI at Hofstra.*

When TR returned to Oyster Bay from his campaign tour on the eve of the national presidential elections in 1900, he was greeted by a wildly enthusiastic reception. The local newspaper reported:

> There was a monster parade, the number participating being estimated all the way from two to four thousand. Villages were represented from all sections of the island and never has Oyster Bay been through such a demonstration. The people came on foot, on wheels, in carriages and on special trains.[13]

The Republican ticket, of course, was elected, and two days later Roosevelt was "serenaded" by his Oyster Bay neighbors. Three weeks after being inaugurated as Vice President, Roosevelt received his second Masonic degree at Matinecock Lodge in Oyster Bay; a month later, he received the third Masonic degree.[14]

The following month, in April 1901, Roosevelt laid the cornerstone of the new Methodist Church in East Norwich, south of Oyster Bay.[15] In June, TR was to be the "centre of attraction" at the dedication of Oyster Bay's new school building. The ceremonies were delayed for almost an hour in uncomfortably humid weather, awaiting the vice president who did not appear until the evening graduation exercises. Roosevelt spoke for fifteen minutes "on the virtues and importance of education and urged the necessity for being manly, honest, courageous, and virtuous."[16]

President Roosevelt on his way to vote in Oyster Bay, c. 1908. *NCM Collection, LISI at Hofstra.*

TR became president on September 14, 1901, after McKinley died from an assassin's bullet. The next year, Sagamore Hill became the summer White House. Governmental offices were located on the second floor of Moore's Building at the northeast corner of South and East Main Street in the business section of Oyster Bay.[17] The family usually spent from late June through September at Sagamore Hill during TR's presidential years. Roosevelt regularly returned to Oyster Bay to vote, coming by train from Washington. Lest we think in terms of today's airplanes or even Metroliner speeds, that trip took between seven and ten hours each way, including a tugboat from Jersey City to Long Island City, which was then the terminus of the Long Island Rail Road.[18]

During and after his presidency, TR had many visitors at Sagamore Hill, with conferences, lunches, occasional reviews of the fleet, and sometimes large gatherings. Most of these visitors and gatherings involved national or state politics and government, but a good many were connected with Nassau County. For instance, he asked to address a meeting of Long Island physicians when they met at Oyster Bay High School in 1905.[19]

Several months after Roosevelt became president, a local community in Nassau honored him by assuming his name. When Greenwich Point, southeast of the village of Hempstead, sought to establish a post office, they were informed that a new name was necessary because there was another Greenwich post office upstate. The name Roosevelt was adopted in March 1902.[20]

In September 1902, Roosevelt held the first reception for his "friends and neighbors" at Sagamore Hill—what the local paper declared to be "one of the greatest days in Oyster Bay's history." Businesses and some private homes were "covered with bunting" and large flags hung across the road every hundred feet from the railroad station to Sagamore Hill. Bands from Brooklyn, Hempstead, and Oyster Bay marched with delegations The president greeted and shook hands with 8,000 people (80 percent of whom were women). Guests then received lemonade or raspberry shrub in a souvenir glass inscribed "Reception to President Roosevelt."[21]

In 1906, Roosevelt was the featured speaker at Oyster Bay's Fourth of July celebration. The program was typical of a small town's celebration, with a band from Port Washington, school children opening ceremonies by singing the national anthem, two baseball games in the afternoon (the home team won both), and fireworks in the evening. The weather kept the crowd down to only 1,500. Though a deluge of heavy rain came halfway through Roosevelt's half-hour speech, he continued in "utter disregard for the rain." He spoke on the "social, political and business conditions of the country and the good work done by the last Congress." The local paper commented that his "speech was characteristic of the man and abounded in truths and good advice."[22]

The night before his term as president ended in 1909, more than a hundred attended a dinner of "President Roosevelt's Neighbors" in Washington, where a Nassau County band played. Thereafter, the Roosevelts lived at Sagamore Hill throughout the year.[23] Visitors still came there, but Roosevelt met others in New York City at the offices of the *Outlook* or later the *Metropolitan*—magazines where he was an editor and for which he regularly wrote articles.

When Roosevelt returned from his African expedition in June 1910, after more than a year abroad, he was greeted with a large parade in New York City, a "reception committee" of 450 on the train to Oyster Bay, and large crowds along the way. In fact, the train had to come to a halt in Roslyn to avoid killing those who had crowded on the tracks. He told the 5,000 gathered in Oyster Bay, "I am glad to see you all again, men, women, and little Oysters [as he called the children of Oyster Bay]. I can't say how much these homecomings to Oyster Bay have meant to me in the last dozen years. I know you all and I do not think there is one among you with whom I am not on a good footing." After indicating how touched he was that so many of his neighbors had come to New York City that morning, he concluded, "But it touched me more deeply to see you all here; to live among you again as I have for the last forty years; to take up my duties. The first duty of a man is in his own family. Before a man can aspire to reform a nation he must turn his attention to the folks at home."[24]

TR's devotion to his family and children, of course, is legendary, and others have focused on this important aspect of his life.[25] I will offer only one example. On July 19, 1905, the headline on the first page of the *New York Times* was, "Roosevelt Off Camping with Ten Youngsters. Flotilla of Four Bound for the Cape of Happy Chance." TR had taken three of his boys, together with several of their cousins and friends, on an overnight camping trip. The *Times* story opened:

> The whereabouts of the President of the United States to-night is more uncertain than at any time since his bear hunting expeditions in the wilds of the Rocky Mountains this Spring.
>
> It is likely, however, that while this dispatch is being written Mr. Roosevelt is sitting by a blazing camp fire somewhere on the shores of Long Island Sound telling hair-raising stories of the hunt and the Western plains to ten listening youths, who make up his party.

This overnight adventure was apparently an annual expedition with the President as the "Admiral in Chief" of the flotilla.[26]

Roosevelt laid the cornerstone for the Doubleday Country Life Press plant in Garden City in August 1910. The impressive Tudor revival-style building was modeled on Hampton Court in England and was designed with extensive landscaped gardens. TR praised Doubleday for moving their printing plant from New York City to the country. As publishers of *Country Life* magazine, Doubleday was practicing what it preached. He spoke of the desirability of spreading "the city work out into the country regions" and felt fresh air and living in the country were especially important for children.[27]

In October 1910, Roosevelt accepted an invitation to address the state Firemen's Convention in Freeport, where he spoke on citizens' responsibilities and paid tribute to the firemen's important work. He had been "greeted with loud cheering from the hundreds of people who lined the sidewalk and roadway" in Freeport. On the grandstand, he delivered a "short witty speech" to the local schoolchildren urging them to "play with all their might" at recess so they would sit still in class![28]

In March 1912, TR was called to jury duty in Mineola. This was shortly after he announced his candidacy for the Republican nomination for president over William Howard Taft. The summons to jury duty may have been a political maneuver to thwart his efforts. He wrote to a political supporter, "I do not quite know why I was drawn on jury duty. Somebody said it was

Theodore Roosevelt on the steps of the courthouse leaving jury duty, 1912. *NCM Collection, LISI at Hofstra.*

on the hope that I would ask to be excused, which of course I should not do." TR did ask to be excused one day for "an important business engagement," but stated he had "no desire to evade or shirk his part." After lawyers in three cases rejected him for the jury, Roosevelt complained to the judge that "he wanted to serve on a jury to show that he was doing his civic duty like any other citizen." When the judge questioned one of the lawyers he reportedly said, "Mr. President, my client is entitled to a jury of twelve men. If you go into the jury box, there will be only one."[29] Photographers followed his every move, and the local paper commented, "it certainly is laughable to watch the antics of their camera fiends. Of course, Teddy enjoys it, you know."[30]

Roosevelt's Bull Moose campaign in 1912, as the candidate of the Progressive Party, brought him back into the political spotlight, but he did not ignore his local supporters. On July 27, for example, he hosted a delegation of eighty supporters from Freeport, shaking hands with each one, showing them his trophies in the North Room, and posing for pictures. He asked that his comments "to his friends and neighbors" not be quoted, but the reporter indicated that they "showed that he is kept in close touch with the situation from the small County of Nassau to the limits of the United States." One of the campaign songs had the refrain, "Has anyone here seen Teddy/Teddy of Old Nassau."[31]

After Roosevelt's defeat and Woodrow Wilson's victory, the editor of the *Hempstead Sentinel* reflected, "There may be some who believe that Roosevelt's ambition has been satisfied. Mighty few, however. He has almost wrecked a party [i.e., the Republican Party] which heaped honors upon him."[32]

Oyster Bay again brought out the flags and bunting to welcome Roosevelt home after his expedition to Brazil in 1914. Although he was not in good health, he consented to "meet and greet his townsmen and neighbors." A short parade was followed by speeches in the center of town.[33]

Roosevelt continued to be active in politics. He declined the Progressive Party's presidential nomination and campaigned for Republican Charles E. Hughes for president in 1916. To the delight of his neighbors, he chose to "close the campaign" by being with the "Home Folks" at the Lyric Theatre in Oyster Bay.[34]

With the entry of the United States into war in 1917, Roosevelt spoke vigorously in support of Liberty Bonds and the Red Cross. He reviewed the thirty units of the Nassau Sheriff's Home Defense force, the Sheriff's Reserves, at the fair grounds in Mineola in May 1917. In an address, TR urged everyone in the crowd "to do all in their power to aid . . . the country in the war and to purchase Liberty Bonds to the limit of their ability."[35] Later that year, TR spoke at three meetings in Hempstead, inaugurating the county's Red Cross membership drive, urging the county "to do its full share and a little more than its full share." He noted that the county had met its quota in the Y.M.C.A. drive and bought more than its share of Liberty Loans.[36] Roosevelt later chaired the opening meeting of a fund-raising drive for the Nassau County Red Cross at the Garden City Hotel, in May 1918. The *Brooklyn Daily Eagle* reported that he "was truly in his element, being among friends." Roosevelt addressed 250 "prominent men and women" and particularly urged summer residents to contribute: "they have no business to come if they haven't subscribed heavily to the Red Cross fund! If they only subscribe in New York [City] I hope they spend the summer in New York. I want them to distinctly understand that we expect them to subscribe here."[37]

In September 1917, Roosevelt visited the Mineola Army Aviation Field where his youngest son, Quentin, had trained. Roosevelt flew in the observer's seat for half an hour in the new Liberty Motor military biplane. The plane attained a speed of more than 100 miles per hour, flying at more than 5,000 feet. When the plane landed, he waved to all and said, "It was remarkable; it was a great pleasure. I thank you all."[38]

The Roosevelt family regularly attended Christ Episcopal Church in Oyster Bay and Edith Roosevelt, TR's wife, was particularly active in some of its women's organizations. TR spoke at the church's 200th anniversary in 1906, and on several other occasions.[39] After the presidential years, when the family lived at Sagamore Hill all year round, TR regularly distributed Christmas gifts to children at the Cove Neck school which his sons had attended. He also spoke on Arbor Day one year and praised the Boy Scouts. Incidentally, TR himself organized a Boy Scout troop in Oyster Bay and had receptions for the Scouts at Sagamore Hill.[40]

Theodore Roosevelt died at Sagamore Hill on January 6, 1919 and was buried in Youngs Cemetery in Oyster Bay two days later. The following Sunday, Nassau County's Congressman Fred C. Hicks gave the memorial address at a service in the Tabernacle in Washington, D.C.[41]

Soon after TR's death, his cousin, Emlen Roosevelt, purchased land adjacent to the cemetery for the Roosevelt Bird Sanctuary (see note 4 below). The Republican Club of Nassau County began to hold memorial dinners on the anniversary of Roosevelt's birth, and the Boy Scouts, headed by the National Scout Commissioner, initiated a Memorial Pilgrimage to his grave on the Saturday closest to his birthday. Others made pilgrimages to the grave on the anniversary of his death. On the centennial of Roosevelt's birth in 1958, there were federal, state, and Nassau County commissions to celebrate the anniversary. Vice President Richard M. Nixon opened the TR centennial year in Nassau County.

The Theodore Roosevelt Association purchased Sagamore Hill in 1950 after TR's widow had died. The home was opened to the public in 1953 at ceremonies attended by presidents Dwight David Eisenhower and Herbert

Hoover. Sagamore Hill was donated to the federal government in 1962 and is now a National Historic Site, administered by the National Park Service—the only such site in Nassau County.

When Robert Gaston Herbert was commissioned to create murals for the Nassau County Courthouse under the auspices of the Works Progress Administration (WPA) in the 1930s, one of the four significant events he chose to depict was Roosevelt laying the cornerstone for the building. (The other courthouse murals depict seventeenth and eighteenth century events.) There are other memorials to Roosevelt in the county. The Oyster Bay Historical Society, for example, placed a plaque on the presidential office building in Oyster Bay in 1963. There is a Theodore Roosevelt Elementary School in Oyster Bay. In 1984, a two-foot high bust of TR was erected in front of the Oyster Bay Town Hall.[42] Hofstra University has a Theodore Roosevelt Hall which was built and named in 1957 while his daughter-in-law, Mrs. Theodore Roosevelt, Jr., was on the then college's Board of Trustees.

Theodore Roosevelt's activities in the local arena of Nassau County were certainly *not* the major accomplishments of his career. Yet he clearly loved Sagamore Hill and his adopted home town of Oyster Bay, and was an involved citizen of the county in its first two decades. As his friend and biographer, Hermann Hagedorn noted, "He never, if he could help it, refused any invitation to address these Nassau County neighbors of his."[43] Whether speaking to children at the Cove Neck elementary school or officiating at a Red Cross Drive at the Garden City Hotel, he was active in a wide range of civic activities—an exemplary first citizen in the local arena.

Notes

The chronology in the appendices of *The Letters of Theodore Roosevelt,* edited by Elting E. Morison, 8 vols. (Cambridge: Harvard University Press, 1954) was helpful in initially pinpointing dates and events for this paper. The *New York Times* index also proved useful. (My "Chronology of Theodore Roosevelt's Nassau County Events" is deposited in the Long Island Studies Institute Nassau County Conference files.) I am grateful for the assistance of Victoria Aspinwall in locating newspaper articles in the Nassau County Museum's microfilm collection of newspaper files in the Long Island Studies Institute at Hofstra University.

1. Sagamore Hill was completed in 1885. TR's widow, Edith Carow Roosevelt, lived in the home until her death in 1948.

2. Among the recent biographies and books are H. W. Brands, *TR: The Last Romantic* (New York: Basic Books, 1997); James G. Barber, *Theodore Roosevelt: Icon of the American Century* (Washington, DC: Smithsonian, 1998); and Edward J. Renehan, Jr., *The Lion's Pride: Theodore Roosevelt and His Family in Peace and War* (New York: Oxford University Press, 1998). We are still awaiting the second volume of Edmund Morris's biography. The Centennial of the Spanish American War, in 1998,

resulted in several books, as well as the reprinting of TR's writings on the war. See Theodore Roosevelt, *The Rough Riders,* edited by Richard Bak (Dallas, TX: Taylor Publishing, 1997); *Pocket Diary: Theodore Roosevelt's Private Account of the War with Spain,* edited by Wallace Finley Dailey (Cambridge: Harvard University Press, 1998); Jeff Heatley, *Bully! Theodore Roosevelt, the Rough Riders and Camp Wikoff, Montauk, New York, 1898* (Montauk: Montauk Historical Society and Pushcart Press, 1998); and H. Paul Jeffers, *Theodore Roosevelt Goes to War, 1897-1898* (New York: John Wiley & Sons, 1996).

Sherwin Gluck, *TR's Summer White House, Oyster Bay* (Oyster Bay: Privately printed, 1999), was published after this article was written. It documents Roosevelt's activities in Oyster Bay during the summers of his presidential years (1902-1908), by reprinting correspondence from the Theodore Roosevelt Papers and contemporary newspaper articles, primarily from the *New York Times.*

3. Richard Nixon quoted Theodore Roosevelt's "In the Arena" in his speech resigning the presidency on August 4, 1974; Nixon also quoted the passage as an epigraph for his memoirs, *In the Arena: A Memoir of Victory, Defeat, and Renewal* (New York: Simon and Shuster, 1990). The lines come from Theodore Roosevelt's "Citizenship in a Republic," an address he delivered before the Sorbonne in Paris on April 23, 1910, after his African expedition. It was printed in contemporary newspapers and can be found in *National Edition: Works of Theodore Roosevelt,* edited by Hermann Hagedorn (New York: Charles Scribner's Sons, 1926), 13: 506-29, and *The Man in the Arena: Speeches and Essays by Theodore Roosevelt,* edited by John Allen Gable (Oyster Bay: Theodore Roosevelt Association, 1987), 50-74, quotation at 54.

4. Theodore Roosevelt's *Notes on Birds* is conveniently reprinted in the *Nassau County Historical Journal* 14 (Spring 1953): 83-85. Roosevelt's first publication, co-authored with his classmate Hal Minot following a summer trip after his freshman year, was *The Summer Birds of the Adirondacks in Franklin County, N.Y.* As President, Roosevelt established fifty-one bird reserves. See Edwin Way Teale, "Long Island Bird Life," in *Long Island: A History of Two Great Counties,* edited by Paul Bailey, 2 vols. (New York: Lewis Publishing, 1949), 2: 171-72, 187. The twelve acre Theodore Roosevelt Memorial Bird Sanctuary, adjacent to Youngs Cemetery, west of Oyster Bay Cove Road, was established in 1919 by TR's cousin, W. Emlen Roosevelt who donated it to the National Audubon Society in 1923. See also John A. Gable, "Theodore Roosevelt: Long Island's President," in *Between Ocean and Empire: An Illustrated History of Long Island,* edited by Robert B. MacKay, Geoffrey L. Rossano, and Carol A. Traynor (Northridge, CA: Windsor Publications, 1985), 128-29.

5. The convention vote was 753 for TR and 218 votes for incumbent Governor Frank S. Black whose administration had been tainted by a scandal over Erie Canal bonds. Subsequently, Roosevelt paid back taxes in New York City; the books in Oyster Bay had been closed. See Nathan Miller, *Theodore Roosevelt: A Life* (New York: William Morrow, 1992), 316-18; Edmund Morris, *The Rise of Theodore Roosevelt* (New York: Coward, McCann & Geoghegan, 1979), 677-79, 853-54 n.75; and Morison, *Letters,* 2: 878-80.

6. "Peace Jubilee September 21, 1898," *Theodore Roosevelt Association Journal* 22, no. 4 (1998): 5-6, 10 (reprinted from Heatley, *Bully!).*

7. Quote from an undated clipping in "Theodore Roosevelt" vertical file (newspaper is not identified), Nassau County Museum Collection, Long Island Studies

Institute (the other Long Island communities where he spoke that day were Flushing, Jamaica, Babylon, Islip, Patchogue, Bridgehampton, and Southampton); *Hempstead Inquirer,* November 4, 1898; and Morison, *Letters,* 2: 1,497.

8. Roosevelt received 661,707 votes and Van Wyck, 643,921 (*Congressional Quarterly Guide to U.S. Elections,* 3d ed. [Washington, DC: Congressional Quarterly, 1994], 698); *New York Times,* November 7, 1900 (comparing county's votes for governor in 1898 and 1900 elections). In the 1904 election when Roosevelt ran for president, he received 61 percent of the 13,537 votes cast in Nassau County. His largest margin was in the town of Hempstead where he received 63 percent of the votes; Oyster Bay cast 58 percent of their votes for TR, and North Hempstead, 59 percent (*Port Washington News,* November 12, 1904, 3).

9. Morison, *Letters,* 2: 1,502-3; *Hempstead Inquirer,* September 22, 1899.

10. Edward J. Smits, "The Creation of Nassau County," *Long Island Historical Journal* 1 (Spring 1989): 179.

11. *Oyster Bay Guardian,* October 13, 1899. See also the later account by a participant of TR's visit to the Suffolk County Fair in Riverhead, Natter S. Funnell, "Funnell and Roosevelt Went to Fair Together in Pioneer Auto Excursion," *Nassau Daily Star,* February 26, 1936.

12. Jesse Merritt, "The Laying of the Cornerstone of the Old County Courthouse," *Nassau County Historical Society Journal* 17 (Summer 1956): 15, 16. See also Theodore Roosevelt, "Speech at the Laying of the Courthouse Cornerstone," earlier in this book (76-77); "Gov. Roosevelt Lays the Corner Stone," *Hempstead Sentinel,* July 19, 1900; and *Brooklyn Eagle,* July 14, 1900, 14. Merritt's article does not list his sources, but he apparently relied on the account in the *Brooklyn Eagle.* The speech as reported in the two newspaper accounts has slight variations (not surprising at a time when reporters were dependent on their own notes and unable to record speeches).

13. *Nassau Daily Review,* November 9, 1900.

14. Morison, *Letters,* 6: 1,510; *Oyster Bay Guardian,* March 27, 1901 and April 26, 1901. It was reported that "many visitors were present from other lodges" in March and a more than capacity crowd including "high officials from all parts of the State as well as other states were present, as were delegations from Lodges throughout the 1st Masonic District and places outside" in April. Apparently, it is not unusual for the two Masonic degrees to be awarded in such close proximity. On August 22, 1904, Roosevelt hosted the Masonic Lodges at Sagamore Hill. See Morison, *Letters,* 4: 1,370, 8: 1,466, 8: 1,469; 8: 1,477.

15. *Nassau County Review,* May 17, 1901.

16. *Oyster Bay Guardian,* June 28, 1901.

17. The newspaper reported offices on the second floor of the Oyster Bay Bank Building in 1902 and the next year over a grocery store; see *Oyster Bay Guardian,* July 11, 1902; and *New-York Tribune,* June 7, 1903. John A. Gable, Executive Director of the Theodore Roosevelt Association, indicated that space was rented by the government in various buildings in Oyster Bay; these were for clerical and other government employees and were not used as offices by Roosevelt himself (personal communication, March 9, 1999). See also Gluck, *TR's Summer White House,* 1-3, 13-14.

18. Joseph L. Gardner, *Departing Glory: Theodore Roosevelt as ex-President* (New York: Charles Scribner's Sons, 1973), 4-7.

19. Reviews of the fleet were reported in the *Oyster Bay Guardian* on August 21, 1903 and September 7, 1906. The *New York Times* reported he "appeared to have the time of his life" in greeting the physicians (July 13, 1905).

20. Interestingly, Roosevelt was probably a compromise choice. At a meeting held at Royal Mollineaux's store, the name "Royalston" was adopted (Mollineaux hoped to become postmaster). The newspaper reported that many preferred "Laramie," and in a later vote the name Roosevelt was adopted. Richard A. Winsche, *The History of Nassau County Community Place Names* (Interlaken, NY: Empire State Books, 1999), 86-87, 134.

Roosevelt became the name of a savings bank which was absorbed in 1999 by the Roslyn Savings Bank. Roosevelt Field Aviation Field was named for TR's youngest son, Quentin Roosevelt, who was killed in action over France in World War I; this later became a shopping center and raceway. The Roosevelt National Guard unit on Oak Street, Uniondale, is named for TR's eldest son, Theodore Roosevelt, Jr., who served with distinction in both World War I and II.

21. *Harper's Weekly,* September 27, 1902, 1,342; *Oyster Bay Guardian,* September 19, 1902. The newspaper article also noted security measures and "every precaution taken to prevent any repetition of the Buffalo calamity a year ago" (i.e. the assassination of President McKinley).

22. *Oyster Bay Guardian,* July 6, 1906.

23. The dinner program is in the Nassau County Museum Collection (63.39) in the Long Island Studies Institute at Hofstra University. TR was out of the country on his African expedition for more than a year in 1909-1910, on extensive speaking tours when he ran for president on the Progressive Party line in 1912, and in South America for six months in 1913-1914.

24. *New York Times,* June 19, 1910.

25. See, for example, Hermann Hagedorn, *The Roosevelt Family of Sagamore Hill* (New York: Macmillan, 1954); Edward J. Renehan, Jr., *The Lion's Pride: Theodore Roosevelt and his Family in Peace and War;* Theodore Roosevelt, *A Bully Father: Theodore Roosevelt's Letters to His Children,* with a biographical essay and notes by Joan Paterson Kerr (New York: Random House, 1995).

26. *New York Times,* July 19, 1905.

27. *New York Times,* August 20, 1910. Most of the gardens were paved over for parking lots during a building expansion in the 1940s. See American Institute of Architects [AIA], Long Island Chapter, and the Society for the Preservation of Long Island Antiquities, *AIA Architectural Guide to Nassau and Suffolk Counties, Long Island,* edited by Robert B. MacKay, Stanley Lindvall, and Carol Traynor (New York: Dover, 1992), 10, 12, 13.

28. *Nassau County Review,* October 7, 1910.

29. TR's "business engagement" on March 8 was probably to meet with Charles H. Duell, Chairman on the Roosevelt Committee in New York City, and Elon Huntington Hooker, treasurer of the Progressive Party. See TR letter to Walter Roscoe Stubbs, Governor of Kansas, March 5, 1912, in Morison, *Letters* 7: 519, 543; 8: 1,475; *Nassau County Review* March 8, 1912; *Theodore Roosevelt Association Journal* 9 (Spring 1893): 24. I am grateful to James W. Foote who mentioned this incident in his talk at the Hofstra conference and to John A. Gable for providing references.

30. *Hempstead Sentinel,* March 14, 1912.

31. *Nassau County Review,* August 2, 1912. The song is in the Roosevelt Collection, Nassau County Museum Collection, Long Island Studies Institute at Hofstra University.

32. *Hempstead Sentinel,* November 7, 1912.

33. *Oyster Bay Guardian,* May 22, 1914.

34. *Oyster Bay Guardian,* November 3, 1916.

35. *Nassau County Review,* June 1, 1917.

36. The meeting was held at the armory, with overflow meetings in the Presbyterian and Methodist churches. *Hempstead Sentinel,* December 20, 1917. See also article in *Nassau County Review,* December 28, 1917.

37. *Brooklyn Daily Eagle,* May 15, 1918; *Hempstead Sentinel,* May 16, 1918; *Oyster Bay Guardian,* May 17, 1918; and *Nassau County Review,* May 17, 1918. Roosevelt also spoke for the Red Cross Drive at a Port Washington meeting; see *Nassau County Review,* May 24, 1918.

38. *New York Times,* September 14, 1917. Roosevelt had taken his first airplane flight in 1910 with A. Hoxey in Kansas. While president, he had taken a trip in a submarine in Oyster Bay in 1905.

39. The chronology in Morison's *Letters* lists some occasions: speech at church fair, August 16, 1900, 2: 1,508; speech at Christ Church, September 8, 1906, 6: 1,602; Christmas party and speech on Brazil, December 24, 1914, 8: 1,486; speech at Christmas party, December 24, 1917, 8: 1,493. TR's wife and children were Episcopalian but he remained a member of the Dutch Reformed Church throughout his life.

40. *New York Times,* December 21, 1917; May 6, 1916; he also visited the Cove School on September 14, 1914 (Morison, *Letters,* 8: 1,485). See also Renehan, *The Lion's Pride,* 168-69, 249. Roosevelt entertained Boy Scouts from Glen Cove and Irvington at Sagamore Hill on May 13, 1916 while his wife was marching in a Readiness Preparedness parade in New York City (*New York Times,* May 14, 1916). See also photograph of TR with Nassau Scouts in August 1918 presentation of Scouts who had sold the most Liberty Bonds (Nassau County Museum Collection, Long Island Studies Institute at Hofstra University, photograph no. 1746).

41. Copy of program and address in Nassau County Museum Collection, Long Island Studies Institute at Hofstra University.

42. The original bust was replaced after it was stolen in 1990. *Oyster Bay Guardian,* April 5, 1963; *Newsday,* July 11, 1990.

43. Hagedorn, *The Roosevelt Family of Sagamore Hill,* 167. Hagedorn, TR's friend and biographer, was the first director of the Roosevelt Memorial Association. Hagedorn had published *The Boys' Life of Theodore Roosevelt* in 1918 (New York: Harper and Brothers); *Roosevelt in the Bad Lands* (Boston: Houghton Mifflin, 1921); and edited Roosevelt's *Works* in 1926.

TR wrote his son Archie in 1918, "I receive on average 15 to 20 invitations to speak a day. About one in a hundred is reasonably worth accepting." Quoted by Renehan, *Lion's Pride,* 163. Although Hagedorn's statement about TR never refusing an invitation to speak to his Nassau County neighbors may not be literally true, it conveys the genuine feelings TR had for them. The speeches noted in this essay are some, but not all that he delivered in Nassau County; similarly, he attended more public events than those discussed here.

Sandbar to City: William H. Reynolds and the Planned Community of Long Beach, 1906–1922

Roberta Fiore and Elizabeth Coffin Allerhand

After making and losing millions of dollars through speculation and the successful development of four new neighborhoods in Brooklyn, along with Coney Island's Dreamland pleasure park, William H. Reynolds turned his visionary energy in 1906, to creating Long Beach, Long Island. Reynolds was to be known throughout his life as the "Senator," a title he earned in 1892 as the youngest man ever elected to the New York State Senate. He served only one term, leaving elected political life to return to his career as a builder-developer. Aware of boom and bust cycles of real estate, Reynolds paid $3 million for 1,128 acres on Long Beach island at the bottom of a real estate cycle. His stretch of sandbar, a barrier island on the South Shore, had been first developed in 1880. It was now encumbered with the failing business of the Long Beach Hotel, with its annexed twenty-two "cottages," all polluting the waters. Yet, here on the sand dunes, he proposed to establish an exclusive resort community: The Estates of Long Beach.

On March 5, 1907, Reynolds appeared before the Town Board of Hempstead where he:

> asked for the 1,084 more acres of meadow and marsh on the north side of the beach for which he offered to pay $100 an acre and to widen the channel to the width of 1,000 feet and to a depth of 10 feet at low water. The additional acreage was desired to straighten out the northern boundary and by filling in portions then submerged by the tide water to create sites for building parkways, streets and boulevards.[1] (See Fig. 1.)

The Board told Reynolds that any such purchase would have to go to public referendum.

One of the Senator's many attributes was his rhetorical ability. He went barnstorming through the local villages of the Town of Hempstead asking the rural electorate to vote "yes" on his resort proposal. He promised Hempstead a tremendous tax revenue increase without any more sewage and waste pollution of the waters. In April 1907, after success at the voting box, he legally purchased the 1,084 acres, most of which were under water. It was his genius to be able to look at salt meadow and see a yacht basin with pleasure palaces.

With the success at the ballot box behind him, he was free to start rearranging and creating land by dredging the channel. Not only was he free

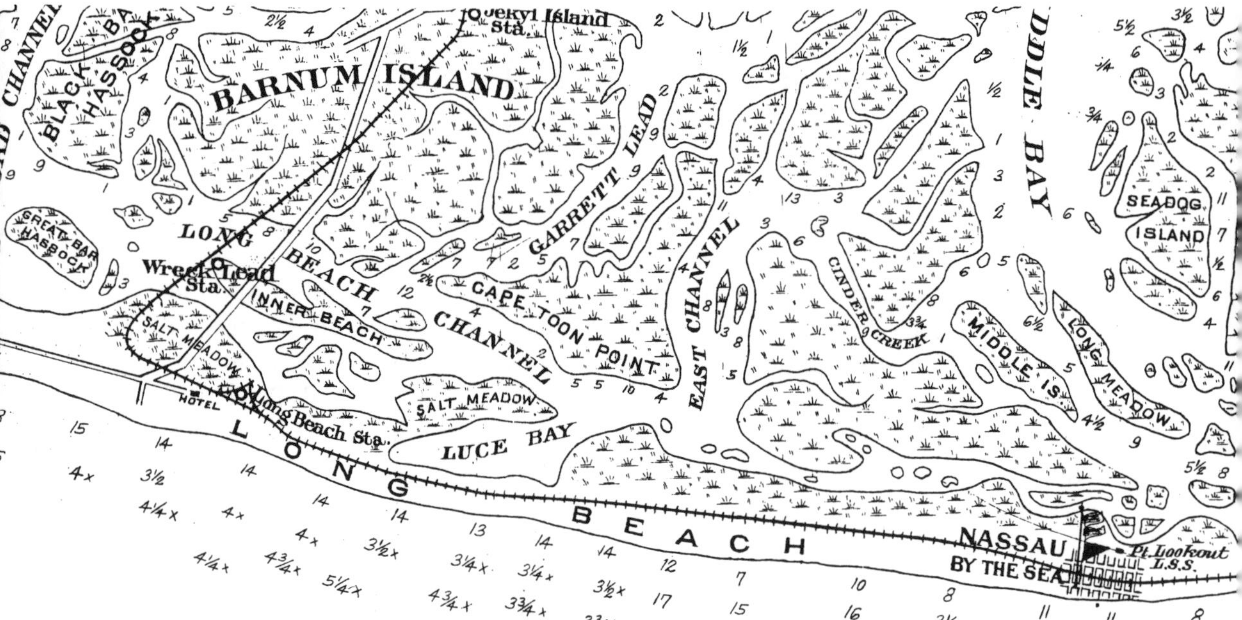

Fig. 1. Map of Long Beach in 1906. Detail from Belcher-Hyde *Atlas,* 1906. *NCM Collection, LISI at Hofstra.*

to create this land, but he was also soon relieved of the burden of the 1880 Long Beach Hotel. "The Largest Hotel in the World" burned to the ground on July 29, 1907. The Senator and his colleagues were on the premises to help evacuate the huge hotel, and fortunately for the eight hundred guests, there was no human life lost.

The island was a barrier reef shaped by the estuaries and inlets. This marshland had an inner and outer beach dotted with bayshacks. There was also an abandoned railroad spur, as well as a United States Life-Saving Station along with a primitive wooden bridge which was the only pedestrian way to the mainland. On the northwest side was the old railroad terminal, and facing the ocean was a tall brick chimney, a casino, and a few cottages, which were all that remained of the recently burned, shingled Queen Anne-style 1880 hotel and its properties.

The dredging of the channel was a massive project. Bulkheads had to be filled in with sand which was dredged up out of the channel, and this effort took two years, from 1907 to 1909. This new land was designed by Charles W. Leavitt, Jr., landscape engineer, and the field supervisor was G. S. Van Der Werken, a civil engineer. Most of the workmen, and their Captain Nelson, were Swedes who lived on board a houseboat-dormitory. The total force was 1,500 men; one workman was killed by the dredging machine. The dredges worked night and day pulling up 60,000 cubic yards of sand a day and in one year the Atlantic, Gulf and Pacific Dredging Company completed two miles of waterway to create Reynolds' Channel.[2]

In 1907, one of Senator Reynolds' promotional events was to have elephants marching along Observer Street (Sunrise Highway) carrying pilings for the bulkheads. They may also have been used to tear down older bayshacks and temporary train tracks. "Two hundred [train] carloads of lumber were needed for the bulkheads." Huge derricks drove the pilings into the sandy marshlands to hold in dredged fill from the channel.[3] This dredging completely altered the topography of Long Beach. Three suction dredges were connected to pipes, thirty inches thick and three-quarters of a mile long. As the dredges scooped sand from the waterway, the mixture of sand and water—20 percent sand and the rest water—was pumped through the pipes back onto the island, the water sluicing and coursing back to the ocean while the sand remained to bring all the hollow spots up to grade.[4]

Senator Reynolds joined the contemporary movement of urban planners when he directed his engineers to reproduce a rectilinear grid on this new land. A modern city was mapped out along generous lines with east-west streets sixty feet wide and boulevards one hundred feet wide. More than two hundred newly created city blocks were each 700 feet long and 200 feet wide.[5]

This new plan can be seen on the March 1907 General Lot Plan as designed by Charles W. Leavitt, Jr. Leavitt planned this rectilinear grid with streets of vitrified brick or macadam to accommodate the new mode of transportation—the automobile. In the plan, each block is numbered sequentially and subdivided into lots. An early price list of the Estates specifies exactly how much each block and every segment is to cost.[6]

The value of this rectilinear grid design in the control of one owner/seller is the ease with which it can be parceled up for sales. In fact, the March 1907 lot plan became the legal record of land sales. On all early contracts before 1911, the lot plan is referred to in the phrase, "Filed, or to be filed with the Nassau County Clerk."[7] This legal instrument stayed in the hands of the Estates of Long Beach until 1911, when it was finally turned over to the County Clerk. This is not a minor oversight; by 1909, three million dollars in land sales had been transacted. Land was swapped between the Long Island Rail Road and the Estates for the most advantageous site for the new railroad terminal, which was built in 1909.

This four-year registration gap during which the map remained under Senator Reynolds' control allowed him to continue to change the land outline and land use. Possibly by 1911, there were enough individual landowners so that Reynolds could no longer assert sole control and ownership. Thus began the idea of incorporating as a village, which was realized in 1914.

By 1909 another General Lot Plan existed displaying Sandringham Colony.[8] (See Fig. 2.) Senator Reynolds was split between his desire to emulate and associate with the plutocrats of the Gilded Age, and his need to sell Estates to the nouveau riche. This resort area was probably conceived with and for August Belmont, Jr. as an Edwardian park estate. It was to be completed with formal lanes of trees shading closely clipped turf, with circular drives laid out for horses and carriages leading to mansions of stucco and cobblestone. Still in existence at 657 Laurelton Boulevard (at the corner of West Bay Drive) is the Senator's model building for this venture—"Cobble Villa"—with covered carriage archway. However, the horse was outmoded by the automobile, and the plutocrat families stayed on the North Shore.

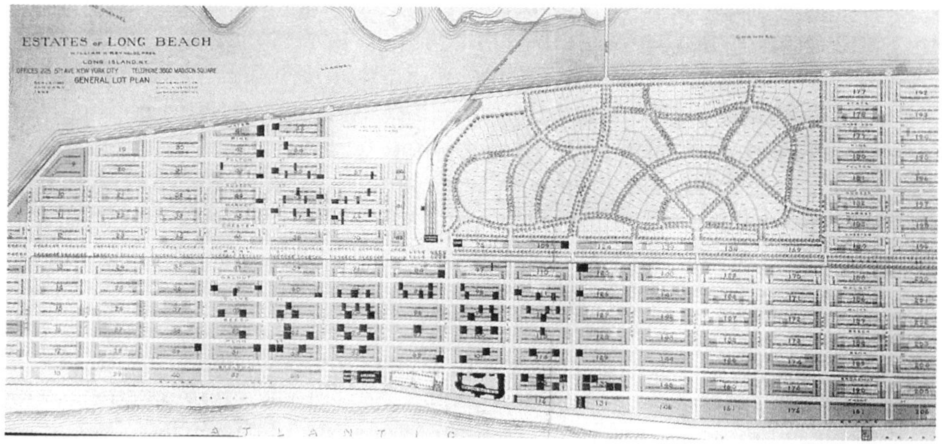

Fig. 2. General Lot Plan, Estates of Long Beach, January 1909, featuring Sandringham Colony. Map courtesy of the Long Beach Museum archives.

All the Estates' homes were built with covenanted restrictions to protect their exclusivity. For although William H. Reynolds' vision was to emulate the style of living of the extremely wealthy, his well-organized sales force on Fifth Avenue in New York City succeeded in selling to the newly rich, upper middle-class homeowners with cultural aspirations. The restrictive covenants also contained the most progressive and innovative design elements. Reynolds was responsible for an infrastructure that featured terracotta water mains to convey to the houses and hotels hot and cold water, fresh water, and salt brine. (The Long Beach Museum, located in a 1909 Estate home at 226 West Penn Street, still has four porcelain tub faucets: hot and cold fresh water and hot and cold salt water.)

To prevent wastewater pollution, no septic tanks were permitted, as the water table is very high; instead, two vaults located to the east and west of the Estates handled the sewage. Easements were reserved for laying underground telephone and electric lines. Every new home builder agreed to have each house built on a minimum of three lots, cost no less than $25,000 (in 1907 dollars), have twenty-foot setbacks, use cement stucco for the exteriors, and have a red roof. Each homeowner further agreed to a $6 annual assessment per lot for cultivation of trees and meridian mall plantings, each lot being graded level for green lawns.[9]

Long Beach villas built before 1922, showing variety of architectural styles. *NCM Collection, LISI at Hofstra.*

New prospective homeowners coming from New York City by special train were often shocked at the barren landscape of Long Beach. The Estates houses, many sparingly trimmed in dark red paint accenting terra-cotta roofs, were perched high on barren sandlots, along red brick streets optimistically named Park, Olive, Walnut, and Beech. Most of these early homes cost more than $25,000, a sizable sum considering the effects of the financial panic of 1907 besetting the merchant bankers of New York City. Yet no expense was spared to bring the latest technological innovations to Long Beach soon after 1907. The infrastructure of gas power, electric lights, telephone lines, and water was built and maintained by one owner, the master builder, Senator Reynolds himself.

The Senator was a showman as well as a politician. He owned and managed the New Montauk Theater in Brooklyn. He introduced George Bernard Shaw's scandalous play *Mrs. Warren's Profession* to the United

States with much notoriety.[10] He enjoyed the company of many actresses and, indeed, in 1892 he did marry a young and beautiful actress, Elise du Beaufort Guerrier.[11] Because of his interests in show business, many theater people were early buyers of Estates homes.

The central attraction of this seaside community, its social center, was a steel-reinforced, concrete boardwalk, fifty feet wide and two and one-half miles long that cost $136,000 per mile to construct.[12] Each mile of boardwalk rested on concrete piles and girders, 1,700 boards to a mile. In many ways, the Long Beach boardwalk was the perfect summer venue for theater people. In formal dress, on parade, one could see and be seen; too public for the richest families, the Long Beach boardwalk was a splendid social setting much sought after by the upwardly mobile. There one found the Band Gazebo for listening to music, the Palm Court and the Lavender Room for dining in the New Nassau Hotel, and the Casino for dancing. All these entertainments could be enjoyed on foot or by Rolling Chair along the wide and handsome boardwalk, lit up at night on both sides by new incandescent light bulbs. Indeed, Reynolds' earlier experiences with Dreamland at Coney Island helped him produce this pleasure resort.

The model of modernity named after the new county, the New Nassau Hotel, was built by Westinghouse and Company. From the granting of the building permit in October 1908 to the opening date, June 1909, intense building labor went on day and night; eight hundred and fifty men worked without a break to create this new glamour spot. Opening day brought 1,084 well-dressed patrons in automobiles to Long Beach. An even more elaborate entertainment pier designed by John Russell Pope in 1909 and to be built by Paul J. Rainey, was projected but never erected.[13]

William H. Reynolds created and changed corporate entities yearly, always one step ahead of the bank. Knowing that his fifteen-year bonds from 1906 were coming due in 1921, he had to change his business strategy. He opened a new market (Westholme) for people of modest means to purchase smaller "Reynolds' homes," tract houses with less stringent covenants. His next subdivision was the West End of Long Beach, where prefabricated bungalows were reassembled on streets named after states. Each street featured a model named after that street, e.g., the "California" on California Street, the "New Yorker" on New York Avenue.

During World War I, the New Nassau Hotel was used for de-embarkation purposes. The United States Army at Camp Upton transported by barge military style houses from Yaphank, Long Island, for its enlisted personnel. Inventively, they adopted the nickname "The Walks" as there was no vehicular access to their front doors.[14] After the war, these houses remained and, like the West End homes, they became summer bungalows.

All covenants and restrictions on residences were lifted in 1918 to facilitate home sales. After the end of World War I, the prestigious auctioneer Joseph P. Day sold lots at auction, a modern sales concept.[15] These sales, combined with the all-year round Westholme and Eastholme segments of the village, bolstered Long Beach's development. New homeowners had a greater commitment to settle in Long Beach because it was easily accessible and provided a healthier climate for their families.[16] Its new citizenry inspired Reynolds to construct a Town Hall, complete with a clock tower which was a beacon to vessels navigating his channel. Residents responded by supporting a business district, building houses of worship, schools, a hospital, and a library. Long Beach endorsed the use of the motor vehicle, the building of bridges, and macadam roads. Reynolds' next contribution to progress was the Lido Golf Course and the addition of an electric trolley for transportation.[17]

In 1921, the Estates of Long Beach went bankrupt. The 1906 bond issue came due and could not be paid off. Frank Bailey, a cohort of Reynolds for many years and president of the Title Guarantee and Trust Company, bid against Reynolds, hoping to wrest control. Irving T. Bush backed Reynolds with $400,000 solely on a handshake. William H. Reynolds scrambled for the money, succeeded in raising it, and never forgot Bush's support or Bailey's personal betrayal.

By 1922, village life had changed. Many of the homeowners refused to go along with the Senator's autocratic style and private ownership of the infrastructure. In order to maintain control of Long Beach, he pushed political buttons and, seemingly overnight, had the village status changed to city and himself made mayor.

The new twentieth century saw a number of planned communities developed in New York State, but Long Beach remains unique. It was created virtually out of nothing, using the most innovative designs and materials. Its success reflects the personal achievements of one man who in sixteen years turned a sandbar into a city and lived to govern it.

Notes

1. David B. Tolins, *History of Long Beach*, January 1932, serialized chapters for *The Long Beach Life;* 1-12 chapters, editor Eugene Blumenthal, typed manuscript from "The Long Beach Voice," 1972, on microfilm in Long Beach Public Library, 40-41.

2. Henry Isham Hazelton, *The Boroughs of Brooklyn and Queens, Counties of Nassau and Suffolk, Long Island, New York 1609-1924*, 3 vols. (New York: Lewis Historical Publishing, 1925), 3: 884-85.

3. Hazelton, *Boroughs*, 885.

4. *Brooklyn Daily Eagle*, 1908 (newspaper article in Long Beach Museum archives, unknown author and date). The editor of this newspaper, George F. Dobson, was a major investor in the Estates of Long Beach. His staff reported regularly on Long Beach events.

5. *Brooklyn Daily Eagle*, 1908 article.

6. Official Price List, Estates of Long Beach, William H. Reynolds, President, issued Saturday, April 20, 1907 (copy in the Long Beach Museum archives).

7. Contract leases, 1907-1911. Copies from Nassau County Clerk's Office on deposit with Long Beach Museum archives.

8. The January 1909 General Lot Plan of Long Beach features Sandringham Colony. In Long Beach Museum archives.

9. Contract leases, 1907 and on, in Long Beach Museum archives.

The minimum $25,000 cost of a house in 1907 dollars would be more than $400,000 in late 1990 dollars. See John J. McCusker, *How Much Is That in Real Money?* (Worcester, MA: American Antiquarian Society, 1992), 332; and *Statistical Abstract of the United States* (Washington DC: Government Printing Office), 489. (Editor's note.)

10. "The Unauthorized Biography: William H. Reynolds, Doer of Dreams," written c. 1925, unknown author (photocopy of typewritten manuscript in the Long Beach Public Library); chap. 10, p. 9.

11. "Unauthorized Biography," chap. 6, p. 28.

12. "Unauthorized Biography," chap. 5, p. 20.

13. Prospectus of *The Paul J. Rainey Pier, At Long Beach* (New York and Providence RI: Dean and Shipley, bankers, 1909), copy in the Long Beach Museum archives.

14. Bruce Lambert, "Without Streeets and Loving It," *New York Times*, June 13, 1996, B-1, 6.

15. Joseph P. Day, auctioneer, auction sales brochure with sale homes and land displayed; copy in the Long Beach Museum archives.

16. Julius C. Bierwirth, Vice-President of New York Medical Society, *Long Beach— America's Healthiest City,* 1920 brochure with climate comparisons; copy in the Long Beach Museum archives.

17. Edward J. Farrell scrapbook (in possession of the authors). Mr. Farrell was a realtor who invested in the Lido Hotel and the Canals of Lido Corporation.

Farmingdale's History: A Reflection of Nassau County's First Century

William J. Johnston

The County of Nassau and the Incorporated Village of Farmingdale were established as governmental entities only five years apart: 1899 for Nassau and 1904 for Farmingdale. Both shared long histories prior to their official creation. The eastern portion of Queens County, which was to become Nassau, had settlements as early as the 1640s,[1] and Thomas Powell settled in his Bethpage Purchase, which includes present-day Farmingdale, in 1687.[2] This essay will attempt to note certain similarities in the history of Farmingdale, especially in those last hundred years, to that of Nassau County. It is not a mirror reflection, as each community in Nassau obviously has distinctive historical characteristics, but there are still a sufficient number to be worth citing.

From Thomas Powell's settlement in 1687 until the arrival of the Long Island Rail Road in 1841, the area of contemporary Farmingdale and environs was almost totally rural and largely Quaker. Farms and woodlots of the various Powell descendants covered much of the Bethpage Purchase area, a tract approximately five miles north to south and about three miles wide. The first roads were constructed to connect the farmhouses of the Powell family members.[3] The predominance of agriculture was a feature of the life and economy of eastern Queens and Suffolk Counties throughout this period.[4] This era lives on at Old Bethpage Village Restoration, once the farm of Joshua Powell.

The first civil subdivision of Thomas Powell's Bethpage Purchase of 1695 was the creation of Hardscrabble School District 16 in 1814. Shortly before the arrival of the railroad in 1841, a land developer named Ambrose George had renamed the settlement Farmingdale. The train schedule in 1841 notes Farmingdale as "late Bethpage," the original name selected by Thomas Powell.[5] The settlement in the area of Farmingdale station grew slowly but steadily. A year after the arrival of the railroad, a Methodist congregation was formed (1842),[6] and a postmaster, John Monfort, was appointed by President James K. Polk in 1845.[7] As with Nassau County, there is a history even to the naming of Farmingdale, but once chosen, each has endured.[8]

In the years following the Civil War, a brickyard north of the hamlet was built.[9] This facility supplied the bricks for A. T. Stewart's planned community of Garden City. In 1875 an Episcopal parish, St. Thomas, was established.[10] Two volunteer fire companies were formed in the latter half of the

1880s: the Hook and Ladder Company in 1886, and the Water Witch Engine Company in 1889.[11]

At the time of Nassau County's establishment in 1899, the hamlet of Farmingdale was still part of the Town of Oyster Bay, which dates from 1653. Residents of Farmingdale had to travel by horse-drawn conveyances or endure a two-part train ride, changing at Mineola, to transact business at Town Hall. Unlike the lengthy effort over several decades to establish Nassau County,[12] the Village of Farmingdale was founded in a relatively short time in 1904. On April 14 of that year a petition was filed with William H. Jones, Supervisor of the Town of Oyster Bay. Supervisor Jones issued a "Public Notice" on May 18 calling for a hearing to be held at the "building known as Town Hall in the present unincorporated Village of Farmingdale on the tenth day of June 1904, at 3 o'clock in the afternoon." At the hearing a petition protesting the proposed incorporation was introduced by twenty-five taxpayers, but was rejected as not meeting the "form prescribed by statute" by Supervisor Jones, who then set an election for July 20. Eighty-seven voters went to the polls on that mid-summer day in 1904. Forty-six voted for incorporation, and thirty-seven opposed. It appears that the formation of the Village was not met with the enthusiasm that Nassau County had enjoyed on its creation some five years earlier![13] The new village numbered 1,047 residents. By the next federal census in 1910, the population had increased to 1,567. By comparison Nassau's residents numbered 55,448 on its first census in 1900.[14]

By 1930 the village's population had climbed to 3,373.[15] After World War II the village shared in the explosive wave of suburbanization that had started a few miles west, in Levittown, in 1947. This is reflected in the growth of the Farmingdale Public Schools, a district which serves not only the village but also portions of the Town of Oyster Bay in West Farmingdale, South Farmingdale, North Massapequa, and Massapequa Park, and also East Farmingdale in the Town of Babylon, Suffolk County. In 1952 all 2,902 students in grades K-12 attended the Main Street School, albeit on split-sessions. Ten years later, there were six K-6 elementary schools, two junior high schools (grades 7-9), and a senior high school, serving in total almost 14,000 students. Virtually every available tract of land was developed for residential purposes in that era. Although Farmingdale has some homes dating from the nineteenth century, and even one from the seventeenth century (Thomas Powell House), approximately 60 percent of the school district's homes date from the 1950s and 1960s.. Farmingdale's population was 4,492 in 1950 and peaked at 9,297 in 1970. Nassau County also experienced a tremendous surge of population growth in these two decades In 1950, the county population numbered 672,765; twenty years later it reached 1,428,838.[16] Today the

Today the population, according to the 1990 census, has leveled off for both the county (1,303,389) and the village (8,022).[17]

When Farmingdale incorporated as a village in 1904, there were few residents who could not claim Anglo-Saxon ancestry, perhaps 2 percent or less of the total of 1,047.[18] This figure began to increase in the immigration wave felt by this county following World War I, particularly for Italian-Americans. By the time of the suburbanization surge following World War II, this wave of newcomers, mostly war veterans and their families from New York City, many with southern and eastern European roots, overwhelmed the old stock. This was reflected on the county level also, in the election of Frank Gulotta in 1949 as district attorney, the first Italian-American to hold countywide office.[19] Farmingdale has shared this increasing diversity in the last half-century, by routinely electing village, school, and library officials of varied ethnic backgrounds.

This welcoming tolerance of diversity had one brief but dark interruption in both Nassau and Farmingdale. In the mid-1920s the Ku Klux Klan had a short period of activity in several villages of Long Island. Their activities were not directed at a traditional target, African-Americans, but at Roman Catholics and Jews, particularly those who were foreign born.[20] A large rally attracting hundreds was held north of Farmingdale in early October 1923, and the Klan openly distributed bags of candy and fruit following the lighting of the community tree on the grounds of Main Street School on Christmas Eve, 1923.[21] Klan intervention colored village and school board elections in Farmingdale in the mid-1920s. By 1926 the *New York Times* observed, "Long Island seems to be recovering from its belief in the Ku Klux Klan. . . . Thus has good sense returned to Long Island."[22]

One strong voice toward that "good sense" was that of Jesse Merritt, a lifelong Quaker, who in 1920 founded the *Farmingdale Post,* the village's first local paper. Mr. Merritt consistently battled the Ku Klux Klan through

Newspaper editor and historian Jesse Merritt was Clerk of the Nassau County Board of Supervisors, 1917-1923. The Nassau County Museum Collection is the Jesse Merritt Memorial Library and this 1965 painting by Pat Sowecke is in the Long Island Studies Institute. *NCM Collection, LISI at Hofstra.*

his editorials, insisting that "Farmingdale must not lose that tolerance that John Bowne, Peter Zenger, and Lady Deborah Moody had championed so long before."[23] Mr. Merritt, incidentally, was the first official historian of both the village (1920) and the county (1939). Two of the targets of the local Klan in the 1920s have evolved as influential factors in contemporary Farmingdale. The Roman Catholic Church of St. Kilian, founded in 1896 by ten families, largely German farmers, now numbers more than six thousand families. Jewish professional and business leaders have played a part in village life for decades, especially since 1948, when the Farmingdale Jewish Center was founded.

About the time of the establishment of Nassau and Farmingdale as governmental entities at the beginning of this century, industry began to rival agriculture in Farmingdale. In addition to the previously mentioned brick works, other Farmingdale area businesses of this era included some six pickle works, a glass bottle plant, a picture frame factory, several wholesale florist greenhouses, a fertilizer works, a truck factory, and even a car manufacturing company. World War I brought the aviation industry beginning with the Lawrence Sperry Aircraft Company in 1914. Later firms in this field included Seversky Aviation, Grumman, Republic, Ranger, Fairchild, and Liberty Aircraft Products.[24] World War II and the ensuing Cold War brought tremendous growth to Long Island aviation firms, with 100,000 working in their plants by 1945, about one-quarter at Republic alone.[25] This era largely closed with the dissolution of the Soviet "Iron Curtain." Republic, by then Fairchild-Republic, closed in 1987; its name lives on through Long Island Republic Airport, now a busy general aviation facility. The old factory area is now the site of a multiplex cinema, a sports complex, and a proposed shopping mall. In 1994 Grumman was acquired by the Northrop Corporation, based in California. This effectively ended an era for Long Island, which was the "Cradle of Aviation."

The changing Long Island economy has brought challenges to the downtown retail centers as shopping malls were established in the suburbanization era following World War II. Farmingdale's Main Street has been developing commercially since the arrival of the railroad in 1841. By the time of incorporation in 1904, the section north of Conklin Street to Melville Road was almost totally commercial.[26] The area south of Conklin developed more slowly; it was not until after World War II that the section from Conklin to the Village Hall became exclusively commercial. Farmingdale's Main Street had been a regional shopping area unrivaled in eastern Nassau for much of the twentieth century. Local residents had to travel only for major purchases, such as furniture, to stores in Hempstead or Jamaica.

The period of this "golden era" of Main Street retailing was likely the quarter century between the development of Levittown in 1947 and the opening of Sunrise Mall in Massapequa in 1973. Farmingdale during that period was not only growing quickly in population, but all of eastern Nassau was keeping pace. The Farmingdale Chamber of Commerce operated a holiday season bus service to bring stranded, non-driving housewives from their new homes in Levittown, Island Trees, and other developing areas of eastern Nassau to Main Street shops, and stores stayed open every weekday night in December until Christmas Eve.[27] One early threat to Main Street's retailing prosperity was the opening of the Abraham and Straus department store in Hempstead in 1955, and then Mid-Island Plaza in Hicksville (now Broadway Mall) a year later. A much greater negative impact took place in 1973 with the opening of Sunrise Mall in Massapequa, followed by numerous discount stores in the Route 110 area of East Farmingdale. Farmingdale has countered this competition, to a degree, by concerted effort by the Chamber of Commerce and the village government. Shops tend not to compete with those in regional shopping centers but rather to meet the needs of contemporary families. Restaurants, take-out food services, laundry and dry-cleaning shops, convenience stores, and child care facilities have taken the place of the clothing, shoe, and variety stores of the past. The village government reacted to the growth of auto traffic in the immediate postwar years by constructing four large parking fields in the areas behind the stores on Main and Conklin Streets. Municipal improvements such as "turn of the century" street lighting, shade trees, and brick sidewalks on Main Street have recently enhanced the retail area. Nassau County's "Operation Downtown," which is seeking to address the problems of Nassau's older commercial cores countywide, has assisted with part of the funding for this effort.

The role of the Long Island Rail Road (LIRR) in the story of Farmingdale since 1841 when the first train arrived has already been noted. On May 25, 1896 a new station opened, one that is still in service. On the 150th anniversary of LIRR service in 1991, the structure was added to the National Register of Historic Places. Throughout the 1990s it has been undergoing restoration as part of a community effort to bring it back to its original glory of a century ago. The exterior is largely completed, and most of the work still to be done is in the interior of the waiting room. In the early days of Nassau County and the Village of Farmingdale, this station would have been known, in today's parlance, as an intermodal hub. From 1909 to 1919, in addition to train and taxi service, Farmingdale station was an important stop on the "cross-island" trolley line, with service to Huntington and Amityville. The line came south on Broad Hollow Road (Route 110) from Huntington, swung west on Conklin Street (local name for Hempstead Turnpike), then turned south on Main Street, in the heart of the village, toward Amityville. The increasing number of automobiles, including those of jitney operators during

Long Island Railroad Station in Farmingdale, c. 1910. The brick tower was added for the Cross Island Trolley. Korten photograph, *NCM Collection, LISI at Hofstra.*

and immediately after World War I, was a significant factor in ending the trolley service.[28]

The Otten brothers of Farmingdale, much like the Wright brothers of Dayton, were in the bicycle repair business originally. The Farmingdale brothers saw their future in 1907 as they began to repair automobiles. At the time the Southern New York Volunteer Firemen's Association met for a convention, parade, and tournament in 1911, their program advertised two additional auto repair garages, that of Leo Kappertz (Farmingdale Garage) and H. F. Sands' Turnpike Garage.[29] The popularity of the private motorcar apparently blossomed quickly in Farmingdale.

The first roads in the area connected the forms of the early Quaker settlers of the Bethpage Purchase. A survey by Samuel Willis completed in 1768 reveals that by then a trail connected Hempstead to present-day Farmingdale. By the mid-nineteenth century this road, planked in some sections, had become a toll road. Its name has been shortened from Hempstead-Bethpage Turnpike to Hempstead Turnpike. A more famous road which connected the Farmingdale area to central Nassau was the Vanderbilt Motor Parkway, also a toll road, and renowned as the route of the Vanderbilt Cup Race. The road, which by 1911 connected Queens to Ronkonkoma on a forty-three mile route, passed just north of Farmingdale through what is now Bethpage State Park.[30] Robert Moses, "the master builder," was instrumental in planning and constructing several major roadways that link the Farmingdale area to other parts of Long Island as well as New York City. These would include the Northern, Southern, and Bethpage Parkways, and the Long Island and Seaford-Oyster Bay Expressways.

As previously noted, the Farmingdale (originally Hardscrabble) school district was established in 1814. Several major local events took place in

The Main Street School in Farmingdale was built in 1912. Korten photograph, c. 1915. *NCM Collection, LISI at Hofstra.*

education in the early twentieth century shortly after the founding of Nassau County and Farmingdale's incorporation as a village. In 1911 the Farmingdale Board of Education decided to close the four-room wooden schoolhouse on Main Street and erect a brick structure in its place. This new building, later known as the "south wing" of Main Street School, endured until 1961. The thrifty school board members of 1911 had the old schoolhouse salvaged and rebuilt as residences on Nelson Street. In 1913 the Farmingdale school trustees decided to begin a secondary program, one of the earliest in eastern Nassau. (For its first one hundred years, the district had offered only an elementary program.) Grades nine through twelve were added one year at a time from 1913 to 1916, with the first high school commencement taking place in June 1917, with two graduates. The number of students who stayed to complete high school was low in the early years. A decade after the first graduation in 1927, there still were but nine graduating seniors.[31] As has been previously noted, growth of the school and also the general population was slow but steady until the postwar suburbanization era. Sixty years after the first graduation at Farmingdale High School, there were more than 1,200 in the class of 1977.

In 1912 the State Legislature established a school of agriculture just northeast of the village of Farmingdale. This became the first public institution of higher learning on Long Island. The school has had several official names during its eighty-seven year history as its mission has changed to meet the needs of a changing Long Island. Today it is the State University of New York at Farmingdale College of Technology, and it offers several four-year programs leading to a bachelor's degree as well as two-year associate degrees. In 1946 the Industrial-Technical Division was established off-campus at the old Nazareth Trade School, a former orphanage on Conklin Street founded by the Sisters of St. Dominic in 1900.[32] Today technology is the major mission of the college; the last agriculture students were graduated in 1987 and the livestock and farm equipment sent to the remaining state agricultural schools upstate. At Long Island Republic Airport the college has recently inaugurated an aerospace department.

Through various phases of history Farmingdale has shared in the experience of Nassau County and all of Long Island's settlements: a long era of farming; the growth of small industries; heavy dependence on aircraft manufacturing; rapid suburbanization; and now the depletion of space for further development. The parallels are not perfectly congruent, but Nassau and Farmingdale together share many facets of a rich heritage.

Notes

1. Edward J. Smits, *The Creation of Nassau County* (Syosset: Friends of the Nassau County Museum, 1979), 7.

2. Iris and Alonzo Gibbs, *Harking Back, An Account of the Bethpage Purchase and Sundry Long Island Events, Persons, and Places* (Waldoboro, ME: Kinsman Publications, 1983), 18.

3. Gibbs, *Harking Back,* 40.

4. Bill Bleyer, "Farming Takes Root," in Newsday, *Long Island: Our Story* (Melville: Newsday, 1998), 194.

5. *Brooklyn Eagle-Kings County Democrat,* October 16, 1841, 1.

6. Dorothy B. Ruettgers, *Farmingdale United Methodist Church, 1842-1992* (Farmingdale: Farmingdale Methodist Church, 1992), not paginated.

7. Junior Historical Society, *Farmingdale's Story: Farms to Flights* (Farmingdale: Howitt School, 1956), 119.

8. Smits, *Creation of Nassau County,* 22.

9. Junior Historical Society, *Farmingdale's Story,* 101.

10. Junior Historical Society, *Farmingdale's Story,* 51.

11. *Fortieth Anniversary, Volunteer and Exempt Fireman's Benevolent Association of Farmingdale* (Farmingdale, 1979), 16.

12. Geoffrey Mohan, "Nassau's Difficult Birth," in Newsday, *Long Island: Our Story,* 232.

13. Archives, Village of Farmingdale (mimeographed copy), 20.

14. Mohan, "Nassau's Difficult Birth,"232.

15. Junior Historical Society, *Farmingdale's Story,* 75.

16. *Historical Population of Long Isand Communities* (Hauppauge: Long Island Regional Planning Board, 1982), 20; David Behrens, "The New Frontier, in Newsday,

Long Island: Our Story, 323. The privately-owned Thomas Powell House is located at 33 Merritts Road.

17. *World Almanac 1998,* 430 (county), 409 (village).

18. Archives, Village of Farmingdale, 1900 Census.

19. Michael Dorman, "A Vote for Ethnic Americans," in Newsday, *Long Island: Our Story,* 332.

20. Drew Fetherston, "Waves of Immigrants," in Newsday, *Long Island: Our Story,* 292. Also see Frank J. Cavaioli, "The Ku Klux Klan On Long Island,"*Long Island Forum* 42 (May 1979): 100-104; "People, Places, and the Ku Klux Klan on Long Island," *Long Island Forum* 49 (August 1986): 159-67.

21. *Farmingdale Post,* October 5, 1923, December 28, 1923.

22. David Behrens, "The KKK Flares Up on LI," in Newsday, *Long Island: Our Story,* 293.

23. Myron H. Luke, "Portrait of a Long Island Historian: Jesse Merritt," *Nassau County Historical Journal* 48 (1993): 7.

24. Junior Historical Society, *Farmingdale's Story,* 97-113. (See also the essay in this volume by Roy Douglas, "The Origins of Airplane Manufacturing in Farmingdale, New York, 1917-1928, 229-40." Editor's note.)

25. Joshua Stoff, *Long Island's Aerospace Heritage* (Interlaken, NY: Heart of the Lakes Publishing, 1989), 49-57.

26. "Farmingdale," (map); Sanborn Map Company, 1910.

27. *Farmingdale Post,* November 26, 1955.

28. Vincent F. Seyfried, *The Cross-Island Line, The Story of the Huntington Railroad* (Garden City: Privately printed, 1976), 95-113.

29. *Official Programme,* Southern New York Volunteer Firemen's Association, October 3-5, 1911.

30. Gibbs, *Harking Back,* 41.

31. Junior Historical Society, *Farmingdale's Story,* 28.

32. Junior Historical Society, *Farmingdale's Story,* 37-38.

From Soup to Nuts: Laughter in the Suburbs
Alan King and Billy Crystal

Joseph Dorinson

Brooklyn has an image leavened with humor. Manhattan has an image silhouetted in skyline. Bronx has an image punctuated by a less than pleasant cheer. Although Ogden Nash dismissed the Bronx with a "no thonks," the borough paints a picture. What about Long Island in general? Nassau County, in particular? The profile of this place, however vibrant and prolific, eludes us. When the Islanders, a splendid hockey team in the 1980s, won four consecutive National Hockey League titles, it appeared that Nassau would take from this the image of a winner. Unfortunately, the team fell on hard times. A positive new identity for Nassau would have to come from other sources.

A brief look at Long Island's history helps us to understand the reason for the lack of image. The first settlers, English Puritans and Quakers, came from the Connecticut Valley and from New England outposts, attracted by fishing and farmland. With its proximity to both the sea and New York City's trade, Long Island beckoned seductively. Kenneth T. Jackson, the preeminent historian of suburbanization in America, explains its spectacular growth: "the robber barons sought security in a country estate, an impressive physical edifice that would represent more stability than any urban residence." Jackson cites Long Island's North Shore as a prime example of the passion for country residence. Men of substance, such as John S. Phipps, Marshall Field, and John Hay Whitney, "built lavish mansions with square pavilions, balustraded arcades, and hundreds of acres of lawns, ponds, gardens, and polo fields."[1]

Owners of Georgian manor houses, these magnates represented only a tiny portion of the total population. The middle class and common workers would come later; ethnic, racial, and class exclusion delayed their arrival. Country clubs, for example, the Meadow Brook Country Club, sent a clear signal to outsiders: Keep out. The "unwashed" trickled in, however, as a support staff for the elites. Abetted by successive improvements in transit systems—bridges, trolleys, railroads, and automobiles—suburban growth on Long Island was facilitated. A combination of new immigrants and low cost land spurred industry. Doubleday Publishing came to Garden City in 1910; Glen Cove spurred the manufacture of leather and canvas goods; Port Washington had sand pits. Increased demands for consumer goods sparked the growth of wholesale and retail marketing in Freeport and Hempstead.

The Franklin Shop in Hempstead emerged as Nassau's first department store. Blessed with beaches and parks, and anticipating Frank Capra, local realtors crowed, "It's a wonderful life," as the masses joined the classes.

Between 1920 and 1930 suburbs expanded throughout the nation and Nassau County nearly trebled in population. Lured by "the green light of the orgiastic future," Jay Gatsby drove his yellow Rolls Royce into West Egg, i.e., Great Neck, in F. Scott Fitzgerald's *The Great Gatsby.* Another real—as opposed to fictional—outsider, Abraham Levitt, and his sons, William and Alfred, paved the way for a mass influx. This Jewish family started their development in Rockville Centre in 1929, fanning out to Manhasset in 1934, then in Norfolk, Virginia in 1941, and Hawaii in the war years, 1943 to 1945. After World War II they built 2,250 homes in Roslyn in one year, 1946. That same year the Levitts accumulated a large stretch of potato farms in the Town of Hempstead.[2]

Using innovative techniques, new power tools, and pre-assembled parts, the Levitts put up a tremendous number of houses, sometimes thirty in a single day. The first houses were designated as rentals at $60 per month for a Cape Cod with four rooms. After 1949 these were offered for sale. A survey found 82,000 residents in 17,400 houses. Low prices most certainly lured buyers. The middle class flocked to Levittown to purchase Cape Cods for $7,900 and ranches at $9,500. Minus down payments, closing costs, and extras, these homes loomed as true bargains. Add a free Bendix washer to sweeten the deal and the number of pilgrims in search of a new life mushroomed. An eight inch television set paid over a thirty-year period was an attractive option. Thus, by underselling competitors, the Levitts still managed to earn a $1,000 profit on each house.[3]

The Levitts provided swimming pools (nine), playgrounds (sixty), and baseball diamonds (ten). Social critics and architectural mavens lamented the "cookie cutter lots," the drab uniformity, and the single-class community.[4] African Americans, it must be observed, were excluded; however innovative in other spheres, the Levitts refused to tackle the race problem. With the Levitts showing the way, Long Island suburbs exploded. The promised land was just an automobile ride or railroad stop away. During the years 1950 to 1980, New York City lost 800,000 people, many of whom settled in Nassau County.

To chronicle this demographic shift a new paradigm was needed, preferably one with a comic sensibility. Enter Alan King, laughing. The odyssey of America's foremost suburban comic and that of his younger partner in fun, Billy Crystal, mirrors the journey to and from Long Island and serves as the meat and potatoes of this essay.

Alan King's most recent book, *Name-Dropping,* taken together with an article in the *New York Times,* offers an excellent insight into his suburban experience. Born in Manhattan's Lower East Side and raised in Brooklyn, he dropped out of high school to pursue a career in show business. His parents, Bernie and Minnie Kniberg, were European immigrants who came to America in search of a better life. A union man and member of the International Ladies Garment Workers Union (ILGWU), Bernie revered David Dubinsky and the New Deal. In an earlier book, King quipped:

> With the coming of the New Deal my father joined the Democrats. In our house we had two pictures on the kitchen wall. One was a colored print of Moses on the Mount and the other was a rotogravure of Franklin Delano Roosevelt, and until I was fourteen years old I didn't know who came first or who was more important.[5]

The father passed his politics on to his son, but could never earn a steady living or respect from his in-laws, so he remained an angry *luftmentsh* (dreamer).

Alan grew up angry and tough. At age fourteen, he appeared on Major Boses's Amateur Hour singing a depression era favorite, "Brother, Can You Spare a Dime?" in dirty face and torn knickers. Applause and laughter primed his comic pump, and, once bitten by the bug of entertaining, he could not stay in the classroom. Soon he was exiled from his Brooklyn school.

At age fifteen King went to the Catskills. Hired as number three comic, porch tummler (clown), beauty contest emcee, he quickly moved up to comic number one. He spent summers in the Borscht Belt and winters in Lakewood, New Jersey. Hired by the Gradus Hotel, he complained, "When you work for Gradus, you work for gratis."[6] The proprietor was not amused. King also worked for the Tisch family who owned Laurel in the Pines, Lakewood's poshest hotel. He copied every successful comic of the 1940s era, Milton Berle, Jackie Miles, Phil Foster, Jan Murray, Danny Kaye, Jerry Lester, Danny Thomas, and Jack E. Leonard.

King proved adept at memorizing movie dialogue, which he exchanged with another movie fanatic, Sammy Davis, Jr. Both fledgling entertainers experienced the poison of prejudice. King tried to assimilate but could not, and eventually he learned to wear his Jewishness proudly. At age sixteen, he went to Canada where he became a boxer. After twenty wins he fought a black boxer named King. He lost, badly, but he won a new moniker—King. After this savage beating Alan turned to comedy; he preferred to use his wits instead of his fists.[7]

King's talent was first recognized while performing at Georgie Jay's 78th Street Tap Room in Manhattan, where newspaper columnist Walter Winchell saw his act. Soon King was seen among the stars. He opened for Frank Sinatra at the Steel Pier in Atlantic City on Memorial Day, 1944. He stretched twelve minutes of comedy into eighteen, punctuated with laughter; Sinatra was not amused.[8] Despite this inauspicious beginning, their friendship grew, unal-

Alan King (*center*) at Hofstra University's Frank Sinatra Conference in 1998. Hofstra President James M. Shuart is on the right and Vice President J. Richard Block is on the left. Photograph by Ginny S. Greenberg, Hofstra University Relations.

tered even by political differences based on personal loyalties. They argued over the Kennedys who courted, then rejected, Sinatra, the self-styled "saloon singer."

Serving as the keynote speaker at Hofstra University's Frank Sinatra Conference in November 1998, King told many of his favorite stories about the singer, including this brief exchange:

> Waiter: "Mr. Sinatra, would you like some water?"
>
> Frank Sinatra: "I'm thirsty, not dirty."

King concluded his keynote address in tears and with the words, "I'll always have the music—but I miss the man."[9]

Moving to Long Island may have brought heavy debt and major problems but it also gave the comedian much new material. He had married his childhood sweetheart, Jeannette Sprung, at the East Midwood Jewish Center in 1947. The young couple moved to an apartment in Long Beach; later, they bought a house on a cul-de-sac in Rockville Centre for $22,000. King remembers it as "an upscale Levittown." *Tsores* (trouble) soon followed, providing grist for the comic's humor mill.

As a frequent guest on Ed Sullivan's celebrated CBS television show, Alan King vented his anger in more than ninety appearances. He poked fun at suburban zoning laws which, he claimed, ran a line through his home which meant his kids were zoned for another school district. King quipped, "They tried to explain to me that if my kids would sleep in the garage, they could go to the Rockville Centre schools."[10] Keeping up with the neighbors was no easy chore: the Kings had to mow their lawns to group specifications. Feeling oppressed, King wanted to let his grass go.

Obsessive cleanliness and finished basements also triggered King's comic wrath. Whenever he left his bed at 5 a.m. for the bathroom, he claimed, he returned to find that his wife had made the bed. There was no sleep for the weary in an upward mobile home. As for finished basements, King observed, "it's so wonderful to walk into a house with an eight-foot ceiling and a basement with a four-foot ceiling and spend an evening like Quasimodo or Toulouse-Lautrec." As many homeowners discover, you never have enough room. Adding rooms sparked King's description of how "the open porch became a closed-in-porch. The garage became a study. I had a $22,000 house and lived there for 11 years. We figured out I put $50,000 into that $22,000 house. And you know how much I sold it for? Twenty-two thousand dollars. That's absolutely true."[11]

Equally true and palpably painful were the ground rules for husbands about to host guests, handed down by imperious wives:

> 1. Don't sit on the sofa. I just puffed up the pillows.
>
> 2. Stay off the carpets, the pile is up.
>
> 3. Don't go into the bedroom. I want to keep it clean.
>
> 4. Hurry up and take a shower—but don't use the towels.
>
> So what happens? A man ends up dressing in a dark closet. And all night long he walks around with a damp skin blotting himself with a Kleenex.[12]

The visitors suffer too. King's narrative resonates with anyone lost in Yonkers or on Long Island. Listen.

> Meanwhile . . . the guests are trying to follow their hostess' directions to the house. Even if you ever received good directions—which is unlikely—it would be virtually impossible to find these places in the suburbs. . . .
>
> Today they stick a street between two trees, and even the people who live on the street are not too sure of its name. Every one of these places is called something like Featherbed Road or Poinsetta Place, and someone I know found his thrill on Blueberry Hill.[13]

For sure, it was not "Fats" Domino because of the "Gentleman's Agreement" and restrictive covenants.

For forty plus years, King's family has lived in a mansion formerly owned by Oscar Hammerstein. What's a mansion? King asks rhetorically. "According to the press, if you have a four-bedroom house, it's a mansion. Six bedrooms, it's an estate. I'm looking at my rose gardens right now. My rose gardens are on more land than my house in Rockville Centre was on."[14] In stark contrast to tenement life in New York with eight million kids on every block, the King family had to take their kids in a station wagon to find playmates.

Despite his carping, King winds up favoring Long Island. Why? Because you have the excitement of New York with the ambience of Beverly Hills and Bel Air on Long Island. With golf and tennis everywhere and New York City very near, who could ask for anything more? Although his business was moving to California, King opted to stay. Besides, King countered: "Half of it [the Golden State] is burning down, the other half is choking to death."[15]

Why didn't the King family move to Manhattan? They wanted their cake of culture and the bread of community and felt a sense of community is absent in the "Big Apple." Long Island, on the other hand, spans a James Joyce club and a bowling league. "Only in Long Island is garbage worth more than in its original form." Keenly aware of the drug problem which afflicted his sons in their teens, King hails community leaders who have devised a solution, namely, halfway houses. "They said we've got to build these halfway houses—halfway to your house, not my house. People in Great Neck said build them in Roslyn, people in Roslyn said build them in Hewlett, and then the temples said the churches."[16]

Unlike younger comedians, such as Jay Leno and David Letterman, King did not join the comic demolition derby at the expense of Amy Fisher and Joey Buttafuocco. This tragedy turned funny to be sure, but adultery and consensual sex with a Litvak Lolita are not unique to Long Island. Weirdos, King argues, can be found all over America. There are no free rides. Everyone pays dues. There are trade-offs. King's children prefer Greenwich Village, on a fire escape.

King continues to mock the absurdities of life on Long Island, like paying $41 for a loaf of bread in the Hamptons or taking three hours plus to reach the beach. Nevertheless, as reported in the *New York Times,* King prefers a walk in the sun on Long Island Sound and sand to Palm Beach in velvet slippers.[17]

In his latest book, the Long Island-based humorist provides minimal information about his current habitat. Picking up the slack in the final chapter, Jeannette, his upwardly mobile wife, adds kitschy commentary on life in Nassau County. Flushed with her husband's success, she expresses disenchantment with the incongruity of a $35,000 car parked in front of their $25,000 home in Rockville Centre, and the juxtaposition of oversized TV sets larger than the rooms in which they reside.[18] This no doubt prompted their move to Great Neck.

In the house of Hammerstein, they encountered trouble. As teenagers, the King boys turned to drugs, but no mention of this trauma is found in the book. Instead, we are invited to meet celebrities and trace the family's itineraries to exotic places. Evidently averse to airing dirty laundry, King discourses quite frankly on politics. Unlike many migrants to suburbia who switched politics from Democrat to Republican, King remained true to father Bernie's bent. Starting as a Norman Thomas Socialist, Bernie transferred loyalties to the Democratic Party of Franklin Delano Roosevelt. King remains a staunch defender of his father's faith. He cites meetings with Harry Truman and Adlai Stevenson, two of his heroes. He campaigned for Hubert Humphrey in 1960 and joined the Kennedy camp, where both John and Robert evoked King's enthusiastic support.[19]

Because of Harry Belafonte, Alan King marched with Dr. Martin Luther King, Jr., from Selma to Montgomery, Alabama. Flanked by a host of celebrities and common folk, King experienced fear. Spat upon by national guardsmen and sheltered in a Catholic monastery, he grew angry. He pushed for civil rights under the aegis of Dr. King and both Kennedys. Their deaths by assassination fueled his fury.[20]

Never content to be just a stand-up comic or a political fellow traveler, Alan King ventured into the movies. Movies meant action. Movies also established connective tissue with Billy Crystal and the big picture of life in modern America. Starting in films in 1955 with *Hit the Deck,* a clichéd remake of the three sailors on leave formula, King had a small role.[21] He played a gangster in *The Helen Morgan Story* (1957) opposite Paul Newman. *Bye Bye Braverman* (1968) converted King from *gonif* (thief) to rabbi. He actually played two rabbis: one, an old-world talmudist, the other a hip, new-age Oxford-accented hustler.[22]

In 1980, King gained star-billing as a garment center tycoon, Max Herschel, in *Just Tell Me What You Want.* Like the real-life King, Max bemoans rural America because basically he's New York City, urban, Jewish. Yet, he lived in a palatial estate on Long Island. Married to an alcoholic *shiksa* (Dina Merrill) and involved with a sultry mistress (Ali MacGraw), Max suffers. This film, directed by Sidney Lumet, conveys a dark vision of assimilation, social mobility, and moral rot.[23] A number of mediocre films followed. Then magic in a bottle of lightning struck in 1988 with *Memories of Me*. This memorable movie paired Alan King and Billy Crystal. Producer and star, Alan King likened it to his King Lear.[24]

Billy Crystal grew up in Long Beach, Long Island. His father managed the music shop in the Commodore Hotel. An avid Yankee fan, Crystal Sr. took his young son to Yankee Stadium on May 30, 1956. At his first game, Billy found a hero, Mickey Mantle. When he played baseball in high school, Crystal affected a limp just like Mantle's. The baseball idyll ended when his dad died suddenly in 1963.[25]

After high school, Billy attended Marshall University. During a summer vacation in 1966, he fell in love with Janice Goldfinger. Their first date was a night game at Shea Stadium on July 30, 1966. He transferred to Nassau Community College where he majored in theater. He directed and starred in *The Fantastics*. He moved on to New York University where he studied film under Martin Scorsese. After college, he married Janice and moved back to Long Beach where he earned his daily bread as a substitute teacher. His wife gave birth to a daughter, Jennifer, and for a time Mrs. Crystal became the breadwinner while Billy played Mr. Mom. At night, he ventured into New York to perform at comedy clubs such as The Bitter End in Greenwich Village. In an interview with James Lipton, Crystal confided: "I had to rehearse material for a fraternity party on my eighteen-month-old daughter. Aside from a little dribbling, her feedback wasn't that positive."[26] In his autobiography co-written with Dick Schaap, Crystal traces his start in show business. He got a few laughs on the way to the hospital, prenatally. "It was the best womb I ever played." At age six, he imitated his relatives while hanging up their coats. Influenced by television, Billy and his two older brothers, Joel and Richard, honed their own comedies based on what they saw. For example, they converted Mel Brooks's 2,000-year-old man into the 2,000-year-old teenager. Later, he drew inspiration from the insipid but campy Joe Franklin Show. Teaming up with two students, Dave Hawthorne and Al Finelli whom he befriended at Nassau Community College, Billy began to write and act in comic sketches. They worked the college circuit for $150 per night. Billy's first solo gig was a fraternity party for $25. Twenty minutes built around a Howard Cosell-Muhammad Ali routine became one hour of material. From that point, Crystal would work alone.[27]

Dick Schaap needed a comic to grace a *Sport* magazine banquet honoring Muhammad Ali in 1975. Since Robert Klein could not make it, Schaap, close to panic, took Billy on the rebound. So this timid, some-time substitute teacher on Long Island sat on a dais with Neil Simon, George Plimpton, Melba Moore, and Ali. Crystal strode to the microphone to perform:

> "Muhammad—may I call you 'Mo'?"
>
> "Sure, Howard, but don't call me Larry or Curly."
>
> "How fast are you, Mo?"

> "I'm so fast, Howard, I can turn off the light and jump in the bed and be under the covers before the room gets dark."[28]

It was a sensational debut.

Billy shlepped his family to the West Coast to launch a film career. Stand-up led to the role of Jody, a homosexual on *Soap,* an evening soap opera. In 1984, he joined the cast of *Saturday Night Live.* As a writer/performer/host, he created an amazing array of characters: Sammy Davis; Rooster, an aging black baseball player; an old Jewish weatherman; Buddy Young, a stereotypical comic; Penny Lane, a transvestite piano player; gullible Ricky; self-abusive Willie; and Fernando in his Hideaway, a hilarious synthesis of Fernando Lamas and Joe Franklin.[29]

Billy Crystal hooked up with Alan King in a poignant film which the younger comic wrote called *Memories of Me* (1988). King plays a Jewish Lear who is alienated from his family until an unwanted reunion with his son reestablishes his humanity. Some viewers found the film a bit maudlin, a danger whenever comedians try tragedy. This cinematic venture brought together the two Jewish comics, one from Brooklyn who lived on Long Island, the other from Long Island who lived in Los Angeles. A close friendship issued from this not-so-brief encounter. Crystal pumped King for information about the history of entertainment, and the latter dropped names and topped the younger comic in their verbal *manos a manos.*[30]

In *Mr. Saturday Night* (1992), a vastly underrated film, Crystal deftly synthesized comedy and tragedy. He mined his Long Island past, his association with Borscht Belt comics, and the Hollywood experience to craft a self-destructive yet highly creative figure, Buddy Young, Jr. The protagonist Young finally finds fulfillment in Florida, working the senior circuit not too far from his transplanted roots in Long Beach, while his comrade in fun, the King of the Crabgrass Frontier, continues to live in Great Neck with occasional forays into Florida.

If we seek an historical narrative of Nassau County suburban life coupled with comedic commentary, we find it more in the memories of the Brooklyn expatriate (Alan King), not from the antics of the native son.[31] "City Slicker" Billy Crystal found national recognition at another time, in another place, East of Eden, west of the moon, and far from Long Island.

Notes

1. Kenneth T. Jackson, *Crabgrass Frontier: The Suburbanization of the United States* (New York: Oxford University Press, 1985), 88-89.
2. Jackson, *Crabgrass Frontier,* 234.
3. Jackson, *Crabgrass Frontier,* 234-36.
4. Jackson, *Crabgrass Frontier,* 236-37.

5. Alan King with Kathryn Ryan, *Anybody Who Owns His Own Home Deserves It* (New York: Hearst Avon Books, 1962), 19.

6. Alan King with Chris Chase, *Name-Dropping: The Life and Lies of Alan King* (New York: Hearst Avon Books, 1996), 26.

7. King, *Name-Dropping,* 21-38.

8. King, *Name-Dropping,* 110-11.

9. Jon Weiner, "The Birth of Sinatra Studies," *Lingua Franca,* February 1999, 35, 37. King was not alone in tears. This writer also succumbed to sentiment as noted in the same scintillating article, 39.

10. James Barron, "Alan King's Love-Hate Relationship: An Angry Comedian with 50 years on L.I.," *New York Times,* August 30, 1998, sec. 14, LI, 13.

11. Barron, "Alan King's Love-Hate Relationship."

12. King, *Anybody Who Owns His Own Home,* 42-43.

13. King, *Anybody Who Owns His Own Home,* 43.

14. Barron, "Alan King's Love-Hate Relationship" 13.

15. Barron, "Alan King's Love-Hate Relationship," 13.

16. Barron, "Alan King's Love-Hate Relationship," 13.

17. Barron, "Alan King's Love-Hate Relationship," 13.

18. King, *Name-Dropping,* 204.

19. King, *Name-Dropping,* 120-27.

20. King, *Name-Dropping,* 128-33.

21. This genre is discussed in Dennis Carpenter and Joseph Dorinson, *Is Anyone Here a Sailor?* (Great Neck: Brightlights Press, 1995).

22. King, *Name-Dropping,* 136, 139.

23. David Desser and Lester D. Friedman, *American-Jewish Filmmakers: Traditions and Trends* (Urbana: University of Illinois Press, 1993), 193-95.

24. King, *Name-Dropping,* 101-2.

25. Rick Lyman, "In The Bronx with Billy Crystal; Facing Fifty with Memories of Mick," March 13, 1998 in *New York Times Biographical Service* 29, no. 3 (March 1990): 376-78.

26. Bravo: Billy Crystal Inside the Actors Studio, Bravotv.com, 1.

27. Billy Crystal with Dick Schaap, *Absolutely Mahvelous* (New York: G. P. Putnam's Sons, 1986), 20, 33-42.

28. Crystal, *Absolutely Mahvelous,* 11.

29. Crystal, *Absolutely Mahvelous,* 9-14.

30. King, *Name-Dropping,* 150-51.

31. Polarized perceptions of suburbia in American culture and their altered states are deftly captured by Samuel G. Freedman in his article, "Suburbia Outgrows Its Image in the Arts," *New York Times,* February 28, 1999, sec. 2, pp. 1, 26-27.

Women in the Clergy in Nassau County: Breaking Through the Stained Glass Ceiling

Linda F. Burghardt

Women . . . God . . . leadership.

Three little words that dare, declare, plead, forebode, and challenge.

Three little words that inspire fear, defy tradition, provide comfort, and offer hope.

Three little words that speak of enormous change, and in so doing tell a story of Nassau County more deeply enmeshed in our consciousness and our culture than we fully understand.

Historians are fond of saying that wherever there have been communities of faith, there have been women there to shape them. But the truth is that despite small markers on the rutted road of religious leadership, for thousands of years women have been barred from gaining positions of any real authority in the religious world. Yet struggling against the dual forces of scriptural admonition and cultural pressure, women in the last hundred years have risked personal taunts and traumas, and sometimes even bodily harm to follow their devotion to their faith.

The result is a population today of female clergy in Nassau County burgeoning with fresh ideas, new perspectives, and renewed spiritual energy. But how did it get that way? How did the women themselves create the inner well of spirit that nurtured them in their quest? How have women leaders shifted the religious, cultural, and social agendas in churches and synagogues throughout Nassau County? And what does this bode for the future?

Listen to the voices of today's women clergy as they speak for themselves before the backdrop of our shared history. You will hear courage in their clarity, and doubt overcome by ambition in their words. And as time passes and the texture of their story becomes more richly endowed, you will witness how these changes in religious leadership hold the promise of change for all of us.

For nearly four years Linda DiSantis has been one of three ministers at the Unitarian Universalist Congregation at Shelter Rock in Manhasset. But when she graduated from Hofstra University in 1970 as a French major, she planned an entirely different life for herself. "I was raised as a Catholic," Reverend DiSantis said in an interview, "and I planned to become a teacher. I got married young, had a couple of kids and followed my husband's job from city to city."[1] But in the early 1980s Reverend DiSantis moved back to Long Island with neither her marriage nor her faith intact. Everything in her life was shifting. "I heard from neighbors about a Unitarian church in Garden City, and I went there to look it over. At the end of the first evening, I decided to join."

In 1985, buoyed by the fact that one-third of the ministers in the Unitarian Church were female, Linda DiSantis decided to pursue a degree from Union Theological Seminary in New York City and become a minister herself. She was ordained in 1990.

"Today over 50 percent of those preparing for the ministry in my faith are women," the Reverend DiSantis says. Nationwide, 33.9 percent of total enrollment in all theological schools is female, up from 10.2 percent in 1972.[2] "While this is certainly something to celebrate, the worry is that the so-called feminization of the industry is contributing to a lack of pay increases," Reverend DiSantis says. "The Unitarians have been ordaining women since 1865, but the truth is these women were relegated to the shabbiest, most struggling congregations on the frontier."

Reverend DiSantis landed her first job, her first settlement as it is called, at Washington Cross Church in New Jersey. She spent six years there, filing for divorce during her tenure. Shortly after receiving the decree, she moved to Manhasset and accepted the position of minister at Shelter Rock.

Is acceptance of women in Nassau County more prevalent than in New Jersey? "Soon after becoming the minister at Washington Cross, I was asked to help the congregation bring sexual misconduct charges against my predecessor," Reverend DiSantis explained. "Sometimes women are offered ministerial jobs following men who had some sort of sexual misconduct or power inequality issue with the congregation. It's as if the congregation believes hiring a woman will prevent a recurrence. I don't see any of that happening here."

Indeed, as far back as three years ago, *Newsday* commented that women in the clergy had become so commonplace on Long Island they no longer warranted any special notice. "Twenty years ago clergywomen were practically unheard of," wrote Susan Hartman. "A decade ago they were pioneers. Today, they're business as usual in most of Judaism and most Protestant sects." Rabbi Jill Kreitman of the Community Synagogue in Sands Point is quoted as remarking, "Being a clergywoman is becoming a pink collar job."[3]

Yet despite this publicized acceptance, DiSantis says she still encounters special treatment as a woman. "It's especially true at weddings," she recalls, "and it mostly comes from women, older women in particular. They tend to pat me on the head and murmur, 'Very good, dear,' something they would never do to a man."

Among the three Unitarian churches in Nassau County, two have male ministers, and one has two women and a man. In Suffolk County, both Unitarian churches have female ministers.

"Women in the ministry have a different way of understanding power than men," Reverend DiSantis says. "We believe more in collaboration, not the old hierarchal paradigm where the clergyman is on top of the congregation. We believe in empowering people to become involved, to help make decisions with us."

The Reverend Joan Brown Campbell puts it a different way. "Women are less in love with power," asserts the general secretary of the National Council of Churches, an umbrella organization of thirty-two Protestant denominations that represents an estimated forty-five million Christians. "This has brought clergywomen closer to their congregations."[4]

"In our society today," Reverend DiSantis comments, "people expect women to be nurturing and caring. When we are strong leaders, with open opinions and a directive style, it upsets them. For us, cooperation works."

Other mainline Protestant denominations in Nassau County besides the Unitarian Church welcome women ministers but have been hampered by declining church membership. "We have two ministers for every position that opens," says Ann Du Bois, a personnel coordinator for the Presbyterian Church.[5] On Long Island, where the Protestant population predominated through the first half of the twentieth century, demographers estimate that half of today's 2.7 million residents are Catholic, 20 percent Jewish, and 30 percent Protestants and others.[6] *Compton's Encyclopedia* states that nationwide, 64 percent of Americans are Protestant, 25 percent Catholic, and 2 percent Jewish. The remaining 9 percent belong to other major faiths or have no religious ties.

Reverend DiSantis believes that like most other Nassau County clergywomen, she has a different agenda than her male colleagues. "When the issue of [President] Clinton's sex life first came up," she said, "I delivered a sermon about inequality of power. I wanted my congregation to understand the difference between infidelity and sex with a young woman. Some members of the congregation were openly angry. One man accused me of giving what he called a 'woman's sermon.' What he was attacking was the fact that I raised an issue at odds with mainstream patriarchal thought."

Where did this ability come from? Reverend DiSantis looked into her childhood for the answer, but failed to find it. "My mother lied to me when she said I could do anything," she says. "I wanted to believe her, but when I started my work as a minister, people chided me. 'How can you leave your children?' they demanded. And the fact is, if you ask my daughter how it was when I was in theological school, she will have nothing good to say."

Today, with both her children away in college, Reverend DiSantis said her job is a twenty-four-hour commitment. "I don't really see how it can be anything less," she says. "It's my whole life."

Not all women who go into the ministry take on the heavy burden of leading a congregation. Julie Parker, who is the daughter, wife, and sister of ministers, and a minister herself, chose a different path. As the Protestant chaplain at Hofstra University for the last eight years, Reverend Parker works only two days a week, instead of the sixty to ninety hour workweeks common to congregational clergy. The rest of the time she spends with her son, seven, and her daughter, five. She is an ordained minister in the United Methodist Church, which began ordaining women in 1956, eighteen years before the Lutherans and the Episcopalians, but some sixty years later than the Baptists[7] and one hundred years after the Congregationalists.[8]

"Campus ministry is a wonderful way for women with families to serve in the clergy," she said in an interview.[9] "The culture here in Nassau County is pervasively secular, and we fit in very easily, much more so than in other less metropolitan areas of the state, where clergywomen are less welcome."

A 1983 graduate of Hamilton College, where she majored in English, Parker found her way to the ministry through a direct route. "In college I had an inkling I wanted to become a minister, and in my senior year I voiced this fledgling idea to my campus chaplain. He was encouraging and told me about a missionary program in Washington, D.C., which I applied to immediately." When she told her parents, she recalls, her mother cried. "And they were not tears of joy," she pointed out. "My mother told me about all the things we couldn't afford to buy when I was small, when my family was living on my father's small minister's salary. She told me she wanted something better for me. But I told her I couldn't think of anything better."

Today Reverend Parker is married to the minister of the First Presbyterian Church in Freeport. She was ordained a deacon in 1987, then spent two years as associate pastor at Grace Church in Valley Stream, where she was ordained an elder. "I'm among the first generation of women who joined the clergy in significant numbers," Reverend Parker says. "I was a teenager before I met my first woman pastor. I think it's great for today's little girls to see a woman in the pulpit."[10]

Does she find resistance to women as ministers? "Yes," she said, "great resistance." Yet the objections often come from a surprising source—other women. "My theory is that many of these women want a strong, caring man in their lives. If they don't have it at home, they look for it in church." Yet Reverend Parker's experience in religious leadership tells her that what these congregants are resistant to is the idea of a woman, not so much the woman herself. "It's analogous to race relations," she said. "Once you meet the person on an individual basis, the prejudice often evaporates."

Reverend Parker believes women in the ministry in Nassau County have distinctly different goals from men. "Women are keenly aware of disempowered people," she says. "Our experience of being relegated to the margins colors everything we do. Now that some of us are beginning to move toward the center, we are interested in helping those who are still outside." The problem, as she sees it, is that society hasn't kept pace with the changes in people's lives that resulted from women's entry into the workforce. "It's similar to the social upheaval at the turn of the century, when families moved from the country to urban areas in droves. The services they needed in the cities simply didn't exist. When I went to enroll my son at Hofstra child care, I found a waiting list of two hundred children. Society, once again, is just not keeping up with change."

Hence many women in the clergy in Nassau County are choosing to achieve their goals in part-time positions. "Women who want to lead a congregation can certainly do so," she said, "but for those of us without wives, we often find our skills are best used as part-time chaplains, working for hospitals, prisons, or universities. The fact is women in the clergy are doing what we always did—teaching, helping, counseling. But today we have new status, a new name, and a better place in the community."

Bonnie Steinberg, who is the rabbi at Temple Isaiah in Great Neck, is keenly aware of the value of this new status. "The fact that I am here as a rabbi, not as a social worker, is a political statement," she said in an interview.[11] A native of Belmont, Massachusetts, Rabbi Steinberg is the daughter of a psychiatric nurse and a textile manufacturer, and a graduate of Brandeis University and Hebrew Union College. She studied anthropology in college until a friend literally dragged her to a freshman course in Judaism and opened her eyes to a profession she says has brought her "many difficulties but far more joys." She explains, "I made a transition inside myself, and instead of perceiving other cultures as incredibly important, my own culture and people became primary."

Bonnie Steinberg became the first woman rabbi on Long Island at the age of twenty-seven. She was ordained in 1979, at a time when there were only twenty rabbis who were women in the United States. Today there are more than 330.[12] The Reform movement was the first to ordain a woman rabbi in 1972; the Conservative movement followed in 1985.[13]

Yet despite her status as pioneer, Rabbi Steinberg had to go through twenty-three job interviews to find a position. "Years later, a colleague told me that when he went in for his interview right after I finished mine, he heard someone say, 'Too bad she's a woman. She'd make a great rabbi.'" Some interviews were even cancelled when the organization found out she was a woman.

Half the female rabbis surveyed by the Commission for Women's Equality of the American Jewish Congress in 1993 believe they haven't been offered a job because they are female, and, like their Protestant counterparts, they have trouble getting hired by the bigger, wealthier organizations. A full

48 percent said they are paid less than male rabbis with similar positions.[14] "It's important that people think of me as a rabbi who is a woman, not a woman rabbi. That implies the real rabbis are men. But we're all rabbis," Rabbi Steinberg asserts.

Job equality in the clergy is a long way off, says Adair Lummis, faculty research associate for the Center for Social and Religious Research at Hartford Seminary in Connecticut. "While the number of women entering seminary has doubled since 1980, the total number of ordained women remains at only 11.1 percent, whereas women now account for 25 percent of lawyers and 21 percent of doctors."[15]

"Some people simply can't handle the woman factor," Rabbi Steinberg says. "My class in rabbinical school was the first to have any significant numbers of women—nine out of forty," Steinberg recalls. "Today, the ratio is close to 50/50."

Like most clergywomen, Rabbi Steinberg delivers sermons, officiates at weddings and funerals, runs a religious school, administers a budget, and comforts the ailing. Yet at the same time she cares for her two school-age sons and nurtures her marriage. Confronted daily with other people's problems, she must find a way to solve her own as well. And that, she says, has nothing to do with being a woman. "I remember reading about a pianist who had a sex change operation, and afterward many of his bookings were cancelled. I wondered why. Didn't he still play the piano just as well?" In fact, some congregants in her temple think she does it better. "Many people have told me they like the feminine presence in the pulpit. I tend to think out loud, to get everyone involved in decision-making. But I also have goals that I might not have if I were male," Rabbi Steinberg said.

These goals include trying to change the liturgy to add female stories and gender-neutral pronouns, and to encourage more collaboration on ideas. "Not every congregation wants to do this," Rabbi Steinberg says. "There is a classical way of being in the pulpit that suits many men but does not fit my style. Men are just more frontal, that's all. But people tell me I'm a rabbi who's a real human being. To me that's a real success."

While Rabbi Steinberg chose the clergy as her first and only career, for Angela Archer, minister at the North Shore Presbyterian Church in Great Neck, becoming a minister was a choice made after other worlds had been conquered. "When I made my vocational decision, becoming a member of the clergy was not an option for women," says the Reverend Archer, an African American, who was a nurse for twenty-five years before being called to the ministry.[16] "Preaching women have been in our culture for many years, but ordained preaching women were not accepted until the 1970s."

"I joined the ministry after challenging myself professionally in other ways," Reverend Archer said in an interview. "I was a church person while

I was raising my four children, and I'm a church person now. What got me interested in the ministry is that my home church constructed a new building, and I helped it happen. Then I survived a near-fatal car accident. That summer I went back to school."

After earning her degree from Union Theological Seminary in New York City, Reverend Archer was ordained in 1996. "I was well-established in my work as a nurse, and I could have stayed there and made a nice living," she says. Instead, she chose to answer the call to the ministry. But it was not as big a change as she expected. "Women look at the challenges of the ministry in a unique way and come to different conclusions than men as to how to approach problems," she said. "I'm a mother, a homemaker, a wife. I have a large stake in nurturing. I've been concerned for the inner spirit my whole life." Men, she said, are geared to "building, building, building. They want to see results in material ways."

Originally from Virginia, Reverend Archer believes our busy Nassau County lifestyles often fail to provide support systems for people's emotional needs. "That's why they need the church," she said. With her community health experience, Reverend Archer fell right into step making pastoral visits and immediately felt at home in the ministry. Yet as a woman, she has seen many barriers to getting hired for a job. In the church and synagogue directory of the Great Neck telephone book, for example, her church is listed as having a minister named as "Angelo Archer."[17] A typographical error? Most likely. An assumption of gender on the part of the proofreader? Perhaps.

Nevertheless, the Ordained Clergy Study, conducted in 1995 by the Center for Social and Religious Research at Hartford Seminary, reported that male ministers are likely to be hired as a sole pastor for their first position, while women are more often offered positions as assistants or associates. In addition, female ministers earn at least $5,000 a year less in salaries and benefits than their male counterparts.[18]

"Many congregations in Nassau County struggle when they are presented with a woman candidate," Reverend Archer said. "I almost always see a longer space of time for women between completing ordination and getting a position—up to a year for women, three or four months for a man." Reverend Archer believes most churches will let a woman do everything but preach. "Women can get jobs as associate pastors, but senior pastor—now that's hard. There's a definite line of demarcation when it comes to power. Some churches are becoming more liberal in their thinking; others are not."

In her doctoral dissertation for Harvard, the Reverend Paula Nesbitt documented how male and female clergy are placed on different career paths. "Most commonly, women move laterally, from assistant to assistant job, while men move directly into rectorships. This speaks of cultural, sexual and structural arguments similar to those of secular occupations," she said.[19] Yet

Reverend Archer feels strongly that faith communities can be fragile and are more likely to be held together by a woman minister. "Church communities need a great deal of care and nurturing. The roles assigned to us when we come into the world have love at their center. Isn't that the guiding principle of every religion?"

Perhaps that is so. But in the words of the Reverend Campbell, director of the National Council of Churches, "Women have broken ordination barriers, but resistance to a woman as pastor, as one who speaks the word of God, is still there. The culture hasn't changed. There is still a lot of work to be done."[20]

Notes

1. Interview with Reverend Linda DiSantis, November 27, 1998.

2. Eileen Lindner, ed., *Yearbook of American and Canadian Churches* (Nashville: Abingdon Press, 1998), 14.

3. Susan Hartman, "True Calling: Women Clergy Bring Something Special to Their Congregations," *Newsday,* October 8, 1996, B29.

4. Quoted by Debra Nussbaum Cohen, "Women Bring New Dimension to Several Aspects of Ministry," *National Catholic Reporter,* February 11, 1994, 6.

5. Quoted by Joseph Carey, "Women of the Cloth: How They're Faring," *U.S. News & World Report,* December 3, 1984, 76.

6. John Rather, "In Church, Changing of the Guard," *New York Times,* September 20, 1998, sec. 14, p. 1.

7. Julie F. Parker, *Careers for Women in the Clergy* (New York: Rosen Publishing Group, 1993), 2.

8. Rosemary Radford Reuther and Rosemary Skinner Keller, eds., *Women and Religion in America, Volume 3, 1900–1968, A Documentary History* (San Francisco: Harper & Row, 1986), 340.

9. Interview with Reverend Julie F. Parker, November 18, 1998.

10. After this essay was written, but while this book was in preparation, the Reverend Parker began doctoral studies at Yale University in September 1999 after her husband, the Reverend William Crawford, became minister of the Larchmont Presbyterian Church in Westchester County in July 1999. (Editor's note.)

11. Interview with Rabbi Bonnie Steinberg, November 9, 1998. (Rabbi Steinberg was the Jewish chaplin at Hofstra University, 1979-1985. Editor's note.)

12. "Religion," *Working Woman,* November-December 1996, 75.

13. Parker, *Careers for Women in the Clergy,* 5.

14. Hartman, "True Calling," 30.

15. Hartman, "True Calling," 29.

16. Interview with Reverend Angela Archer, December 2, 1998.

17. *Yellow Book,* Great Neck edition, 1998-99, 14.

18. Hartman, "True Calling," 29.

19. Quoted by Bob Keeler, "A Calling, A Struggle: Women Priests and the Quest for Equality in the Patriarchal World of Religion," *Newsday,* August 18, 1994, B4.

20. Quoted by Cohen, "Women Bring New Dimensions," 6.

A Century of Authors and Literature

Janet S. Wagner

In the past one hundred years, Nassau County has been the home of some of the most respected poets, novelists, children's authors, essayists, and journalists in twentieth-century American literature. Historically, the Long Island region has not only produced wonderful writers, but it has itself often been the subject of literary works. "A survey published by the Suffolk County Cooperative Library System in 1993, lists approximately 200 books of fiction set here, some dating back to the 1800s. The list includes *Gatsby* published in 1925 and John Steinbeck's *The Winter of Our Discontent* published in 1961."[1] All of the authors discussed here, however, were born in, resided in for at least a brief period, or currently live in Nassau County, and many of them incorporated their environment into their work. I have included a selected bibliography of the works by Nassau County authors mentioned in this paper.

Important literary activity blossomed early between the borders of what was to become known as Nassau County, and I must mention two eminent poets who pre-date its establishment. At a time when the borders were still fluid, Jupiter Hammon from Lloyd Neck (which remained part of Oyster Bay until after the Civil War) was the first published black poet in America. His eighty-eight-line broadside poem of 1760 entitled "An Evening Thought" pre-dates works by Phillis Wheatley by almost ten years. Hammon, a slave of the Lloyd family, published religious works, and his "Address to the Negroes of New York" was widely distributed.[2] And, of course, in the nineteenth century, we had William Cullen Bryant (1794–1878), described in the *Dictionary of Literary Biography*, as "a poet of historic importance . . . because he was the first American writer of verse to win wide international acclaim."[3] Bryant moved to his country home, Cedarmere, in Hempstead Harbor (now Roslyn Harbor), in 1844 and is buried in the nearby Roslyn Cemetery on Northern Boulevard. Of special interest to us today is the fact that he was held in such esteem that "Bryant" was one of the names put forth as a suggestion for the name of our county before "Nassau" was finally selected. As a historical note, the bill creating Nassau County was introduced by George B. Wallace, "a well known lawyer, *author,* and publisher."[4]

We can begin our historical view of the literary scene in Nassau County with the Roosevelt family of Sagamore Hill in Oyster Bay. At the turn of the century, Theodore Roosevelt, soon to be our twenty-sixth president, was still governor of New York State and nominee of the Republican Party for the vice-presidency. On July 13, 1900, he laid the cornerstone of the county courthouse in Garden City.[5] A prolific author who wrote more than thirty books, Roosevelt lived until 1919. His twentieth-century publications include collections of his articles and essays, including *History as Literature*, *Fear God and Take Your Own Part*, and *African Game Trails*, as well as reminiscences of the West and an autobiography.[6]

Theodore was not the only published author in his family. From childhood, Corinne Roosevelt Robinson, his sister, had continuously produced a large body of sentimental and religious poems, and in 1921, she published a reminiscence entitled *My Brother, Theodore Roosevelt.*[7] TR's children, Alice Roosevelt Longworth and Theodore Roosevelt, Jr., collaborated on the compilation and selection of the poetry included in *The Desk Drawer Anthology: Poems for the American People* (1937). Scribner's Sons had already published *Crowded Hours: Reminiscences of Alice Roosevelt Longworth* (1933). Edith, his second wife, published a family history and a jointly written description of family travels entitled *Cleared for Strange Ports* (1927), and Kermit, his son, published several books on hunting, reminiscences of his brother Quentin, and his experiences in World War I.[8]

Frances Hodgson Burnett was born in England on November 24, 1849. Although she is now chiefly known as a children's writer, the author of *Little Lord Fauntleroy*, *A Little Princess*, and *The Secret Garden*, among others, she actually wrote primarily for adults. After spending many years of her life traveling between England, the European continent, and the United States, in 1909 she settled in an Italianate villa in Plandome where she resided (with the exception of winters spent at her home in Bermuda) until her death in 1924.[9]

Living in the next town was Charles G. Norris (born in 1881), "the author of eleven provocative novels [who] has been unduly neglected by critics since his death in 1945, although during his lifetime his work was highly praised by some of the leading literary figures of the day."[10] The author of *Salt* and *Brass* and other novels dealing with controversial social and political issues, he was the brother of the more famed novelist Frank Norris and the husband for thirty-six years of Kathleen Norris (born in 1880), herself the author of very popular short stories and seventy novels.[11] His support and encouragement made her name "a household word" as the author of *Mother* and subsequent works. *Mother* first appeared as a short story in the *American Magazine*. Enlarged to a novel and serialized in the *Ladies Home Journal*, it eventually went into twenty-five editions, sold 900,000 copies, and established her reputation.[12]

The Norrises came to Port Washington in 1913 and remained there for a few years. Initially they took two small bungalows together with Mrs. Norris' sister, Theresa, and her husband, the poet William Rose Benet.[13] Friends of the Norrises in the literary, theatrical, and political worlds included the Frank Doubledays, Peter Finley Dunne, H. L. Mencken, George Kaufman, Charles Lindbergh, and Herbert Hoover among many others.

When Charles and Kathleen Norris gave up their house on Vandeventer Avenue in 1914, Sinclair Lewis and his new bride, Grace Hegger, moved into it and named it "Wrenn House," after one of his works. According to Mark Schorer, "The details of the life they lived there are to be found in Grace Hegger's books and, only a little less literally, in the last chapters of *The Trail of the Hawk,*" parts of which were completed on the commuting trains between Port Washington and Pennsylvania Station. While there, Lewis wrote three stories for the *Saturday Evening Post:* "Commutation: $9.17," about suburban snobbery; "The Other Side of the House"; and "If I Were Boss." The Lewises left Port Washington in December 1915.[14]

Ring Lardner, born in 1885, established his journalistic reputation as a reporter of the daily events of major-league professional baseball between 1908 to 1913. But it was his short stories that were read by millions, and he became one of the most respected writers of the twenties. In early 1921, the Lardners moved into their house on East Shore Road in Great Neck (which he referred to as "The Mange") where they lived until 1928. A local publication proclaimed: "To live in Great Neck is synonymous to being a national success!" To give the flavor of the area at that time, the following is a list of just some of the celebrities living close by: Solomon Guggenheim, Vincent Astor, Walter P. Chrysler, O. H. P. Belmont, Alfred P. Sloan, and Harry Sinclair. Neighbors of the Lardners included Ed Wynn, George M. Cohan, Leslie Howard, Basil Rathbone, Groucho Marx, Oscar Hammerstein II, Clifton Webb, Marilyn Miller, Eddie Cantor, and others.[15]

The Lardners' close friends in the area were the F. Scott Fitzgeralds. From their back yards, Lardner and Fitzgerald used to watch the opulent parties held on neighboring estates, which of course provided inspiration for their literary work. F. Scott Fitzgerald, born in 1896, lived in Great Neck from mid-October 1922 to April 1924 at 6 Gateway Drive in a house rented for $300 per month. It was there in the summer of 1923 that he began a draft of what became *The Great Gatsby*, using the Great Neck environment as material for the novel. While there, he revised *The Vegetable*, a stage comedy published in April 1923, which ran in New York for only one week in November, leaving him with a substantial debt. His 1924 essay, "How to Live on $36,000 a Year," provides a humorous account of the Fitzgeralds' life style in Great Neck, and explains the reason for their debts.[16]

Living only a few miles away, Christopher Morley had a much deeper and longer attachment to Nassau County. Born on May 5, 1890 in Haverford, Pennsylvania, and reared in Baltimore, he attended Haverford College and studied modern history at New College, Oxford, as a Rhodes Scholar. From

Christopher Morley's Knothole Writing Studio, 1970s. The Latin quotation from Erasmus is "How busy you are in your library which is your Paradise." *NCM Collection, LISI at Hofstra.*

1913 to 1917, he worked for Doubleday, Page and Company in Garden City, learning the book trade. After a brief stay in Philadelphia, where he worked as editor of the *Ladies Home Journal* and columnist for the *Philadelphia Evening Public Ledger*, in 1920 he established a lifetime residence in Roslyn Estates, where he wrote in a one-room cabin known as "The Knothole," now located in the North Hills park that bears his name. Although he worked to produce the "Bowling Green" column in the

Christopher Morley at work, c. 1950. *NCM Collection, LISI at Hofstra.*

New York Evening Post, he continued to publish his own works as well, and, from 1924, acted as a contributing editor of the *Saturday Review of Literature*. In 1926 he became a judge for the Book-of-the-Month Club, and therefore, a major influence on the literary tastes of America.[17]

Doubleday published a twelve-volume *Haverford Collected Edition* of his works in 1927 which reflected his persistent interest particularly in Walt Whitman and Joseph Conrad.[18] In addition to journalism, fiction, and poetry, he had a life-long passion for the theater, wrote plays, and, in 1940, founded, with producer David Lowe, the Millpond Playhouse in the Roslyn War Memorial Building, now the Bryant Library, with which he was associated until his death in 1957.[19]

Morley was obsessed with a sense of place, writing often of Roslyn, which he referred to as "Salamis." In *The Man Who Made Friends with Himself*, the village of "Wending Ways" is actually Roslyn, his home for thirty-seven years. "Salamis Station" represents the Roslyn Station for the steam train of the Oyster Bay Branch of the Long Island Rail Road, while "Marathon" corresponds to Manhasset. "Wending Heights" stands for Roslyn Heights as distinguished from Roslyn Estates, where Morley lived at "Green Escape," on a street known as "The Birches" where, as he described it, "the birch trees stood up in slanted clusters, like white china middling rods in pools of absinthe."[20] Morley was not the only author in his family. His wife, Helen Fairchild, was an author of children's books and his daughter, Blythe Morley, published *The Intemperate Season* in 1948.

Morley's contemporary, Harold Stearns (1891–1943), was the "acclaimed chronicler of American culture," a journalist, editor, and essayist who published seven book-length studies after World War I, including *Civilization in the United States* (1922) and *Rediscovering America* (1934). Hemingway depicted him in the character of Harvey Stone in *The Sun Also Rises*. Jeanne Welcher describes him as "a copious writer judicious, tolerant and incisive. . . . For a generation, Stearns examined and brought to public consciousness American attitudes of the era." In 1937, he married Betty Chapin and moved to Locust Valley.[21]

Shortly after his famous transatlantic flight in 1927, Charles Lindbergh was taken under the wing of Captain Harry F. Guggenheim who ran the Foundation for Aeronautical Research. He was invited by the Guggenheims to live with them at *Falaise*, their home in Sands Point, while he wrote his first account of the historic event, entitled *We* (1927). *The Spirit of Saint Louis,* a more thorough version of the flight, published in 1953, won the Pulitzer Prize. In 1939, he and his wife, Anne Morrow Lindbergh, author of *Gift from the Sea* and several volumes of poetry, letters, and diaries, returned from Europe and resided for a short time in the Joseph Lloyd Manor House, now an historic house museum, where Jupiter Hammon had once served.[22]

An author with an interest in the local area, Alonzo Gibbs, born in 1915, was educated at Hofstra University and at Columbia University. An employee of Grumman Aerospace and contributing editor of the *Long Island Forum,* he authored novels and verse, and, with his wife Iris, co-authored a number of local histories, including *Bethpage Bygones* (1962) and *Harking Back* (1983).[23]

Described as "a poet of domestic detail,[24] Hilma Wolitzer, born in 1930 and a resident of Syosset, began to write at the age of thirty-five. She has been the recipient of a scholarship to the Bread Loaf Writers Conference, Guggenheim and National Endowment for the Arts fellowships, and awards from the American Academy and Institute of Arts and Letters Award in Literature. Her novels include *Ending, Introducing Shirley Braverman,* and *Hearts,* and she has published juvenile literature as well. Her daughter, Meg Wolitzer, born in 1959, is also an author whose first novel, *Sleepwalking,* written when she was twenty-three, won much critical acclaim.[25]

A native son of much celebrity and even more mystery, Thomas Pynchon was born in Glen Cove on May 8, 1937 and graduated from Oyster Bay High School as class salutatorian at age sixteen in 1953. His family history can be traced back to the eleventh century and figures prominently in New England history. In fact, it is the subject of Nathaniel Hawthorne's *House of the Seven Gables.*[26] In 1963, he published *V.*, judged by the *Saturday Review* to be "the most masterful first novel in the history of literature."[27]

Michael Hartnett notes that Long Island appears in three of Pynchon's works. In "The Secret Integration," Pynchon transferred the experience of growing up on Long Island to the Berkshires; in *V.*, "Pynchon's narrator describes the Five Towns area . . . as afflicted with a kind of 'geographical incest'"; and in the short story, "Lowlands," his only short story set on Long Island, it "also takes on confining qualities."[28]

Despite his esteemed position in the literary world, only one known photograph of him exists (from his 1953 high school yearbook), and Pynchon goes to great lengths to maintain anonymity.[29] In his expository monograph entitled *Understanding Thomas Pynchon,* Robert D. Newman states that "Pynchon's works . . . [coincide] with the post-World War II literary redefinition of realism and [place] Pynchon at the forefront of contemporary fiction writers."[30] His current whereabouts are unknown.

Recognized as a major contributor to children's literature, Johanna Hurwitz was born in 1937 in the Bronx and resides in Great Neck. A former librarian, she writes poetry, reviews books, and is the winner of many awards and honors. Her books, which now number more than fifty, are "lighthearted novels for elementary and junior high school readers" including such titles as *The Hot and Cold Summer, Teacher's Pet,* and *The Rabbi's Girls.* Many of the ideas for her books are drawn from her life on Long Island.[31]

Writing in an altogether different genre is Michael Crichton, whose family moved to Roslyn shortly after his birth in 1942. An article in *Current Biography* describes him as a novelist and filmmaker who "has become one of Hollywood's most valuable literary properties. . . . Crichton abandoned his plan for a career as a physician to become the author of such bestsellers as *The Andromeda Strain* and *The Terminal Man*, works . . . whose suspenseful plots are never overwhelmed by their scientific data and 'technospeak.'"[32] His latest work is *Airframe* (1996).

An author familiar to all of us is Nelson DeMille, born in New York in 1943, raised in Elmont, and currently a resident of Garden City. He is a Hofstra University graduate, honored by Hofstra, Long Island University, and Dowling College, who has worked as carpenter, house painter, and in other trades, but is now a prolific novelist and freelance writer. His well-known 1990 novel, *The Gold Coast*, one of four set on Long Island, takes place on the North Shore and was described in the *Washington Post Book Review* as "a cautionary tale of soul-selling by a Wall Streeter seeking release from the stupefying boredom and compromise of upper-crust life. DeMille is a gifted eyewitness and so at home with his material we never doubt that he got it from the source."[33] Mr. De Mille has observed that, "Long Island is incredibly diverse for a land mass this small. Go to the Midwest and drive through Kansas and Oklahoma and it's pretty much the same . . . I've lived here all my life and I find this place extremely rich in raw materials for a novelist."[34]

Susan Isaacs was also born in 1943, in Brooklyn. A novelist, screenwriter, political speech writer, and magazine editor, she has lived in Manhasset and now Sands Point. Her first novel, *Compromising Positions*, "went beyond bestseller and Book-of-the-Month Club selection status to bring in higher-than-hoped-for amounts for paperback, foreign and movie rights."[35] It was followed by a succession of successful novels, and, most recently, by *Brave Dames and Wimpettes: What Women Are Really Doing on Screen and Page*, a "lively romp through books, movies, and TV."[36] Susan Isaacs echoes Nelson DeMille when she declares that "Long Island offers the universe. Because of its richness, it's so alive. Maybe North Dakota is alive, but not to me."[37]

Nineteen forty-three must have been a very good year, because it was also the birth year of historian Doris Kearns Goodwin, whose *Wait Until Next Year: A Memoir* (1997) describes her childhood in Rockville Centre in the 1950s, her love for baseball and the Dodgers, and, for her, "the end of an era and the end of childhood."[38]

The subject of much discussion and acclaim, Alice McDermott, whose most recent book, *Charming Billy*, won the National Book Award in 1999, attended Sacred Heart Academy in Hempstead. *That Night* (1987), her second novel, was a finalist for the National Book Award, the Pulitzer Prize, the PEN/Faulkner Award, and the Los Angeles Times Book Award. It is set in suburban Levittown during the early 1960s and told from the point of view of a ten year old child for whom this is an initiation into the "failures of love and the realities and many disappointments of the adult world."[39]

A less familiar name, but one we will be hearing more of is Jillian Medoff, who lived on Long Island for only six months. In her first novel, *Hunger Point* (1997), she created "Lindsey Point," a community close to Great Neck. In explaining her choice, she stated, "I think the thing about the Island that gives it such a unique sensibility is that it's so close to New York. It has a witty, gritty sense of irony that you don't find in many suburbs. You grow up very fast on Long Island because it's so close to New York."[40]

I want to take a moment now to focus on Nassau County poetry and poets. For example, we have not yet mentioned Howard Griffin who was born in Wheatley (north of Old Westbury) in 1915. Mr. Griffin worked as secretary to W. H. Auden and as a reviewer for the *Saturday Review of Literature*. His published works include *City Cadence*, *A Dialogue with W. H. Auden*, and *Overseen Objects and Other Fears*.[41] Nor have we mentioned Donald Everett Axinn, a name familiar to all of us who use the Axinn Library at Hofstra University, who is both a novelist and a poet. His works include, among others, *Sliding Down the Wind* (1977), a collection of poetry, and his most recent novel, *The Ego Makers* (1998).

A number of excellent collections of poetry by diverse groups of local poets have been compiled. *In Autumn: An Anthology of Long Island Poetry*, for instance, contains several poems devoted to specific Nassau locations.[42] Let me list a few with which you may be familiar:

"Westbury" by Arthur Dobrin
"Sherry the Klepto at Work in Roosevelt Field" by Arleen Ruth Cohen
"6 am in Sea Cliff" by Laurie Catterson
"Roslyn Pond" by Joseph Stanton
"Old Brookville" by Jennie Hair
"Beach at Sea Cliff" by Elaine Preston
"Spring Comes to Roslyn Heights" by Weslea Sidon
"Massapequa" by Daniel Thomas Moran

To my great amusement, I also came across a collection in a special edition of the *Long Island Quarterly* (1993) entitled *New Covenant: Poems by Long Island Poets for the Clinton Administration*, to which twenty-three poets contributed, several from Nassau County.[43] As an example of community-based literary initiatives, I bring to your attention *Long Island Stories: A Collection of Stories and Verse About Life Experience on Long Island (1914-1994)* published by the Massapequa Public Library, a compilation of writings by members of the "Senior Connections Writing our Stories Program."

We are all well aware that the East End of Long Island has become a mecca for authors of all genres. Nassau County residents should have no regrets, however, since our environment is bursting with creative literary energy. For example, in a 1997 directory of authors published by the Glen Cove Library, I counted thirty-four authors listed as residents of Glen Cove and the surrounding villages of Sea Cliff, Oyster Bay, Locust Valley, Roslyn Heights, Old Brookville, Mill Neck, and Roslyn Harbor (a relatively small geographic area in Nassau County). The list included writers of fiction and non-fiction, poetry, newspaper and magazine writing, TV and radio scripts, book reviews, sports, children's literature, biography, exercise, health, and travel.[44]

And to demonstrate that our area is very much a part of the contemporary national literary consciousness, for good or for bad, a play opened on Broadway in 1999 entitled *The Mineola Twins*, an "overview of nearly 40 years in the social history of American women."[45] Originally titled *Minnesota Twins*, Pulitzer Prize winner Paula Vogel realized that sounded too much like a baseball team, and chose Mineola for its "white suburban" appeal.[46]

It is quite apparent that the Nassau County literary scene is alive and well as we celebrate our centennial. No doubt the next century will be equally distinguished. I would like to end with a lovely description of a scene on Manhasset Bay, which appears at the closing of *The Great Gatsby* and illustrates the timeless beauty of all great literature, in this case as it describes the place where we live:

> And as the moon rose higher the inessential houses began to melt away until gradually, I became aware of the old island here that flowered once for Dutch sailors' eyes—a fresh green breast of the new world. Its vanished trees, the trees that had made way for Gatsby's house, had once pandered in whispers to the last and greatest of all human dreams; for a transitory enchanted moment man must have held his breath in the presence of this continent, compelled into an aesthetic contemplation he neither understood nor desired, face to face for the last time in history with something commensurate to his capacity for wonder.[47]

Notes

1. Phil Mintz, "L.I. in Literature: Gatsby & Beyond," *Newsday* March 9, 1997, sec. E, p. 6. Steinbeck was awarded the Nobel Prize in Literature in 1962. Other, less distinguished, but popular works set on Long Island include Peter Benchley's *Jaws* (1974) and *Naked Came the Stranger* (1969) by Penelope Ashe, pseudonym of twenty-five Newsday staffers. Portions of Kenneth Roberts' historical novel, *Oliver Wiswell* (1940), are set on Long Island during the Revolutionary War. In the process of

my research, I discovered a previously unpublished short story entitled "Long Island Sound" written by William Carlos Williams in 1961 and reproduced in the *William Carlos Williams Review* 7, no. 2 (Fall 1981): 1-3, with an introduction by Theodore R. Graham. It had been unpublished because Mrs. Williams considered it pornographic, although that would probably not be the judgement of most readers in the 1990s.

2. Oscar Wegelin, "Biographical Sketch of Jupiter Hammon" in *America's First Negro Poet: The Complete Works of Jupiter Hammon,* edited by Stanley A. Ransom, Jr. (Port Washington: Kennikat Press, 1970), 21-33.

3. David Tomlinson, s.v. "William Cullen Bryant," *Dictionary of Literary Biography*, 3: 30. See also Diane Tarleton Bennett and Linda Tarleton, *W. C. Bryant in Roslyn* (Roslyn: Bryant Library, 1978).

4. Jesse Merritt, *The Historical Importance of Nassau County, Long Island* (Farmingdale, NY: "At the Sign of the Turf and Twig," 1940), not paginated (emphasis added). Cedarmere is now owned by Nassau County and is open seasonally.

5. Merritt, *Historical Importance.* (See also his speech above, 76-77. Editor's note.)

6. See Selected Bibliography below and "The Works, Letters, and Papers of Theodore Roosevelt," by John Allen Gable in *Theodore Roosevelt: Many-Sided American,* edited by Natalie A. Naylor, Douglas Brinkley, and John Allen Gable (Interlaken, NY: Heart of the Lakes Publishing, 1992), 646-48.

7. *The Call of Brotherhood* appeared in 1912 and other collections of poetry followed in 1914, 1919, 1924, and 1930. Mrs. Robinson lived in New York City, but was a frequent visitor to Sagamore Hill, and was often there in emergencies, as in 1917 when she helped to nurse TR back to health. See Peter Collier and David Horowitz, *The Roosevelts: An American Saga* (New York: Simon and Schuster, 1994), 218.

8. Titles included *The Long Trail* (1921), *Quentin Roosevelt* (1921), *The Happy Hunting Grounds* (1920), and *War in the Garden of Eden* (1919). See Selected Bibliography below for full bibliographical information.

9. Phyllis Bixler, *Frances Hodgson Burnett* (Boston: Twayne, 1984), 1-18. The house burned in 1935; the property was later owned by Leroy and Rose Grumman. See also Bea Tusiani, "Last Stop Plandome: Frances Hodgson Burnett," in *Long Island Women,* edited by Natalie A. Naylor and Maureen O. Murphy (Interlaken, NY: Empire State Books, 1998), 246-57.

10. Richard Allan Davison, s.v. "Charles G. Norris," *Dictionary of Literary Biography* 9: 248.

11. Margaret Haller, "Main Street, Port Washington, 1914," *Journal of Long Island History* 5, no. 2 (Spring 1965): 26.

12. *National Cyclopaedia of American Biography,* s.v. "Norris, Kathleen L. Thompson," C: 366.

13. William Rose Benet won the Pulitzer Prize for poetry in 1942 and was the elder brother of Stephen Vincent Benet (Haller, "Main Street, Port Washington," 27).

14. Mark Schorer, *Sinclair Lewis: An American Life* (New York: McGraw-Hill, 1961), 221. See also "Sinclair Lewis in Port Washington," Port Washington Public Library, February 1999, no pagination.

15. Jonathan Yardley, *Ring: A Biography of Ring Lardner* (New York: Random House, 1977), 238-42.

16. Mary Jo Tate, "Great Neck," in *F. Scott Fitzgerald: The Essential Reference to his Life* (New York: Facts on File, 1998), 104-5. See also Joann P. Krieg, "Remembering Great Neck," *Long Island Historical Journal* 7, no. 1 (Fall 1994): 111-17; and Roger Wunderlich, "*The Great Gatsby* As Long Island History," *Long Island Historical Journal* 7, no. 1 (Fall 1994): 119-24.

17. See Helen McK. Oakley, *Christopher Morley on Long Island* (Roslyn: Christopher Morley Knothole Association, 1967); and Helen McK. Oakley, *Three Hours for Lunch: The Life and Times of Christopher Morley, A Biography* (New York: Watermill Publishers, 1976).

18. It should be noted that Whitman, in his late teens and early twenties, taught school in Woodbury and other locations in Nassau County, but he is most often associated with and considered to be a son of Huntington in Suffolk County, where his birthplace (246 Old Walt Whitman Road, Huntington Station) is now a New York State Historic Site. See Joann P. Krieg, *Long Island and Literature* (Interlaken, NY: Heart of the Lakes Publishing, 1989), 27-38; and Joann P. Krieg, *Whitman, A Chronology* (Iowa City: University of Iowa Press, 1998).

19. Mark I. Wallach and Jon Bracker, *Christopher Morley* (Boston: Twayne Publishers, 1976), 20. The Nassau County Centennial Conference at Hofstra included a dramatic presentation of one of Morley's comedies, *Soft Shoulders,* which had been a hit at the Millpond Playhouse in 1940.

20. Wallach and Bracker, *Christopher Morley,* 79, 80.

21. Betty Chapin, "Harold Stearns' Brief Halcyon," *Confrontation* (Long Island University), November 1985, 58-60.

22. Leonard Moseley, *Lindbergh: A Biography* (New York, Doubleday, 1976), 127-28.

23. *Contemporary Authors,* New Revision Series, s.v. "Gibbs, Alonzo (Lawrence)," 5: 212-13.

24. Martha Saxton as quoted in "Wolitzer, Hilma," *Contemporary Authors,* New Revision Series, 18: 488.

25. *Contemporary Authors,* New Revision Series, s.v. "Wolitzer, Meg,"18: 491.

26. An ancestor, William Pynchon, was the model for William Slothorp in *Gravity's Rainbow*. He arrived in the New World in 1630, served as treasurer of the Massachusetts Bay Colony, and wrote theological text that ran counter to orthodox Calvinism. Calvinism, as a rational system, figures strongly in Thomas Pynchon's work. Robert D. Newman, *Understanding Thomas Pynchon* (Columbia, SC: University of South Carolina Press, 1986), 1-2.

27. Ihab Hassan, review of *V.* by Thomas Pynchon, *Saturday Review* 46 (March 23, 1963): 44.

28. Michael Hartnett, "Thomas Pynchon's Long Island Years," *Confrontation,* November, 1985, 46. These Pynchon stories are included in his *Slow Learner: Early Stories* (Boston: Little Brown, 1984).

29. To illustrate: When *Gravity's Rainbow* (considered to be his masterpiece) shared the National Book Award for fiction in 1974 with Isaac Bashevis Singer's *Crown of Feathers,* rather than make a public appearance, Pynchon sent "Professor" Irwin Corey, a renowned double talker, to accept it for him.

30. Newman, *Understanding Thomas Pynchon,* 5.

31. *Contemporary Authors,* New Revision Series, s.v. "Hurwitz, Johanna," 44: 198-200. See also Meliss Beery, "For Her, Childhood Joys Never End," *Newsday*, July 7, 1998, sec. B, p. 2; and Donna Kutt Nahas, "Lending a Guiding Hand by her Children's Books," *New York Times* January 17, 1999, Long Island sec. 14, p. 12.

32. *Current Biography Yearbook 1993,* s.v. "Crichton, Michael," 140.

33. Consuelo Saah Baehr as quoted in *Contemporary Authors,* New Revision Series, s. v. "DeMille, Nelson (Richard)," 62: 131. See also William B. Falk, "Nelson DeMille, Storyteller," *Newsday,* August 13, 1997, sec. B, p. 4.

34. Quoted in Mintz, "Long Island in Literature," (see note no. 1 above).

35. *Contemporary Authors,* New Revision Series, s.v. "Isaacs, Susan," 20:239; see also 65: 126-29.

36. These include *Close Relations, Almost Paradise, People Like You and Me,* and the screenplay for *Compromising Positions.*

37. Quoted in Mintz, "Long Island in Literature," 6.

38. Review of *Wait Till Next Year: A Memoir,* The Book House of Stuyvesant Plaza, http://www.bhny.com/staff25.htm, Internet, accessed March 16, 1999.

39. *Contemporary Authors,* New Revision Series, s.v. "McDermott, Alice," 40: 296; see also Dan Cryer, "Will Success Spoil Alice McDermott?" *Newsday,* March 25, 1998, sec. B, p. 6; and Robert Towers, "All-American Novel," *New York Review of Books,* January 21, 1988, 26-27.

40. Quoted by Mintz, in "Long Island in Literature," 6.

41. Iris and Alonzo Gibbs, "Howard Griffin: Long Island Poet," parts 1-3, *Long Island Forum* 45 (April-June 1982): 63-69, 90-93, 116-21.

42. *In Autumn: An Anthology of Long Island Poetry* (Northport, NY: Birnham Wood Graphics, 1994).

43. *Long Island Quarterly* is published by Birnham Woods Graphics, Northport. Other collections by poets from Nassau County that may be of interest are *Long Island Girl* by Carmela Delia Lanza and Albert Scofield Knorr's *Share My Fire.* See bibliography below.

44. Antonia Petrash, *Directory of Local Authors* (Glen Cove: Glen Cove Public Library, 1997). Because of space restrictions, I have not included authors of travel or photographic works in this survey of Nassau County literature.

New names of authors keep surfacing. Alice Hoffman, who was raised in Franklin Square, has published nine novels. Phoebe Eng's new book, *Warrior Lessons*, describes the experiences of an Asian American growing up in Westbury during the 1970s. Mary Gordon, who grew up in Valley Stream, has written several novels and books of essays. Cynthia Blair, who lived in Sea Cliff for many years before moving to Stony Brook, wrote two novels and many books for young adults.

45. Vincent Canby, "A Mad History of Women as Told by Twin Barbies," *New York Times,* February 28, 1999, sec. 2, p. 6.

46. Alex Witchel, "After the Prize is the Pressure: Now What?" *New York Times*, February 7, 1999, sec. 2, p.5.

47. F. Scott Fitzgerald, *The Great Gatsby,* 1925 (New York: Cambridge University Press, 1991), 140.

Selected Bibliography of Works by Nassau County Authors

Ashe, Penelope. *Naked Came the Stranger*. New York: L. Stuart, 1969.
Axinn, Donald E. *The Ego Makers: A Novel*. New York: Arcade Publishers, 1998.
——. *Sliding Down the Wind*. Chicago: Swallow Press, 1977.
Benchley, Peter. *Jaws*. Garden City: Doubleday, 1974.
Benet, William Rose. *The Dust Which Is God, A Novel in Verse*. New York: A. A. Knopf, 1945.
Bryant, William Cullen. *The Complete Poems of William Cullen Bryant*. New York: Frederick A. Stokes, 1894.
Burnett, Frances Hodgson. *Little Lord Fauntleroy*. New York: Scribner, 1886.
——. *The Little Princess; Being the Whole Story of Sara Crewe*. New York: C. Scribner's Sons, 1905.
——. *The Secret Garden*. New York: F. A. Stokes, 1911.
Crichton, Michael. *Airframe*. New York: Alfred Knopf, 1996.
——. *The Andromeda Strain*. New York: Knopf, 1969.
——. *The Terminal Man*. New York: Knopf, 1972.
——. *Timeline*. New York: Knopf, 1999.
DeMille, Nelson. *The Gold Coast*. New York: Warner Books, 1990.
Fitzgerald, F. Scott. *The Great Gatsby*. Edited by Matthew J. Bruccoli. New York: Cambridge University Press, 1991.
——. "How to Live on $36,000 a Year." Essay in *Saturday Evening Post* 196 (April 5, 1924): 22, 94, 97.
Gibbs, Iris and Alonzo. *Bethpage Bygones*. N.p.: Kinsman Press, Inc., 1962.
——. *Harking Back: An Account of the Bethpage Purchase and Sundry Long Island Events, Persons and Places*. Waldoboro, ME: Kinsman Publications, 1983.
——. "Howard Griffin: Long Island Poet." Parts 1-3. *Long Island Forum* 45 (April-June 1982): 63-69, 90-93, 116-21.
Goodwin, Doris Kearns. *Wait Until Next Year: A Memoir*. New York: Simon and Schuster, 1997.
Griffin, Howard. *Conversations with Auden*. San Francisco: Grey Fox Press, 1981.
——. *Cry Cadence*. New York: Farrar, Straus, 1947.
——. *Overseen Objects*. Geneve, Switzerland: Druck Press, 1972.
Hammon, Jupiter. *America's First Negro Poet: The Complete Works of Jupiter Hammon of Long Island*. Port Washington, NY: Associated Faculty Press, 1983.
Hurwitz, Johanna. *The Hot and Cold Summer*. New York: Morrow, 1984.
——. *The Rabbi's Girls*. New York: Morrow, 1982.
——. *Teacher's Pet*. New York: Morrow Junior Books, 1988.
Isaacs, Susan. *Brave Dames and Wimpettes: What Women Are Really Doing on Page and Screen*. New York: Ballantine Publishing Group, 1999.
——. *Compromising Positions*. New York: Times Books, 1978.
Knorr, Albert Scofield. *Share My Fire*. Fort Smith, AR: South and West, 1966.
Lanza, Carmela Delia. *Long Island Girl*. San Francisco, CA: Malafemmina Press, 1992.
Lardner, Ring. *How to Write Short Stories*. New York: Charles Scribner's Sons, 1924.
Lewis, Grace Hegger. *Half a Loaf*. New York: H. Liveright, 1931.
Lewis, Sinclair. *Our Mr. Wrenn*. New York: Harcourt, Brace and Company, 1914.
——. "Commutation: $9.17, A Story." *Saturday Evening Post*, October 30, 1915, 6.
——. "If I Were Boss, A Story." *Saturday Evening Post*, January 1, 1916, 5, 14.
——. "The Other Side of the House." *Saturday Evening Post*, November 27, 1915, 11.

——. *The Trail of the Hawk.* New York: Harcourt, 1915.
Lindbergh, Anne Morrow. *Gift from the Sea.* New York: Pantheon, 1955.
Lindbergh, Charles A. *The Spirit of St. Louis.* New York: Scribner, 1953.
——. *We.* New York: G. P. Putnam's Sons, 1927.
Longworth, Alice Roosevelt. *Crowded Hours.* New York: C. Scribner's Sons, 1933.
Longworth, Alice Roosevelt and Theodore Roosevelt [Jr.]. *The Desk Drawer Anthology: Poems for the American People*, 1937. Reprint; Freeport, NY: Books for Libraries Press, 1969.
McDermott, Alice. *Charming Billy.* New York: Farrar, Straus and Giroux, 1998.
——. *That Night.* New York: Farrar, Straus, and Giroux, 1987.
Medoff, Jillian. *Hunger Point: A Novel.* New York: Regan Books, 1997.
Morley, Blythe. *The Intemperate Season.* New York: Farrar, Straus and Company, 1948.
Morley, Christopher. *The Haverford Edition of Christopher Morley.* 12 vols. Garden City, NY: Doubleday, Page and Company, 1927.
——. *The Man Who Made Friends with Himself.* Garden City, NY: Doubleday and Company, 1949.
Norris, Charles Gilman. *Brass; A Novel of Marriage.* New York: R. P. Dutton and Company, 1921.
——. *Salt, or, The Education of Griffith Adams.* New York; E. P. Dutton and Company, 1918.
Norris, Kathleen Thompson. *Mother.* New York: Macmillan Company, 1911.
——. "Mother." *American Magazine* 72 (August 1911): 415-27.
——. *Ladies Home Journal* 29 (June-September 1912).
Pynchon, Thomas. *Gravity's Rainbow.* New York: Viking Press, 1973.
——. *Slow Learner: Early Stories.* Boston: Little, Brown, 1984.
——. *V., A Novel.* Philadelphia: Lippincott, 1963.
Robinson, Corinne Roosevelt. *The Call of Brotherhood, and Other Poems.* New York: C. Scribner, 1912.
——. *My Brother, Theodore Roosevelt.* New York: C. Scribner's Sons, 1921.
——. *Service and Sacrifice, Poems.* New York: Scribner, 1919.
Roosevelt, Edith Kermit Carew. *Cleared for Strange Ports.* New York: C. Scribner's Sons, 1927.
Roosevelt, Kermit. *The Happy Hunting-grounds.* New York: C. Scribner's Sons, 1920.
——. *War in the Garden of Eden.* New York: C. Scribner's Sons, 1919.
Roosevelt, Quentin. *Quentin Roosevelt.* Edited by Kermit Roosevelt. New York: C. Scribner's Sons, 1921.
Roosevelt, Theodore. *African Game Trails.* New York: C. Scribner's Sons, 1910.
——. *Fear God and Take Your Own Part.* New York: George H. Doran Company, 1916.
——. *History as Literature and Other Essays.* New York: C. Scribner's Sons, 1913.
Roosevelt, Theodore, [Jr.], and Kermit Roosevelt. *East of the Sun and West of the Moon.* New York: Blue Ribbon Books, 1926.
Stearns, Harold. *Civilization in the United States.* New York: Harcourt, Brace and Company, 1922.
——. *Rediscovering America.* New York: Liveright, 1934.
Steinbeck, John. *The Winter of Our Discontent.* New York: Viking Press, 1961.
Wolitzer, Hilma. *Ending.* New York: Ivy Books, 1974.
——. *Hearts.* New York: Farrar, Straus, and Giroux, 1980.
——. *Introducing Shirley Braverman.* New York: Farrar, Straus, and Giroux, 1975.
Wolitzer, Meg. *Sleepwalking.* New York: Random House, 1982.

About the Editors and Contributors

Liz Coffin Allerhand was a Classics major at Wellesley College and worked at Yale University as an historical editor on the St. Thomas More Papers. After she moved to Long Beach, her work experience as an art and architectural book editor led her to study the rich local housing stock and architecture of Long Beach as a cultural treasure. First a student of Roberta M. Fiore, she moved on to write about the early twentieth-century architectural history of Long Beach. At present they are collaborating on a biography of William H. Reynolds.

L. D. George Angus, M.D., F.A.C.S. is Director of Trauma at the Nassau County Medical Center, a Clinical Assistant Professor of Surgery at New York College of Osteopathic Medicine, and Assistant Professor of Surgery at SUNY Health Science Center of Brooklyn. He is the co-author of numerous articles in medical journals and has been a presenter at scientific meetings. His co-author, **Dina Fahmy, M.D.**, is a Research Fellow at the Nassau County Medical Center.

Stanley D. Berliner, M.D., F.A.C.S. is Director of General Surgery at the Day Op Center of Long Island in Mineola, and Attending Surgeon at North Shore University Hospital in Manhasset and Glen Cove. He is also Clinical Associate Professor of Surgery at The Albert Einstein College of Medicine in the Bronx. He is on the editorial board of *Hernia, Journal of Hernias and Abdominal Wall Surgery* and has published numerous articles in medical journals.

Linda F. Burghardt is a freelance journalist whose articles have appeared in the *New York Times*, the *Chicago Tribune*, the *USA Today*, *Newsday*, the *San Francisco Chronicle*, the *Christian Science Monitor*, the *Atlanta Constitution*, and other publications. She teaches journalism in the Department of Continuing Education at Queensborough Community College. Her article, "On the Frontiers of Feminism: The Life and Vision of Letty Cottin Pogrebin," appeared in a previous Long Island Studies Institute conference volume, *Long Island Women: Activists and Innovators* (1998).

Patricia T. Caro is a geographer who is on the faculty of Nassau Community College. She previously taught at Hunter College, C. W. Post Campus of Long Island University, the University of Oregon, SUNY Albany, and in Switzerland. She is the co-author of *Atlas of California* and *A World View*, a seventh grade social studies textbook, and has published articles on European geography.

Adrian R. Coren, M.D., F.A.C.S. is an orthopedic surgeon who has been in private practice. He is Emeritus Director of Orthopedic Surgery and the Total Hip Clinic at the Nassau County Medical Center and Associate Professor of Clinical Surgery at the State University at Stony Brook. Dr. Coren was Chief of Orthopedic Surgery at Hempstead General Hospital and Central General Hospital and Attending Surgeon at Mid-Island Hospital and Downstate University in Brooklyn.

Mildred Murphy DeRiggi is an historian with the Nassau County Division of Museum Services who administers the Nassau County Museum Collection at the Long Island Studies Institute. Her article, "The Wright Sisters: Seventeenth Century Quaker Activists," appeared in a previous Long Island Studies Institute conference volume, *Long Island Women: Activists and Innovators* (1998). She has published articles in the *Nassau County Historical Society Journal* and has spoken at local historical organizations.

Joseph Dorinson is Professor of History at the Brooklyn Campus of Long Island University. His specialties in the field of popular culture span sports history, humor studies, Brooklyn and Jewish history, and World War II movies. He is the co-editor of *Jackie Robinson: Race, Sports, and the American Dream* (1998), and numerous articles, including two in previous Long Island Studies Institute conference volumes: "The Suburbanization of Brooklyn: Persistent Without Plan," in *Long Island: The Suburban Experience* (1990), and "Marianne Moore and the Brooklyn Dodgers," in *Long Island Women: Activists and Innovators* (1998).

Roy Douglas has taught social studies at William H. Taft and Forest Hills High Schools in New York City for thirty years. He received his B.A. in history from Dowling College and an M.A. in history from New York University. He is one of the founders of the Long Island Republic Airport Historical Society. He has published articles on aviation history in the *Long Island Forum* and reviewed books on aviation history for the *Forum* and the *Long Island Historical Journal.*

Roberta M. Fiore is one of two official city historians of Long Beach. She was the founder of the Long Beach Historical Society in 1980 and currently serves as President and Chairwoman of its Board of Directors. She initiated a local history program in the school system in 1993, and was responsible for Long Beach's *75th Anniversary Commemorative Photo Album.* She continues to research Long Beach history and is working to restore a Reynolds' Estate house as the Long Beach Museum.

Kenneth Foreman is the Curator of the Historical Society of the Bellmores and previously had been the Executive Vice-President. He is a retired aeronautical engineer who was in charge of an advanced concepts research laboratory at Grumman Aerospace Corporation. He has authored more than one hundred technical papers, reports, and articles, and holds five United States patents. He has published many articles on Bellmore history in *Bellmore Life* and the *Long Island Forum,* and is the author of *A Profile of the Bellmores* (1994). His article, "Justice in Hempstead Town (1873-74)—The Samuel Jones Murder Case," appeared in the first Long Island Studies Institute conference volume, *Evoking a Sense of Place* (1988).

Jack David Gorvoy, M.D. is Professor of Clinical Pediatrics at the Albert Einstein College of Medicine, and has a joint appointment in the Department of Medicine, Long Island Jewish Medical Center, New Hyde Park. He is Medical Director and on the Board of Trustees of the Nassau-Suffolk Cystic Fibrosis Chapter. He is the co-author of numerous articles in medical journals.

Marjorie Freeman Harrison, a lifelong Nassau resident, is currently writing her doctoral dissertation, "Postwar Political Identity in Suburbia: Nassau, Long Island, N.Y., 1948-1971" at Columbia University. A library media specialist at Lawrence High School and teacher union publicist, Ms. Harrison has contributed to a number of scholarly anthologies and reference books, including the *Encyclopedia of New York City* and the *Dictionary of American Biography.* Her article on the "Demise of the Shoreham Nuclear Power Plant" appeared in the Hofstra conference volume, *Contested Terrain: Power, Politics, and Participation in Suburbia* (1995).

William J. Johnston has been Historian of the Village of Farmingdale since 1990 and program coordinator for the Farmingdale-Bethpage Historical Society for more than two decades. He has been active in the state Association of Municipal Historians, serving as state conference Chairman in 1994, and has been Chairman of the Long Island Historians Association since 1996. Before his retirement, Mr. Johnston was an administrator in the Farmingdale public schools. He has written numerous articles on Farmingdale history including a booklet, *Historic Farmingdale.*

Thomas J. Kelly was the chief designer and the Father of the Lunar Module. Born in Brooklyn, he grew up in Bellmore and graduated from W. C. Mepham High School. During his more than forty years at Grumman, he was a propulsion engineer, Engineering Manager for Grumman's $2.3 billion Apollo Project Lunar Module, and held a number of executive positions including vice president of space shuttle programs and President of the Space Integration Division before he retired in 1992. He received NASA's Distinguished Public Service Medal in 1973 and was the recipient of an honorary Doctor of Science degree from the State University of New York at Farmingdale.

John B. Kiernan has been Commissioner of the Nassau County Department of Recreation and Parks since 1990. His career in public service began in 1971 as a legislative assistant to State Senator John D. Caemmerer; later he was Chief Council to the Senate Transportation Committee and to the Legislative Commission on Critical Transportation Choices. Mr. Kiernan was elected Supervisor of the Town of North Hempstead in 1982, and served through 1989. In 1993, he was appointed to the Nassau County Commission on Government Revision (Charter Revision) and chosen by the Commissioners to be the Chairman.

Martha Kreisel is Assistant Professor of Library Services (Humanities Reference Librarian) in Hofstra University's Axinn Library. She has published two indexes on photography books, a bibliography on papercutting, and co-authored annotated bibliographies to Civil War books and works on Lewis Wickes Hines. Her article, "Candace Wheeler and the New York Exchange for Woman's Work," appeared in the Long Island Studies Institute conference volume, *Long Island Women: Activists and Innovators* (1998).

Joann P. Krieg is Professor of English at Hofstra University where she teaches American literature and American Studies. She is the author of *Long Island and Literature* (1989), *Epidemics in the Modern World* (1992), and *A Whitman Chronology* (1998). Dr. Krieg is editor of *Walt Whitman, Here and Now* (1985) and has edited several Long Island Studies Institute conference volumes including *Evoking a Sense of Place* (1988), *Robert Moses: Single-Minded Genius* (1989), and *Long Island Architecture* (1991).

Dorothy Horton McGee is the Historian of the Town of Oyster Bay, Chairman of the Town of Oyster Bay Landmarks Preservation and Bicentennial Commissions. She serves on the board of a number of historical organizations and is the recipient of many awards, most recently the Franklin Delano Roosevelt Local Government Historian's Professional Achievement

Award (1999), Office of New York State Historian, and Supervisor Venditto's Award to a Woman in Government (1999). Miss McGee is the author of several books including *Sally Townsend, Patriot,* biographies of Alexander Hamilton and Herbert Hoover, and a book on the signers of the Declaration of Independence.

James M. McKenna is the Site Director of Old Bethpage Village Restoration and has been associated with the Nassau County Museum for more than two decades. A graduate of Hofstra University, his B.A. is in American history. He is one of the founders of Company H, 119th New York Volunteers, a Civil War living history association. His interests in military studies and Long Island history have joined to form an interest in Long Island's role in our nation's defense.

Natalie A. Naylor is Professor in Hofstra's New College where she has taught courses in American social history, including Long Island history. She is Director of the Long Island Studies Institute and has edited or co-edited several of the Institute's conference volumes, including *Theodore Roosevelt: Many-Sided American* (1992), *The Roots and Heritage of Hempstead Town* (1994), *To Know the Place: Exploring Long Island History* (1995), and *Long Island Women: Activists and Innovators* (1998). She has also published articles on educational history and Long Island history.

Thomas Palmieri, M.D., F.A.C.S. is a practicing physician specializing in hand surgery and upper extremity surgery. He is Associate Professor of Clinical Surgery at the Albert Einstein College of Medicine and Attending Surgeon at Long Island Jewish Medical Center, North Shore University Hospital, and St. Francis Hospital. He has published numerous articles in medical journals and is the author of *The Injured Hand—Evaluation and Treatment* (1973) and *The Medical and Surgical Treatment of Arthritis of the Hand and Wrist* (1998).

Herbert D. Rosenbaum is Professor Emeritus of Political Science at Hofstra University where he taught from 1952-1991, and chaired the Political Science Department for many years. His dissertation at Columbia University was "The Political Consequences of Suburban Growth: A Case Study of Nassau County, New York." He is the author of *A First Book in Politics and Government* (1972) and co-edited Hofstra conference volumes on Franklin D. Roosevelt and Jimmy Carter.

Ruth Shackelford is an Assistant Professor of History at Long Island University in Brooklyn. She received her Ph.D. from Harvard University and previously taught at CUNY, York College, and at Hofstra University. Her dissertation was "To Shield Them From Temptation: Child-saving Institutions and the Children of the Underclass in San Francisco, 1850-1910." Her current research uses statistical analysis to investigate the relationship between urban institutions and single mothers.

James Shelland is an adjunct mentor in history and political science at Empire State College, based at SUNY, Old Westbury. He had previously taught at Hofstra and C. W. Post Colleges, Adelphi University, and was a high school social studies teacher in Glen Cove and Great Neck. His Ph.D. dissertation at the New School for Social Research was "The County Executive: A Case Study of the Office in Nassau County, New York."

James M. Shuart has been President of Hofstra University since 1976. He is a graduate of Hofstra (class of 1953) and received his Ph.D. from New York University. He began his administrative career at Hofstra in 1959. Dr. Shuart became Nassau County Commissioner of Social Services in 1971, and served as Deputy Nassau County Executive in 1974 and 1975. He has continued his involvement in civic and governmental affairs, serving on numerous boards and commissions, including the Long Island Association, Long Island Regional Planning Board, and the Health and Welfare Council of Nassau County. He was Chairman of the Nassau County Property Tax Relief Commission, and was a member of the Nassau County Charter Revision Commission.

Edward J. Smits is the Nassau County Historian, Planning Coordinator for the Museums at Mitchel Center, and was chairman of the Nassau County Centennial Committee. Beginning as a curator with the Nassau County Historical Museum, for more than two decades he was director of the Nassau County Division of Museum Services and developed Nassau's outstanding museum system. Mr. Smits is the author of *Long Island Landmarks* (1970), *Nassau Suburbia, U.S.A.* (1974), and of numerous articles in historical publications. His article, "Legislative Reorganization in Nassau County," appeared in the Hofstra conference volume, *Contested Terrain: Power, Politics, and Participation in Suburbia* (1995).

Jon C. Teaford was the Joseph G. Astman Distinguished Conference Scholar and gave the conference keynote address. He is Professor of History at Purdue University, where he teaches political and urban history and has won awards for his teaching. He is the author of numerous articles in journals and many entries for encyclopedias and biographical dictionaries. Dr. Teaford's seven books include *City and Suburb: The Political Fragmentation* *of Metropolitan America, 1850 to 1970* (1979), *The Unheralded Triumph: City Government in America, 1870-1900* (1984), and *Post-Suburbia: Government and Politics in the Edge Cities* (1997).

Janet S. Wagner is a Reference Librarian in Hofstra University's Axinn Library. Her B.S. degree at Queens College was in literature and her M.A. at Hofstra University in American History. Her M.A. thesis, "Modern Times, Factors of Success and Failure," was on a mid-nineteenth century Long Island anarchic utopian community. She is the co-author of *Guide to Roslyn* and *Index to New York Theatre Critics' Reviews, 1973-1986* (1987). Professor Wagner chaired her department from 1988-1998, and has been very active in professional organizations; she is currently on the executive board of the Long Island Library Resources Council.

Hugh A. Wilson is Associate Professor of Polticial Science at Adelphi University where he was Director of the Institute for Suburban Studies, 1974-1985. His research interests include suburbia, Blacks and public policy, the transition of welfare states in Europe and North America, and the heterogenization of European states. His most recent article, "Does Affirmative Action for Blacks Harm Whites? Some Evidence from the Higher Education Arena," was published in *The Western Journal of Black Studies.* His article, "The Family in Suburbia: From Tradition to Pluralism," appeared in the Hofstra Conference volume, *Suburbia Re-examined* (1989).

Richard A. Winsche was a curator and later historian for the Nassau County Division of Museum Services from 1960 until his retirement in 1992. He administered the museum's reference library and manuscript collections, researched and wrote reports on historic sites and buildings. He has written numerous articles for the *Long Island Forum,* the *Journal of Long Island History,* and the *Nassau County Historical Journal.* His article, "Evolution of the Gould/Guggenheim Estate at Sands Point," appeared in the Institute's *Long Island: The Suburban Experience* (1990), and his book, *The History of Nassau County Community Place-Names,* was published in 1999 by the Long Island Studies Institute and Empire State Books.

B. George Wisoff, M.D., F.A.C.S. is Attending Surgeon Emeritus at St. Francis Hospital and an Affiliate at Long Island Jewish Medical Center. He is a Fellow of the American College of Surgeons and of the American College of Cardiology. His specialty is cardiothoracic surgery. He was Professor of Surgery at SUNY, Stony Brook and has co-authored more than fifty articles in medical journals.

Index

References are to page numbers; pages of photographs, maps, and tables are in *italics*.

L

M

N

O

P

Q

R

The Long Island Studies Institute

The Long Island Studies Institute is a cooperative endeavor of Hofstra University and Nassau County. This major center for the study of local and regional history was established in 1985 to foster the study of Long Island history and heritage. Two major research collections on the study of Nassau County, Long Island, and New York State are located in the Special Collections Department on the University's West Campus, 619 Fulton Avenue, Hempstead, New York 11549. These collections—the Nassau County Museum collection and Hofstra University's James N. MacLean American Legion Memorial collection—are available to historians, librarians, teachers, and the general public, as well as to Hofstra students and faculty. Together, they offer a rich repository of books, photographs, newspapers, maps, census records, genealogies, government documents, manuscripts, and audiovisual materials.

In addition to its research collections, the Institute sponsors publications, meetings, and conferences pertaining to Long Island and its heritage. Through its programs, the Institute complements various Long Island Studies courses offered by the University through the History Department, New College, and University College for Continuing Education.

The Long Island Studies Institute is open Monday-Friday (except major holidays), 9–5 (Fridays to 4 in the summer). For further information, contact the Institute, 516-463-6411. The Institute also houses the historical research offices of the Nassau County Historian and Division of Museum Services (516-463-6418).

Long Island Studies Institute Publications

Heart of the Lakes Publishing/Empire State Books:

Aerospace Heritage of Long Island, by Joshua Stoff (1989).

Algonquian Peoples of Long Island from Earliest Times to 1700, by John A. Strong (1997).

Blessed Isle: Hal B. Fullerton and His Image of Long Island, 1897-1927, by Charles L. Sachs (1991).

Evoking a Sense of Place, edited by Joann P. Krieg (1988).

From Airship to Spaceship: Long Island in Aviation and Spaceflight, by Joshua Stoff (1991). For younger readers.

From Canoes to Cruisers: The Maritime Heritage of Long Island, by Joshua Stoff (1994). For younger readers.

History of Nassau County Community Place-Names, by Richard Winsche (1999).

Long Island and Literature, by Joann P. Krieg (1989).

Long Island Architecture, edited by Joann P. Krieg (1991).

Long Island: The Suburban Experience, edited by Barbara M. Kelly (1990).
Long Island Women: Activists and Innovators, edited by Natalie A. Naylor and Maureen O. Murphy (1998).
Making a Way to Freedom: A History of African Americans on Long Island, by Lynda R. Day (1997).
Nassau County: From Rural Hinterland to Suburban Metropolis, edited by Joann P. Krieg and Natalie A. Naylor (2000).
Robert Moses: Single-Minded Genius, edited by Joann P. Krieg (1989).
Roots and Heritage of Hempstead Town, edited by Natalie A. Naylor (1994).
Theodore Roosevelt: Many-Sided American, edited by Natalie A. Naylor, Douglas Brinkley, and John Allen Gable (1992).
To Know the Place: Exploring Long Island History, edited by Joann P. Krieg and Natalie A. Naylor (rev. ed., 1995).
"We Are Still Here!" The Algonquian Peoples of Long Island Today, by John A. Strong (1996; 2d ed. 1998).

Long Island Studies Institute:

Bibliography of Dissertations and Theses on Long Island Studies, by Natalie A. Naylor (1999).
Calderone Theatres on Long Island: An Introductory Essay and Description of the Calderone Theatre Collection at Hofstra University, by Miriam Tulin (1991).
Cumulative Index, Nassau County Historical Society Journal, 1958-1988, by Jeanne M. Burke (1989).
Exploring African-American History, edited by Natalie A. Naylor (1991, 1995).
Nassau County at 100: The Past and Present in Photographs, by Linda B. Martin (1999).
To Know the Place: Teaching Local History, edited by Joann P. Krieg (1986).
Vignettes of Hempstead Town, 1643-1800, by Myron H. Luke (1993).

Greenwood Press:

Contested Terrain: Power, Politics, and Participation in Suburbia, edited by Marc L. Silver and Martin Melkonian (1995).
Suburbia Re-examined, edited by Barbara M. Kelly (1989).

The Institute collections and reading room are on the second floor of the Library Services Center on Hofstra's West Campus, 619 Fulton Avenue, Hempstead, NY.